STRANGE COMPANY

*To Hibino Takeo and
Nakamura Takashi*

Cover design:
Ingeborg Claessens, Audiovisueel Centrum Rijksuniversiteit Leiden.

VERHANDELINGEN
VAN HET KONINKLIJK INSTITUUT
VOOR TAAL-, LAND- EN VOLKENKUNDE

122

LEONARD BLUSSÉ

STRANGE COMPANY

CHINESE SETTLERS, MESTIZO WOMEN
AND THE DUTCH IN VOC BATAVIA

SECOND IMPRESSION

1988
FORIS PUBLICATIONS
Dordrecht-Holland / Providence-U.S.A.

Published by:
Foris Publications Holland
P.O. Box 509
3300 AM Dordrecht, The Netherlands

Sole distributor for the U.S.A. and Canada:
Foris Publications U.S.A.
P.O. Box 5904
Providence R.I. 02903
U.S.A.

First impression 1986.

ISBN 90 6765 211 3

© 1988 Koninklijk Instituut voor Taal-, Land- en Volkenkunde, Leiden

No part of this publication may be reproduced or transmitted in any form or by any means, electronic or mechanical, including photocopy, recording, or any information storage and retrieval system, without permission from the copyright owner.

Printed in the Netherlands

CONTENTS

Preface	VII
Abbreviations	IX
Glossary	XI
I Introduction	1
II The Story of an Ecological Disaster: The Dutch East India Company and Batavia (1619-1799)	15
III Trojan Horse of Lead: The Picis in Early 17th Century Java	35
IV Testament to a Towkay: Jan Con, Batavia and the Dutch China Trade	49
V Batavia 1619-1740: The Rise and Fall of a Chinese Colonial Town	73
VI The VOC and the Junk Trade to Batavia: A Problem in Administrative Control	97
VII The Caryatids of 17th Century Batavia: Reproduction, Religion and Acculturation under the VOC	156
VIII Butterfly or Mantis? The Life and Times of Cornelia van Nijenroode	172
Notes	260
Literature	271
Index of Personal Names	284
Index of Geographical Names	289
Subject Index	293
Sources of the Illustrations	301

PREFACE

The English word "hobby" has been naturalized in the vocabularies of many Western languages to such an extent that few people are aware of its original meaning: a medium-sized horse. Indeed, the hobbies one engages in are like horses. Once broken in, they enable their rider to make excursions at a slightly more elevated plane, and permit him a wider range of action, than the pair of sturdy boots the economic historian R.H. Tawney advised his contemporaries to don. Hobbies do not always accompany one's original intentions as boots accompany one's feet; sometimes they may run out of control. However, they may teach the rider a lesson. The French describe the horse in these terms: "le cheval, la plus noble conquète de l'homme". Indeed the conquest may work both ways. In the course of revising the contents of this book I was reminded of the leaps and bounds with which the seven chapters were originally conceived as hobby excursions from my main area of study.
    Between 1973 and 1975 with a grant from the Japanese Ministry of Education I worked at the Research Institute of Humanities of Kyoto University on the early history of the Dutch East India Company within the world of the Far East. Professor Hibino Takeo, my supervisor at the time, enlisted me for a seminar on the Overseas Chinese in eighteenth century Java, which he was directing together with Professor Nakamura Takashi of Tenri University. My main task was to collect Dutch printed material on the subject and while engaged in this project my interest was awakened for Hua-chiao studies.
    Whether the seminar itself ever resulted in a publication, I do not know. I hope that Professors Hibino and Nakamura will consider this collection of essays as an albeit insufficient repayment for their inspiring teaching.
    I am especially grateful to Prof. I. Schöffer who suggested to me that I should revise and publish these essays in book form. His valuable comments as well as those made by Prof. E. Zürcher have led to improvements in argument and style. George Winius, Robert Ross, Gregory Ralph and Eloise Van Niel provided at various stages advice on English usage, but I especially want to thank Judy Marcure for her thorough revision of the text. Chiang Shu-sheng, Ingeborg Claessens, Jennegien Nieuwstraten, Carin Compeer, M.Th. de Kock-Ververda, and the staff of the KITLV gave the book its final form.

ABBREVIATIONS

Archival Collections

ARA	Algemeen Rijksarchief (National Archives), 's-Gravenhage
AS	Arsip Nasional (National Archives), Jakarta
GA	Gemeente Archief (Municipal Archives), Amsterdam
HR	Hoge Raad (Archives of the Supreme Court), ARA, 's-Gravenhage
KITLV	Koninklijk Instituut voor Taal-, Land- en Volkenkunde (Royal Institute of Linguistics and Anthropology), Leiden
MMPH	Maritiem Museum Prins Hendrik, Rotterdam
RU	Rijksarchief Utrecht (Provincial Archives), Utrecht
VOC	Archives of the Dutch East India Company, ARA, 's-Gravenhage

Source Publications

Bouwstoffen	J. Mooij (ed.), "Bouwstoffen voor de geschiedenis der Protestantsche Kerken in Nederlandsch-Indië", Weltevreden, 1927-1931. 3 Vols.
CCT	"Ch'ing-shih-lu Ching-chi Tzu-liao Chi-yao" (A compendium of economic materials in the veritable records of the Ch'ing dynasty), Peking, 1959.
Coen	H.T. Colenbrander and W.Ph. Coolhaas (eds), "Jan Pietersz. Coen; Bescheiden omtrent zijn bedrijf in Indië", 's-Gravenhage, 1919-1953. 7 Vols.
CWT	"Ch'ing-ch'ao Wen-hsien T'ung-k'ao" (Ch'ing encyclopedia of historical records), Shanghai, 1936. 2 Vols. [Reprint.]
Daghregister	J.A. van der Chijs et al. (eds), "Dagh-Register gehouden int Casteel Batavia vant passerende daer ter plaetse als over geheel Nederlandts-India 1624-1682", 's-Gravenhage/Batavia, 1887-1931. 31 Vols.
GM	W.Ph. Coolhaas (ed.), "Generale Missiven van Gouverneurs-Generaal en Raden aan Heren XVII der Verenigde Oostindische Compagnie", 's-Gravenhage, 1960-1985. 8 Vols.
HFCH	Wang Hsi-ch'i (ed.), "Hsiao-fang-hu Chai Yü-ti Ts'ung-ch'ao" (Collected texts on geography from the Hsiao-fang-hu studio), Shanghai, 1877. 3 Vols.
Hirado Diaries	"Diaries kept by the heads of the Dutch factory in Japan 1633-1640", Tokyo, 1974-1985. 5 Vols.

HMC	Chou K'ai (ed.), "Hsia-men Chih" (Gazetteer of Amoy), Taipei, 1961. 5 Vols.
Opkomst	J.K.J. de Jonge et al. (eds.), "De opkomst van het Nederlandsch gezag in Oost-Indië; Verzameling van onuitgegeven stukken uit het Oud-Koloniaal Archief", 's Gravenhage, 1862-1909. 13 Vols.
Plakaatboek	J.A. van der Chijs (ed.), "Nederlandsch-Indisch Plakaatboek, 1602-1811", Batavia/'s Hage, 1885-1900. 17 Vols.
Realia	J.A. van der Chijs (ed.), "Realia; Register op de generale resolutiën van het Kasteel Batavia", Leiden, 1882-1886. 3 Vols.

Periodicals

BKI	Bijdragen tot de Taal-, Land- en Volkenkunde van het Koninklijk Instituut voor Taal-, Land- en Volkenkunde.
TBG	Tijdschrift voor Indische Taal-, Land- en Volkenkunde uitgegeven door het Bataviaasch Genootschap van Kunsten en Wetenschappen.
VBG	Verhandelingen van het Bataviaasch Genootschap van Kunsten en Wetenschappen.

GLOSSARY

arak	(Ind.), locally produced spirit, commonly fabricated from sugar cane or rice
baly	(Dutch), basket or tub, varying unit of packaging tea or porcelain
catty	(Ind. kati), weight measure equal to 16 taels, i.e. 625 grams
chan-ch'uan 戰船	(Chin.), war vessel
ch'eng 城	(Chin.), wall or walled town
ch'ien 錢	(Chin.), copper coin with a hole in the middle; 1000 ch'ien is equivalent to one tael
chin 金	(Chin.), gold; also used as joint venture denotation by Amoy shipping firms
ch'uan-chu 船主	(Chin.), nachoda or captain of Chinese junk
ch'u-hai 出海	(Chin.), nachoda or captain of Chinese junk; literal: he who puts to sea
condrin	(Dutch condrijn), Japanese monetary unit; 100 condrin is the equivalent of one tael
couban 小判	(Dutch), derived from Japanese ko-ban; Japanese golden oval-shaped coin equal to 18 grams of gold
daimyo 大名	(Jap.), feudal lord
dalem	(Ind. dalam), princely residence
desa	(Ind.), village
duit	(Dutch), copper coin; eight duit is equivalent to one stuiver
freeburgher	see vrijburger
Generale Missive	(Dutch), general report sent twice a year by GG and Council to the the Gentlemen XVII in Holland
Heren XVII	(Dutch), Gentlemen XVII, the directors of the Dutch East India Company
Hoge Regering	(Dutch), High Government, GG and Council of the Indies
hsiao-ch'uan 小船	(Chin.), small vessel
Hsi-yang 西洋	(Chin.), Western Ocean, denoting the western littoral of the South China Sea
hua-ch'iao 華僑	(Chin.), Overseas Chinese
huo-ch'ang 火長	(Chin.), pilot
i-lu-p'ing-an 一路平安	(Chin.), literal: peace all along the road
intramuros	(Span.), literal: within the walls, the inner city
juffrouw	(Dutch), literal: miss, but in VOC usage denoting the wives of the higher echelon offi-

kampong	(Ind.), suburban quarter, village
kana 仮名	(Jap.), Japanese syllabary
keng 更	(Chin.), measure of distance and time; 10 keng is equal to 24 hours
klenteng	(Ind.), temple, probably derived from Chinese kuan-yin ting 觀音亭, pavilion dedicated to the goddess Kuan-yin
kongkuan	(Chin. kung-kuan), Chinese Council
kraton	(Ind.), royal palace
Mardijker	(Dutch), derived from Indonesian orang merdeka, free man; Christian population group of Indonesian descent
nachoda	(Persian na-khuda), captain of an Asian vessel
Nan-yang 南洋	(Chin.), Southeast Asia; literal: Southern Ocean
njonja	(Ind. nyonya), lady
Ommelanden	(Dutch), surrounding country, hinterland of Batavia
on-shin 音信	(Jap.), letter, communication
opperhoofd	(Dutch), chief factor or head of a trading factory
orang baru	(Ind.), newcomer, literal: new man
otemba お転婆	(Jap.), tomboy, headstrong woman, from Dutch ontembaar
oya koko 親孝行	(Jap.), filial piety
pangeran	(Ind.), noble title often used to denote a prince
pasar	(Ind.), market
payong	(Ind.), umbrella, parasol; a status symbol in the VOC hierarchy
picul	(Ind. pikul), weight equal to 62.5 kilogram
plak(k)aat	(Dutch), ordinance issued by the colonial government
pothia 保長	(Chin. pao-chang?), Chinese sugar miller or supervisor on a plantation
prahu	(Ind.), small local craft
Quewie 契子(或僧仔)	(Chin. ch'i-tze), Chinese travelling merchant.
rixdollar	(Dutch rijksdaalder), 2.5 guilders
ryomandokoro 両政所	(Jap.), the two governors of Nagasaki
schuitsilver	(Dutch), unrefined Japanese silver equal to 4.3 tael or about 15 guilders
shahbandar	(Persian), harbour master
shang-ch'uan 商船	(Chin.), coastal trading vessel
sjambok	(Persian chabuk), slave lash
sobat	(Ind. sahabat), friend
stuiver	(Dutch), coin; one guilder is equal to 20 stuiver
Sumkon 心肝	(Chin. hsin-gan), literal: heart and liver
tael	Chinese ounce; weight equal to 1/16 catty; also monetary unit of the same weight of sil-

(cials with the exception of the wife of the GG who is denoted mevrouw)

Glossary

	ver (Chin. liang; Jap. ryo) 両; 1 tael = 10 mace = 100 condrins
tan 反	(Jap.), varying length measure for a roll of cloth
Tang-soa 唐山	(Chin. T'ang-shan), mountains of T'ang, meaning China
t'ieh li mu 鉄力木	(Chin), iron-strength wood
toutocq 都督	(Chin. tu-tu), provincial commander of the Chinese regular army
towkay 頭家	(Chin.), chief
ts'ai-fu 財富	(Chin.), clerk and treasurer in charge of the cargo
ts'ai-tung 財東	(Chin.), financier
tsu 族	(Chin.), lineage
Tung-yang 東洋	(Chin.), Eastern Ocean, denoting the eastern littoral of the South China Sea
vrijburger	(Dutch), free citizen, not-employed by the VOC
wang 王	(Chin.), king
wangkan(g) 艎舡	(Chin. huang-kung), small junk
wayang	(Ind.), theatre play
wo-k'ou 倭寇	(Chin.), short bandits, derogatory term for Japanese
ya-men 衙門	(Chin.), public office of the magistrate
yang-ch'uan 洋船	(Chin.), ocean-going craft
yang-hang 洋行	(Chin.), Ocean Guild; the shipping corporations trading with Southeast Asia
yashiki 屋敷	(Jap.), residence, estate
yü-ch'uan 魚船	(Chin.), fishing vessel

Chapter I

INTRODUCTION

The publication in book form of these essays, which were originally written for different occasions, allows me to introduce the main themes of this "travel guide" into Oud-Batavia, and to examine the conceptual and research procedures followed.[1] People and places are the twin pillars on which this book is built, but the emphasis as the title of one of the chapters suggests is on people. I have not attempted to write an urban history in its proper sense. The birth, growth and decay of Batavia, her appearance, her urban élite and their particular life style, have already been studied by others. Instead, I have focussed on an underlying theme: studying the long-term relationship between colonial ruler and subjects in Batavia. In each chapter, one facet will be analysed of the process of interaction between the Verenigde Oost-Indische Compagnie (VOC) - the Dutch East-India Company which founded Batavia in 1619 and ruled the town until its bankruptcy in 1795 - and two specific groups of the town population: the Chinese and the mestizo wives of the Dutch Company servants and freeburghers. The selection of these two reference groups is not altogether the result of a personal whim. They do have something in common. If mestizo women were the indispensable companions of Dutch male individuals in the tropics, the same kind of relationship could be perceived between the Dutch and the Chinese communities in Batavia. Would the East-India Company have survived in Java without the help of "de verwijfde hoop" (the effeminate breed) as the peaceful, long haired Chinese were derogatorily called? These two relationships on individual and group levels can indeed be best characterized as "Strange Company".

Social Change

It would be hard to find an ancien régime account of Batavia which does not devote ample space to a stereotypical description of the exotic, industrious business partners of the VOC, the Chinese, and Jan Compagnie's no less impressive, indolent, Portuguese-speaking, female bedpartners, who spent their lives in "pracht en praal" (pomp and circumstance). As an understanding of such stereotypes cannot be separated from the knowledge of their genesis, I set out to explore how the two groups came about and have attempted to lay bare the roots of their relationships with the VOC. The mosaic of biased generalisations contained in the literature and archival material concerning the town in general, the Chinese, and the "Dutch" women in particular, was subjected to rigorous historical analysis. This means that the case-studies collected here do not merely deal with motion within and interaction between seemingly fixed social groups and a monolithic administration, but focus on change in established patterns of social relationships in economic, religious or family life. Indeed the succession of differences in the course of time in these social relationships, the entities concerned (the VOC administration and the two reference groups) and, last but not least, the site (Batavia), furnish the three vital elements which have enabled me to make propositions concerning the nature of empirical change in this colonial society. In the first section of the book, social change will be studied in the context of the changing economic structures of the VOC and the Chinese community in the town; in the second section, attention is paid to changing patterns of social relationships within the household, by analysing the role and function of mestizo wives.

The investigation of social change does not necessarily take place at macro-level; analysis can be practised on the micro-level as well. The study of the function of a leaden coin, for instance, helps us to establish how European and Chinese commercial exchange developed on the local market. The biographical study of a Chinese entrepreneur inquires into his sphere of action and the objectives he shared with the Dutch. The life history of a Batavian widow shows how a significant theme - the social position of women in Batavia - can be inductively understood through the life and experiences of an individual connected with it.

Source Materials

It goes without saying that the feasibility of this kind of research depends upon the availability of source materials. A great deal has appeared in print concerning Batavia in the past three hundred years. Although an archival enthusiast, I have to admit that printed source materials and secondary sources have provided the bulk of evidence for the five interpretive studies on social change in economic and religious life in this book. This is not surprising as the stereotypes are created and/or propagated in these sources. Rather I have attempted to make use of source publications in a somewhat different way than others have done before me. It strikes me that several source publications tend to be used via their indices for reference purposes only. Often it is not realized that these indices were originally drawn up for purposes fundamentally different from the objectives of today's historian. For instance, the original index of the Plakaatboeken, a series of VOC ordinances edited by J.A. van der Chijs, classifies objects and events into categories used by the dominant VOC administration itself. Clearly the assumptions of the trade-oriented Company administration as reflected in their choice of categories, were quite different from ours. This, of course, does not mean that it would be impossible for today's historian to organize many previously unrelated observations through the use of a conceptual framework of his own, and thus gain insight into social processes which were not understood by those who experienced or witnessed them. Bearing this in mind, I plowed through source publications such as the Plakaatboeken, the Realia (Resolutions by the High Government), and the Acta of the Church Council, and treated them as serial sources in which the answers to specific questions could be found. This enabled me to infer how the situation may have been defined by segments of the Batavian population such as the Chinese or the mestizo women, and to contrast their views with those of the authorities.

The two biographical studies in this book have been written mainly on the basis of archival research. On micro-level it is almost impossible to carry out original archival work on social change in family life without having full access to the records kept in the former Landsarchief, the Arsip Nasional in Jakarta. Only in Jakarta are the pertinent sources for this research available, such as the records of urban institutions like the Bench of Aldermen, the Council of Justice, the Orphanage Board, the Polder boards or that indispensable tool for tracing economic and social activities of individuals, the Notarial Archives. Yet, for a number of reasons sufficient evidence concerning the heroine of my biographical study, Cornelia van Nijenroode, could be collected in the Algemeen Rijksarchief (ARA), as well as provincial and municipal archives in the Netherlands. This lady was enmeshed in so many weighty political and juridical issues that she looms large in the policy making reports of the Batavia High Goverment that were sent to Holland. Moreover, as she started legal proceedings against her husband at the High Court of Holland, the VOC archives as well as those of the High Court yield considerable precious information about her career.

The Locality and Its Functions

In view of the fact that the study of social change involves the observation of the dynamics of social behaviour among specific groups in one locality at successive points in time, it may be clarifying to delineate at this point both the basic functions of Batavia, and thereafter to examine the specific character of the relationship that existed between the VOC and the population of this urban society.

As a result of a colonial decision imposed from above, Batavia was founded in 1619 on the ruins of the former principality of Jakarta. Occupation and domination are the elements inherent in any colonial establishment's foundation; however, in the case of Batavia, the native population either chose to follow their own rulers and fled to nearby Banten, or they were simply chased away. Batavia castle, a fortress commanding the roadstead, was erected as the administrative headquarters and the commercial entrepot of the monopolistic trading activities of the VOC in Asia. Batavia town was established in the shadow of the castle's ramparts with a dual function in mind: it was to provide the necessities of the Company's personnel and it served as a bait to lure the native inter-archipelago trade into range. After the area was occupied and, as we have seen, the native population expelled, policies of immigration and legislation were followed to put the colony on a more permanent footing. As the numbers of Dutch settlers were insufficient, traders from all over the Southeast Asian region were welcomed by the VOC authorities to establish themselves in Batavia. Most favoured among these were the Chinese, who were not only encouraged but even coerced into moving into town on account of their industrious qualities and the access they could provide to intra- and extra-archipelago trade networks. Sharing Batavia's economic orientation, the Chinese needed little further inducement and settled on their own initiative, not only as traders in town but also as farmers in the immediate surroundings. Thus the conquerors welcomed the traders, who in turn were followed up by the real settlers, the exploiters of the soil.

Historians of European overseas expansion like Holden Furber and J.H. Parry characterize the 17th and 18th centuries as the "Age of Partnership". They refer thereby to the trading settlements on the coast of the Indian subcontinent where European traders lived shoulder-to-shoulder with their Asian counterparts, under the rule of local potentates. Such equal partnerships never existed in Batavia between its Dutch and Asian populations. Yet, in the first fifty years when the town faced a constant menace of attacks from the Javanese hinterland the Dutch and Chinese at least shared a notion of common destiny. Although the Chinese lived according to their own customs under their own chiefs in Batavia, in ultimo they were subject to the legislation of the Dutch business organisation on whose territory they had become established.

Institutional order involves a variety of spheres such as the religious, the economic and the political. As this order depends upon the successful interrelation and coordination of role behaviour between individuals, groups or social institutions, it is a living arrangement and therefore subject to change in a newly established settlement still in search of an identity. Change can occur on a personal, organizational, or for that matter cultural, plane in different ways: gradually through fads and fashions or suddenly in the form of a revolution. Because an institutional arrangement per se is meant to preserve order, change is not always that obvious to those who participate in it. There may be a discrepancy between appearance and reality. This is quite apparent in the case of Batavia, where heterogeneous groups came to live together under an institutional arrangement which did not necessarily reflect their true relationships. For these merchant groups, stability within the family, religious, economic, and political spheres, was of utmost importance. Contractual arrangements which could prescribe and rationalize reciprocal economic behaviour between the different groups in the market were fixed but the economic and social spheres were less stable than they appeared on first sight. When the interests of ruler and subject diverged or clashed, the social consensus arrangement was inevitably affected and the possibilities for the VOC administration to impose sanctions approved by the parties concerned weakened. This explains the legalistic attitude of the Batavian High Government and the extreme severity with which it sometimes meted out punishments to its Non-European subjects.

It is within this context that the words of the advocate of free trade, Adam Smith, are relevant: "The Government of an exclusive company of merchants is, perhaps, the worst of all governments for any country whatever" (Godée Molsbergen 1936:53). Was Smith referring merely to exclusive practices on the marketplace, or did he imply that the welfare of the people might be sacrificed for the well-being of the Company? Batavia, the headquarters to the biggest European monopolistic business organisation in Asia, constituted a good test of his assertion.

The Plural Accommodation

From the outset, the population of Batavia consisted of different (ethnic) groups who lived more-or-less segregated, according to their own customs, but who met at the marketplace, each group carving its own niche within the local economy. In this respect, Batavian society did not differ much from the type of society found in the harbour principalities of Java, where culturally heterogeneous groups lived in separate wards under their own chiefs.

This "patch-work quilt" model of economic accommodation and cooperation has been called a "plural society". As a result of internal and external factors the colours of the quilt do not readily fade or merge. Each group involved realizes that giving up identity also means giving up collective stakes, each group has to be reckoned with in the economic sector and therefore its economic interests are jealously protected. Although plural society is primarily used as an economic concept, it may be applied to social and political objectives as well.

The British colonial administrator and historian, J.S. Furnivall, was the first to apply the concept of plural society to Southeast Asian society (Furnivall 1939). He described the forms it had taken in the early decades of this century in the Dutch Indies. At the time, administrative regulations and all kinds of accommodations had been worked out to effect a relatively stable society. Contending interest groups were firmly held in check by a colonial government, which sought to control and channel any economic developments that could possibly upset the structural arrangement. Furnivall defined plural society as: "a society comprising two or more elements or social orders which live side-by-side, yet without mingling in one political unit" (Furnivall 1939:446).

Seventeenth century Batavia constituted the first directly administrated territory where the Dutch were forced to come to terms with the phenomenon of an extremely heterogeneous society within an urban context: it was a plural society avant la lettre. The VOC administration in Batavia accepted cultural differences within colonial society insofar as these did not conflict with the norms and values of its own dominant Dutch culture; a conscious policy was even followed, aimed at resisting assimilation of the various groups from the point of view of divide et impera. In short, Batavian society, made up of several contending groups under a western ruler, was haunted by many troubles foreign to other social structures.

As the town was built up from scratch in 1619, the VOC administration set up an institutional framework modeled upon the relatively democratic structure of the contemporary Dutch town. An administrative grid was superimposed upon a diverse population of Dutch burghers, Chinese, Japanese, mestizo's, Balinese, Ambonese and slaves and was expressed in such urban institutions as the Bench of Aldermen, the Orphanage, the sheriff's office, et cetera. As explained in Chapter II, these institutions were only a shadow of their Dutch counterparts and possessed only superficial independence; in reality they were dominated by the VOC through its functionaries who presided over them.

Security was a matter of continual concern for the Company. W.E. Mastenbroek, who in 1935 published his doctoral thesis "De historische ontwikkeling van de staatsrechtelijke indeeling der bevolking van Nederlandsch-Indië", has demonstrated that the Batavian population was categorized according to religion. Within the classification scheme, race played a secondary role for the administration. In Chapter VII, "The Caryatids of Batavia", I have specifically explored how this religious bond was used as pledge of loyalty to the colonial ruler.

The exclusivist practices on which the VOC was founded, were less than beneficial to the development of robust political institutions or, for that matter, a healthy and independent urban economy. Only those individuals who coupled their fate with that of the Company or who plundered it from within were able to build up considerable fortunes, a state of affairs as valid for the Dutch as for the other inhabitants of the town, the Chinese included. O.D. van den Muijzenberg, who has devoted a theoretical study to the usefulness of the plural society concept for social research, notes that members of this type of society cannot be said to have common interests, "because common is what we have collectively, what we share without dividing it up: at best members of a plural society have like interests" (Van den Muijzenberg 1965:9).

Unlike their Dutch fellow citizens of Batavia, the Chinese were also part of the Chinese trade networks, serving interests alien to those of the VOC. The Chinese of Batavia always remained embedded in and drew strength from their own South China Sea trade network which spread from port towns like Amoy, Swatow or Canton all over East and Southeast Asia. Seen from this perspective, Batavian society harboured the ingredients for the potential collision of local interests between the subjects and the administration; moreover, the relationship between the VOC and the Chinese bore the seeds of a potential cultural conflict between two socio-economic systems.

The two hundred years of the VOC's administration of the town may be described initially as a rather fluid cooperative arrangement for commercial ends which finally crystallized into a fixed position when the interests of the Company clashed with opposing forces among its subjects, the Chinese in particular.

Historiographical Notes

This less-than-cheerful picture of Batavia as a segmented society heavily dominated by Company interests is confirmed by the established Dutch historical literature on the city. The town never had an idealized mythical past like "Golden Goa" for instance - not even in the eyes of our 19th century ancestors. Dr. Frederik de Haan, the archivist of the Landsarchief, who in 1922 published the standard work on Batavia's history on the occasion of its tricentennial celebrations, struck no unexpected chord when he digressed to describe some of the darker sides of the town's past - although he may not have followed precisely the guidelines of the commemoration committee who had commisioned him to write the book. It seems that the author of "Oud Batavia" had a peculiar character: productive and hard-working as a historian, if sometimes bad tempered when employed in research in the archives. He nearly succeeded in sealing off access to the Landsarchief in between 1905 and 1922, the period he held sway over this treasure house. De Haan managed to put together and combine in an elegantly styled and ironically toned narrative whatever he deemed of interest in connection with the town's history during the VOC administration. The result, a three-tome magnum opus, is no less a feat of scholarship than his earlier four-volume study on the local history of the Priangan region, upon the completion of which he remarked that he had "squeezed all the records for that district like lemons so that there was not a drop left for others to extract" (Coolhaas 1980:54).

However, there are striking differences between "Priangan" and "Oud Batavia": while the earlier work is encyclopedic in character and constitutes a collection of extensively annotated case studies, the urban history shows more unity but lacks references. It is often said that this is related to the fact that "Oud Batavia" was meant for the educated general public. I would not be surprised if there were more to the story: witness the doggerel in which the writer mocked that anybody

I Introduction

dabbling in the history of the VOC could write about it without doing any original research simply by fleecing De Haan's works.

> Elkeen schrijft in onze dagen
> Over d'Oost-Indische Compagnie
> En waarom zou men niet slagen?
> Wees brutaal, ook zonder studie!
> Zóó moet het elken beunhaas lukken
> Hij heeft DE HAAN maar kaal te plukken. (Nieuwenhuys 1984:10.)

Freely translated:
> These days everybody's writing
> The history of the VOC
> Succeeding too, and without citing
> Their sources on the Dutch oversea
> Those dabblers who this would dare
> Have only to pluck THE ROOSTER bare.

This indeed happened. Novelists, journalists and popular historians have shamelessly cribbed from "Oud Batavia". At the same time De Haan's inimitable style and encyclopedic knowledge have damped the enthusiasm of many a scholar who might otherwise have chosen the town as his or her field of research. A few people who have faced the challenge and by doing so have broadened our knowledge of Batavia should be mentioned. Historians owe much to P.C. Bloys van Treslong Prins' exhaustive genealogical studies. In addition to his numerous publications, his card files can be consulted in Jakarta and The Hague (Bloys van Treslong Prins 1934-1939). In the pre-war period, V.I. van de Wall did research on the country houses located in the neighbourhood of the town (Van de Wall 1943). This research, which also dealt with the history of the families residing in estates, was unfortunately cut short by the author's early death. In 1954, H.A. Breuning published a delightful survey in the Heemschut series, "Het voormalige Batavia", which has been recently - and deservedly - republished. This small book draws heavily from "Oud Batavia", but the architectural education of the writer gives the book its own particular style, balance and succinctness. "The Social World of Batavia", the first English language book-length study of the town, published in 1983 by Jean Gelman Taylor, has been written on basis of secondary studies in the Dutch language, among whom De Haan looms largely. The central thesis in Taylor's book, the emergence of family networks as the main interest group in the town and the role that women played in them, is a well-developed synthesis of earlier theories propounded by such writers as De Haan, Lequin and Furber. "The Social World of Batavia" is highly recommended as a general introduction to Batavia's history. Having surveyed the most important historical literature on the town, we can now turn to the subject matter of the present study, which is introduced below.

Subject Matter

The Ecology
The opening chapter invalidates earlier theories which account for the insalubrious conditions in Batavia and explores how a complex of political and economic policies raised havoc with the ecology of the surround-

ing territory of Batavia, the Ommelanden, bringing death and disease within the walls of the town and ultimately its downfall as a port city. This chapter does not deal in particular with the Chinese inhabitants or mestizo women but further elaborates on the dominant character of the VOC administration which denied its headquarters sufficient flexibility to adapt to changing circumstances. When the Company fell apart, so did the town.

The Chinese
Chapter III, "Trojan Horse of Lead: The Picis in Early Seventeenth Century Java", is the offshoot of an earlier study, "Western Impact on Chinese Communities in Western Java at the Beginning of the 17th Century", which dealt with the initial confrontation between Dutch and Chinese interests in Banten and the subsequent incorporation of this town's Chinese community into the Dutch trade network centered on Batavia (Blussé 1975). Not only is the old myth of the impact of imported European silver on the local market debunked, but also, and more importantly, the chapter examines how the European and Chinese trade networks were related and how they functioned. The case study on the lead coins sheds light on one aspect of the economic cooperation that emerged between the Dutch and the Chinese on Java. How such cooperation worked on a personal level is further examined in Chapter IV.

It is not mere coincidence that the Chinese who was enfranchised by the administration to produce the picis also joined forces with the Dutch in other areas. The case of Jan Con is a tabloid monument to the new type of Chinese élite that emerged in Batavia. The theme of cooperation is examined in a broader framework in the following chapter.

Chapter V, "Batavia, 1619-1740: The Rise and Fall of a Chinese Colonial Town" was written in reaction to the ethnocentric bias displayed by some Indonesian historians who write about the history of their capital with little or no reference to its important Chinese heritage. Consequently it caused a stir when presented in an earlier version at the second Dutch-Indonesian Historical Conference at Ujung Pandang in 1978. Of course, this chapter deals with more than the Chinese legacy. My main objective was to analyse how shifts in economic interests within the VOC as well as among the Chinese were able to throw the existing mode of cooperation out of balance. The writing of this article forced me to re-evaluate the procedures I had previously followed in the collection of data. Having reached my conclusions on the basis of qualitative evidence, I wondered whether the argument concerning the large numerical presence of the Chinese in Batavia and their relative importance within the economic sectors like tax-farming could be further shored up by presenting quantitative evidence. Shortly afterwards, Marie-Sybille de Vienne sent me a copy of her thesis on the Chinese in the Indonesian Archipelago in the 17th century, which she had just defended at Paris University (De Vienne 1979). Her calculations of the share of the Chinese in the tax-farming activities and the inter-archipelago trade of Batavia which were based upon quantitative data derived from the published diaries or Daghregisters of Batavia castle (1624-1682) not only concurred with the outcome of my own research, but also showed what could be achieved in this respect.

The use of statistics for collecting, tabulating, presenting and analysing quantitative data for economic purposes is an inherent part of any modern business organisation. The archives of the VOC are a case

I Introduction

in point. Moreover, the High Government in Batavia also used statistics for administrative purposes if we agree on the 17th century definition of statistics as "the art of reasoning by figures, upon things relating to government" (Finley 1985:25). From 1671 on, the administration took an annual census of the Batavian population, which for more than a century, was duly reported to the Gentlemen XVII in the Netherlands. Abbreviated versions can be found in the printed Daghregisters during the ten years which followed, up until 1682. In the Overgekomen Brieven en Papieren series, the appendices to the General Reports (Generale Missiven) of the High Government, copies of the other censuses are presented in their original complete form. The graphs in Chapters II and V were drawn on the basis of the evidence collected from these annual census reports in the Algemeen Rijksarchief. At a later stage, a student of mine at the History Department, Albertine Bollemeijer, analysed the data of the census reports made at ten-year intervals with the help of a computer, calculating issues such as the sex ratios of the different population groups, their distribution over different wards of the city and so on. The outcome of this research, combined with the annotated computer printouts of the census categorized according to the wards of the town, will be published separately in the Intercontinenta documentation series of the Centre for the History of European Expansion (Leiden University). The computer-produced pie diagrams in Chapter V indicating the relative size of the Chinese population group are an "amuse gueule" of what is to follow.

I was prompted to investigate the Dutch East India Company's policies towards the Chinese shipping link with Batavia for several reasons. This subject, dealt with in Chapter VI, is full of paradoxes. Why were the Chinese allowed to sail their own ships to Batavia by the VOC which continually strove to monopolize the sea routes of Asia? Why was there a difference of opinion between the Gentlemen XVII in the Dutch Republic and the High Government in Batavia with regard to the desirability of establishing a direct trade link to China? And finally, why did this trade suffer a steep decline during the last decades of the eighteenth century? Three sources in particular have been useful in providing answers to these questions: the correspondence between the Governors-General in Batavia and the Directors in Holland give information on the changes in priorities in the trade with China, while the Plakaatboeken yield many data on the way in which this was actually carried out. Chinese data, mostly derived from the Hsiamen-chih, the local Gazetteer of Amoy, provide for the Chinese side of the story (HMC 1961). Once again, quantitative data have buttressed the qualitative evidence. The graph of yearly arrivals in Batavia was composed from the annual lists of arrivals and departures of Chinese shipping in the Overgekomen Brieven en Papieren Series. In collaboration with J. Oosterhoff (Erasmus University) and A.C.J. Vermeulen (Leiden University) these shipping lists as well as all available data on goods imported and exported via the Chinese shipping link have been processed by computer. The result will also be published separately in the Intercontinenta series.

Even though I subscribe to the dictum of the well-known French historian of the ancien régime, Lucien Febvre: "Il faut compter", it should be pointed out that little statistical evidence has been used so far by other historians of Oud-Batavia. Their doyen, Frederik de Haan, actually confessed that he thoroughly disliked statistics. He deemed official tallies like the census "confused and always incorrect", and consequently excused himself with a sigh of relief from the dreary task of quantification (De Haan 1935 I:99). De Haan was right in pointing out that the official figures of capitation tax tickets (hoofdbriefjes) quoted in the Company sources are totally unreliable. Every Chinese citizen had to carry such a ticket on his person to prove he had paid his monthly tax. The Chinese captain who farmed the capitation tax from the administration continuously played down the actual number of his subjects, and many Chinese must have tried to avoid paying the tax altogether. These data therefore have little value. The same goes for the statistics on the Chinese passengers arriving at and departing from Batavia. The nachodas or chief merchants of the Chinese junks made sure that the number of passengers always tallied with the official quotas set by the Company - even when these quotas were actually exceeded. However, in the case of the yearly census of Batavia's population one faces an altogether different situation. The census was made by wijkmeesters, wardmasters, who every year counted the number of people living within their own wards, never more than a thousand people in a single ward. In the course of longer periods of time, occasional lapses in the calculation were rectified, and apart from the representation of the frequently migrating Chinese, we arrive at quite reliable data. The same goes for the figures of incoming and outgoing ships, or goods sold and purchased by the Company.

Women
To this point, we have been speaking of the Chinese population group, which constituted the largest ethnic group of the free civilian population. When we examine the case of the wives of the Dutch burghers in Batavia, one should rather speak of a social category. Starting out as individual members of an aggregate of Asian women, these ladies guaranteed the survival of the Dutch establishment in town and in the process pressed their own distinctive stamp on this segment of Batavia's population. Jean Gelman Taylor has given considerable attention to the emergence of a local Dutch élite in her book. She employs the time-honoured Dutch term of Indischman (she writes Indiesman), for all those more-or-less European citizens who adapted completely to colonial life in the tropics, creating in the process a culture of their own.

Asian women with European status, who as wives to Company servants and freeburghers ensured the continuity of the Dutch local presence in general and the preservation of private fortunes in particular, were objects of ridicule to many a contemporary European writer. Chewing betel nuts, and inevitably surrounded by female slaves who scratched their backs, these women seemed to spend their life in idleness. The German mining engineer Elias Hesse summarized Batavian life as follows: "Batavia is a paradise for women, as they have most of the fun; for their husbands life is a patient, though crowned, suffering, as they have to suffer the plight of caring for their wretched in-laws. It is a hell to the slaves as they are very sharply disciplined." (Hesse 1930:110). The reputation of the town as a paradise for women has been hard to eradicate, not in the least because historians have described the lifestyle of the women rather than studying their social position.

Quite remarkably, ecclesiastical sources have not yet been well evaluated by historians of the ancien régime in Southeast Asia. This is well-illustrated by the fact that F.W. Stapel, the editor of Pieter van

Dam's manuscript on the history of the East India Company (which was written in the second half of the seventeenth century) decided to leave out material on clerical matters because he deemed it of little importance. It is just as significant that eventually it was a cleric, Van Boetzelaer, who published the missing material "on account of its importance to the history of the Dutch mission in Indonesia". I believe it is high time that historians of colonial society start using the church archives for other than strictly mission-oriented goals.

Through its apparatus of social control, the censura morum, or the sermons from the pulpit the Church has left the historian with a treasure trove of material on social life in Batavia. With the help of these records, which were quite inexplicably neglected by De Haan, Taylor and others, I have tried to provide an answer to the question of how Asian wives became actually acclimatized to "Dutch" society in Chapter VII, "The Caryatids of Batavia". The data derived from the Acta of the Batavian Church Council inform us in detail about the procedures used to integrate Asian women into "Dutch" society. Yet, this evidence originates from the moral judges and not from the women themselves. How women actually saw and experienced the limitations of their social position is suggested in Chapter VIII.

The length of this last chapter may be advanced as an excuse for devoting here a few reflections on the nature and reach of the biographical approach, and on the insights this genre presents to the student of the history of a specific group within colonial society. Hypotheses are only the pieces of scaffolding which are erected around a building during the course of construction, and which are taken away as soon as the edifice is completed. As I was dismantling the scaffolding of the study on the Caryatids, the idea struck me that part of it could be used once more and provide the skeleton for a biography.

Ever since Plutarch portrayed the Bioi paralleloi (Parallel Lives) the educated public has perceived the biographical approach as a literary genre with an edifying, exemplary function. But until quite recently, biography equally represented the conventional idea of the meaning of history, i.e. teaching moral lessons to the present generation. If our forefathers looked at history as a mirror of the past, this implies that morality was a timeless phenomenon to them. Nowadays historians would be inclined to say that, due to this timelessness, the traditional biography was ahistorical in character.

The modern historian is no longer primarily interested in drawing moral lessons from the past, he is seeking to arrange the evidence in a logical order through the discovery of some degree of coherence between divergent events. In this historical analysis he leans heavily upon abstract concepts derived from the social sciences. They provide part of the scaffolding, as he deals with events occurring and people living in a previously existing society, and he attempts to explain them in terms of that particular society. Will this "collective" approach, which takes a cross bearing from social structures (stable ties between individuals or groups) and social processes (movements within these structures), eventually result in the demise of the individual-orientated biographical approach? I do not think so, for two quite different reasons.

First of all, personalities of "historic import" will always remain in the limelight due not only to our curiosity about them, but also to their own actions. These men or women quite consciously court other people's interest by writing memoirs or by leaving behind (often carefully sorted) collections of personal papers. Important people simply will not allow us to overlook them. Secondly, whereas the hero's faits et gestes formerly were treated as almost self-containing entities, nowadays the individual's lot is sketched against a backdrop of the era and the civilization that produced him - every individual, after all, is a social being. It goes without saying that this modern "life-and-times" approach better enables us to enter into the inner workings of society and the age in which the hero lived. From this point of view, the historical biography is eminently suited to give us a glimpse of the mentality of a group through the portrait of one of its members.

Individual voices transcend the individual's lot; they tell us about the society which has given them their shape, expression and particular ring. The life story of an individual should give body to social constructs and consequently fill up the gaps that are likely to remain open within the impersonal frameworks of social historiography which, wishing to conceive of larger connections, attaches labels to people who may have something in common with regard to a standard of living or mentality.

Anthropologists, accustomed to dealing with comparatively small groups, are generally conscious of this. Whenever they intend to create a representative picture of the attitudes of a given social group, they do not fail to apply the inductive method and to present one or several life stories noted down through interviews.

But what courses are open to the historian of Southeast Asia who would like to record views of people from a more remote past? Not only will he soon discover that the particular social group, such as the women of ancien régime Batavia, of which he intends to compile life stories participated in a society quite different from today's, but more importantly, it may turn out that few or no traces of individual members can be found.

History has been defined as an attempt to recreate the significant features of the past on the basis of imperfect and fragmentary evidence (Barraclough 1955:29). Because the sources are insufficient, it often is impossible to recover the data needed to formulate adequate answers to the questions. In that case one has to extrapolate. Heroes tend to be served on platters, even if the serving comprises only the head; with "the woman in the street" it is different: here, the contrary is the case and the researcher is forced to go in search of data concerning persons who consciously or unconsciously have left little behind.

To unlock the past, well-aimed questions must be posed with a view to the possible location and character of the source materials one is looking for. Like the fisherman who adapts the shape, the reach and the mesh of his nets to the kind of catch he is after, as he gazes at the grey sea that covers his objective, the historian is aware of the fact that a nice haul is a question of calculated luck and patience, and that he might encounter something unexpected - a mermaid for instance.

While I was searching for and sifting evidence about the position of women in seventeenth century Batavia, I continually ran across references concerning one particular woman, who has been portrayed in totally different ways, in one case as a shining example of filial piety, in the other as an untamed shrew. The question soon posed itself: was she actually a paragon of dedication, or an androphague - a butterfly

I Introduction

or a mantis?

The reader is at liberty to interpret the life story of Cornelia van Nijenroode as a moral lesson, a social analysis or an indictment of the subordinate position of women in the past. My primary objective has been to comprehend certain problems and aspects of the "human condition" in Batavia during the ancien régime, be they legal, social or "événementiel" through the life story of one woman.

Some of the occurrences analysed in connection with the Chinese and the women of Batavia in the coming chapters have been used by other authors in a rather peripheral way - as events belonging to the history of the VOC. But although I have frequently made use of VOC sources, my intentions regarding their application have been different from the VOC historians. Stitching my own observations together with what I have extracted from the evidence, I have tried to provide an insight into the historical context of the social structure in which these groups were embedded. Who controlled this structure, how were the relationships institutionalized, and what were the roots of possible conflicts; these are questions I have attempted to answer.

Perhaps more than in any other branch of history, the history of European expansion overseas evokes feelings of admiration, surprise or even indignation. It is my sincere wish that this study may contribute to a better understanding of the social realities of the historical relationship between colonial rulers and their subjects.

Batavia, coat of arms.

Batavia, Queen of the East.

Chapter II

THE STORY OF AN ECOLOGICAL DISASTER: THE DUTCH EAST INDIA COMPANY AND BATAVIA (1619-1799)*

> Cities and Thrones and Powers
> Stand in Time's eye,
> Almost as long as flowers
> Which daily die;
> But, as new buds put forth
> To glad new men,
> Out of the spent and unconsidered Earth
> The Cities rise again.
>
> Rudyard Kipling

Introduction

The vista that greeted the early-nineteenth-century visitor to Batavia as he disembarked from the launch that had brought him over the shoals of the Batavian roadstead was not a cheerful one. It was as if he had entered a ghost town. Weitzel wrote at the time: "The City of Batavia is not anymore the famous metropolis of yore. The great majority of all the most important buildings and houses have been pulled down, with the exception of the warehouses. Of the castle only rubble heaps remain. The larger part of the town walls have been razed, the city gates have been demolished. The town is but a village surrounded by wide canals [...] the Prinsenstraat being no more than a shaded road along which a few houses can be found near the centre." (Weitzel 1860:8-10).

In 1815 another visitor, Couperus, described a canal to the left of this street: "This is the formerly beautiful Tijgergracht, but all the manifold edifices which used to occupy the area in between this canal and the Prinsenstraat have been levelled to the ground. Who would recognize it as the Tijgergracht which Valentijn celebrated in 1726, only eighty years before, as follows: 'The Tijgergracht possesses uniformly beautiful buildings, the most exquisite of the town. The beauty of this elegantly planted straight canal surpasses anything I have ever seen in Holland. Although one may find along the Heerengracht in Amsterdam or elsewhere more beautiful palaces or wider canals, all [these canals and streets] however do not match the delight and the satisfying and pleasing view that this canal and the others of Batavia offer to the eye' [...]." After rambling on for a while about the lost splendour of the town, Couperus concludes: "the migration of the European nations, if I may put it like that, has of course resulted in new settlements elsewhere, i.e. [the higher-lying regions of] Rijswijk, Noordwijk and Weltevreden".[1]

These impressionistic sketches may suffice to illustrate the fact that at the turn of the nineteenth century a fundamental change had taken place in the morphology of Batavia. Like a snake shedding its skin, the town population had crept out of the city walls that had encircled it for almost two centuries, beginning a new life about ten kilometers inland in a garden city with a totally different layout. In this chapter I would like to focus in depth on the origins and causes of the conditions that forced the Dutch, in the interests of their own survival, to make the move to Weltevreden during the government of Marshall Daendels.

Current Views on the Causes of Decay
What were the causes of the process that turned the "Queen of the East" into the "Graveyard of the East"? This question has only been answered in part and unsatifactorily. Medical specialists of the past stressed in their analysis the bad climate of the city, the low, hanging, poisonous mists, the polluted canals and of course the main object of their interests: exotic diseases with sinister names like remitterende rotkoortsen (intermittent rotting fevers), roode loop (red diarrhoea), febres ardentes, malignae et putridae, and mort de chien.

Company officials also sought to put the blame primarily on nature: the unhealthy climate of a marshy region in the tropics, the lack of fresh water, and the formation of a sandbank in front of the river mouth as a result of the eruption of the nearby Salak volcano in 1699. They rarely criticized the politics of the Company itself, but rather focussed on the manner in which their predecessors had built the town in the Dutch manner, with houses in a row and a number of canals bordered by shady trees. Here the main argument was that, due to overcrowded quarters, insalubrious conditions developed which were exacerbated by the canals. The stench of these polluted waters could not be dispersed by the wind because it was blocked by the rows of houses and trees.

Even though Raffles is often cited with reference to the problems of the city - he was after all one of the first non-Dutch writers to touch upon the matter - his analysis is not trustworthy. Perhaps this was because it was no longer a vital issue by the time of his arrival in 1811. The migration of the Dutch population out of the lower town had already taken place a few years earlier, during the administration of Governor-General Daendels. In his "History of Java", Raffles rakes all the above arguments together and adds a scathing, sarcastic commentary which is plainly meant to ridicule "mijnheer" - as he used to call the Dutch. He buttresses his account with unreliable statistics, however, which undermines his argument. If we may believe the data he presents, Batavia would have lost, between 1730 and 1752, no less than 1,119,375 inhabitants, which would amount to the total extinction of an entire Batavian population every five months for a period of twenty-three years (Raffles 1817 II:viii). Other reports like those of C.S.W. van Hogendorp (1833) and Keuchenius (1875) have come closer to the source of the problems by pointing at the malfunctioning irrigation works in the Ommelanden (the hinterland of Batavia) and possible faults in their structure.

All these reports and inquests describe symptoms and not the real causes of Batavia's decay. The nineteenth century explanation which still prevails is that the Dutch designed their own doom when they constructed in a tropical area a town whose lay-out was similar to that of the cities in the Low Countries: city walls, canals and houses in a row.

II The Story of an Ecological Disaster

This explanation, however, does not stand up to an examination of the historical facts. Batavia was a perfectly healthy city during the first hundred years of its existence, and, according to Jean-Baptiste Tavernier, boasting "la plus belle eau et la meilleure qui soit au monde" (Van Gorkom 1913:182). Some historians have recognized this and have hastened to say that although this may be true, the state of the town's sanitation was completely thrown out of balance as a result of the eruption of the Salak volcano, which partly blocked the course of the Ciliwong River, the waters of which supplied the town, and polluted it as well. Further scrutiny of archival material shows, however, that the mortality rate suddenly increased only in 1733, which is thirty-four years later. So this argument can also be discounted.

Restating the Problem
The problem that underlay Batavia's demise - its transformation from a healthy city into a graveyard - should not be sought primarily in the Dutch layout of the town or in natural disasters. They should be sought in the Ommelanden, the city's hinterland. The rash and thoughtless development of the Ommelanden for the sugar cultivation, followed by a crisis in the export of this product, resulted in important changes in the natural irrigation system of the plains and eventually affected its ecological balance.

It has been rightly stated that in terms of town-hinterland relations, port cities can only achieve sustained growth after the political pacification of the countryside and its exploitation through modern techniques of production (Telkamp 1978:41). It was the tragedy of Batavia that this exploitation was mainly meant to support the trade policies of the Dutch East India Company (VOC) and not the city itself. The burgeoning of the Ommelanden and the absence of answers to the challenges that faced the town community were the direct result of the lack of an independent, institutional framework for the town during the rule of the VOC. In other words, it is not sufficient to attribute the disturbance of the equilibrium to a single cause. Rather, insight can only be achieved through the study of simultaneity among several processes, which in this case are, as we shall see, mainly of an institutional, economic and ecological character.

Organization

To the reader of the enthusiastic accounts of Batavia by travellers who visited it at the end of the seventeenth century, the city may have been close to the four considerations that Aristotle, father of civic planning, deemed necessary for the situation and planning of the ideal town: health, defence, suitability for political activity, and beauty.[2] I shall discuss these four points in turn in the chronological treatment of the town's history below, but it should be emphasized that, save for the names, Batavia in fact lacked all those political institutions that gave her Dutch sister cities inner strength: its citizens lacked all political power or privilege. The VOC directorate denied the town and its population the right to become a real town. It never intended to deal with Batavia other than as its headquarters, its place of rendezvous in Asia. The government regulation of April 26, 1650 actually states that "the administration of the city should depend in general and in particular upon the proper direction and leadership of Governor-General and

Council" (Van Deventer 1886:210). Always and everywhere the mighty government made its hand felt. The firm decision to treat Batavia as a kind of super trade-factory, explains why the town's lot was tied in such an inextricable way to that of the trade institution which had created it: Batavia intramuros survived the VOC for a mere decade.

Having touched briefly upon the organization of the town and its inherent weaknesses, a few words should be said about the spatial arrangement of the town and its function, before we engage upon a chronological treatment in which the three concepts of function, spatial arrangement and organization will be employed and the ways in which they interacted will be considered.

Demography
Regarding the demography of the town, which was closely tied to its spatial arrangement, we are still very much in the dark. There are qualitative treatments available of several of the most important population groups, such as the Balinese (Lekkerkerker 1918), the Mardijkers (De Haan 1917) and the Chinese (Hoetink 1917, 1918, 1922, 1923), and one interesting but nonetheless sketchy article on Jakarta's ethnic profile, which touches briefly on the Company period (Castles 1967). The figures presented below have been made on basis of quantitative data derived from the annual census of Batavia. They describe better than words the life cycle of the town. Fig. 1 on the population of the town and the Ommelanden may roughly parallel the thermometer charts of a hospital patient. It clearly illustrates the decay of Batavia intramuros starting with the 1730s.

As is the case with so many other colonial cities, the "native" population of Batavia was mainly segregated on the unplanned outer fringes of the city, although the Chinese homes were spread throughout the city until 1740. The population groups shown in Fig. 2 are only the

Fig. 1. Total population inside and outside Batavia (based on Overgekomen Brieven en Papieren series, VOC archives).

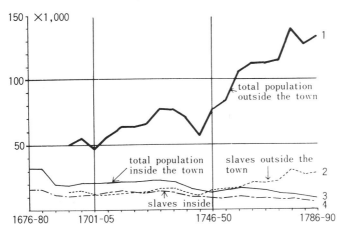

Fig. 2. The major population groups at Batavia (based on Overgekomen Brieven en Papieren series, VOC archives).

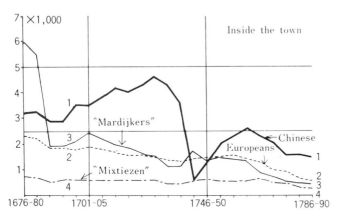

most important ones numerically. As for the other groups, it will suffice here for the time being to mention them briefly, by quoting the rather slanderous account of the former governor of Malacca, A. Couperus, for curiosity's sake and to demonstrate the mutual feelings of distrust that reigned in the late eighteenth century: "The other inhabitants of Batavia are Malays, Bugis, Macassarese, Ambonese, Timorese, Bengali, Ceylonese and others. It would be circumstantial to treat all these different nations one by one. I shall honestly say that the Ceylonese have a false character, the Javanese (Malays) are lazy and slow, the Bugis sly and cruel, the Timorese superstitious, the Ambonese haughty and vain, the Macassarese cruel, the Malays slow and the Bengali thievish, all of them being lascivious people."[3] Domestic slaves made up nearly half of the city population and lived throughout the town. They originated from Malabar, Bengal, Sumatra, Bali and above all Sulawesi. On an average, three thousand slaves were imported into Batavia annually.

The Functions of the Town and the Main Interest Groups
Batavia was founded in the footsteps of trade. As stated above, it was meant to function as the headquarters of the VOC, "Het magazijn derzelver producten". Soon enough (business) transactions also came to link Batavia to the countryside and to the ports of the native shipping networks in the archipelago, as I shall show in Chapter III in my study concerning the picis. It grew out into an emporium, with its own staple-market, for the inter-archipelago trade, and became in the course of time a centre for the hinterland that was initially opened up piecemeal but was after 1680 literally overwhelmed by Western and Chinese exploiters.

Before we engage upon the chronological treatment of the life cycle of Batavia intramuros, let us dwell for a moment on the interest groups that were tied to the different functions of the town. It will then become perfectly clear that there was little room for private enterprise apart from the Company. De Haan described the situation well: "In the Company period, officialdom was the wielder of power as well as of intellect, the proprietor of capital and large landownership. The freeburgher class on the contrary, being small in number, without direction, had to confine itself meekly to what was decided by the authorities or had to take with a smile the kicks that the government happened to administer." (De Haan 1935 I:426).

It was of course in the interest of the directors of the VOC, the Gentlemen XVII, in Holland, that the rendezvous should pay for its own maintenance. It soon turned out to be a costly undertaking for the Company itself. For years on end, the factory's balance was in the red. To the apparently grossly underpaid Company officials serving in the VOC headquarters, however, Batavia turned out to be a source of wealth. They literally plundered the resources of the Company through private trade or smuggling, and entered into local investments with embezzled funds.

As an emporium, the town was supposed to provide an income to the Dutch freeburghers who were needed for the maintenance and supply of the Company headquarters. Their income was drawn mainly from the service sector, brewing, bar-tending, and so on, and from private trade. As the freeburghers tended to undermine some of the Company's dealings, the Gentlemen XVII did everything in their power to thwart or confine the activities of the private merchants. They chipped away at the foundation upon which these citizens should have based their livelihood.

On account of their skill as handicraftsmen, fishers, and agriculturalists and due to their experience in inter-archipelago low-expense trade, the Chinese served the networks that were generally situated outside the grasp of the Company. As I shall show in the following chapters, this population group actually became the real citizenry of Batavia, nevertheless remaining without political power, until it was considered a menace and massacred in 1740.

As for the entrenchment of the town in its agrarian (regional) system, the Ommelanden provided good opportunities for investment and a source of income to the Batavian Company elite. Rich Company officials came to possess and exploit the land by having the labour performed for them by slaves and Chinese tenants. Batavia came close to what Werner Sombart called "a consumption city": it derived its maintenance not so much from products fabricated in town and sold in the countryside, but rather on the basis of legal claims, such as taxes and rents without having to deliver anything of value in return.[4] The demands of the Gentlemen XVII for huge quantities of export products such as sugar and coffee undermined any attempt or possibility for a balanced approach to the opening-up of the Ommelanden, or indeed any town-hinterland relations of that order.

The town's three functions - headquarters, trade-emporium and urban centre to an agrarian hinterland - were interlocking, but unfortunately the Gentlemen XVII regarded the real development of a free-economy centre as a threat to their own interests. This becomes apparent from the organization of the town government which did not provide political power or privilege to the burghers. Thus the opportunity to create a real town community was not taken. As a result, there were eventually only two interest groups left, after the burghers and the Chinese had been shut out because they were too influential or too

II The Story of an Ecological Disaster

sizeable: the Gentlemen XVII in the Republic did everything they could to milk the colony and turn its debit into a credit balance, and the Company officials did the same to line their purses. This policy at least temporarily wreaked havoc on the ecology of the Ommelanden in the eighteenth century. To what extent these two groups ever fully realized what the consequences of their actions were remains an academic question.

The Beginnings

In 1610 Jacques l'Hermite received permission from the Pangeran of Jakarta to build a trade factory for the Dutch East India Company. In the summer of 1618 Governor-General Jan Pietersz. Coen moved most of the Company's belongings from Banten to this trade factory after his attempts to monopolize the Banten market had misfired. At the end of the year, the Dutch, who had begun to fortify their trade post, were attacked by the combined forces of the English and the Pangeran of Jakarta and his allies. On May 30th, 1619 the native army was soundly beaten, the English had left, and the kraton, the palace of the Pangeran, was levelled to the ground. Out of its ashes rose the Dutch castle city of Batavia, which by 1660 had attained its final form. The position of Batavia castle and its town was as follows: on its northern side it

The roadstead of Jakarta around 1600

Batavia and surroundings anno 1670.

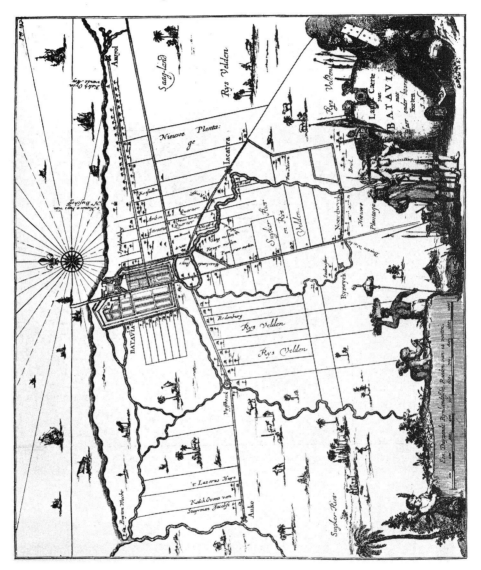

II The Story of an Ecological Disaster

bordered on the Batavian roadstead, which is well-shielded from the seaswell by a multitude of small islands that wreathe the bay and protect the anchorage within. To the south the town looked out over the wild landscape of a marshy but fertile plain which rose gently to the feet of the high mountains in the background and was covered with woods and intersected by fast-running rivers.

Batavia castle was a square fortress with four bastions lying at the mouth of the river Ciliwong. It housed the administrative buildings, the living quarters of the higher servants of the Company, the barracks of the garrison, a little church, and the warehouses.

Batavia-town formed a rectangle of about 2250 metres in length and 1500 metres across. It was cut into two almost equal parts by the river Ciliwong or Grote Rivier as the Dutch used to call it. Each part of the town was in turn intersected by two canals running parallel along the longest sides of the rectangle, and these were themselves intersected at right angles by several cross-canals. Eight streets - all of them thirty feet wide - further emphasized the grid pattern of the town. All Batavia was finally enclosed by high coral rock walls with twenty-two bulwarks. Four gates led to the bridges that spanned the surrounding deep city moat.

External Challenges
First I shall focus upon the military challenges from outside Batavia's walls, the effect they had upon the supply of foodstuffs for the city population, and upon town-hinterland relations. In 1628, less than ten years after Batavia was established, the troops of the Sultan Agung of Mataram appeared before the city, the walls of which were at the time only partly completed. For two consecutive years the Javanese tried to capture the town but all attempts failed because the Dutch fleet cut off the supply of food that had to reach the besiegers by sea. During the siege, all population groups of Batavia took part in the defence of the town and mounted sallies against the enemy. A veritable esprit de corps was achieved among the different nations of the town, if we may believe the enthusiastic contemporary records. Repulsing the Mataram troops did not, however, mean that the menace of violence from outside had disappeared. Nearby Banten, where most of the followers of the Pangeran of Jakarta had sought refuge, continued to render the Ommelanden unsafe for the next fifty years.

In the early days, short reconnaissance trips were undertaken via the rivers in the vicinity of the town in search for timber. The heavily forested land, however, remained unexplored and unexploited. Consequently most food supplies had to be shipped in from overseas. Rice was imported from Siam, Burma and in later years from Mataram.

After an armistice was concluded with Banten in 1639, market-gardens were laid out in the shadow of the town walls but even there the Chinese gardeners were not quite safe from Bantenese vagabonds. The construction of three canals in western, eastern and southern directions eased the transport of timber and foodstuffs to the city and stimulated the emergence of an infrastructure for the development of the hinterland. In 1656, war broke out again with Banten; all ten sugar mills and twenty-three brick factories just outside town were razed by the enemy. As a security measure, the government decided to order the various Indonesian peoples that had come to live inside the walls, out of the city. The Javanese, the Ambonese and the Balinese were settled in separate kampongs outside the walls, but they nonetheless had to be provided with sufficient protection against aggression from outside.

A line of defence works was constructed an hour's distance from the town: Antjol in the East, Anké in the West, Jakatra, Wilgenburg and Rijswijk to the South. Along the roads and the canals leading to these five strongholds the ground was cleared for cultivation to ensure the food supply (rice and market-gardening) and to some extent for export crops like sugar. Around this time we find the first reports by Company officials like Van Hoorn, Demmer and Cuneus on "the desirability of stabilizing an agricultural colony".[5] Chastelein, an early eighteenth century Ommelanden landowner, confirms that it was not until the conclusion of the peace treaty with Banten of 1659 that "we could for the first time discover these lands and bring some order to them. Not much headway was made until 1670, but after that year this region took on a different aspect" (Chastelein 1876:179).

From 1660 onwards plots of land were sold to Europeans who did not work the land themselves but instead leased them out to Chinese tenants or employed slaves. The price of the land was set according to the distance from the city. Some of the more remote regions were issued to the chiefs of the "native populations" who, as mentioned above, lived in kampongs outside the walls. The captain of the Balinese, for instance, received a large plot near Tangerang in 1667. This was granted on condition that certain corvée services would be rendered and products like rice would be delivered at set prices. In this way the government tried to populate the deserted regions around the town. By 1680 a second line of defence works was completed at some twenty kilometres distance from the town, namely at Tangerang in the West, Tanjongpura in the East and Meester Cornelis in the South. This region came mainly to be used, as we shall see, for sugar cultivation.

Internal Challenges
A second challenge to the authority of the VOC government in Batavia came from inside the city. The so-called freeburghers, free townsmen not in the service of the Company, who had taken part in the construction of the town and its defence, wanted to have their burgher rights confirmed. They desired a city government, a vroedschap of their own, which could not be manipulated by presiding Company officials. The letter which they sent in 1649 directly to the States-General of the Dutch Republic (thus bypassing the Governor-General in Batavia and the Gentlemen XVII in Amsterdam) in fact represented the culmination of a running feud between the burghers, the Governor-General and the Gentlemen XVII, which had been fermenting since the founding of Batavia in 1619.

The founder of the town, Jan Pietersz. Coen, was quite impressed with the powers of endurance of the Portuguese colonies in Asia, which, cut off from their mother country, but due to their economic independence, were still able to withstand Dutch aggression. Therefore, Coen deemed it absolutely necessary that a strong and sizeable colony of Dutchmen should be established at Batavia. To make this possible, he proposed that the freeburghers be granted relative freedom in private trade and city government. His proposals were brushed aside, however. During the 1640s this discussion was revived when Governor-General Van Diemen noticed the feeble economic base supporting the Batavian citizenry. He put the question bluntly. Would their lordships, he asked the Gentlemen XVII, please make it clear what ideas they actually had about the colony? The main point of the answer from Amsterdam - and it took the directors of the VOC several years to formulate it - can be summarized as follows: "We are on the horns of a dilemma. A Dutch colony is indeed highly useful, nay, indispensable for the political status of the Company. Experience has shown, however, that these colonies cannot exist unless freedom of movement and freedom of trade is permitted to the colonists. This would certainly have a detrimental effect on the mainstay of the Company, its trade. The strong maintenance of this trade was the motive that resulted in the issue of the octroy by the States-General to the VOC. Therefore, the stabilization of a real colony with burghers trading privately cannot be in the interest of the Company." And, as if they had not made their ideas clear enough, they went on to do so in a letter dated October 14, 1651. They wrote: "We must remain the masters of the enterprise, even if that means the disposal of the Batavian citizenry".[6] At the time the latter amounted to no more than a few hundred males and their families.

Thus all requests from the Dutch citizenry for representation elected from their members were brushed aside. They had to live under institutions which were similar in name only to those back in Holland. All administrative organs in Batavia were presided over by Company officials, mostly members from the Council of the Indies. According to Van den Berg, who devoted an interesting article to examining the strivings of the early Batavian citizenry for more political privileges and economic independence, in the first decades of the town's existence the citizenry was of more importance than is commonly supposed (Van den Berg 1904:30-63). A burgher mentality definitely existed, which manifested itself in a feeling of association with the lot of the town, as is clearly indicated from the statements of these people: it also was their town; they had fought for its freedom against Mataram. Valentijn still perceived some of this burgher pride when he arrived for the first time in Batavia in 1685, the year in which the isolation of the town from its Ommelanden had finally come to an end. "Most beautiful was at New Year's day the traditional parade of Batavia's citizen soldiery, which still occurred at the time. Soon afterwards it fell into disuse." (Valentijn 1724-26 IV:107.)

The consequences of the severe stand by the VOC directorate began to make themselves evident much earlier than this, however. In 1654 the well-being of the free citizenry had already gone downhill to such an extent that the Gentlemen XVII asked the Governor-General whether he could not take some measures to lighten their burden. Henceforth the burghers lived subject to the whims of the successive Governors-General.

This also becomes clear if we make some further inquiries into the ways by which justice was administered and government was executed. Roman Dutch law was administered in town. It was full of loopholes, because the government was confronted with circumstances that were totally different from those in Holland. Special provisions had to be made for institutions such as slavery, which were all issued as ordinances, edicts and so on. They were collected during the tenure of Governor-General Van Diemen and published in 1642, entitled "De Bataviasche Statuten".[7] It should likewise be added that appointed chiefs, or kapiteins, of the different native populations of the town had the right to punish petty crimes in their own fashion.

Any decision that was taken by the Council of the Indies - the de facto VOC government of Batavia - was issued by plakkaat or ordinance. "The result", as a seventeenth century landowner, Cornelis Chastelein, wryly remarked, "is that they are heeded only as long as they remain posted. Once they are stripped off the walls, they are forgotten." (Chastelein 1876:182.) Thus all typical Dutch urban institutions - the Bench of Aldermen, the trustees and orphanage trustees, the polder board - which were often viewed with admiration by foreign visitors as a proof of righteous Dutch government were like a Potemkin village. The Company held the town in its iron grip. Governor-General Van der Lijn (1645-1650) is said to have spontaneously remarked, "I would rather serve the heathen and the Turks than the Company" (Oost-Indische praetjes 1663:3). He was certainly not the only one who thought so.

Concluding, we can say that during the first sixty years of the town, the Company pressed its organizational stamp firmly onto its headquarters on Java. Thereby it completely bound the city's functions to the business of the Company. The spatial layout comprised a walled port town with Europeans, Mestizos, Chinese and a few other small Asian groups living inside the town with their slaves, and the Javanese, Ambonese and Balinese living in kampongs in the direct vicinity. The relationship with the hinterland was established when the two concentric defence lines were drawn. The space in between the first line and the city was used mainly for market-gardening, while the space between the first and second defence line came to be reserved for cash crops. This set the framework for the next thirty years during which the town was destined to reach its zenith - thanks to the economic success of the Company itself as well as the exploitation of the Ommelanden for cash crops.

The Ommelanden and Sugar Cultivation

During the period between 1680 and 1720 a real bonanza was discovered. The Ommelanden were opened up in Wild West fashion with the help of a steady flow of Chinese coolies who came in droves to Java after the Chinese imperial government lifted the maritime prohibitions in 1684. As I shall describe in Chapter V the role that the Chinese played in the Ommelanden, I shall now limit myself to only a few general remarks, which may serve to introduce the ecological disaster of the 1730s and the massacre of the Chinese in 1740. Batavia's natural surroundings underwent a fundamental change when the Ommelanden were cleared of their forests. Apart from the fields reserved for rice cultivation, the plain was refashioned to support sugar cultivation, which was strongly promoted by the High Government through measures such as high purchase prices and liberal credit. At first farmers were encouraged to plant new crops by the promise of high profits. As soon as overproduction occurred the Heren XVII ordered a clamp-down on production, setting quotas and lowering purchase prices. This policy towards the sugar cultivation indicates the pattern which, in most cases, became the Company's trademark when involved with agriculture. It does not matter whether we are dealing with pepper or other spices, coffee or indigo; the same trick was used everywhere throughout the seventeenth and eighteenth centuries. The sugar bonanza in the Ommelanden lasted until the early 1720s, ending then not only because of soil-exhaustion and the growing scarcity of firewood for the sugar cauldrons, but also because quotas had been set. There were at least two reasons for this fixation of the output: the disappearance of several outlets in Asia, and competition for the European market from the much cheaper West Indian sugar.

The important change inherent in sugar cultivation for a landscape is well-known from early examples such as Madeira and the West Indies. It devours forests, pollutes the water and exhausts the often delicately balanced tropical soil if practised in the ill-advised way which was almost always adhered to in past centuries. It can thoroughly destroy the natural equilibrium of an area. That is exactly what happened in the Ommelanden. A timber producing area lost the major part of its forest cover to sugar mills that needed wood for fuel. Situated near the rivers, the sugar mills polluted the fresh water flowing into Batavia.

In this respect the findings of a reconnaissance party that was sent to the higher reaches of the Ommelanden rivers in 1701 should be noted. Its mission was to investigate, two years after the eruption of the Salak volcano, the causes of the pollution of the water that streamed through the city. Upon returning, the expedition leaders reported that they had found the upper reaches of the Ciliwong River clear all the way down to the (sugar) land of Cornelis Chastelein (Leupe 1878: 484-505). The pollution of the Tangerang River must also have been due to the sugar mills in that region. Thus water pollution had little to do with the Salak volcano. It is true, however, that a sandbank formed in front of the mouth of the Ciliwong river as a result of the débris that washed down the river immediately after the eruption. This sandbank has often been cited as the main culprit behind Batavia's unhealthiness - but as we have shown, this is a misinterpretation of the evidence. In the years following the Salak eruption, a decrease in the volume of water supplied by the Ciliwong to the town did become noticeable, but, as was pointed out by the investigation team of 1701, this was probably due as much to the diversion of water for irrigation purposes as to the eruption. The real shortage of water in the town became apparent only in the late 1720s, and this was typical of an ecology robbed by sugar cultivation of its capacity to retain moisture between wet spells. Here all the evidence converges. As sugar mills were closed down due to the crisis on the sugar-market and the erosion of the soil, the river irrigation system fell into decay and roving bands of unemployed coolies started to render the countryside unsafe.

Monsoon or Mookervaart?

In his "History of Java", Raffles cites a reply to queries about the unhealthy nature of Batavia dated October 14, 1753 (Raffles 1817 II:ix). This reply is without doubt the report by Doctor J.A. Paravicini to Governor-General Mossel.[8] Paravicini was an adherent of the so-called miasma theory, according to which illnesses could be spread by noxious vapours. This theory remained an accepted one far into the nineteenth century and generated the absurd notion of the killing vapours of Batavia's canals. Paravicini very scrupulously investigated the causes of the sudden increase in mortality after 1733. He designated the Mookervaart, a canal dug in that year as the obvious culprit, but he personally thought the fact that so many people had died was due rather to the evil influence of the irregular monsoon.

Batavia and surroundings anno 1740.

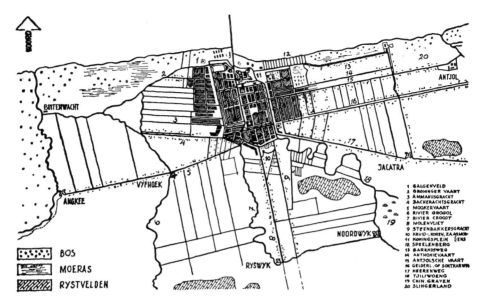

In 1732 Governor-General Diederik Durven ordered the Mookervaart to be dug in order to regulate a better water supply to the town. The digging of the new canal not only spread illness and death among the Javanese navvies and the population of the desas in the neigbourhood; it also brought death into Batavia. Although the volume of the water-supply was increased, it remained virtually stagnant. Thus an even greater amount of river silt from the Ommelanden - a result of the soil erosion - was deposited along the canal-network of the city, where it became mixed with the muck and trash of the inhabitants, the folhas nonas horas.[9] The so-called Modder-Javanen (mud-Javanese) from Cirebon came once a year to divest Batavia's canals of the excess mud. Eventually this turned out to be an endless task which resulted only in certain death for the pitiable corvée labourers. Consequently the canal cleaning was given up in the eighties.[10] As the Mookervaart derived most of its water from the rivers that it crossed, these now silted up at their outlets near the sea. Stagnant pools, breeding grounds for mosquitoes, formed around the city: malaria became endemic. Other illnesses that spread included typhoid and dysentery. Fig. 3 shows the disastrous increase in mortality. However, the Ommelanden themselves did not become a chronic threat to the health of Batavian population. Diversification of the cultivated crops in the second half of the eighteenth century brought about a recovery of this area from the crisis of the late 1720s. The inept construction of the Mookervaart, meant to alleviate the sufferings caused by a decreased water supply, paradoxically resulted in the destruction of the ecology of the town's direct surroundings.

Fig. 3. Mortality of Europeans in Batavia, 1716-1767, based on Semmelink 1885:387-8.

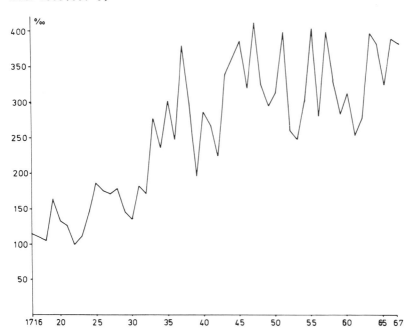

After 1730 building activities increased south of the city, as wealthy burghers started to move out to the more healthy region of Weltevreden. Although Governor-General Van Imhoff tried to improve the sanitary condition of the town during the 1740s, these attempts had little effect as the real character or origin of the illnesses were not known at the time.

There were two hospitals in town for Company servants and burghers. One was situated inside the town and was nicknamed De Moordkuil (the death-pit)[11], while the other was outside. On average, one in four patients died inside the town and one in twelve outside. A contemporary observer remarked in relation to this that in the hospital of Lyon, the best of Europe, one out of 15 patients died, in Hotel Dieu in Paris because of the crowded conditions one out of four (Stavorinus 1785 III:412). The high mortality became visible in and outside the town: Stavorinus speaks about empty houses and desolated gardens. He also cites one of James Cook's officers as having said that the mere thought of Batavia's unhealthiness would keep any other nation from attempting an attack. What it felt like to live in such a town is made clear by the following anecdote: in a letter to his mother, the Company servant J. Bergsma explained how he had unearthed the bodies of a Dutch couple who had been killed by their own slaves. He adds: "meanwhile I called for coffins, which are always ready over here. Because it often happens that one has dinner with someone tonight, and is present at his funeral tomorrow; the day after tomorrow it will be auction day, two days later he will be forgotten."[12]

The European Connection

This discussion concerning the causes of the sudden increase in mortality of Batavia's population would be incomplete if a recent and interesting article on the recruitment of VOC personnel by the maritime historian J.R. Bruijn were not given careful consideration. Discussing the high mortality among sailors in Europe during the 1730s, he also touches upon the sudden outbreak of illness in Batavia. "Many sailors were so ill upon their arrival in the Orient that they had to be admitted right away into the hospital. Data about the number of patients and deaths in the Batavian hospital show a steep increase after 1733, especially regarding deaths. The illnesses that erupted on board continued to rage ashore, and their victims in fact should be added to the number of deaths during the voyage itself." (Bruijn 1976:223.)

If this assertion were true, the consequences would be far-reaching indeed. It would mean that Batavia's unhealthiness and the steep increase in mortality in 1733 had little to do with the local situation. And as if trying to show the influence of sea power upon Asian medical history, Bruijn indeed concludes that "the causes for the high mortality rate among Company personnel in Asia should not be sought in Asia" (Bruijn 1976:247).

As we have seen, local and contemporary sources do not agree with this bold theory; an abundance of qualitative and quantitative data stress the primacy of endemic factors. Closer scrutiny of other data also shows this position to be untenable. It would lead us into a long and fruitless discussion if we were to call into question whether all those sailors that were admitted to the hospital really entered it directly on account of illnesses that they had already acquired on board. Neither this nor the opposite can really be proven. I would argue rather that sailors, weakened by the long six-to-seven-months voyages and the deficient diet on board, were the first to fall prey to the raging epidemics in the town. This thesis can be proven by way of a rather simple calculation on the basis of figures for the percentage of sailors that died on board the ships that arrived in Batavia, and the percentage of Company servants (mostly sailors and soldiers) that died in the Batavian hospitals. If, during 1729, 1733 and 1737 illnesses of unprecedented fierceness were raging on the ships then the death toll on board should indicate this fact. There indeed was a steady increase in mortality aboard the ships: 8.8% in 1729, 10.4% in 1733 and 11.8% in 1737 (Bruijn, Gaastra and Schöffer 1979 II:402). This increase however is negligible if we compare it to the increase in deaths among the patients in Batavia's hospitals: 14.2% in 1729, 25.5% in 1733 and 36.4% in 1737. These data make it clear that the high death toll in the hospitals was due to local causes.

It should be stressed, however, that a high mortality rate does not necessarily lead to the evacuation of a city, or even less so its demise. Calcutta, after all, was as unhealthy as Batavia. The causes for Batavia's final decay should also be sought in the economic side of the matter. This takes us back to the functions of Batavia as headquarters of the Company and as a centre of inter-archipelago trade.

II The Story of an Ecological Disaster

The End of an Era

We have seen how the well-being of the Batavian burghers came to depend on the whims of the Governors-General. The implications of this become clear if we study the policies of some of these viceroys in the latter half of the eighteenth century.

Before he was appointed Governor-General in 1742, Gustaaf Willem van Imhoff handed over to the VOC directorate a colonial programme which outlined the means by which he planned to restore the perilous affairs of the Company in Asia (Heeres 1912). Among the many things that should be considered for improvement, he mentioned the situation of Batavia, which at the time was recovering from the after-effects of the Chinese massacre of October 1740. As so many people before him, Van Imhoff stated that Batavia owed its existence to its function as the headquarters to the Company. Trade and settlement had always come second. The trade (by this, he meant private trade) had often come close to smuggling, due to the Company monopolies. Now it was time, he maintained, to rethink Batavia's position and permit its burghers a free and protected trade in Asia. Van Imhoff did not ignore the political organization of the colony in his plan. It was his opinion that the Batavians should be authorized to choose their own city council or vroedschap. But like most of his ideas, these remained only plans on paper.

Van Imhoff's successor, Jacob Mossel (1750-1761) has generally had a bad press in Dutch historical writing (Coolhaas 1958). The reasons are not hard to find. During his tenure he introduced the so-called "Reglement ter beteugeling van pracht en praal" in which he prescribed to the Batavian population in 124 articles exactly what kinds of diamonds, clothes, hats, they were to wear; how many slaves were allowed to follow them in the streets, and so on, according to rank and status. When the ideas of the French Revolution became en vogue in Batavia, a people's gathering declared these regulations null and void and "unworthy of a free Batavian". Consequently Mossel, by virtue of his representing all that stands for the evils of the ancien régime, was made into a scapegoat. He has also been criticized for having made private trade impossible, but here the curious problem arises that Batavia underwent a period of prosperity during his reign, the high mortality rate notwithstanding. It is striking how writers on the subject have parroted each other in this case. A century ago J.K.J. de Jonge described Mossel as the man who only wanted to leave the "trash" (afval) of the Company's trade to the burghers. Most historians have blindly accepted this verdict without checking it against the sources.

Mossel actually was a brilliant "economist", as his contemporaries called him. He did indeed forbid private trading between Batavia and the Indian subcontinent, but he was fully in favour of leaving a large share of the trade at Batavia to private entrepreneurs. "As the Company is a distinguished merchant", he wrote, "it must also engage in a distinguished trade and neither in a universal nor a common one. It must be a privileged trade." To this "privileged trade" he reckoned the opium and spice trades, navigation to Europe and the commerce in copper, pepper and textiles. Mossel was quite apt at selling his arguments to the seventeen businessmen in the Republic, who were interested mainly in protecting their monopoly. "We must not engage in an all-embracing trade" - he continued - "because there is no way in which we could conduct it on a profitable basis. [...] Those articles that can be

The Dutch Reformed Church at Batavia, second half 18th century.

II The Story of an Ecological Disaster

better dealt in by private traders than by the Company should be left to them; because just as they live from the scraps [not trash!] of what the Company leaves to them, in the same way the Company can also exist on its own share, and must partly exist from the profits that the people gain by this [private] trade." (Opkomst X:213-4.)

Mossel's intentions were better understood by his contemporaries. In an unsigned manuscript dated 29 September 1794, probably written by the Commissioner-General Nederburgh, the decay of Batavia is explained in relation to the policies of Mossel's successors. According to him, Mossel had a good understanding of the growing commercial interest of the British, and therefore "He aimed at counteracting their trade potential, and promoted private trade to which the fortunate situation of Batavia in connection with the total eastern aspect of the Indies seemed to be entitled. [...] At the time the atmosphere in the city was just as insalubrious as it is nowadays, but private traders were not apprehensive; they quickly found buyers for their cargoes and were protected against vexations by the local officials."[13] The tenor of this piece is that after Mossel's death his successors again restricted all trade to Company channels as the VOC's general condition declined and that they levied too high taxes which totally ruined the citizenry.

"Around 1780 the most respectable neighbourhoods of Batavia had already changed into caverns and ruins - by then there was no trace left of the prosperity and bloom that this capital still enjoyed only twenty-five years ago, and if I may trust the impartial testimonies of people who have experienced the whole march of events - there was already nothing but a shadow left of the rich and great Batavian citizenry which had so flourished under Governor Mossel", the same anonymous writer concludes. The decay of Batavia had definitely set in.

Fernand Braudel has pointed to the sudden transition, "le passage rapide, brusque" of Batavia's hegemony to Calcutta, a city that was growing with the greatest speed and disorder possible. The Duke of Modave's esprit cartésien must have been thoroughly shocked when he typified the rise of the city as follows: "C'est, dit-on un effet de la liberté, comme si cette liberté était incompatible avec l'ordre et la simétrie" (Braudel 1979 III:459). At the same time Batavia was gradually being strangled to death by the monopolists of an all-but-bankrupt Company. Braudel is not the first to have contrasted the towns. In 1799 Dirk van Hogendorp wrote: "How many firms have not made considerable fortunes over the last twenty to thirty years in Calcutta, Madras and Bombay! I wager I can name more than a hundred persons who have gained in these towns more than a hundred thousand pounds sterling each. [...] And how many people have scraped together fortune here during the same period? None but a very few Company servants, who were so lucky as to have been appointed to profitable positions." (Dirk van Hogendorp 1799:131). He wisely did not add that his father, a notorious money-grabber, was one of these happy few. In conclusion we may say that a vicious spiral of mismanagement and disease resulted in the old city's ruin.

The Decision to Move

Batavia's position as a capital underwent a fundamental change during the eighteenth century. On Java the Company was gradually transformed from a maritime power into a territorial power which increasingly derived its income from tributes in the form of payments by its Javanese vassals. For this reason proposals were made during the 1780s to move the headquarters to the more healthy regions of Surabaya or Semarang. The main idea was that the Company could make its authority better felt in the most populous part of Java. An establishment at Semarang would guarantee a steady supply of rice and timber, but most of all "the mightiest feudal princes of the Company" (the Susuhunan of Solo, the Sultan of Yogyakarta and the Prince of Madura) would be within striking distance. One official duly noted, "We might present the courageous Javanese every now and then with a spectacle of military exercises carried out by healthy and crafty soldiers. Now they see the gates of Batavia guarded by spectres in the shape of soldiers and they know better than anybody else that we lose so many people every year that Batavia is no longer able to launch any sort of military campaign either afloat or ashore."[14]

Governor-General Van Overstraten who inherited the bankrupt estate of the Company in 1797, did not deem it wise to push forward this radical project and he quickly started to move his offices out of Batavia into the higher-lying region of nearby Weltevreden by 1800. He had to, since no additional Dutch civil and military personnel could be brought in from Europe because of the blockade by the English at the time. It was a matter of move or die. Thus, the capital changed from port city to garrison town. This operation was fully executed by Daendels in 1809. He also administered the coup de grâce to Batavia intramuros by having the castle, the walls and the outer fortresses of the town demolished and its canals filled up.

It was not until the beginning of the present century that, to paraphrase Kipling, out of the spent and unconsidered earth of the long defunct VOC emporium a modern business city rose again along the seashore.

Chapter III

TROJAN HORSE OF LEAD: THE PICIS IN EARLY 17TH CENTURY JAVA*

Introduction

Non-Western "primitive" economic practices have often been misunderstood by anthropologists and historians alike because sources have been carelessly treated and examined out of their historical context in order to build up a persuasive functional framework through which a given society can be explained.

A well-known victim of this heavy-handed treatment of evidence is the potlatch ceremony of the Kwakiutl Indians, the ceremonial feast at which people gained prestige by destroying or giving away wealth and property. The problem is that subsequent research has diminished the scientific validity of the data collected on the ceremony: as the Kwakiutl population declined following the advent of white man, the number of potlatches did not - leaving anthropologists with the impression that the ceremony occupied a position of much more importance in Kwakiutl culture than it really did. It is not surprising then that one serious researcher exclaimed in despair: "Any generalization about the nature of a potlatch should bear a date" (Dalton 1965:64).

The study of primitive money-stuff has been treated in much the same sloppy way until George Dalton, quoted above, set the stage for a new approach. As a result there has been a revival in interest in the study of primitive money. Surveying the harvest, one feels that Marion Johnson's studies about the cowrie currencies of West Africa are particularly good examples of a balanced treatment of historical and anthropological materials. She has shown that the cowries are in no sense a primitive money, "but a sophisticated form of currency capable of adaptation to the particular needs of West African trade" (Johnson 1970:17).

Research into "primitive" media of commercial exchange is of utmost importance to us right now as a new fad of academic research excites the historical profession: the study of the specie and bullion flows. Citing impressive evidence and statistics, bullion enthusiasts tell us and even expect us to believe that the yearly supplies of silver brought by the European sailing vessels swamped the coasts of the Asian and African trading communities in the 16th and 17th centuries.

In this small case study I shall show among other things how the silver flow was actually channelled and dispersed at a particular place and period by the use of lead cash much despised by contemporaries and historians alike. Western Europe's extraordinary dissipation of South America's silver treasures in its early colonial phase might be akin to a gigantic Kwakiutl potlatch, but let us not fall into the same methodological trap; rather let us study the phenomenon on basis of pertinent sources. In this case, these are plentiful and are available in the archives of the Dutch East India Company (VOC) if one takes the pains to look for them among the huge quantity of reals-of-eight- and guilder-accounts and official reports these archives contain.

I shall not limit my discussion here to the function of the picis or caixa[1] as a medium of commercial exchange in Java. After all, it is well known that also on Africa's beaches the Europeans had to adjust to local trading practices of accounting through "sortings" and "ounces". I shall show how the Chinese, and later the Europeans, actually made use of the coin's function as a medium of exchange in order to penetrate Java's economy. As we proceed, the unusual features which have made the picis so suitable for this job will become clear. I shall then focus on these features and analyse them in close connection with the underlying organization upon which they depend. Through such an analytical study, the picis will hopefully serve - in Braudelian terms - as an indicator and a source of illumination (Braudel 1979 I:383).

Numismatic Notes

After his return to Holland from Portuguese Goa, Jan Huygen van Linschoten drew up his Guide Bleu to the East for Dutch sailors: the "Itinerario". When Cornelis de Houtman and his men arrived on Java's shores in 1596 they were confronted with a problem: Sunda Kalapa, highly recommended by Van Linschoten, "The principal port of the island [...] where there is no money other than a [Chinese] coin of copper called caixa" (Van Linschoten 1910 I:78) in the meantime had changed its name into Jakarta and had lost its position of pre-eminence to nearby Banten.

Upon anchoring at the Banten roadstead, the Dutch received a brief explanation of the trade customs in this town, "but", relates the chronicler of this first Dutch expedition to the Orient, "when our people understood that all trade was done in leaden caixas while they had brought only [silver] reals-of-eight and merchandise, they feared they had to sail to another shore where the reals might be more in demand" (Rouffaer 1929:20). The local trade official, or shahbandar, however reassured the Dutch, remarking that a favourable rate of exchange could be arranged. Moreover, Banten's yearly production of 25,000 bags of pepper was more than enough to satify all customers.

In the following days, the exchange rate became an increasing thorny issue as it became less and less favourable. The Dutch merchants, bogged down in negotiations, asked about the origin and use of this particular leaden coin, which had become such an obstacle to the swift exchange of silver reals for pepper. They were told that the picis (as the Javanese called them) were fabricated from an alloy of lead and copper dross and cast in the Ch'üan-chou region in China. The Chinese traders had only recently introduced the picis to the Banten market as a substitute for the much more expensive copper ch'ien which Van Linschoten had mentioned. From a grammatically incoherent sentence in the same report (which serves to show that the meaning of the received information was not fully understood at the time) it nonetheless becomes evident that the coins were introduced in 1590, after the Chinese "king Hammion" had realized that during the preceding twenty years coins of his predecessor, "the king, i.e. Wontai by the name of Hoyen, had by their vast quantity filled the archipelago" (Rouffaer and IJzerman 1915:122). The Dutch were told that the lead coin was not circulating in

Leaden picis coin and copper ch'ien.

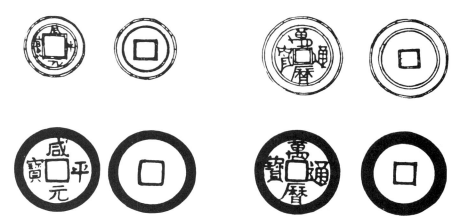

China itself.
   Fortunately another travelogue has left us an illustration of both a Chinese copper ch'ien and a leaden caixa (Commelin 1646 I:111). Two generations of numismatists have attempted to analyse the illustration of these two coins with respect to origin and character. The most complete study is without doubt the commentary to the "Appendix of weights, measures and coins in the East Indies" by the editors of the "Eerste schipvaart", which really constitutes a recapitulation of all preceding numismatical research (Rouffaer and IJzerman 1915:216-38). In this commentary, a reconstruction by J.P. Moquette, then numismatic conservator of the Bataviaasch Genootschap, is shown. He identifies the period of issue of the copper coin as the Wan-li period (1573-1629). The "false" period of issue of the leaden counterfeit coin turns out to be the Hsien-ping period (998-1004) of the Northern Sung dynasty. Moquette fails to identify the names of the "kings" quoted above and the editors of the source publication state that it is now up to Sinologists to identify them. The editors personally believe these kings to have been Fukienese viceroys (onderkoningen). In this, they seem to have overlooked Schlegel's original but rather far-fetched suggestions concerning this problem (Schlegel 1899:521). In Wontai, king, Schlegel recognizes Huang-ti, emperor (Cantonese wong-tai, Fukienese hong-te). Hoyen he identifies as Huyen, the name of the Annamese king, who set himself up as an emperor. For Hammion he provides the intricate explanation that this was the name of an unidentified usurper with the surname, Hsien, in Fukienese Ham. In my opinion, however, there is little doubt about that name: we are dealing here with the Hsien-ping coin that Moquette identified. Hammion simply stands for king Hsien-ping, in Fukienese Ham-pi-ong or Ham-peng-ong. According to Schlegel, the Chinese, seeing that coins from Vietnam had been circulating throughout the archipelago, began to manufacture the picis themselves.
   Whatever Vietnamese influence there may have been in the area, I

personally believe that it was the large drain on copper coins, which were in great demand overseas, which forced the Chinese to manufacture a leaden substitute. It should not be forgotten that the export of copper coins was severely prohibited by the Chinese authorities, especially in the last decade of the 16th century when they became particularly scarce. Yet in spite of the government's efforts, the flow of coins continued, and smugglers found the export of money, either genuine or counterfeit, no less profitable a business than trading commodities (Chan 1967:226).

Two pieces of information, in the report of the first voyage from which I quoted, require closer consideration. It is stated that the number of Chinese coins circulating in Southeast Asia considerably increased over the two decades prior to 1596. This coincides with the new Chinese overseas trade expansion which followed the lifting of the maritime prohibitions in 1567. The same source also tells us that picis were cast in China but not used there. Chinese sources disagree on this last point. Due to the increasing scarcity of copper coins during the second half of the Ming dynasty (1368-1644), leaden coins were made by counterfeiters, often not even through normal casting processes but rather by cutting them into shape. These coins were processed in Lung-hsi, in the province of Fukien, and Hsin-ning in Kwantung. They were meant for illegal export but were nonetheless also used in China itself at a special rate in relation to the copper cash (P'eng 1958:476).

Picis as a Medium of (Commercial) Exchange

Having paid attention to the composition and origin of the coin, I shall now turn to its role as a medium of commercial exchange. It lies outside the scope of this paper to analyse the functioning of the Banten market, not least because this has already been done in detail elsewhere.[2] Still, a short sketch is appropriate here in order to place the picis in a proper setting.

The transformation of Banten into a "port of trade" (in the Polanyian sense) was a matter of several decades only.[3] It had been a small fishing village when it was occupied by Muslim followers of the sultan of Demak in 1527. After ties with this suzerain had loosened, Banten gradually established its hegemony over western Java and soon surpassed nearby Sunda Kalapa as a trade centre. Situated close to the Sunda Strait, it was an ideal barter-beach for the monsoon traders from the Indian Ocean and the Southern China sea. Trade was carried out under the supervision of Superintendents of Trade or shahbandar, who mediated between the pangeran of Banten and the foreigner traders and regulated the accounting. By taking preemptive measures, the Banten administration was able to exercise some control over the market prices. Along with its "port of trade" function, Banten also gained a second trade opportunity when a growing Chinese demand promoted the increase of the pepper cultivation. The town thus also became the outlet for the pepper production in its hinterland and several nearby areas on Sumatra.

The "Tung-Hsi-Yang k'ao", an early 17th century Chinese description of the trade with Southeast Asia, mentions that lead coins were circulating in Banten, but for obvious reasons does not indicate that they were a Chinese export product: the export of lead was also forbidden. It describes the trade of Banten as follows: "The western bar-

III Trojan Horse of Lead

barians [the Dutch and English] visit this port every year to engage in trade. They use silver coins. The natives use lead coins. When our junks arrive in Banten, the traders from the other countries have not yet appeared. We exchange our cargoes for silver and lead coins. When the products of the other countries have arrived, then we use this silver and lead money to purchase their merchandise" (Chang 1981:48).

The story of Chinese and Western influence on Banten is actually one of the impact of the "price-making market" - characterized by competing groups of buyers and sellers whose activities are governed by market prices - on the "port of trade", where the administration prevails over the "economic" procedure of competition. It took about 25 years and some adaptations in the administrative structure before the Banten rulers were able to come to grips again with the prices of the pepper market, via the establishment of a monopoly in 1618.

These two and-a-half decades coincide roughly with the period in which the position of the Chinese changed from that of "external" to "internal" traders. This internalization was the result of their increasing authority in matters of executive government (as shahbandar or as counsellors of the regent), and on account of the control they had established over the local economy as intermediaries in the pepper trade. The business acumen of the Chinese and their original position as the largest customers of the pepper production, but above all a "secret weapon" - their Trojan horse - enabled them to penetrate the local economy and transform its mode of supply and exchange.

Through the introduction of a very cheap coin, which as a medium of exchange was marvellously adapted to the need of the "common man Kromo", the Chinese were able to insinuate themselves between the producers in the hills and the purchasers in the pasar. Local dealings gradually became monetarized and Bantenese of all walks of life had to learn to count in picis. In an economic sense, this was a leap forward as it meant a transition for the hinterland from local bartering to becoming part of a monetary circuit centering on Banten. The constructiveness and efficiency this innovation brought to the pepper trade is demonstrated by virtue of the fact that it was eventually extended to the other domains of trade.

The question how external Chinese money came to be used internally is an intriguing one indeed. From old Chinese sources we know that copper cash was already used for several centuries in the trade along the Java coast. One of the striking differences between the copper cash and the brittle leaden picis is that the former was also used for the religious, decorative and ceremonial purposes. Due to their durability, their relative rareness and their great age, they were viewed as jimat, talismans, highly valued in the eyes of the Javanese and as a result, they were often withdrawn from circulation (Millies 1871:6).

The efficiency of the pepper cultivation with its supply and purchase network of Chinese intermediaries who climbed into the hills, gasping for breath with strings of leaden picis hanging from their yokes instead of waiting in the plains until the harvest might be sent down for sale, brought the market economy of the plains into the hinterland. The scourge of monetarized agricultural society, credit, must have taken its first victims around this time, as it became possible to borrow picis outside the harvest season.

Here follow a few examples of prices in picis. They show the extreme cheapness of the coin. It should be added that the counting was not

Chinese pepper merchant.

actually as bothersome as one would think at first sight. Picis were always carried around in strings of fixed quantities[4]: 1 atak = 200 picis; 1 peku = 1,000 picis; 1 bungkus = 10,000 picis and 1 keti = 100,000 picis.

Around 1600, a slave owner who hired out his slave received 1,000 picis (1 peku-string) a day, food excluded, or 800 picis, if food was provided, which enables us to set the price of a daily meal at 1 atak (Fruin-Mees 1920:44). In Banten the reward for killing a thief caught in the act amounted to 8 peku (Keuning 1938 I:88). In 1625 one chicken cost in Mataram 1 peku (Mac Leod 1927 I:289). Chinese purchasers in 1596 bought eight bags of pepper in the mountains for 1 keti and sold them for 4 keti at the market (Commelin 1646 I:76).

Market prices fluctuated depending on supply and demand of the merchandise but they also depended on the quantity of picis available. The English merchant John Saris writes in 1613 that "a pecco is of divers value, according as cashes rise and fall. [...] upon the departing

III Trojan Horse of Lead

of the Junckes, you shall see 34 and 35 pecoes for a real, which before the next yeere you may sell for twentie two and twentie for a real, so that there is a great profit to be made; but the danger of fire is great" (Purchas 1905 III:507).

The late arrival of a junk in April 1604 made another English trader, Edmund Scot, mutter: [It] "was thought to be cast away, because she tarryed so late, for they use to come in February and March, but by reason of her coming, cashis kept all the year at a very cheap rate, which was a great hindrance to us in the sales of our prize goods, for when Cashis were cheape, and Reals deare, we could not vent a piece of stuffe at halfe the value we did at our first comming" (Purchas 1905 II:462).

On the other hand, in 1618, Jan Pietersz. Coen expressed his dissatisfaction about the expensive rate of the picis. He wrote in a letter to the Gentlemen XVII: "Everything in Java is valued according to caxas. Formerly one real might provided us with 30,000 caxas, and now we hardly receive 8,000, so that the expensiveness of the pepper becomes very annoying to Your Lordships. All expenses have risen four times as high as they used to be in former times; the Javanese however do not advance by this, as a bag of pepper went for 35,000 caxas when we bought a bag at 1.25 real, the exchange rate being one real to 28,000 caxas, and now that one bag costs 5 reals [the exchange rate being one real to 8,000 caxas] a bag of pepper fetches 40,000 caxas, which is a little more than they used to cost 4 to 5 years ago." (Coen

Pepper trees.

I:394). It should be added that the quoted exchange rate of 1:30,000 - Saris even speaks of 1:34,000 - was seasonal and not very representative. On average, the picis were exchanged at a 1:15,000 to 1:20,000 rate in Banten after the Westerners had settled there. In places more distant from the centre of the monetary circuit, rates were of course different. See for instance the above-quoted expensive chicken from Mataram, where the exchange rate in 1625 was 1:7,000. In 1596 on their way to Java the leaders of the first Dutch journey to the East exchanged reals for picis at the rate of 1:8,500 in Sumatra (Mollema 1935:211).

The Qualities of Imperfection

All contemporaries agreed on the baseness of the coin, which was so fragile that if one dropped a peku string by accident, 10 or 12 picis would be smashed. Willem Lodewijcksz, who must have been a precocious scientist who engaged in experiments, informs us that if submerged overnight in salt water "they so stick to each other that half of them break when you want to disengage them" (Rouffaer and IJzerman 1915: 122). Jacob van Neck, the leader of the second expedition to Asia, fully agrees, he calls them "dreck" (filth) and states that even properly used picis did not last for more than three or four years (Keuning 1938 I:87).

Quite a few historians and economists have fallen victim to such negative remarks about this imperfect currency, and prefer to focus on the introduction of western money into Indonesian society. By doing so, they have overlooked not only the great innovations that the picis actually brought to Java's population by serving as a medium of exchange, if only for a short period, but also the coin's function as the gateway into Java's subsistence economy, which lacked a coinage of its own; "money is also a way of exploiting someone else inside and outside his own home, and of accelerating the whole process of exploitation" (Braudel 1979 I:388).

P. Bakker who in 1936 published an interesting doctoral thesis on money circulation within the native (inheemse) society of the Netherlands Indies, makes a serious false step before embarking on the safer story of Western penetration into the economy. At the beginning of the first chapter, he cites a letter from Coen, who wrote to the Board of Directors in the Netherlands in March 1618: "As over a long period the junks from China have brought only a few cashes, - because the pangeran wished to see them banned on account of their snooheyt (wicked, base quality) - the caxas have become so dear that one cannot obtain more than 8,000 for 1 real, while this formerly used to be 30,000 for 1 real; and those used to be of better make than the ones that circulate nowadays!" (Coen I:332). Bakker then implies that the Chinese trade, because of its wicked nature, declined: "for the westerner a very curious phenomenon that money becomes dearer when trade decreases - that is, the trade with China where the cashes were imported from" (Bakker 1936:2). Actually the Chinese trade did not decrease; the supply of picis was curtailed.

The real was the medium of exchange on the external (uitheemse) market while the picis fulfilled the same function in the internal (inheemse) sphere, as Bakker points out. Because of its high intrinsic value, the silver real was out of reach of people of small means. Moreover, as a medium of commercial exchange the real was possessed of a peculiar quality. Each year the Chinese carried away almost all the silver coins that were circulating on the Banten market, since they never considered them as money but rather as a scarce commodity. Curiously, Bakker denies money status to the picis. According to him, they were just a commodity to the Chinese, not a medium of commercial exchange. He deemed this coin "not durable enough to be used as money".[5]

Elsewhere I have taken exception to M.A.P. Meilink-Roelofsz's views on the reals as the medium of commercial transactions in Banten, particularly when she holds that the increased supply of reals led to a protracted inflation of the silver coins on the Banten market (Blussé 1975:44). As I have stated, the depreciation of the real was wholly due to the amount of Chinese picis available. The Banten market was dancing to the tune set by the circulation of the picis and not to that of the European real.

P. de Kat Angelino describes a similar phenomenon in Bali at the turn of this century, which illustrates my point of view, provided we take into account one point of difference: that the Chinese planters on Bali did not manipulate the supply of kèpèng (Chinese copper coins) from outside. "Now the time of the coffee crop had come. The Chinese had to pay for all their purchases with kèpèng; the pickers coming from far and near all demanded their wages in kèpèng. If the Chinese or the rich Balinese coffee planter did not have enough coins, but a lot of silver money, then he was forced to change. The kèpèng became expensive and the rijksdaalder (rixdollar) cheap, so that in those seasons a rixdollar was only worth 1,500, 1,250 - yes, even 900 kèpèng." (De Kat Angelino 1921:70.) The normal exchange rate was 2,000 kèpèng to one rixdollar.

As far as money is concerned, the commodity price level in a market economy is decided primarily by the quantity of its supply and the velocity of its circulation. Within this conceptual framework we may raise the question: what made the picis so extremely well-suited for the job? The answer is: exactly those points of imperfection which were most severely criticized by the Dutch. The reason why their baseness turned out to be a blessing in disguise will be explained below.

Supply
Every year, eight to nine small, or four to six large, Chinese junks carried a cargo of "grove waren" (coarse commodities) to Banten. These commodities consisted of porcelain, ironware, gold thread, piece goods, and large quantities of picis. These leaden coins were used primarily to pay for daily necessities and for the purchase of pepper. The arrival of the Chinese junks in Banten coincided with that of the pepper junks from Jambi and also with the arrival of the canoes filled with pepper which made use of the rain-swollen mountain rivers in February to descend from the hilly Banten hinterland. Picis were also handed out to agents who stayed throughout the year in Banten to buy pepper for the following season at a lower price by purchasing it in advance of its production. This form of credit-allowance bound the producer to the Chinese purchaser, who drew upon a yearly supply of picis from China and was able to sustain this practice year in and year out. As an oversupply of picis would have resulted in an increase of the pepper market prices, it was in the pepper trader's interest to balance the supply with the demand. How closely demand and supply were attuned to each other may be perceived from the above quotation of Scot's remarks con-

cerning a junk which unexpectedly arrived later in March.
Even if the Chinese merchants in Banten did not exercise any control on the supply of picis - which is likely judging from the traditional economic behaviour of the Chinese, who never let themselves be hampered by self-imposed restrictions - still it is a fact that the pepper market was expanding[6] and the money circuit was widening. All over Java and gradually also in the coastal areas of Sumatra, Borneo and Celebes the picis came to be accepted as a medium of commercial transaction. The greatest guarantee against oversupply was the base character of the coin. We have already seen Lodewijcksz's remark that the picis decayed after a few years of intensive use. A description of Batavia dating from 1782 puts it in even stronger terms: "It [picis] is so brittle that one cannot drop it without breaking part of it, which has been intended by the Chinese, as they fear that the islands might become over-filled with this money, which would make it decrease in value. Consequently they make it so flimsy that a considerable portion of this money yearly becomes useless." (Batavia 1782:52). Thus eventual oversupply was balanced by the built-in obsolescence of the coin.

Velocity of Circulation
As the pepper cultivation increased and the planted surface area widened, greater amounts of picis came into the hands of the planters, a development which in turn promoted market transactions in Banten's hinterland. It became possible to buy commodities at the pasar, or on credit with the Chinese the whole year round. If it had not been for the baseness of the coin, we would not have any idea about its circulation velocity, for the simple reason that the Javanese had to be attentive in their use of this coin, as it could not be well preserved. It taught them a new attitude towards money. Leaden picis were not the same kind of money-stuff as the silver and copper coins which were often treated as treasures; these were frequently buried by the owner to be occasionally dug up and spread out in the sun in front of his dwelling: Jemur, "showing off", as this was rightly called. The consumer had to use the leaden coins on short notice or take the risk that his money would dissolve almost like ice in his hands. Hoarding, the enemy of circulation, was not to be recommended in Banten either on account of the recurring cases of arson in this town which became a serious hazard. The coins would have melted!
All these "qualities" - though imperfect - made the picis well adapted to the daily needs of an elementary money economy.
Before I am suspected of blind admiration for the "consuming" qualities of this proto-capitalist coin, I must also point out the picis' major drawback: its weight. Geographically, the eventual monetary circuit of the picis may have been impressive, as it covered most of Java and the coasts of Celebes, Borneo and Sumatra, but the actual circulation took place around the axes and centres along the coast. Cumbersome to carry in large quantities on land, it would almost be a contradiction in terms to say that the leaden coins were easily transported over great distances.
On the passage from China to Java, picis probably fulfilled the same role that sugar and copper - or even cowries - were to play later on in VOC ships: stowed below lighter commodities, they acted as ballast and a commodity at the same time. That the weight of the coins was given due consideration by Chinese sailors may be perceived from a Chinese

functionary's observations on Fukienese coastal trade in the 19th century: "The province of Fukien being on the borders of the sea, its distance from some other provinces is great; and the merchants who resort hither with their goods, finding it inconvenient to carry back such a weight of coin, exchange it for silver as a more portable remittance" (Davis 1836 II:433).

On land, picis became a heavy load on the back of the merchant or his porters. In the case of Banten it is hard to imagine what deals other than the purchase of the coveted pepper would have motivated the transport of large quantities over considerable distances. The cost of transport must have become a considerable item in itself. This is expressed in the enormous difference between the purchase and sale prices of pepper. If we want to get a clear insight into the profits that the Chinese merchants actually made, we must deduct not only the cost of transport of the pepper from the hills to town, but also the cost of the transport of the picis into the hills, not to mention the interest rate at which the money was probably lent to the small merchant. The picis were always cumbersome to carry just as cowries were in Africa. "Their most important use may always have been as market currencies, to facilitate exchange within the market rather than to carry from one market to another." (Johnson 1970:46.)

In the beginning of 1618, pangeran Aria Rana di Manggala of Banten and his Chinese collaborators were able to manipulate the circulation of picis in the region and to gain control over the supply from China. As a result, the coin became dearer, as is explained in Coen's letter cited above. The Dutch, realizing that all their efforts to gain control of the Banten pepper market and to establish a monopoly had been in vain, drew their own conclusions and moved their warehouses to nearby Jakarta. But, before matters had taken this course, the pangeran asked Coen whether the VOC could help him in establishing a new small silver currency which might take the place of the lead picis. Elsewhere, I have regarded this request as probably being part of the manipulative strategems of the Banten ruler (Blussé 1975:45). On second thought, there may be much more to his demand. As the pangeran consolidated his control over the circulation of the local currency, he must have realized that the circle would not be closed until the production of money also came under his control. He was able to drive the exchange value upwards, but part of the proceeds in reals disappeared again as the Chinese traders upon whom he depended for the supply of new picis took the silver away to China. In other words, he was sitting on a melting mountain of lead, which did not bring him the profits he had hoped for. In his attempt to introduce small silver coins, we can see a genuine attempt to change to a higher plane of development, i.e. to connect the internal market with the external one.

In fact, this plan would have turned out to be futile due to the great Chinese demand for silver, which would have put too great a strain on a silver coinage at the Banten market, but also due to important political changes that were brewing: one year later the Dutch threw up a blockade and cut off Banten's trade after the English-Bantenese attempt to dislodge them from their castle in Jakarta had misfired.

Theoretically speaking, one might add that it would also have been almost impossible to carry out monetary reform. The standard of living in Banten was not yet high enough to support a silver coinage. Thus the "imperfect" picis continued to be used in the region.

The VOC Rides Two Horses

The Dutch East India Company at last had the opportunity to introduce its own currency after it had withdrawn from the Banten market in 1618. At its new establishment, Batavia, it used a wide range of copper and silver coins. Pepper was brought in from Jambi and Palembang on Sumatra and paid for in reals. The much-hated picis were foresworn in the Company's dealings, although it was virtually impossible to eradicate them from the pasar. Dutch copper duiten only very gradually replaced them. Thus it seemed a foregone conclusion that, as far as the VOC was concerned, the role of the picis was finished. Matters, however, turned out differently. The coin was to emerge again as a promotor of trade, this time for the Dutch and the Chinese who had come to live under their protection in Batavia.

In August, 1633, Governor-General Hendrick Brouwer wrote from Batavia to the Gentlemen XVII that over the previous year the outside demand for lead had risen remarkably. The Batavian government had reduced a bit the sales of lead from its warehouses to drive up the price and within a few months it actually rose from 6 to 9 real a picul. Then a contract was made with Jan Con, the greatest Chinese entrepreneur in the city. He would purchase 200 piculs of lead at the fixed price of 9 reals a picul, on the understanding that the Company would not sell any lead as long as he still had in store. Jan Con quickly sold out his portion and when he again came knocking at the door of the VOC for more, it was decided that the considerable increase in demand merited a closer look. The reported findings and measures that were consecutively taken are perhaps best expressed by Brouwer himself:

"It turned out that the lead was transported to Banten, Ceribon and Japara. Finally we understood that it was primarily used to fabricate Javanese cash or picis, which are drawn in great quantities along the coasts of Java and Borneo, where they have become scarce because for a long time only a few Chinese junks have come here. Now as we once more found that we alone dispose of [stocks of] lead and consequently are the masters of the price, we have actually arranged for cashmakers, who are all Chinese, to be drawn hither in order to increase our trade. After much deliberation we have agreed to provide nobody but Bencon [the captain of the Chinese] and Jan Con with a contract on the following conditions:

They shall not export lead in kind, on penalty of forfeiture. They may export the mentioned picis free of duty. The [normal export-]duties amount to 20% as lead is considered to be war-ammunition. They shall pay money down, 12 rials of 48 stuivers each for every picul of lead, on the understanding that we shall cede to them one hundred piculs and that no one else without their consent is allowed to fabricate picis in Batavia. Since June 5, the date the contract was entered into, they have already received five hundred piculs, so that they will be able to work up three to four thousand piculs of lead into picis a year, as several coiners have been drawn from Banten, Ceribon and Japara to Batavia." (GM I:388).

The quotation shows that the picis had become so totally internalized within the Javanese economy that they were even fabricated on the

III Trojan Horse of Lead

island itself. The VOC, because of its unique position as supplier of lead, decided to attract Java's trade to Batavia through the sale of picis. This policy was supported by such measures as the freedom of tolls, and a monopoly for the picis-maker cited above. Curse had given way to praise. Next to their own monetary circuit the Dutch cleared the way for the "imperfect" one.

Insufficient sources make it impossible to furnish hard quantitative data which can illustrate how much indigenous shipping was drawn to Batavia due to the manufacture of the picis. In the Daghregisters of the years 1631 to 1634, very little Indonesian shipping is mentioned until October 1634. After this month we see a sudden rise in arrivals. Unfortunately, only rarely is it mentioned what the ships carried away. In one of the few instances this information is given, it is said that nine ships returned to East Java "with a great quantity of Batavian picis" (Daghregister 1631-1634:461). The journal of 1635 is lost. The journals of 1636 and 1637 show that Indonesian shipping to Batavia by that time had become quite intensive. Return loads are more often reported and, indeed, consisted mostly of Chinese commodities and picis. It should be remembered that the VOC tried to direct all Chinese shipping headed for the Indonesian archipelago to Batavia, to strengthen the town's position in the interarchipelago trade. The contract with Jan Con was regularly renewed at ever-increasing rates (14.5 reals a picul on October 22, 1633, 15 real a picul on September 20, 1636). This favourable arrangement did not last very long.

Governor-General Van Diemen wrote in a letter on December 9, 1637, that the picis export had run into some competition: "The license for the purchase of lead and the manufacture of picis will be continued for one more year. However, the English - we have been apprehensive already for quite some time lest this might actually happen - have received from England a lot of lead on account of its high price here. Consequently, the neighbourhood as far as Banten (where they fabricate picis) and even Japara, Makassar, Jambi, Palembang and also Martapura has been overloaded with lead by them to such an extent that sales in Batavia have decreased considerably. Jan Con would have been forced into cutting down his working force of picis-makers by one half, if we had not given the matter close attention. Accordingly, in order to stimulate the demand and check the English lead [supply], we have arranged by the resolution of August 3 that Jan Con shall from now on pay 12.5 reals - it used to be 15 reals - provided that he will sell 6,000 picis instead of 4,200 picis a real of the same size, shape and alloy as before. This has resulted in such a demand that Jan Con has trouble in accommodating the demands of the merchants and is sending for more picis makers in Banten, Ceribon and Japara's." (GM I:640). Thereupon Van Diemen remarks that 2,212 piculs of lead had been minted into picis during the past 12 months. This was far below the originally estimated quantity of 3,000 to 4,000 piculs.

By December 1638 it again turned out that only 2,550 piculs of lead had been sold to the picis makers. The English and Siamese merchants had brought new loads to Japara and had inflated the picis even further. Even the above-described safety mechanism inherent in the picis' low-quality was no obstacle against these oversupplies. The rate of the coin slumped to 10,000:1 in Japara, while in Batavia the rate was still 6,000:1. The Dutch were then willing to sell lead for as little as 8.5 real a picul. The picis were to be sold at a rate of 12,000:1. Absolutely convinced of the indirect benefits the sale of picis brought, as it drew Indonesian shipping to the Batavian market, Van Diemen wrote: "It is necessary to check the supply by the English, Danes and others and to fabricate the lead coin only in Batavia. Even if the profits that we derive from it remain scanty for the moment, it will probably change for the better." (GM I:713). This expectation was not fulfilled. The rate of the picis dropped to 14,000:1 at a purchase price of the lead of 6.5 reals. Production of lead picis was stopped and on July 14, 1640 (Plakaatboek I:445) the Company concluded a contract for the fabrication of copper picis, which met with a sharp rebuke from the Gentlemen XVII when they heard about it. The latter wrote that Batavia had infringed the prerogative of the States General to mint coins (Plakaatboek II: 120). Copper coins had to be minted within the bounds of the monetary circuit of the Republic.

Although in 1640 the VOC gave up the casting of leaden picis in Batavia, it had attained its main goal: Indonesian shipping and trade which had initially shunned Batavia's port had been attracted to the Company's emporium, and the town had become embedded in the interarchipelago trade network. As a medium of exchange, the leaden coin disappeared relatively soon from Batavia's markets. The lessee of the vegetable market complained in 1664 that the leaden picis were not circulating any longer among Batavia's citizens. "This made it difficult for him to straighten out accounts."[7]

Elsewhere on Java in more isolated areas the picis remained widely used far into the 18th century and continued to play their intermediary role. Indeed, in the princely territories picis or wang baru were the standard payment for a day's labour on the part of coolies, porters or sedan chair carriers. It was the prerogative of the shahbandar of Semarang, Ceribon and Surabaja to farm out their manufacture.

A list of current weights and measures in the archipelago, drawn up in 1765, mentions several money circuits where the leaden coins were still in use. One real would buy 4,000 picis at Palembang (Sumatra), 8,000 at Sumenep (Madura). On the Northeast coast of Java only copper duiten were used, in the Oosthoek (the eastern extremity) of the island and on Bali the copper kèpèng were circulating. However, at Cirebon and Banten, leaden picis were still fabricated. "The picis which are manufactured here are composed of 1/5 of tin and 4/5 of lead. Their value is calculated in relation to an imaginary real of 56 stuivers, divided into four times 14 stuivers. Two stuivers are equal to 100 picis. That means 12 picis for 1 duit and 25 picis for 2 duiten. One real's worth of picis weights 4 catties or 5 pounds. It is a very unstable means of payment, considerably increasing and decreasing in value."[8]

Judging from the contents of a Yogya babad ("Babad Bedhah", British Library Add. MS. 12330) the coin even found its way into everyday expressions. It describes how in order to be first in queue to congratulate the young sultan Hamengku Buwono IV on his wedding, some of his senior relatives jostled with each other "as though scrambling for picis", gugup kasesa lir rebut picis - in other words, like the vulgar masses behaved when picis were thrown to the ground as tokens of royal largesse on feast days.[9]

According to Van der Chijs (1869:145) the picis had vanished by 1780 and given way to the copper coins of the Company. A new monetary period dawned for which Van Hoëvell has coined the appropriate name "De Koperen Eeuw" (the Copper Age) (Van Hoëvell 1860:16).

Chapter IV

TESTAMENT TO A TOWKAY:
JAN CON, BATAVIA AND THE DUTCH CHINA TRADE*

Introduction

Among historians, Southeast Asia's Overseas Chinese have never enjoyed much popularity. They are in many respects a "People without a History", having left behind no substantial deposit of experience and having failed to produce a school of historians to write their own history from an insider's perspective. Apart from their ethnic and cultural background, what distinguishes the hua-chiao from the indigenous peoples of Southeast Asia is the intermediary role that these immigrants have continued to play within the different territories, colonies or states of the area over the last few centuries. Acting as middlemen and brokers - and therefore necessarily discreet in the handling of personal relations - they have traditionally hidden their own aims and motives from the "outer world", and thus eluded the understanding of their contemporaries.

It may not come as a surprise, then, to learn that indigenous historians of Southeast Asia tend to characterize the hua-chiao, on the basis of their intermediary function, as profiteers or henchmen of foreign capital and political influence. For ideological reasons, historians from mainland China have tended either to depict their kinsmen as victims shanghaied into contract labour by wicked capitalists in the past century, or as unfilial souls who have forsaken their own ancestors and the mother country. In other words, in China itself, the push-and-pull factors behind overseas emigration are obscured by the political rhetoric used. This is by no means a new phenomenon, but rather dates back to the turn of the century, if not long before. The unvarnished truth is more likely that whenever China turned (and turns) its attention towards the Overseas Chinese, it has done so only to exact gain from these lost children, who generally enjoyed and continue to enjoy a higher standard of living. Entrapped in this historical situation, the Overseas Chinese are bound to be misunderstood and to be depicted in stereotypes portraying them as a materialistic group who conspire for possible profits and demonstrate willingness to collaborate with foreign capital.

It is not all that easy to replace these deeply ingrained stereotypes with more acceptable and discerning generalizations. The best way to achieve such a perspective would be to focus on the often insecure life conditions of the hua-chiao in Southeast Asia, and, on basis of case-studies, to analyse how they interacted at different times with their immediate environment. Recently, notable attempts have been made in this direction by Charles Coppel (for religion), Claudine Salmon (for literature), Leo Suryadinata (for prosopography) and by the enfant terrible of Overseas Chinese historiography, Wang Gungwu, who is well-known for his indefatigable assertions that no common denominator exists for the "Overseas Chinese".[1]

The dearth of evidence concerning the sayings, thoughts, deeds and sufferings of the hua-chiao poses a problem for the researcher who attempts historical reconstruction, especially if he selects a not-too-recent period for investigation. To resolve the problem, he will have to collect the data from less than obvious sources. In the wake of historians such as B. Hoetink and Iwao Seiichi, I have learned to value the Dutch East India Company (VOC) archives as a preserve within which to collect information concerning the history of the Chinese emigration into 17th and 18th century Southeast Asia. Employing this kind of evidence, I shall attempt to reconstruct a single career as a vehicle for portraying in brief compass "la condition humaine" of the overseas Chinese in early-modern colonial Batavia.

A Puzzling Character

In the Generale Missive of December 18, 1639, Governor-General Antonio van Diemen informed his superiors in Holland, the Gentlemen XVII, that "the Great Chinese Merchant Jan Con" had passed away suddenly, leaving behind an insolvent estate (VOC 1129,f.91). He added that this Chinese citizen of Batavia owed no less than 27,636 and 3/8 rials to the Company. As no will existed, a special committee of curators was appointed to compensate as evenhandedly as possible the swarm of creditors that alighted on the late business tycoon's possessions.

In this context, the admonitions of one of Van Diemen's predecessors, Pieter de Carpentier, who introduced the same Jan Con fourteen years earlier to one of his inferiors have an ironic ring indeed; he said: "Consider this man well recommended by me, provide him with all favours and faith, and make use of his services insofar as you deem this to the benefit of the Company. Yet always follow the maxim that the Company's capital never should be put in Chinese hands, even if it should appear advisable to do so. In this way you will always remain master of the gross of your affairs and eliminate the risk of having trust repaid with bad faith; thus will you also protect good people from making poor decisions." (VOC 852,14-6-1625).

Pieter de Carpentier was obviously warning against the confidence game that the Overseas Chinese were known to play with Company servants. This behaviour is known nowadays as the "con" and is a way of obtaining money under false pretenses by the exercise of fraud and deceit. Yet, one wonders whether this man called Con, as suggested by De Carpentier's premonitions, actually embezzled funds; or was he perhaps given too much leeway by the Dutch authorities in town?

Judging from remarks by Van Diemen regarding Jan Con in the above-quoted Generale Missive, the Governor-General did not seem to feel himself deceived by the Chinese merchant. On the contrary, he showed surprise that this entrepreneur who had been so instrumental in many important contractual engagements with the Company, since the foundation of Batavia in 1619, should have died as poor as a churchmouse, the more so, since according to investigations by the curators, Jan Con did not seem to have spirited away large sums of money. The Governor-General even gave the deceased a last tribute. He deemed him to have been "a very diligent, courageous man of firm decision, a great asset to this Republic" (VOC 1129,f.91v). By "Republic" of course, he meant the VOC's establishment in Batavia.

How can these conflicting tales of great losses and, at the same time, considerable profits be harmonized? An attempt will be made to answer this riddle. Jan Con's faits et gestes will be traced and examined within the larger context of institutional developments such as the building of the colonial city of Batavia, the establishment of direct trade links with China, and the creation of a consumers' market for the Company's merchandise in the Indonesian archipelago. In all these undertakings, the Chinese came to play a crucial role and were entrusted with credit or were advanced large quantities of money. Initially, guidelines and experience were lacking. It was only in the course of time that proper procedures were worked out. This question of interactivity between the Company and Chinese in which money transactions figured to a large degree is mirrored in the career of the hero of this biography. If Jan Con died intestate, this essay may serve as a belated testament to this early towkay, or entrepreneur.

The Setting

The instrumental role that Batavia's Chinese citizens played in the early years of the town's history is by no means a neglected topic. Frederik de Haan has pointed out their important contribution to the city's development in "Oud Batavia" (De Haan 1935), while the two biographical essays on Su Ming-kang (alias Bencon, 1580-1644), the first Chinese Captain of Batavia, by the sinologist B. Hoetink provide an impressive variety of documentary evidence on this particular individual and the Chinese community he governed (Hoetink 1917, 1923). Bencon was not only a respected leader and mediator among his own people, but he was also well-liked by the VOC establishment. He frequently received highly placed Dutch guests at his residence. Among them was Jan Pietersz. Coen, the founder of Batavia, who used to visit him in the evening. The Chinese Captain's personality is suggested in the words of a contemporary who called him a "better mandarin than merchant" (beter een staatsman als een coopman) (Hoetink 1917:375). Indeed, the records show that the Captain shared the responsibility for most of his business dealings with others who were more proficient in that respect, one of them being a good friend of his with the rather striking name of Jan Con. Bencon acted as the respected figurehead of the Batavian Chinese Community and the perfect advocate of its interests, while Jan Con was one of the "movers and doers" who operated outside the limelight of the official circuit and who consequently figures less prominently in the archives of the VOC. Incidentally, the two had no kinship ties, their names being Dutch corruptions of their original Chinese names. From his tombstone we know Bencon's Chinese name; the closest I have been able to come to a reconstruction of Jan Con's original Chinese name is through two barely readable Chinese characters scribbled in a notarial document next to his signature which he used to write in Dutch. The characters would be pronounced in Canton dialect: Sum kon, meaning heart and liver, or sweetheart. It may have been a nickname.[2]

The writing of a biography of a typical Chinese or towkay like Jan Con, who at the outset of his career did not place all his eggs in the lone basket of formal collaboration with the Dutch authorities, certainly poses some perplexing problems. If it is agreed that every individual is a social being and therefore continuously interacts with his surroundings, the question logically arises as to how one traces the steps of an individual like Jan Con. As a labour broker, he worked most of the time with his own people, and in general he only met with the Dutch when making contractual agreements like those concerned with tax farms or public-works projects. It is when those contacts occurred that we find most evidence about him. As a consequence, we are confined to the use of partial (Dutch) sources for our study into the hua-chiao world of motives and forces; a strange world which is not easily understood in the terms of the official VOC interpretation of social reality.

Like many a first-generation hua-chiao, Jan Con was basically a man of several worlds. He had chosen for a new life overseas and had more or less adapted to the local situation - first under the pangeran's rule in Banten, and later under the aegis of the VOC in Batavia - but he still retained obligatory ties with Tang soa, the mountains of T'ang, as the Chinese emigrant nostalgically called his native country. Having committed an unfilial deed by leaving the ancestral grounds, he could only compensate for this offence by regularly remitting funds to his kinsmen. These relatives at the same time were potential pawns in the hands of grafting officials who intended to extort money from people like him.

Jan Con's ties with the mother country were still further strengthened by virtue of the fact that he was a labour broker in Batavia, hiring coolies who were shipped every year from Fukien to Batavia on Chinese junks. He engaged these Chinese as skilled and semi-skilled labourers to supplement the masses of slaves and chain-gangs recruited by the VOC to dredge canals and erect defence-works. He also employed Chinese coolies in the lumber trade and on sugar plantations. Consequently, Jan Con had to perform a balancing act as he served different worlds, each with their own interests: the VOC, the Chinese community in Batavia, and his relatives in his home province.

Building an Enterprise

When the Dutch occupied the dalem (residence) of the ruler of Jakarta on May 30, 1619, they found to their dismay that the local population, with the exception of a small Chinese community, had followed their prince on his flight to his allies in Banten. Although this freed the colonial administration from the necessity of dealing with a potentially rebellious population, the consequences were nevertheless grave. A ruler without subjects is like a rider without a horse. To provide the new settlement with the necessary labourers, traders, fishermen, farmers, gardeners and craftsmen, Batavia's founder, Jan Pietersz. Coen, made an all-out effort to lure Chinese from elsewhere. As he would remark a few years later, no people served the Dutch better in this respect and were easier to attract at the time than the Chinese (Opkomst IV:280).

Among the first Chinese immigrants was the carpenter, Jan Con, alias Gonthay. This man was classified as a "shaven Chinese" - that is, a convert to Islam. He managed to flee from nearby Banten, which technically remained at war with the Dutch. Banten's roadstead was

IV Testament to a Towkay

blockaded by Dutch ships, so that its main artery, the overseas trade, was effectively brought to a halt. Especially those local Chinese traders who acted as middlemen and procurers for the Dutch in the Banten pepper trade and who had invested money for the purchase of pepper in the countryside suffered great losses. For them, the flight to Batavia with the many opportunities this new town offered, constituted an easy escape from obligations in Banten. At the same time, this midnight flit ensured them the assistance of the VOC, to which they still owed large sums of money.

To help him set up a new career, Jan Con was given in loan a stand of coconut trees on August 1, 1620 (Hoetink 1917:360). He was soon involved in supplying wood for the public works of Batavia. This timber trade was a very dangerous occupation. It was carried out on the islands and in the forests around the new settlement by small groups of Chinese lumberjacks, who had to be continuously on the alert against attacks by marauders from Banten. Since he employed many of these lumberjacks as well as many of the coolies who worked on the construction works in Batavia, it is not surprising that, together with Bencon, the Captain of the Chinese, Jan Con was selected to levy the tax on gambling which was introduced in 1620. As the Chinese were the main gamblers in town, Jan Con was in sufficiently close touch with these gamblers to make sure that the winner paid him and Bencon a 20% tax on the gains.[3]

Chinese gamblers.

The two community leaders carried out their task so well that Coen implicitly ordered that Jan Con should be given preference above others at the following auction of the tax farm on gambling (Coen III:10). The normal procedure for farm acquisition was to bid highest at the auction which was held annually at the residence of the Chinese Captain on New Year's Eve. The new tax on in- and outgoing native products such as Borneo and Sumatra camphor, edible bird's nests, rhinoceros horns, diamonds and bezoar, which amounted to 600 reals, also came into Jan Con's hands on March 1, 1622 (Coen III:826).

The first overall survey of the various taxes parceled out in Batavia dates from 1644 (Daghregister 1643-1644:5-6). Judging from the yields of the different farms on that list, it is clear that Jan Con must have farmed some of the most important taxes in the early years. Information regarding these tax farms and an occasional reference to a large delivery of wood, such as 600 logs of teak, leave us with the impression that Jan Con enjoyed good fortune in business (Coen III:829).

He was less fortunate in his personal life. When his wife was discovered with a Chinese lover called Soecko, Jan Con and Bencon took the law into their own hands. They locked Soecko up and extorted heavy compensation from him. By so doing they, of course, trespassed upon the legal powers of the Company's administration. The year before, a group of coolies had accused Bencon of various extortionistic practices - saying that he "possessed the disposition of a snake and a dog, as he fleeced and devoured them, hide and hair" - but their charges were to no avail (Hoetink 1923:14). As the allegations were found to be true in the case of Soecko, both community leaders were sternly reprimanded for "these private apprehensions, and threats of inflicting harm".[4] The fact that Jan Con had lost face when his wife's adultery became public was probably considered a mitigating circumstance. In any event, a few months later in the autumn of 1622, the opportunity arose for him to redeem his bad behaviour.

On October 13, the towkay sailed to the Banten Roads on a special mission for the Indian High Government; he was charged with enquiring into the possibilities of starting peace negotiations with that town's ruler. The pangeran refused to receive the emissary, as he could not produce a letter of credence or any other proof of his official capacity. As a result, Jan Con returned to Batavia nine days later no wiser than he was when he left it.[5] This episode is significant because it set the tune for the negotiations which were held in the years to come. Almost all these pourparlers with Banten took place via the Overseas Chinese network until an armistice was reached in 1639. The Batavian High Government did not wish to risk the loss of face involved if its formal emissary would obtain no hearing at the kraton, while at the same time the pangeran did not wish to appear too eager for peace and therefore put out his feelers through "Chinese creatures" of his own.

These assignments further improved Jan Con's position vis-à-vis the Hoge Regeering to such an extent that he and Bencon approached the Governor-General with a special request on behalf of the Chinese citizenry on New Year's Eve. "On account of the tenderness and the indigence of the Chinese of Batavia", they asked for a two-year delay of the announced increase in the land rent. To emphasize their humility and peaceful disposition they added in almost the same breath that they agreed with the Government's wise decision to forbid the citizens of Batavia to carry keris or other stabbing weapons in the town (31-12-1622,

Coen III:930). Governor-General Coen, who was approaching the end of his first term, not only granted the request of the two Chinese community leaders but even rewarded them handsomely for their services to the town over the preceding three years. He presented them with 600 rials worth of cloth each; a third Chinese received a less generous gift (23-1-1623, Coen III:946).

The Governor-General must have felt that his policies towards the Chinese had paid off and, as if to prove this point, another influential Chinese, Lim Lacco, also fled from Banten to Batavia. Despite having conspired against the Dutch with the pangeran when the Company still had a factory in Banten prior to 1619, Lim Lacco showed his willingness to change partners in this way. In point of fact, he had no alternative, as his business in Banten had gone bankrupt. Like Jan Con, he still owed the Company large sums of money as he "had not been able to collect debts from lesser merchants on account of the war" (28-1-1623, Coen III:956). Apparently both men had received money in Banten from the Company to purchase pepper, which they had not been able to deliver. "Hoping for redress", Lim Lacco and Jan Con begged for remission of these debts and as an act of generosity, Coen acceded to these requests as well before embarking on the voyage home.

By the spring of 1623 Jan Con had cleared his books and was able to further expand his business enterprises. In June of that year, he added one more tax farm to his resources - the very profitable one on cattle for slaughter (2-6-1623, Plakaatboek I:113). He continued to play a prominent role in negotiations with Banten, now assisted by Bencon's son-in-law, Intche Mouda, and Lim Lacco - who was probably better informed about the political situation - at the kraton of Banten (Daghregister 1624:32-3, 42). This happy state of affairs came to an end, however, when a Chinese deputation from the governor of Fukien province in China visited Batavia in the spring of 1624; the deputation seems to have taken offence at Jan Con's untiring energy.

The Long Arm of the Chinese Emperor

The main motive behind the Chinese mission to Batavia was to protest against the rapacious activities of the Dutch on the Fukien coast. The governor of this Southeastern Chinese coastal province had been confronted over the preceding two years with high-handed behaviour by the Dutch sailors. These were under the command of Admiral Cornelis Reyersen who had constructed a fortress between Taiwan and Fukien on the Pescadores archipelago. From that base, Reyersen attempted to force an entrance into the Chinese market. His troops made occasional sallies, plundering the coast of Fukien to press demands. They also did not shrink from kidnapping coastal inhabitants who were used as coolies for the construction of the fortress on the wind-swept Pescadores. Only a few of these unfortunates survived the ordeal and the subsequent voyage to Batavia, where they were finally bought out of slavery by Chinese community leaders as an act of mercy (Groeneveldt 1898:224).

A more covert motivation for the Chinese mission to Batavia was to find out who was masterminding the Dutch actions. It was an accepted belief among the Fukienese authorities that there was an Overseas Chinese who incited the "Red Barbarians" to their uncivilized actions.

It was the task of Bencon and Jan Con to find out about the intentions and status of the Chinese ambassadors after these had presented

Batavia in 1628.

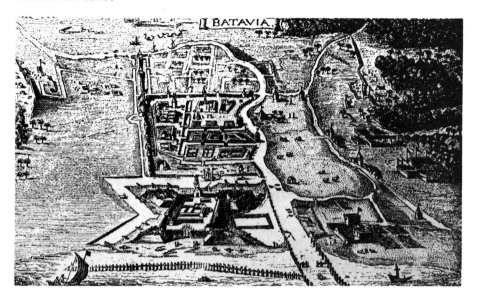

their credentials to the Hoge Regeering on 1 January, 1624.[6] But on their side, the ambassadors were also not idle. Recognizing Jan Con's prominence in the town, they appear to have thought that he was after all the black dalang (puppeteer). In politely couched terms, they accused him of misdemeanor and advised him to return forthwith to his home province if he wished to avoid reprisals against his family and friends.

On May 4, 1624, Jan Con capitulated. He appeared at a meeting of the Governor-General and Council and, upon informing them that he was suspected by the Fukien authorities, asked permission to leave. He wished to travel as a private citizen, with no commission from the VOC, and he planned to leave his possessions in the care of his friends (VOC 1082,f.360). The request was granted on account of his good behaviour. It is not difficult to discover why the authorities were content with the leaders of the Chinese community. This population group had paid seven times more for the construction of the recently finished eastern city wall than all the other citizens together.[7]

By the time Jan Con was ready to leave, the shift of the monsoon had occurred, so he had to wait for the next season. Perhaps this was to his advantage, as, in the meantime, matters on the Chinese coast took a decisive turn. In the summer of 1624, the Dutch evacuated the Pescadores and moved to Taiwan, where they built a new fortress, this time outside the jurisdiction of the Chinese. As Reyersen's successor, Martinus Sonck, had no idea how he was to open trade with Amoy in Fukien province, he asked the Governor-General to send "somebody like Jan Con, [Lim] Lacco, or another able Chinese, as well as silk and

IV Testament to a Towkay

gold specialists, embroidery craftsmen, druggists, et cetera".[8]

When De Carpentier transmitted this request to the Batavian Chinese and asked them whether they were prepared to assist in this venture, he met with a stony refusal. "No one is willing to do so", he wrote in his next letter to Taiwan, "everyone balks at the idea, even though affairs on Taiwan seem to be on the right footing. Not only do they [the Chinese] fear they will fall into disgrace with the local grandees [the authorities in China] but they are also afraid they will arouse hatred among 'the men in the street' if they serve us faithfully. On the other hand should they show themselves disloyal to us, they would also not receive much credit, gratitude or recompense." (Hoetink 1923:5.) It was clear that the ambassadors had fostered fear of the far-reaching powers of the Dragon throne among the Chinese of Batavia. Under these circumstances Taiwan seemed too near to China.

A Balance Sheet

At this particular point, Jan Con decided to speak his mind. This is one of those very rare moments when the sources give us the opportunity to almost hear a man think aloud. He may have spoken out on earlier occasions but this time the tenor of his words is clearly reflected in the records. In June 1625, a few days before he was to board the junk of nachoda (ship-master) Teggouw, he had an interview with the Governor-General and spoke freely on several matters of concern to him. He apologized once more for his departure; in his words, "he had to defend himself against the sinister complaints lodged against him in connection with the Dutch" so that he might "liberate his friends who had been molested because of this". Then he expressed his views on issues we have already touched upon in passing. He recommended that "one should be particularly careful with the Chinese in Batavia and keep them steadily at work. One should neither postpone activities for long periods of time, nor allow them to rest for three months after one month of work. Every month, as the opportunity arose, one should keep some works running, so that these simple souls might earn their daily bread." (Daghregister 1625:164-5). Here speaks an apprehensive employer. It had not escaped Jan Con's notice that the Javanese trade with the town had recently slumped with the result that not enough rice was imported to feed the large number of Chinese in town (Res GG and C 28-7-1625, VOC 1085).

Jan Con may even have felt a bit embarrassed about the gap that would be left in the informal leadership of the community after his departure. He recommended "that the government of the Chinese should no longer be entrusted to one or two persons, but instead to at least three of them, as this would result in less collusion and oppression, because two more easily agree with each other than three" (Daghregister 1625:165).

He did not expect that the peace negotiations with Banten would yield results. In his opinion, the person to watch in this respect was Lackmoy, the Chinese counsellor of the pangeran. Initiatives undertaken by that influential man could, however, lead to something concrete.

His last piece of advice concerned the China trade. It was his conviction - although, of course, he put it in somewhat milder terms - that the Dutch should stop their belligerent behaviour immediately. Dutch attempts to blockade Chinese trade with the Spanish enemy in the

Philippines had only resulted in the development of other shipping routes and faster vessels for this commerce. He further maintained that the only way to lure the Fukienese traders to Formosa was to offer them favourable terms such as a guaranteed 30% profit on the purchase price of their merchandise in China. Samples of the goods the Dutch wished to purchase should be displayed to public view, with the price tags attached.

It would seem that Jan Con's proposals were carefully considered. The "iron rice bowl" employment he proposed for the coolies in Batavia could be guaranteed only if enough funds were available for new public works such as the digging of new canals, a sine qua non for the drainage of the town's marshy soil. A last-minute deal was arranged with the Chinese headmen and the nachodas of the Chinese junks in the roadstead to amass the necessary capital. All the Chinese in Batavia, the crews of the junks included, were charged a surtax of three rials each, realizing a total of 9000 rials, which was to be used for employing the coolies (Res GG and C 28-7-1625, VOC 1085). These "voluntary contributions" were exacted almost every year from 1625 onward, until the fortification of the city was finished in 1640. The money eventually found its way back into Chinese hands in the shape of wages or payments for building materials that were transported from the islands in the bay to the city. More important even than these contributions were the proceeds from the collection of the capitation tax (1.5 rial a month) which every Chinese citizen had to pay in order to remain exempt from service in the militia. According to De Haan, the yield of this tax comprised half the total income of the Batavian administration in the early 1630's (De Haan 1935 I:61).

De Carpentier had great expectations for Jan Con's activities in connection with the development of the Dutch trade with China - but these could only be realized if the latter could settle his own affairs first. De Carpentier therefore sent a letter to the Governor of Taiwan in which he heralded the imminent arrival of the "daring and resolute merchant [...] with great notions about the promotion of the Company's affairs and those of the Chinese and himself". De Carpentier added the note of warning quoted at the beginning of this essay. No large sums of money should be put in the hands of "this merchant for whom no business can be too extensive" (14-6-1625, VOC 852). The Governor-General also showed that he was a good listener, for at the suggestion of Jan Con he issued an order to guarantee to the Chinese traders in Taiwan a 30% profit on the original purchase price of their merchandise (17-7-1625, VOC 852).

A few months later, Commander Frederik de Wit, who was in charge of the Taiwan trade factory, replied to Batavia that he had not yet seen the towkay. A vague message had been passed on via an intermediary that the latter was not eager to cross the Taiwan Strait. This was confirmed by Fukienese merchants who bluntly informed De Wit that Jan Con would have nothing to do with the Company's trade on the island. The commander was sorry to hear this as he foresaw great difficulties in purchasing merchandise in China. He feared that nobody but Jan Con possessed the know-how to select the suitably appealing items such as horsetails, gongs, girdles and knives for specific markets, like the islands of Timor and Solor (29-10-1625, VOC 1087). He even sent a letter to Jan Con who was still defending himself before the provincial authorities in China, begging him to visit Taiwan first before returning to Batavia (21-11-1625, VOC 1090,f.183).

His wishes were not fulfilled. Six months later, the Governor-General explained why Jan Con never showed up in Taiwan and had not even been able to answer De Wit's letter. He had been blackmailed by the mandarins and remained mute "out of awe and pure fear" (3-5-1626, VOC 853). This silence was maintained for no less than three years. Jan Con may have returned to Batavia that same spring, but the Company sources do not mention him for several years. It seems more likely therefore that he remained in China. The next reference to him is found in the Diary of Zeelandia Castle, the Dutch headquarters in Taiwan (Blussé, Van Opstall and Ts'ao 1986:9). It mentions that on December 19, 1629 "the merchant Jan Con, who spent many years in Batavia" had been so kind as to present a gift from Governor Putmans to the "toutocq" (the military commander of Amoy). At that occasion he asked Putmans to advance four hundred rials for the purchase of merchandise in Amoy. "He promised to return in a week or so [...]." This definitely would seem an act worthy of Jan Con: conducting private trade while wearing the cloak of an emissary on a "tribute mission".

China Tangle

By 1630, Jan Con had cast off his initial scruples concerning his acting as a comprador for the Dutch. He was then willing to undertake commissions for the VOC to purchase and sell goods in China. The fact that this experiment failed was not his fault. A series of letters, too long-winded to repeat here in extenso, bear testimony to the knotty problems in which he became entangled.[9]

A lot of three hundred piculs of pepper was entrusted to Jan Con for sale in Fukien province. Upon delivery in March 1630 it was promptly confiscated by the local authorities. Under normal circumstances an independent Chinese merchant would not have been awarded such an important commission by the Dutch. It was an emergency measure dictated by the fear that the pepper price in China would slump with the impending arrival of the Chinese junks loaded with pepper from Southeast Asia. Not only was the pepper seized, but Jan Con himself ended up in the jail of Hai-ch'eng, a port in the Amoy coastal region. Two months later, on May 7, the Dutch authorities in Taiwan were informed that the unfortunate merchant had been able to free himself. Whether or not he was also able to retrieve the parcel of pepper we do not know. Jan Con then began to purchase export items which were to be forwarded in autumn to Taiwan for shipment to Batavia on a VOC vessel during the northern (winter) monsoon.

In autumn the Dutch authorities were given notice by Jan Con that the desired purchases had been made and were awaiting shipment in the port of Anhai, the headquarters of the local strongman, Cheng Chih-lung.[10] This redoubtable character - also known as Iquan - was a former interpreter for the VOC. He had become a pirate, but had been pardoned not long before by the Chinese authorities to act on their behalf as a coastal commander, under orders to fight his former colleagues, pirates and Dutchmen alike. Such complicated arrangements indicate the labyrinth into which the administration of Fukien had foolishly wandered. We shall not delve deeper into its machinations; suffice it to say that Jan Con's merchandise never reached its final destination due to the depredations of the pirates who brought all coastal trade to a standstill.

In this case the Company recouped part of its losses by seizing all the merchandise Jan Con had stored for his own business at Taiwan. Even so, his remaining debts were estimated at 1338 rials, and later correspondence between the Governor of Taiwan and the Governor-General in Batavia shows that the Governor of Taiwan never failed to bring up this subject until the final payment had been received.[11] However expansive Jan Con's ideas about the China trade may have been, for him personally, they resulted in nothing but losses.

Disgusted with the treatment he had received from all quarters, the towkay signed up once again for a trip to the Nanyang, the Southern Seas, and reached Batavia after an eventful voyage on February 25, 1631.[12] He was accorded a hearty reception by the Hoge Regeering which was eager to hear Jan Con's ideas about the prospects for the Dutch trade with China.

The tenor of his account was gloomy. He did not believe the free and open trade that the Company was hoping for would materialize in the near future for several reasons: the rapid turnover of local officials in Fukien province rendered long-term agreements impossible and the "perfidy of the pirates" brought havoc to the coastal trade. He strongly advised against the use of force, which was suggested at that time by the Governor of Taiwan, Hans Putmans. Jan Con recommended peaceful coexistence with the "pacified pirate", Cheng Chih-lung.[13]

These wise words were not heeded. The Dutch authorities indeed attempted to force Chinese cooperation, and as a result it took two more years and a great loss of men and material before at long last a bargain was struck with Cheng Chih-lung. The events on the China coast will not be discussed further here; they serve to indicate, however, that Jan Con lacked neither foresight nor vision.[14]

Canals and Cash

Having only just settled in Batavia, the towkay put his shoulder once again to the wheel. Other contractors had replaced him during his absence. He had to recover his former position by hard work and vision. His services were no longer needed for diplomatic negotiations with Banten. Lim Lacco played the leading role on that scene with great agility. Together with Bencon and another Chinese called Chili Gonting, Lim had also become the main contractor in town.[15]

Jan Con returned to Batavia to find it the site of bustling activity. Jacques Specx, the new Governor-General, had resurrected many building projects which had been neglected by his predecessor Coen during the sieges of the town in 1628 and 1629. He ordered a canal to be dug on the western side of Batavia castle. Within a few months the number of Chinese in Batavia, which had shrunk to 1,200, swelled to over 2,000. Between March and July 1630, these contributed no less than 16,368 rials to these public works. Batavia town was still situated primarily on the eastern side of the meandering outlet of the Ciliwong, and plans for the town's development had to await the canalization of the river's course. Jan Con shouldered this important job (Brandes 1901: 257). The Company was dependent upon Chinese contractors and labour brokers to ensure that the public works were carried out.[16] A splendid commemoration medal that the Chinese towkays presented to Specx at the end of his short tenure in 1632 testifies to their gratitude. One

The medal presented to Governor-General Jacques Specx.

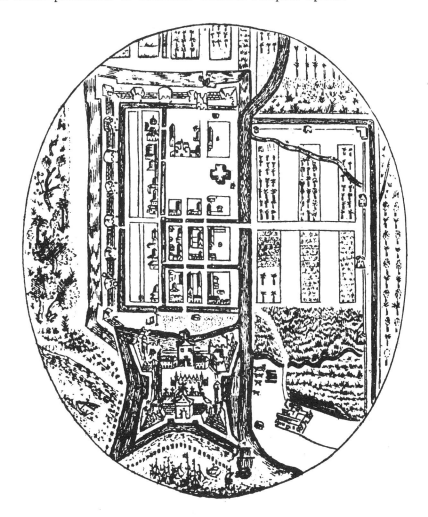

side of the medal shows a map of contemporary Batavia, the other side bears an (illegible) Chinese and a Latin dedication: "In perpetuam gratitudinis memoriam hoc munusculum nos cives Chinenses lubenter meritoque obtulimus insigni heroi Jacobo Spexio Indiarum Orientalium Generali, Patrono nostro observando anno 1632, ady 25, Novembris, Bataviae".[17] Specx' successor, Hendrick Brouwer, further illustrated the indispensable role of the Chinese in his Generale Missive of December 27, 1635. He wrote: "None of the Dutch burghers is willing to contract for building projects such as the dredging of canals or the supply of wood, lime

Pasar Ikan, Batavia.

IV Testament to a Towkay

and stone. Only Chinese are engaged in this sector. Without their help the construction of Batavia's fortification and the city's present lay-out would have required many more years to complete." (Opkomst V:218-9).

Jan Con's record of loyalty and organizational skill must have made him a great asset to the Dutch as they struggled to build a town in a hostile environment. Together with a colleague, in July 1634, he completed at the price of one rial per cubic fathom the digging of a canal that previous contractors had left unfinished. The following month he was awarded another contract to dig the Chinese gracht, the Chinese canal, in town. Canals were not dug for the sake of giving Batavia a Dutch appearance, as is often thought, but out of the necessity to raise the marshy grounds for construction purposes and to fill the pools which still provided a home for crocodiles.[18] On May 13, 1636 the construction of the Rhinoceros Gracht in the western half of the city was contracted with Jan Con's help at a price of 2/3 rial or 32 stuiver per cubic fathom.[19] At the end of that same year, he completed the new Pasar Ikan or fish-market with a special canal added to it to facilitate the landing of fish. According to De Haan, during the same period, the indefatigable entrepreneur also provided the city with a deep moat which surrounded its western and northern sides (De Haan 1935 I:79). Considering the fact that at the same time Jan Con became the chief supplier of lime, stone and wood for the fortification of Batavia castle and Batavia town, it is clear that his projects were most impressive in terms of magnitude, and labour involved (GM I:422). Yet, these projects give us only a partial impression of the man's activities.

Governor-General De Carpentier has been quoted in passing as saying that Jan Con was a man to whom no enterprise was too extensive to undertake. The fact that Jan Con also leased the monopoly on fabricating currency, introduced the cultivation of sugar to the surroundings of Batavia and attempted to start salt production for local consumption may prove his point.

To look at these activities more closely, first of all there was the fabrication of coins. In the 1630's, the High Government hit upon the idea that the mass fabrication of lead coins, the so-called picis, might increase the rapid turnover of trade at the market place and guarantee a profitable outlet for the sale of lead. Jan Con and also, initially, Bencon were enfranchised to fabricate these coins. For several years the venture brought handsome profits to the VOC and Jan Con.

The year 1636 may in some respects be considered as the turning point in Jan Con's career. His friend and partner in many an enterprise, Bencon, decided to relinquish the Captaincy due to his age and ill health.[20] The Hoge Regeering convoked the Chinese headmen and the nachodas of the Chinese junks, seeking their advice with respect to the appointment of a successor. The outcome of this consultation was that Lim Lacco was preferred to Jan Con on July 21 (Res GG and C 21-7-1636, VOC 1119,f.353). The latter must have felt so shattered and insecure regarding his future role that he committed what was for him an uncharacteristic deed. He paid a visit to the wife of Governor-General Van Diemen a few days later and attempted unsuccessfully to bribe her into persuading her husband that the contract on the fabrication of picis, which was up for renewal the following month, should remain in his hands (Res GG and C 30-7-1636, VOC 1119,f.362). The authorities were in a forgiving mood and probably because they never had intended to take away his franchise, Jan Con was awarded the contract (Res GG and C 20-9-1636, VOC 1119,f.407). His initial feeling of relief must have soon given way to feelings of despair, however, when the English started to dump lead coins on the market that autumn (GM I:570). As a result of this practice Jan Con was left with a one year contract for the purchase of lead at a very high price.

Jan-of-all-Trades

Yet, the towkay's spirit was by no means broken. In concert with the authorities he started a whole range of new activities that same year, among which was a a sugar plantation in the Ommelanden of Batavia. Lim Lacco was on the brink of concluding an armistice with Banten, and the Hoge Regering believed it could guarantee Jan Con's employees protection against brigands while they were working outside the city walls in the fields. Imported sugar canes were hacked off at the joints, and 80,000 of these cuttings were laid out in a network of specially prepared gullies and furrows to take root and grow out (GM I:570).

Writing the Directors of the Company in December 1636, Antonio van Diemen expressed his satisfaction at the great strides the city had taken over the previous year in its progress. "Thank God, we have not experienced great disasters, calamities, fires or other difficulties in Batavia", the Governor-General remarked and continued to point out the specific role which the "great merchant Jan Congh" was playing in the development of the town and its immediate surroundings. He expected him to produce a harvest of 2,000 piculs of sugar a year within two years' time, which could in turn be purchased from him at a guaranteed price of 5.5 rials per picul. In the same letter he also mentioned that the Chinese towkay had laid out a salina complex close to the sea, east of Batavia castle, which was to produce 2,000 tons of salt for local use and export. "All this will result in much industry in Batavia to the detriment of our neighbors", Van Diemen concluded, as it later turned out, a bit too optimistically (GM I:570).

The salinas were a costly blunder. It was soon realized that because of high labour-costs in Batavia competition with the saltpans of Eastern Java was impossible. The salt project was therefore abandoned and the investments had to be written off as losses.

The sugar cultivation also experienced growing pains. One and a half years after its initiation it was reported to be progressing well. "[Jan Con] has set up the sugar mills and readied the moulds. The first delivery of sugar is expected soon." (Opkomst V:233-4.) The administration assisted him in many ways, as the references that can be found in this respect demonstrate. A special edict was promulgated which exempted him from paying the tithe of the harvest for a period of ten years (Res GG and C 7-11-1637, VOC 122,f.454). On January 16, 1638, Jan Con bought a plot of land near the southern city gate for 255 rials. He also received another stretch of land on a ten-years' lease near the Gelderland rampart on the condition that he would use it exclusively for the sugar cultivation. Notwithstanding all these efforts the yields were disappointing: in 1638, instead of the projected 2,000 piculs, only a pitiful 22.5 picul of white sugar were sent to Holland. The following year was not much better: the dry monsoon of 1639 scorched part of the harvest, and part of what remained was stolen.[21]

Jan Con's financial resources must have been dealt a staggering blow by these failing enterprises. A complaint made by Bencon that his

IV Testament to a Towkay

friend did not reimburse him for a loan of 3,100 rials within the time agreed may have been a first sign of imminent insolvency.[22] The attempt to diversify operations had failed; Jan Con again became completely dependent upon those building contracts he could conclude with the Company. The administration seems to have been aware of this, for the entrepreneur was not given the opportunity to recoup his losses through his activities as a contractor.

The Ring is Closed

At the end of the wet monsoon of 1638, the Hoge Regering decided it was time to replace the wooden palisades along the western, northern and southern edges of the town with stone city walls which would require less maintenance and could provide more security (17-2-1638, VOC 661). Total costs were estimated at 11,000 rials. Because not only the Company but also the citizens would profit from the greater security offered by these defence works, it was agreed that the town population should share in the expenses. The Company would provide for slaves working at the building sites, while the citizens would be charged the 11,000 rials earmarked for the purchase of building materials. Of this amount the Dutch burghers were to contribute 3,000 rials, while the Chinese had to shoulder the burden of providing the remaining 8,000 rials.

Governor-General and Council met to discuss how this collection should be made. "Exaction" is, however, a more accurate term, as the procedure agreed upon had little in common with a "voluntary contribution". Captain Lim Lacco was ordered to place Chinese notice-boards on the street corners and to exhort his brethren to contribute liberally to the defence works of the town. In addition the wealthy Chinese of Batavia were summoned to the Company headquarters. The manner in which these were encouraged to contribute would have made a mandarin blush. "They were pressed by the use of friendly insinuation and speech to subscribe voluntarily for a share relative to their wealth. Anyone balking at the idea was taxed proportionally to his estimated assets. [...] Chinese who had no possessions worth mentioning were charged four rials to be paid over a period of eight months." The harvest exceeded expectation: more than 9,300 rials were collected from the Chinese alone (GM I:715).

On September 4, 1638 Jan Con invited the authorities to examine the work in progress at the southern and western side of the city. The walls were inspected and declared to have been built according to specification (Res GG and C 4-9-1638, VOC 661). Three days later the remaining works at the northern side of the town were also put out to contract. However, Jan Con was not willing to shoulder this task "and protested he could not survive at a rate of 11 rials per cubic fathom" (Res GG and C 7-9-1638, VOC 661). He even promised a gift of 200 rials to the poor relief fund if he would be excused from carrying out these works. The authorities showed some understanding for his objections: they relieved him "provisionally" of his duties as a supplier of building materials and installed a committee to look into the nature of his complaints.

Several highly placed Company officials assisted by a group of soldiers then tried to establish whether or not his grievances were justified. Temporarily replacing Jan Con, they supervised the activities at

Batavia anno 1650, after the completion of the walls.

Western side:
a Buren
b Vierkant
c Cuilenburch
d Zeeburch
e Groningen
f Overijssel
g Friesland
h Utrecht
i Zeeland
j Nassau
k Diest

1 Chinese hospital
2 Detention house for women
3 Chinese carpenters' wharf
4 Pasar ikan
5 Dutch carpenters' wharf
6 Oud Utrecht

Eastern side:
A Castle
1 Watergate
B Amsterdam
C Middelburg
D Rotterdam
E Enkhuizen
F Gelderland
H Nieuwe Poort
I Hollandia
J Grimbergen
2 Brugstraat
3 New Church
4 Town hall
5 Hospital
6 The Governor's retreat
7 Oud Gelderland

the lime-kilns and the arrival and departure of the prahu and wangkang, native vessels skippered by Bandanese, Chinese and Mardijker burghers, who brought in building materials such as wood and corallite from the nearby Duizend Eilanden (Pulau Seribu). The soldiers probably were needed to act as the eyes and ears of the officials and to ensure an orderly performance of the landing procedures and cargo measurement. In payment the skippers received chits which were converted into cash at the harbour master's office.

One looks in vain for a reference to the committee's findings in the Resolutie-boek of that same autumn. The Generale Missive of December 22, 1638, is not very instructive either, for it reports that 1,438 and 1/4 cubic fathoms of lime and stone had been contracted with Jan Con at the price of 15,821 and 3/8 rials (GM I:714-5). This suggests that the price of 11 rials per cubic fathom had been maintained as if no objection had ever been raised. Thanks to an investigation mounted a year and a half later (after the towkay had died) we know that the Company's attempt to replace him had failed (Res GG and C 5-9-1639, VOC 622). It appears that the officials soon had realized that the only person in town able to run an operation of these dimensions was Jan Con: "geene andere [was] bequaem tot soodanighe groote werck". Short as the experiment may have been, it left no doubts about the necessity of raising the price paid by cubic fathom, although it was difficult for the investigators to specify how much. The upshot of these deliberations was that in order to avoid further delay a very unsatisfactory modus operandi was worked out.

It was probably Director-General Philips Lucasz. who promised Jan Con that the treasury would make up for eventual losses suffered on account of too low a price paid per cubic fathom. The latter agreed to continue his operations at the old rate. Was he reassured by the assertion "that the Company would not prosper by the losses of one of its most capable citizens", or did he simply have no other choice?[23] Whatever the case may have been, as the ring of walls closed around the city, they also created an effective stranglehold around the neck of its contractor.

Jan Con was advanced money on credit and settlements were made every time he completed another stretch of the defence works. In the eyes of the Company servants, issuing Jan Con credit in this way was without risk as the supply of building materials was seen as the mortgage on Jan Con's debts. The authorities were quite pleased with Jan Con's performance. The work was carried out on schedule and according to specification. Curiously, Chinese appear to have been no longer engaged in physical labour at the construction site, a phenomenon which elicited from Van Diemen the remark that "they seemed able to make a better living through pursuits other than digging canals" (GM I:716). Little by little the wooden palisade around Batavia gave way to massive eleven-foot high city walls.

The Hoge Regering reflected on March 25, 1639, after a year of strenuous work that "with the help of God the laudible and memorable construction [...] of a firm and durable city wall was reaching completion". Another surcharge was imposed, this time on all housing in the western city, to alleviate the formidable burden of these public works on the budget of the municipal administration. Those employed in the supply of the building materials also had to contribute: the stonemasons were to pay 1 rial and the lumberjacks 1/4 rial a month (Res GG and C

VOC 662).

In April Jan Con reported that the western city wall stretching from the Overijssel rampart to the Groningen rampart was ready for examination (Res GG and C 14-4-1639, VOC 662). He expected to be paid after the volume of the earthwork used had been measured. His hopes that he would receive the payment in cash were, however, dashed. So much money had been advanced to him for the salinas, the sugarplantation and the construction works, that the payment was simply subtracted from his debts to the Company: he was caught in the grip of his creditors.

In July, the Chinese contractor presented a petition to Governor-General and Council, humbly asking them to be discharged from the tax farm on gambling, which he had contracted at 650 rials a month. The contents of the written petition enable us to gain some understanding of tax farming and how it operated. Jan Con stated that although he had personally contracted the tax farm on gambling from the administration on New Year's eve, he had subsequently subcontracted it out to "Chinese who were dependent upon his activities". The clients who operated their patron's tax farm were losing money on it, except for the busy months of February, March, and April when the Chinese junks with their crews and merchants were in town. In the month of June, when the junks had returned to China, losses amounted to no less than 320 rials and it was apparent that July would even be worse - sufficient reason for the towkay to request to be discharged as soon as possible from the levying of this tax, as "his Chinese [subcontractors] pressed him to do so". The authorities who "did not want to see Jan Con totally ruined and preferred to let him keep the respect of a credit-worthy borrower", gave in to his request.[24] Perhaps they did so because they felt slightly embarrassed by Jan Con's assertion that "the Dutch knew quite well that he had contracted several construction works, tax farms and canal digging projects on which he had suffered considerable losses at different occasions without even informing the Governor-General or having asked for an abatement".

Meanwhile, the wall-building continued at a steady pace, and in August, Jan Con announced the completion of the northern wall between the Groningen and Nassau ramparts. The works were surveyed and measured so that he could receive payment (Res GG and C 15-8-1639, VOC 662).

In the Chinese chronicle of Batavia, the "Kai-pa Li-tai Shih-chi", it is mentioned that with the completion of the walls and the gates of the town, the Chinese inhabitants were doomed.[25] In the particular case of its builder, Jan Con, that was certainly true.

Demasqué

On September 1, 1639, in low spirits, the Governor-General and Council met to take special measures: they had just been informed of the sudden demise of the towkay the previous night. Quick action was advisable. Jan Con was heavily in debt to the Company and creditors were said to be flocking around his estate and demanding repayment. In view of this situation, the board agreed that "it should secure [before it was too late] the remaining property of Jan Con to the detriment of the other creditors", if the Company desired to retrieve some of its outstanding capital. "Jan Con's belongings should therefore be sealed immediate-

IV Testament to a Towkay

ly, confiscated and inventorized, while at the same time it should be assessed how much capital he had loaned, borrowed or put out, here, at sea or anywhere else." All debtors to the Jan Con estate were summoned to report within ten days to the Secretariat in Batavia castle. As there was much work to be done, no fewer than 15 curators were appointed to carry out the above orders: ten Company servants and five Chinese, among whom Bencon, just back from Taiwan, and Jan Con's brother who had arrived from China (Res GG and C 1-9-1639, VOC 662).

On the face of it, this appears to be a case in which the stable door is bolted after the horse was gone, as the expression goes. In retrospect it was not quite as simple as that. In the weeks that followed - and at long last catching a glimpse of reality - the Hoge Regeering was no longer able to keep aloof from what had happened. It had not only to complete the ramparts without the help of its favourite handyman, but it was also presented with the bill for its past policies.

The real state of affairs first became apparent at the building site. Although the city walls had been all but completed, several ramparts were still under construction and in need of considerable quantities of lime, stone and wood. To avoid a delay in the schedule, tenders were immediately invited for the supply of these materials; these were received on September 5. It turned out that no Chinese contractor was willing to supply lime and stone at less than 13.5 rials per cubic fathom; two weeks later that price rose to 14 rials (Res GG and C 5-9-1639, VOC 662). Consequently, in order to avoid losing face, the Company was forced to take these matters into its own hands.

The curators' findings were discussed on September 20. Jan Con was approximately 27,500 rials in arrears with the Company. And although he seemed to have sustained great losses through the failure of the sugar and salt production projects, the evidence also pointed to the administration's involvement in the losses suffered by Jan Con. As culprit the curators designated Director-General Philips Lucasz. who had handled the allowance of credit. They came to the conclusion that Jan Con had been grossly underpaid. In addition to the 4,000 rials which the Company owed in payment of the walls that had been completed in August, another 6,050 rials had to be found for other projects which had not yet been paid for. The Governor-General was so impressed that he allocated these 6,050 rials for the compensation of the "many 'onnozele' [innocent] creditors" who had been hurt by the insolvency (Res GG and C 20-9-1639, VOC 662). In other words, he relinquished the Company's prerogatives over the individual creditors.

In extenuation of the Company's actions, it may be pleaded that Van Diemen was not only willing to concede that mistakes had been made, but he even took steps to avoid similar events in the future. There was no doubt that confidence had been shattered as a result of the towkay's bankruptcy. For the sake of peace and order in town, any repetition of quarrels surrounding (in)solvent estates of Chinese citizens should be avoided at all cost. It was against this background that the Governor-General issued orders for short- and long-term measures.

Learning from Jan Con

One of the long-term measures intended to put an end to the "manifold frauds and malversations committed in the Chinese houses of mourning", was the installation of a body of curators or boedelmeesters for the Chinese in town (26-5-1640, Plakaatboek I:438). It was quite obvious that the Hoge Regering could not be importuned time and again by appeals to mediate in the execution of solvent or insolvent Chinese estates, and therefore a specific administrative body was created to handle these cases. The detailed instructions issued upon the installation of the two Dutch and the two Chinese members of the Boedelkamer bear witness to the importance the government attached to the strict administration of the estates of its Chinese citizens. Soon the social component of this new institution was extended further, when the boedelmeesters, with the consent of the Hoge Regeering, initiated a taxation on Chinese funerals for the sake of financing the foundation of a Chinese hospital in town (13-8-1640, Plakaatboek I:446).

When the Gentlemen XVII in Holland were informed about these sweeping measures, they expressed their approval. "You have settled the administration of the estates of the deceased Chinese correctly, so that henceforth nobody will be wronged and the heirs may receive what they are entitled to", they wrote to Van Diemen (VOC 316,f.350). Indeed, as a result of this institutional reform, the Chinese citizens of Batavia had become formally integrated into the legal framework of the colonial administration.

What immediate measures did Van Diemen take to restore confidence? Here we again encounter the confidence game referred to in the introduction of this essay. The Governor-General ordered a full-scale investigation into the solvency and the borrowing practices of other Chinese merchants who had received credit from the VOC. It was the right moment to do so, for the books had been closed at the end of August and Director-General Philips Lucasz. was in the middle of transmitting his administration to his successor. The outcome of the first investigation was shocking: no fewer than 150,886 rials had been credited to Chinese citizens over the past few years. Van Diemen immediately ordered collection of the debts but his attempts were unsuccessful. Only sixty thousand rials were retrieved and it was feared that at least half of the remaining 80,000 rials would have to be written off as bad debts (Res GG and C 3-12-1639, VOC 662; GM II:74, 122). The outcome of the story was that the creditworthiness of the Chinese in Batavia received a terrible blow: the financial climate was thoroughly undermined. Director-General Philips Lucasz., so tightfisted in his payments to Jan Con, had clearly been too liberal a provider of credit to the other Chinese merchants: While the Dutch burghers (the main moneylenders to the Chinese) asked a monthly interest of 1.5-3 percent, Lucasz. was content with only 6 percent per annum (GM II:122). How could this have happened?

The comment of the investigators is well worth quoting: "Experience teaches us that the Chinese are not content with the small profits on the merchandise they receive from us on credit in small lots to hawk them about. No, it is their main object to lay their hands on capital, which they rashly risk on their ships at sea and even send to China, leaving their creditors in the meantime without interest." (Res GG and C 3-12-1639, VOC 662). This kind of speculative behaviour - a Chinese brand of confidence game - was not only widely practised in Southeast Asia in colonial times but at other periods as well.

In early nineteenth century Canton, the Hong merchants were notorious for their speculation with Western capital; in Republican China this behaviour representative of trading groups chronically devoid of sufficient ready capital was a well known phenomenon. As Carl Crow has described so well in his "400,000,000 Customers", Western firms, neither willing nor able to compete in the local intermediate trade, used to put out their merchandise on credit to Chinese middlemen in the (often vain) expectation that these would open up a consumer market; those firms then were rudely awakened by the discovery that the intermediary immediately sold the entire supply of merchandise far below its real market value. The proceeds of these sales provided the middlemen with ready capital which they could work for their own purposes before having to pay back the first installment (Crow 1939).

In final analysis, this is exactly what had happened in Batavia. The Company as a wholesale organization could not afford to be bothered by small sales on the local market. The Governor-General and Council actually stated that it was not their objective to enter the intermediate trade. "They did not want to open the warehouses for a mere trifle" at the demand of every prospective customer, and as a result, they preferred to entrust Chinese middlemen with selling, regularly providing them with consignments of merchandise (Res GG and C 3-12-1639, VOC 662). It was established that the collective debt of the most eminent Chinese to the Company had amounted to less than 8,000 rials when Philips Lucasz. assumed his duties as Director-General in 1635. During his tenure he had failed to square accounts with these customers every time they returned to fetch a new lot, probably because he had been too credulous and had given in too easily to their unceasing demands. The collective debt rose as a result more than fifteen times (GM II: 122). To put an end to these soft loan practices, Van Diemen issued stern orders that henceforth credit should only be offered to a limited group of thirteen Chinese merchants to a maximum of 2,000 rials per person in the case of the two most prominent ones (Res GG and C 3-12-1639, VOC 662).

The Chinese community of Batavia in fact gained from this volte face of the administration. A loose body of informal rules related to transactions between the VOC and the Chinese merchants underwent important modification and institutionalization based upon a corpus of regulations. These were in turn incorporated into the Batavian Code of Law, (the Bataviaasche Statuten) which was formally introduced in 1642, further institutionalizing the position of the different nations in town.[26]

At this point it seems appropriate to conclude and consider what Jan Con's biography has to tell us and the degree to which he may have been central to these institutional developments.

Conclusion

The hero of this biography was by no means an embezzler. Properly speaking, he may have fallen victim to the confidence game himself. The career of Jan Con - which at first glance seems merely episodic - becomes invested with a deeper significance once we realize his various functions within Batavian society. He lived in a pioneering age where social order in the basic sense of the provision of security to persons and their property was in the process of formation through such important measures as the building of city walls to protect the inhabitants and the creation of a legal framework and safeguards to protect property.

Henri Pirenne demonstrated the contribution of wandering merchants to the revival of trade in 11th century Europe through the use of biographical data he had collected concerning one such wandering merchant, Godric of Finchal. Such an impressionistic picture will not do here. Indeed, we have followed the steps of a wandering Chinese who invented tax farms for the Hoge Regering, was involved in its foreign affairs and trade and finally acted as its handyman in several important projects. However, the sustained investigation into the gradual establishment and institutionalization of social order in Batavia has led us into repeated encounters with Jan Con. He has been a recurring symbol in the real issues which this contribution attempts to address.

The breakdown in Jan Con's commercial fortunes occurred when he let his own interests coincide too closely with those of the Company, and when he trusted that he would not be let down if things went wrong. His sudden death precluded any such salvage operation but more importantly roused the authorities to deal with the Chinese more carefully.

It is easy and tempting to deride the inability of the Batavian authorities to understand the needs of one of its Chinese subjects and to portray Jan Con as a victim or a martyr. It would perhaps be more fitting to wonder at the wisdom of Van Diemen who was able to draw a lesson from these events.

Chapter V

BATAVIA 1619-1740:
THE RISE AND FALL OF A CHINESE COLONIAL TOWN*

The rise and fall of the Chinese colonial town within Batavia was closely related to the transmutation in Batavia's function as a capital. In the early seventeenth century it was founded as the headquarters to a, mainly inter-Asian, maritime trading East India Company at war with the Iberian enemy. As the Company's staple town, het magazijn van derzelver producten, it served both strategic and mercantile goals. From the late seventeenth century onwards, a structural change took place. Wars between the Dutch and their European rivals were over and trade with the fatherland became emphasized at the expense of the Asian "Country trade". On Java, the Company was gradually transformed into a territorial power which derived its main income from a system of "contingenten" and "verplichte leverantiën", or tribute payments. Consequently, Batavia lost most of its dynamic function as a headquarters to a maritime trade empire. The adaptation of the city to its new role of capital to a territorial hinterland did not progress smoothly.

This chapter endeavours to re-examine several issues concerning the rise and demise of the Batavian Chinatown. It attempts to throw light on the historical circumstances in which Batavia took shape, the institutional structure of the collaboration between the Chinese inhabitants and the Dutch East Indies Company, and the fatal developments which brought about the massacre of the Chinese citizens in 1740.

On Collaboration

Historians of modern imperialism, including Henri Brunschwig and Ronald Robinson, have stressed the importance of non-European foundations of European imperialism (Robinson 1972; Brunschwig 1978). Both have convincingly shown that the relatively fast pace at which European powers gained a political and economic foothold on the African continent a hundred years ago was largely due to the skillful use of local collaborating groups as mediators between Europe and the indigenous political and economic system. Both emphasize that the local ruling élite were often quite willing to collaborate with the Europeans, as they thought, rightly or wrongly, that their own influence could be secured, if not extended, through such a "pooling of resources" with the colonizers. The same pattern of collaboration or cooperation (in some cases, the use of the latter term may be preferable) can be discerned in the progressively tightening bond between the Dutch authorities and the local rulers, Inlandse Vorsten, in the Indonesian archipelago during the nineteenth century or even in the early seventeenth century, as illustrated by the initial collaboration between Coen and the unfortunate pangeran of Jakarta, who tried through this collaboration to wrestle himself free from the tight grip of his suzerain, the sultan of nearby Banten.

Collaboration, however, by no means remained restricted to relationships between the colonial ruler and the local indigenous élite. Other partners figured as well: non-indigenous economic "power groups", which were in need of protection, or individuals who attempted to use a career in the colonial service to mount a ladder of success which would have remained inaccessible to them within their own society. The interpreter in colonial societies, for instance, gained influence which often extended far beyond simply translating for others. Good examples of collaborating merchant communities are the Dahoméens in West Africa and the Chinese in Southeast Asia.

I have described the roles played by particular Chinese individuals as collaborators or counterparts of the Dutch merchants in Southeast Asian ports which were, or were not under Dutch jurisdiction (Blussé 1975, 1979). In this chapter I shall focus upon the general mode of cooperation between the headquarters of the Company in Asia, Batavia castle, and the Chinese merchant community in the town of Batavia. Evidence will show that in the period from the establishment of the castle-city in 1619 to the so-called Chinese massacre in 1740, the city of Batavia was, economically speaking, basically a Chinese colonial town under Dutch protection, notwithstanding the misleading image given by its canals and brick gables. Through an elaborate system of political, social, and economic measures, Batavia castle with its warehouses functioned as the "keystone" in the system of Dutch trading posts all over Asia, while Batavia town operated as a "cornerstone" of the Chinese trade network in Southeast Asia. These two aspects coexisted harmoniously and peacefully for a considerable period. Here it might be of interest to glance quickly at the kind of source material and the present state of research concerning the Chinese of Batavia, before we attempt to analyse the character of pre-war 1740 Batavian town society.

Related Source Materials and Studies

Western Languages
A large and varied assortment of information from contemporary eyewitnesses has reached us through published documents and letters written by Company servants or clerics, and travel accounts by European sailors and travellers. In this literature, the Chinese of Batavia are virtually without exception described as a diligent, peace-loving and, at times deceitful, people who had a hand in everything (die overal een hand in hebben) but who were at the same time timorous (vreesachtig van aard). In all these sources it is stated that the Chinese dominated the important economic activities of the city such as fishery, lumbering, construction work, agriculture, horticulture, the markets, handicraft, and the inland and Chinese trade. The taxes which the company levied on the Batavian inhabitants were mainly collected by the Chinese. Only as bartenders did the Chinese acknowledge the superiority of the Dutch, even though the Chinese possessed the monopoly on arak production. The Chinese have been described variously as: "an industrious people [...] on whom the well-being of Batavia completely depends, because without them no markets would be held, neither houses nor defence works would be made" (Reverend Heurnius in 1625); "it is true that without them Batavia's safety and its present state would not have been achieved for many years" (Governor-General Brouwer in 1635); "the Chinese form the foundation [of this colony]" (Governor-General

V Chinese Batavia 1619-1740　　　　　　　　　　75

Van der Lijn in 1650); "without them Batavia would not be half its present state" (François Leguat in 1700); "the Chinese have the greatest trade here, they form most of the excise and customs" (Woodes Rogers in 1712). Today's casual observer might surmise that the Chinese were the Batavian citizens par excellence. However, no further conclusions have been drawn in this direction by contemporaries, since Batavia was after all the headquarters of the Company. To have acknowledged that the well-being of the town depended to a very large degree upon the Chinese community would have amounted to sacrilege.

From source-publications like the Daghregisters, Plakaatboeken, and Realia, a rich harvest of political and economic information on Batavia can be gleaned. Unfortunately, we are less well informed about the modes of Chinese social and economic organization in early Batavia. Only the recently published monograph on temples and communal life in Jakarta by Salmon and Lombard and the unpublished thesis by De Vienne can be considered serious first steps in this field of research (Salmon and Lombard 1977; De Vienne 1979). Chapter VI on the Chinese junk trade offers information on the trade of the Batavian Chinese with China, but hardly anything is known about the existence of Chinese traditional economic institutions like "hang", or guilds, in pre-1740 Batavia. The mutual aid societies that an early eighteenth-century visitor to Batavia, François Leguat, described could have been based on kinship as well as on common place of origin (Kroeskamp 1953:346-71). For information in this respect we shall, for the time being, have to fall back on studies about other Overseas Chinese settlements like Malacca or Nagasaki in the same period, about which we are better informed.

Other studies on the Batavian Chinese, like Hoetink's excellent articles about the Chinese captains and officers of the community (Hoetink 1917, 1918, 1922, 1923), Vermeulen's thesis on the Chinese massacre (Vermeulen 1938), and a couple of studies on the Chinese Raad, the Chinese hospital, and tax-farming by other scholars[1], represent aspects of the Dutch-Chinese cooperation and the channels along which this collaboration took place (with Vermeulen's study of course representing the breakdown in these relations). Consequently, these subjects are characteristic of the situation that I shall sketch.

Chinese Language
For the period we are dealing with, there exist only three important sources which to my knowledge have been translated into Western languages. Two are short accounts by Chinese preceptors who taught in Batavia before, and in Pekalongan, after 1740 respectively (Salmon 1972, Ong 1849). The third is the "Kai-pa Li-tai Shih-chi" (or "The Historical Records of the Foundation of Batavia through the Ages"), a local history which covers the years 1619 up to about 1810 (Hsü 1953). An incomplete and very free translation into Dutch of this chronicle appeared in 1840 (Medhurst 1840) but an annotated English translation is scheduled to appear in the near future. Although this local history has the most information to offer, owing to its length and scope, its contents have generally been judged to be rather disappointing. Its author(s) pay(s) nearly as much attention to the Dutch Governors-General as to the leaders of the Chinese community, and many occurrences which must have been important to the Chinese community are not dealt with at all. The extent to which a lenient or stern policy was adopted by the Dutch "king" - the Governor-General was called wang - toward

The Chinese temple at Batavia.

A Chinese barber.

V Chinese Batavia 1619-1740

the Chinese, and the position of the Chinese leaders as brokers between him and the Chinese community are discussed to varying degrees, and are indicative of the dependent nature of the Chinese settlement. The simultaneous use of Chinese and Western calendars emphasizes the hybrid nature of the text. All these factors contribute to making the Historical Records a document on cooperation. Its main concern is the colonial administration of Batavia and its various institutions "seen from the point of view of local Chinese officials".[2]

Unexplored Sources
Among the many Company documents concerning Batavia in the Arsip Nasional in Jakarta, the largely unexplored notarial archives, which have been preserved intact from the time of the Company till the present, should receive special attention. They contain a wealth of material on Batavia's citizens, without which the definitive study on the city's social and economic history could not be written. As for Chinese documents, there are the still unexplored and pitifully stored Kong koan (Chinese Council) archives close to the klenteng Gunung Sari. Claudine Salmon, who had a brief look at these materials, informed me that most of them date from the nineteenth to the twentieth century. There is little hope that new discoveries will be made elsewhere within the Chinese community, as it seems that many manuscripts and documents were burned by the Chinese themselves during the unfortunate occurrences in 1965, when possession of Chinese language documents could have been dangerous indeed.

A Typological Approach

From the morphological point of view, nineteenth-century Batavia with its distinct kampongs arranged around an administrative (and cultural?) centre may have possessed many traditional Indonesian characteristics, but the castle town of the seventeenth century with its massive structure and isolated position within a hostile foreign territory had little in common with the traditional port settlements on the Javanese coast. When looking for an analogous type of settlement, one is reminded of the medieval princely castle settlement or borough as described by Henri Pirenne. The comparison may seem artificial, but during the seventeenth century Batavia actually had much in common with such medieval colonial castle towns in the Baltic region like Riga and Tallinn (Danska Linna or Danish castle). There, foreign "princes" would build fortifications at strategic places on the crossroads of trade routes and "import" an immigrant urban population, who were to build up a town in the shadow of the walls of the castle. The main function of the town was to supply foodstuffs to and finance the maintenance of the castle's garrison by paying taxes and drawing trade to its markets. Although those in power in the castle jealously guarded certain trade monopolies (in the Baltic case, for instance, grains, and wax) some freedom in overseas trading was also granted to the inhabitants of the town insofar as it ultimately resulted in financial gain for the castle. The lords in the castle took a keen interest in the economic well-being of the town as their own status depended upon it, but at the same time they guarded against its potential military strength and obviously preferred a peaceable and politically passive population.
   Dominated by the castle, the town was controlled by it and could on-

ly assert its independence in the long run by strengthening its ties with the territorial hinterland, which was outside the reach of the lords of the castle. I have deliberately used the example of the Baltic castle town in order to avoid the difficulties inherent in explaining all events in Indonesian history exclusively in Indonesian concepts, which are too often so embedded that it is difficult to discern their real meaning.

Morphologically, the castle town, Batavia, had little in common with the traditional Javanese port towns because of its peculiar physical structure. To this, one could add that it linked the European and Asian markets, and may have introduced new norms and generated new mental and social integration, factors which moved Reed to call seventeenth-century Batavia an example of nascent metropolitan primacy (Reed 1967: 543-62). In many other respects the similarities between Batavia and the Javanese port cities are, however, startling indeed, and this goes a long way toward explaining Batavia's early success as a port city within the archipelago.

European Castle, Chinese Town: Manila and Batavia

Manila and Batavia were the only urban settlements which were literally started from scratch by Europeans during the sixteenth and seventeenth centuries in Southeast Asia. In these castle towns Europeans lived under their own rule and according to their own laws.

I have already briefly mentioned Reed's stimulating essay on the colonial origins of Manila and Batavia. According to him, a new dimension in city life was created in Southeast Asia with the founding of these two cities. However, he does not explore the ethnic composition of these towns, which mainly explains the success of these two urban ventures. It seems relevant to examine this subject here and to analyse the ethnic character of these two cities, particularly as, in fact, seventeenth-century Manila and Batavia had a lot in common. Both castles, Intramuros and Casteel Batavia, dominated towns with populations which were predominantly Chinese. This "Chinese presence" was the result of an imposed colonial decision, as we shall see later. Both castles were directly linked to the Chinese overseas trade network, a network which dated from long before the arrival of the Europeans - they actually owed their locations to it. Both represented links between these networks and new ones: the Mexican and the European trade. Both castles drew their direct incomes from and were supplied by a population of Chinese settlers. In both cases, the scales of interdependence between Europeans and Chinese tipped under the weight of increasing influence wielded by the Chinese. Friction between the European castle and the Chinese perioeci on account of this led to tension and distrust which at times erupted into pogroms. In Batavia one such massacre took place in 1740, while Manila experienced as many as six, respectively in 1603, 1639, 1662, 1686, 1762 and 1819. Aside from these clashes, the rather surprising fact remains that the Europeans actually had little problem dealing with and accepting the Chinese within the "European" urban societies of Manila and Batavia. Dutch seventeenth-century sources mention the "diligent", "peace-loving", and "cowardly" character of the Chinese which made them an easily controlled and dominated urban plebeian class. These traits may have been obvious reasons for the policies of hard-headed colonizers like Coen, who had other things on his mind beside the study of the social organization of the Chinese; today's arm-

V Chinese Batavia 1619-1740

chair historian, however, will probably agree that peace-loving persons do not necessarily make good city dwellers who take tenement houses and crowded quarters for granted.

As a matter of fact the Chinese are, as much as the Europeans, products of a civilization which has produced the phenomenon of the walled city. The word for city in Chinese, ch'eng, actually means "walled city". The average Chinese city was divided into two parts, the yamen and the city, which were the seat of the magistrate or his bureaucratic administration, and the residences of the populace respectively. Exactly the same components could be found in Batavia. With the exception of the capital, Chinese cities had no separate administration but were regarded as the administrative centres of a territory. They were divided into sections over which the government appointed chiefs. Frequently, the largest proportion of the population of a given section was involved in the same business pursuits. There were citizen clubs for group entertainment, social insurance, or mutual aid, hospitals, orphanages, and homes for the aged. The same was true for Batavia, and since all these institutions were native to Chinese society, they were easily introduced into this Dutch colonial city.

Dutch historians have never wearied of singing the praises of their wise forefathers in seventeenth-century Batavia; the latter not only imposed an administrative and judicial grid on Batavia from above to overlay pre-existing Asian structures but also provided the Chinese with a hospital, an orphanage, and a home for the aged. The eventual success of these institutions had, however, little to do with their Calvinist benefactors. They functioned quite simply because they were also part of, or fitted into, the Chinese heritage and needed only a little encouragement to operate within the restless immigrant society as well. The Dutch could thus integrate a Chinese population which did not have to go to great lengths to adjust into the Europeans administrative system.

The resemblances between Manila and Batavia were not coincidental. When Coen founded the rendez-vous, Batavia, he had in mind the creation of a self-sufficient headquarters in the style of Manila. One example in which Coen explains this city's structure may illustrate this: "Around the city of Manila a population of 20,000 families lives, most of them Chinese, also a few Japanese and natives of the country. The Castilians living in the above-mentioned city (which amounts to no more than 1,000 families) draw tribute, tolls and other emoluments from these people and thus maintain their state."[4]

"City" here meant the Spanish castle town or Intramuros. In this respect, Manila and Batavia differed: while the Spaniards emphatically excluded the Chinese from Intramuros and limited their residence to a separate Chinatown called the Parian, the Dutch opted for a different solution. They also built a separate fortress, Casteel Batavia, which acted as the headquarters of the Company, but they chose to live with the Chinese in one city simply because there were too few Dutch freeburghers and because it was necessary to protect the Chinese against attacks from outside. Moreover, they wished to ensure that all Chinese business dealings would pass through the toll gates of the Company. Thus the conditions for a rather unique kind of cooperation were created, which differed considerably from the Manila example.

The Foundation of Batavia and Its Construction

The ultimate choice of a proper place for the Company's rendez-vous was determined by two considerations. It was important that it be situated close to one of the two passages from east to west (Malacca Strait or Sunda Strait), and it should be accessible to the Chinese junks which made an important contribution to the inter-archipelago trade. These considerations, among others, led to the establishment of Batavia in 1619 near the ruined living quarters of the pangeran who, together with his people, had been driven out of Jakarta to Banten. Only a few years earlier, in 1611, Governor-General Pieter Both had received a licence from the pangeran to build a warehouse in the Chinese quarter. In 1619, however, the positions were reversed: Jan Pietersz. Coen pursued a policy which promoted maximum immigration of Chinese and Dutchmen to Batavia. The Chinese began to settle in the "Dutch quarter". The population scheme to attract Dutch freeburghers in great numbers fell through, but the immigration of the Chinese was extremely successful. This success was, however, based upon some questionable measures at the outset like the kidnapping of "immigrants" along the China coast and the forced migration of Chinese from nearby Javanese port cities. After one year, however, the big junks from China started to bring in migrant workers. The building of the city could begin.

The major construction works of the city, like the digging of canals and the building of the city walls and houses were all contracted and carried out by well-known Chinese contractors like Jan Con and Bingam. The Chinese were as familiar with the crafts of brick-making and brick-laying as were the Dutch themselves and photographs made at the beginning of this century, when many old seventeenth- and eighteenth-century houses were still to be found in Batavia, clearly point to Chinese influence on the design of the seventeenth-century Dutch Batavian town house. The Company paid for the reinforcement of the castle, but the citizenry had to shoulder the burden of the expenditures for the fortifications of the town. In 1620 the Chinese were relieved of the obligation to carry earth for the city walls on the condition that they pay a monthly poll tax of 1.5 real (Coen III:648). As a result, they paid five times as much as the other townspeople did for the fortifications of Batavia. For the construction of the town hall, they paid three times as much as all other groups did together (Opkomst V:91; Res GG and C 9-4-1626, VOC 1088).

The Early Population and Colonization Policies of the Company

To lay out and build a city on a marshy plain which is at the same time surrounded by enemies is one problem, but to populate it is a wholly different matter. I have already hinted at the failures of the population policy insofar as Dutch immigrants were concerned. Spinsters and girls from orphanages were shipped to the Indies during the early years. Upon seeing the hundreds of sailors and soldiers, who were eagerly awaiting them at the Batavian roadstead, these ladies seemed to awaken to the fact that they held a strong hand indeed. Letters from the Company officials in Batavia to the Gentlemen XVII in Holland overflowed with reproaches for their having sent these ladies. In the house of God-fearing Coen - the lion's den itself - a young girl entrusted to the Governor-General's tutelage by her father was deflowered by a young

V Chinese Batavia 1619-1740

ensign. Strong action was bound to come. The Gentlemen XVII changed their minds, stipulating that henceforth native girls were to be married as it turned out that "it was of no use for most of the townsmen, and expensive and prejudicial to the interests of the Company, to send Dutch women" (VOC 316, 2-9-1633).

A second problem closely tied to the first was that Dutch freeburghers returned home with their Dutch families as soon as they had made some money. These were not settlers. Through the propagation of marriages between Dutchmen and Asian women, the authorities tried to tie these males to their families and to Batavia.

Paradoxically, the Chinese migrant workers became the first real settlers in Batavia. Many of them attained, in the course of times, sufficient wealth to render themselves independent, and they chose to stay, many of them marrying Balinese women brought in as slaves. This did not escape the attention of the Gentlemen XVII, who wrote to Governor-General Brouwer that they had begun to understand that a Dutch colony could never be secured in Batavia. A colony should be formed with several "Indians" "who might be given the opportunity to settle over there just like the Chinese, who after having resided for many a year in Batavia are now beginning to get accustomed to the local situation. The more these prosper, the more they seek to stay. As regards the Dutch citizenry, we have found the opposite to be true." (VOC 316,3-9-1633). Two years later they reiterated this order and emphasized that Batavia should be peopled with all kinds of folk "and especially the Chinese [...]. We trust that the Chinese trade may blaze the trail for this." (VOC 316,13-9-1635).

The Chinese and the Management of the City

In October 1619, shortly after the city's foundation, Governor-General Jan Pietersz. Coen appointed his sobat and confidant, Su Ming-kang - called Bencon by the Dutch - as headman or captain of the Chinese citizenry, instructing him to settle all civil affairs among his countrymen. With this appointment, the Dutch consciously placed the Chinese under a leader of their own, who was to represent them in dealings with the Dutch authorities. Until 1666 the Chinese were also represented by one or two of their chiefs on the bench of magistrates of the city, which further included three servants of the Company and four freeburghers. Over the years, as the Chinese population steadily increased, other Chinese "officers" called "lieutenants" and "secretaries" were appointed to lighten the task of the captain. At the time of the massacre in 1740, one captain and six lieutenants were in office. We have already seen that the Chinese contributed to the construction of the city by paying exemption money for physical labour. In the 1630s, this poll tax amounted to more than half the total income derived by the Company from the tolls and taxes of the town. By that time, the tax had become a kind of "protection money" which freed the Chinese from serving in the citizen soldiery of the town. The dislike of the Chinese for military service was generally advanced as the reason for the continuation of this tax, but it may also have been a precautionary measure to keep the Chinese unarmed. In his reflections on the situation within the young colony, Governor-General Brouwer stated in 1633 that the Chinese citizens were in all respects superior to the Dutch, but he warned that "they are so full of deceit that we cannot trust them at all" (Opkomst V:214). By 1644, the Chinese contracted seventeen of a total of twenty-one taxes which were levied on such enterprises as gambling, markets, import and export tolls, wayang plays, etc. The auction of these tax farms took place at the house of the Chinese captain at the beginning of every year, until, in 1652, because of the complaints of the Dutch freeburghers about this procedure, it was moved to Batavia castle. According to Nakamura, the Chinese made up through these tax-farms about a quarter of all costs incurred by the headquarters of the Company, the castle and its garrison, and the town (Nakamura 1969: 73). Although Batavia had by no means become self-sufficient, the disproportionately large contribution of the Chinese still represented a major step in this direction.

Problems between creditors and debtors, negligence of orphans (most of whom were born out of alliances with Balinese women), and poor sanitary conditions among the unsettled Chinese immigrants soon prompted intervention by the Dutch. After a first abortive attempt in 1640, the institution of the boedelmeester or trustees was established in 1655. The council of boedelmeesters, which was composed of both Dutch and Chinese members, was to administer the inheritances of Chinese

The Chinese hospital.

citizens who had died without issue or whose children were still under age. From the proceeds of these funds, a Chinese hospital and an orphanage were founded. Thereafter, all Chinese were required to make wills. Through the legal protection of property, accumulation of capital among the Chinese was encouraged, which was an incentive for many Chinese labourers to remain in Batavia. This ultimately resulted in the development of a Chinese property-owning middle class.

Even though they were the only population group which had to pay a poll tax, the position of the Chinese was rather privileged. It appears from complaints that were lodged by 270 freeburghers in 1647 and 1652 that, especially in the area of trade, the Dutch felt that the Batavian government favoured the Chinese over them. They protested to the States-General in Holland as they felt that they could not obtain justice in Java (Van den Berg 1904:30-56). They contended that while the overseas freeburgher trade was becoming more and more restricted by the monopolistic practices of the Company and was therefore doomed to languish, the Chinese with their junks were by contrast free to trade via their inter-archipelago and overseas networks which reached as far as China and Japan. This argument becomes plausible if it is borne in mind that the Chinese junks continued to trade with ports where the Company could not set up a profitable trade because of high expenses, while the areas where the freeburghers were able to trade coincided with those accessible to the Company and thus tended to spoil the Company's trade within its own trade net. The profitable overseas trade enjoyed by the Chinese did not, of course, remain unnoticed by the wealthy servants of the Company, who stimulated it further by lending money at high rates to the Chinese or investing in the trade themselves, with the prospect of earning 30-50 percent in profits. This led to an intertwining of interests of the well-to-do Dutch Company servants and freeburghers and the Chinese traders.

A great deal could be said about the role played by the Chinese as letter bearers and diplomatic brokers in Batavia's relations with Banten and Mataram in the early years of the colony when the Dutch were not yet well-acquainted with the local customs. But for our purposes it may suffice to state that the Chinese were indeed of great help to the Company in this area.

Having digressed somewhat regarding the qualitative share of the Chinese in the city it is time to turn attention to their quantitative portion. Early population data on Batavia are scarce. We know that by 1632 the Chinese already formed the biggest population group, the slave population excluded (Mac Leod 1927 I:336). The number of Chinese was closely tied to the economic ups and downs of the city because of the poll tax they were required to pay. Whenever there was a slump in the junk trade from China - the main source of income for this trading community - a great number of Chinese left Batavian territory for Mataram or Banten where they were not required to pay such high taxes. When this occurred they had to be lured back by lowered, or even abolished, poll-taxes. At the request of the Chinese captain in 1648, Governor-General Van der Lijn lowered the poll tax to 0.5 rial when it appeared in August of that year that only 1,335 Chinese paid it; by December, however, there were 3,077 Chinese in Batavia.[5]

After the 1670s, a period for which more data are available, we see a steady growth in the number of Chinese as compared to other groups. Around 1730, the Chinese comprised 20 percent of the total population

Batavia Intramuros, 1699 and 1739.

Pie diagram of the main population groups, 1699

Pie diagram of the main population groups, 1739

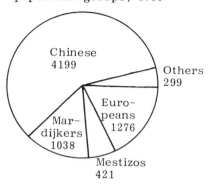

of the city (50 percent if slaves are not taken into account). Between 1680 and 1740, the total number of Chinese doubled, while the total population actually decreased. Consequently, it can be stated that the Chinese presence in the city actually became more and more tangible through the years. The same goes for the rapidly increasing population of the suburbs and Ommelanden. Here the Chinese were, after the Javanese, the second biggest population group.

Within its walls the houses of the Chinese were scattered throughout the city. The Dutch lived in the more respectable neighbourhoods while the other population groups, most of them non-Javanese in origin, like the Mestizos, Mardikas, Makassarese, Balinese, Moors and Gentoos, lived in their own kampongs. The Company did not welcome Javanese into the town of Batavia because of concern that these might include infiltrators from Mataram and Banten, with which it was intermittently at war. It also kept a jealous eye on the number of Javanese that were living in the surroundings and it forcibly turned back natives from Krawang who sought to settle close to the city (Daghregister 1661:223).

Opening Up the Ommelanden

The stereotype, still very widely accepted, of the Chinese deriving his profits from trade and usury, has obscured the important contributions made by this population group to the development of new agricultural territories in the archipelago. Without doubt it can be said that the Batavian Ommelanden were developed by Chinese pioneers. With justifiable pride, the first captain of the Chinese, Su Ming-kang, displayed two lanterns at the entrance of his country house at Mangga Dua which bore the inscription: "The original founder of the region" (Hsü 1953: 25).

By offering incentives such as exemption from poll tax, guaranteed purchase of products by the Company, and the establishment of minimum prices, the Company encouraged the Chinese to take up market gardening and agricultural pursuits in the virgin fields and forests surrounding the city. They also played an important role as harvesters. In the beginning, these activities remained confined to areas where they

Major population groups outside the town (based on Overgekomen Brieven en Papieren series, VOC archives)

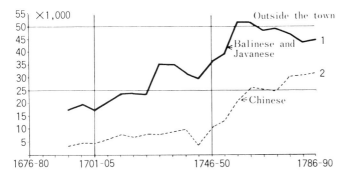

could be reasonably well-protected against marauding bands coming from nearby Banten, but in 1656 there were already complaints that they had settled at too great a distance from the city, making assistance impossible. Consequently, during the war with Banten in the same year, two-thirds of all sugar plantations in the Ommelanden were left in flames (Daghregister 1656-57:18, 194, 233). Sugar cultivation was revived after 1659 (when peace had been achieved with Mataram); it was especially encouraged in the following years as Formosa, the greatest sugar producer to the Company, was lost to the Ming loyalist Cheng Ch'eng-Kung (Coxinga) in 1662. Still agricultural activities in the Ommelanden remained a rather risky affair owing to the unstable relations with Banten.

The almost complete control of agriculture by the Chinese was pointed out by Governor-General Van der Lijn in 1649, who explained that the Dutch freeburghers had no interest in (weijnich lust hebben) engaging in agricultural pursuits, preferring to make their money quickly and to return home to spend it (Opkomst VI:8).

Enterprising individuals like Abraham Pittavin, Isaac de St. Martin, and Pieter van Hoorn, however, set good examples during the 1660s by putting their hand to the plough. Such men brought about a change in the attitude of the Dutch who then found it bon ton to have an idyllic country house. In 1675 Van Hoorn presented a plan for the development of Batavia and its environs into "a colony based on agriculture on Java" and made some slighting references about the Company's "simple commercie".[6] Most agricultural land which came into the possession of the Dutch, however, continued to be leased to Chinese who worked it with Javanese labourers.

A new era of development opened up when Krawang with its sizeable Javanese population was included within Batavian jurisdiction in 1677 and a lasting peace was concluded with Banten in 1683. These events combined with the official reopening of the Chinese trade with Southeast Asia (it had been banned by the Chinese government during the campaigns to annex Formosa which was captured in 1683) created the ideal conditions for an increased immigration of Chinese labourers. It was hoped that these immigrants might open up new lands for the Company.

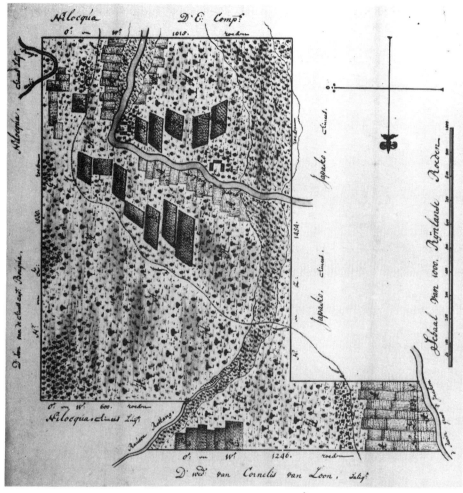

The sugar plantation of the Councillor of the Indies, Wouter Hendrix, surrounded by Chinese plantations, 1732.

A rice paddies
B sugar cane fields
C sugar mills
D mulbury tree garden
E abandoned sugar cane field
F ponds and marshes
G bushes
H cleared area
I the road to Bekasi

And they indeed came in droves. The number of junks from China that anchored each year at the Batavian roadstead grew from three or four to more than twenty. Thousands of immigrants flooded the city. A new rush had started.

Procedures of Dutch-Chinese Collaboration

Recapitulating the Dutch-Chinese relationship and analysing the ways in which the two parties cooperated, we can state that the relationship between the Company and the Chinese population can be subdivided into formal and informal levels. On the formal level, the Chinese were directly subordinate to the captain and his lieutenants. These Chinese officers were the middlemen or brokers in all formal matters in which the Company was concerned. Through taxes and tax farming, the hospital, the orphanage and the boedelmeesters, institutional ties were forged between the Chinese and the Dutch.

On an informal level, the private business interests of the Company servants and the Chinese merchants grew more intertwined, and a great deal of illegal private Dutch trade took place.

The power and influence of the Chinese captain reached its peak around 1685. The newly appointed Governor-General Camphuys had the installation of the new Chinese captain coincide with his own, thus symbolically sharing authority with him. In all wards of the city and in the immediate precincts surrounding Batavia, Chinese wijkmeesters (wardmasters) were appointed along with the Dutch officials of the same rank (who had already been installed in 1655). These Chinese wardmasters were responsible to the lieutenants and ultimately to the captain, the promotor of his people's interests at the "princely castle" and the mediator through whom all matters were channelled. As every Chinese had to pay his monthly poll tax and had to report at least once a year to the house of the captain, the latter remained firmly in command of his fellow countrymen. As long as the Chinese were represented on the Bench of Aldermen they also had some say in matters concerning the town, but after the death of Captain Siqua in 1666, who was the only remaining Chinese member of the bench, there was no new appointment for his seat in this council.

The difference in the social structures the two "partners" adhered to is striking. The Company possessed a bureaucratic, hierarchical structure, which implied that every Company official possessed a specific competency or power. Because of this organizational structure, a certain political and administrative continuity was possible which was not linked to the individual who filled a specific position, although in spite of this structure, nepotism and favouritism were rampant among the Dutch company servants in Batavia during the 18th century.

The political structure of the Chinese community centred around its leader and representative, the Capitein. Initially the captain was chosen and appointed by the Chinese elders in a rather democratic way. The decision was sometimes postponed until the arrival of the trade junks from China to make it possible for the nachodas or skippers to have their say in the choice. By the end of the seventeenth century, however, the élite of the Chinese property-owning class in Batavia had gained a strong grip on this office, so that the captaincy in some instances was even an inheritance from this time onwards and was in some instances even purchased, as was the case with Ni Hoe-kong, the captain at the time of the massacre (Hsü 1953:42).

Thus the efficient functioning of many political matters depended upon a unique relationship of mutual trust and cooperation between the captain and the Dutch authorities, especially since the Chinese were no longer allowed to sit on the bench of city magistrates. It depended equally upon the unchallenged position of the captain as head of and negotiator among his own people.

Rampant Developments

The sharp increase in territory acquired and population settling outside the city from the 1680s onward was not accompanied by adjustments in the administrative machine. The Ommelanden grew into a kind of Wild West avant la lettre. Law and order in these regions were maintained by the two landdrosten, or sheriffs, with their catchpoles, who had been installed in 1651 in order "to prevent thievery, marauding and violence to which the inhabitants were subjected at the hands of vagabonds and highwaymen" (Stapel 1927-43 III:112). The sheriff actually had the same job as the bailiff in the city, but the latter of course was subject to a much closer supervision of his superiors than his colleagues in the Ommelanden

Not long after the rush for the new territories had started, it dawned upon some responsible notables that measures should be taken in the field of administration. In a confidential letter to Director-General Joan van Hoorn, Isaac de St. Martin wrote: "without alluding in any way to the person of the [present] sheriff, I feel that the government and political authority over all the natives should belong in no other hands than those of the Governor-General, or one of the members of the Council [Raden van Indië] whom the Governor-General might designate."[7]

Another enlightened person, Cornelis Chastelein, (who will always be remembered as the man who left to his slaves his estate at Depok) also was not satisfied with the sheriffs who did not exert sufficient control in the distant regions. He tells in 1705 the story of a sheriff instructing a Javanese who had just arrived after a three-day journey from an outlying spot in the Ommelanden to report a murder: "Bring in the body of the victim and also the murderer". It was time, Chastelein said, "that the administration give serious consideration as to how it should deal with the lands or the people that dwell on it and how it should be governed" (Chastelein 1855:68). Thereupon he proposed a political system for the Javanese inhabitants based on desa governments and lurah who would sit together in master-councils to discuss justice in the presence of a political commissary. He foresaw criticism that the Javanese would be given too much power and forestalled it by citing as examples the administration of the Roman empire and also China: "Look at the example of the turbulent Chinese, who have been and remain subdued by the Tartars with a small force. This is because they are governed with the same religion, laws and customs as [before] under the emperor of their own nation. The Tartars keep only the army to themselves without giving the Chinese a say in these affairs, so that always a tight rein can be held on them during an emergency." (Chastelein 1855:80).

In 1715, the Ommelanden actually got their own political commissary (de commissaris tot en over de zaken van den Inlander), whose function it was to keep in touch with the headmen of the Javanese and other people like the numerous Balinese (about the same in number as the Chinese) who lived together in kampong and desa under their own headmen. But strangely enough - one is tempted to say "paradoxically" after the above citation - no adjustment was made for those Chinese who lived at a distance from the city. They remained unattended by their officers in town and its immediate vicinity, and were increasingly at the mercy of the sheriffs and commissaries, a development which was to have grave consequences.

Disruptions in the Cooperation

Historians like Crawfurd, Raffles, Van Hoëvell, De Jonge, Hoetink, De Haan, and Vermeulen have tried to explain the occurrence of the Chinese massacre (of 1740) in various ways.[8] They have differed in opinion about the accidental or the wilful execution of the massacre. All causes and motives they have advanced were of a limited, temporary nature. I shall not repeat the arguments here; suffice it to say that they afford little insight into the developments which took place over a longer period.[9]

These historians were indeed right when they argued that the "massacre" was a consequence of the Chinese revolt outside the city walls, but they have not inquired sufficiently into interrelating factors that may have played a role in the relationship between the Chinese within and without the city walls. They have looked for indications of a conspiracy between insurgents outside the walls and citizens inside, but this would seem a useless quest because not even the law court of Batavia during the trial of the scapegoat Captain China Ni Hoe-kong, was able to prove that such a conspiracy existed in 1741, when there were evidence and witnesses which are obviously no longer available.

In my opinion, the revolt of the Chinese in the Ommelanden of Batavia and the ensuing Chinese massacre should be explained in terms of the deterioration of the Captain's authority vis-à-vis his own people as well as the Company. This breakdown in authority manifested itself in several ways. Many Chinese of the countryside fell victim to a group of usurers inside the city; the Captain was increasingly bypassed when problems arose and, in the end, when he could have helped his countrymen by paying their poll taxes, he neglected to do so. In his "History of Java", Raffles cites Javanese chronicles which hinted at a decreasing legal status of the Chinese. Chinese masters were no longer able to obtain justice vis-à-vis their own slaves (Raffles 1817 II:232).

As a consequence, a vacuum of authority was left in the Ommelanden when the Company also showed itself unable to provide a reasonable degree of supervision there. A series of increasingly arbitrary measures adopted by the Governor-General and Council in Batavia castle followed which were intended to control the "Chinese countryside", a countryside which was no longer represented by the urban Chinese leaders. Bribes and corruption continued to disguise the true situation for some time until a well-intended political investigation and purge by the Gentlemen XVII in 1732 put an end to the reign of Governor-General Diederik Durven and his accomplices. This group had been particularly skillful in extorting from and manipulating the Chinese in the Ommelanden. The explosive situation thus exposed was, however, past redemption. The political powder keg was only waiting for something to

Work in the cane fields.

light the fuse.

The historian of Oud-Batavia, F. de Haan, has observed that the period of the town's greatest prosperity should be designated as that between 1690 and 1730, when the beginning of the decline of the Company could already be observed (De Haan 1935 I:718). This period coincides with a strong development in the sugar culture, and overwhelming immigration of Chinese labourers, the waning political influence of the Chinese Captain among his own people, and increasing corruption.

All these developments were closely related to the opening up of the Ommelanden after the peace treaty with Banten in 1683 and the corresponding development of the sugar culture.

The Small Grocer and the Sugar Cultivation

Sugar cultivation was almost entirely in the hands of the Chinese.[10] Encouraged by the Company, plantations mushroomed in the countryside around Batavia, and by 1710 there were as many as 130 sugar mills belonging to 84 entrepreneurs in the Ommelanden. Among these entrepreneurs were 79 Chinese, 4 Dutchmen, and 1 Javanese. It is plausible that the mills of the latter were also operated by Chinese. All the employees and the Chinese-owned sugar mills, which came to be more and more frequently situated at considerable distances from Batavia, were beyond the authority of the Chinese Captain and Lieutenants in the city and were placed under the direct supervision of the Dutch sheriff and his men. The pothias, or Chinese operators of the sugar mills, however, had to pay a yearly poll tax on their personnel to the Chinese Captain, and it is not difficult to guess how many did so faithfully.

The pothias preferred to reach "compromises" with the personnel of the sheriff, who were willing to look in the other direction in exchange for the bribes they received. Thus the prestige of the Captain decreased and the incidence of corruption increased. The sugar industry must have exercised a very stimulating and pervasive influence on the Batavian economy. Hooyman estimated that in 1781, when the sugar culture had already long since passed its peak and only sixty mills remained, half of Batavia's total population profited from the sugar industry through related supplies of materials, food etc. (Hooyman 1779:246). One can imagine what the impact of the sugar industry must have been on Chinese citizens when it was still at its zenith.

Before long, the great influx of labourers from China led increasingly to problems which could not be solved through those channels which had been created to deal with them. The Company tried to check the supply of Chinese immigrants by putting pressure on the nachodas or junk skippers, and a quota for passenger transport was set as early as 1690. This, however, only prompted the nachodas to bribe port officials who had close contact with the sugar mill operators. Chinese immigrants also were landed on the Thousand Isles in front of the city or on unpatrolled stretches of the Java coast near the city to avoid registration at the house of the captain and to circumvent the immigration quota. The greater the number of illegal workers entering Java, the more the mill operators stood to profit. As these immigrants were unregistered, no poll tax had to be paid. Consequently, these illegal workers, placed in the roles of "outlaws", were completely at the mercy of the pothias, who could always threaten to denounce them to the sheriff. Bribes to the sheriff and his men were their only insurance against discovery. In this way the position of the captain was totally undermined. Finally, even he and his lieutenants, all of whom had invested in sugar plantations of their own, took part in these practices. The result was a vicious circle, in which long-term cooperation was replaced by short-term corruption.

The price policy of the Batavian administration has been severely criticised by De Jonge. He has called it "de handelstaktiek van den kleinen kruidenier" (the trade policy of the small grocer) (Opkomst VIII:cxxxi). Glamann has made some extenuating comments in this respect by showing that the competitive qualities of the Batavian sugar on the Asian market should be taken into consideration (Glamann 1958: 160). The fact that Bengal sugar was cheaper than Batavian sugar goes a long way to explain the changes in the purchase price.

Even if we may show some understanding for these difficulties, the high-handed ways in which drastic reductions in the purchase price or the quantity of purchase were carried out without any explanation to the sugar millers cannot be excused. They are a clear manifestation of the breakdown in communication.

Whenever the demand for sugar decreased, the Company adjusted the purchase price at will, thereby striking a direct blow at the sugar plantations in the Ommelanden. In a letter of March 2, 1705, the Gentlemen XVII still advocated that "the sugar trade should be promoted in every way", but a few years later prices were lowered as a result of the "sugar boom" in the West Indies. A short rise in demand on the European market took place between 1712 and 1716 but afterwards it plunged again. The fall of the Sofi dynasty in Persia (1722) meant the disappearance of the Company's largest customer in Asia.

The Chinese massacre.

V Chinese Batavia 1619-1740

Only by 1734 had the inter-Asian sale recovered to some extent when Malabar came to replace Persia as a customer. Trading sugar was no longer the profitable venture it once had been to the Company, and the Chinese sugar producers were of course the first to foot the bill.

Some complaints reached the ears of the Governor-General and Council, and commissions were set up in 1710 and 1728. Rather than offering constructive solutions, their reports proposed production quotas which were impossible to control, and this practice fueled the already simmering feuds among the members of the Council. These reports - the first was made by Hendrick Swaardecroon and Christoffel van Swoll (Opkomst VIII:157-64), the second by Joan Everhard van der Schuur and Rogier Thomas van Heyningen - have left us valuable information on the number and the output of the sugar mills.[11] Still, they also reveal ignorance about the conditions at the Chinese sugar mills and a total absence of information from the Chinese mill owners themselves.

The apology written in 1710 by Director-General Abraham Douglas, who was in charge of the sugar warehouses and had been criticized by Governor-General Abraham van Riebeeck for driving sugarmill owners into bankruptcy, gives us a rare glimpse into the internal functioning of the Batavian sugar industry. According to Douglas, the sudden bankruptcy of several mill owners had nothing to do with the decrease in the purchase price. It was the Chinese themselves who were exhausting each other, he said: "The Chinese sugar millers, who happen to go bankrupt, are ordinary folk, who have no means of their own and therefore borrow money on interest, not to mention those who engage to rent this or that exhausted estate with sugar mills on it for excessive sums of money. This happens under a certain servitude, which implies that all the sugar cane standing in the fields during the period of rent, must be milled by the tenant at the profit of the owner, not to speak of the other extortions which might subdue these people. Therefore they cannot maintain their position nor keep their credit when they meet the least inconvenience, and they inevitably break. It still has to be proved if this has happened more under my directorship than under that of my predecessors."[12]

It was not only the closure of many sugar mills which resulted in the formation of bands of jobless outlaws who infested the Batavian countryside. From the governorship of Diederik Durven onwards (1729-32) life was made more and more difficult for the Chinese in other ways as well. A contemporary pamphlet, "The Dream of the Revolt in Batavia", shows how this population group lost its privileged position during the thirties and was "squeezed like a sponge" by increased taxes, tolls, and extortions. Tax measures against Chinese foodstalls and lodges in the Ommelanden made life for those who were employed in these trades quite impossible. "The distress of several thousand, young and old, became beyond description. Bereft of land, money, and work they could make only one choice of the three that were left: to beg alms - which would come to very little as there were too many of them -, to starve (which hardly is a pleasure) - they had no intention of doing this -, or to steal."[13]

Little information about the mounting unrest in the Ommelanden found its way to the authorities in Batavia castle. The sheriffs found it wiser to obscure the facts and the Chinese captain, who had no authority or esteem left in the Ommelanden and was at loggerheads with his lieutenants, was not in touch with reality.

Holocaust

In the spring of 1740, a great scandal was exposed concerning the sale of permissiebriefjes (residence permits) by Company servants to the Chinese sugar plantations, and this obliged the Batavian authorities to present a radical - and not very realistic - plan for the forced emigration of Chinese labourers to Ceylon in order to do away with the "Chinese problem" once and for all. Rumours soon spread among the Chinese that these unfortunate exiles were thrown overboard rather than sent to Ceylon, and this became an immediate cause for revolt. Having first plundered the countryside, the Chinese insurgents made their headquarters in a few sugar mills at Tanah Abang, in the Ommelanden, and sent a letter to town stating that they were going to attack Batavia, "in which city so few Dutchmen and so many Chinese live, and where nevertheless [the Dutch] dare to treat the Chinese so harshly and oppress them so unjustly that it can no longer be tolerated. The Chinese nation is forced to unite and with all force declare war upon the Dutch." (Opkomst IX:lvii).

A field battle broke out between the two parties. On one side, the Chinese were entrenched behind "an erected field-work of wood and other material consisting of ox-wagons drawn in line, over which poles were driven into the ground, covered with buffalo hides which were padded with kapok and Chinese paper. The space in between these was filled with earth." Cannons with wooden barrels protruded through the embrasures. Above the camp, banners were flying with inscriptions like "to choose the right day and the right moment", "to assist the poor, the destitute and the oppressed", "only in God we trust" [!], "kill the unjust", and "follow the righteous of olden times".[14]

On the Dutch side, Director-General Van Imhoff and the Councillor Van Aarden marched with an army of European and Indonesian soldiers and six fieldpieces. Through some incredible bungling, whereby the fieldpieces had been left behind by coolies in the paddies and ammunition chests were lost in the fray, the Dutch army's first attack was repulsed. The following morning, October 8, the Dutch forces carried the day on account of superior firepower and a brave sally by the Buginese cavalry. The victory proved of little effect, however, as the city was surrounded by the Chinese army again that same night.

Van Hoëvell, Hoetink, and Vermeulen, who have related these events in detail, stress the complete helplessness of the Chinese Captain Ni Hoe-kong and surmise that he was a dull, effeminate and corrupt person. While that may be true, the real story is more complex. All these developments in fact happened beyond the sphere of influence and power of the Captain in the city. Still, the Captain would not have been able to contend that he had remained unaware of the increasing unrest. Not only did he possess sugar mills himself, but as the court papers reveal, the revolt actually originated on one of his plantations. The mutual trust between the Company and the Chinese colony in the city, which had deteriorated so badly over the last decade as Dutch authority over the Chinese Ommelanden became increasingly ineffective, was totally destroyed as the insurgents stormed the city gates.

Feelings of revenge and fear of betrayal by the Chinese in the city as the Ommelanden Chinese were attacking the city and setting the southern suburbs aflame, erupted in the massacre which continued for three days. A Chinese attempt to free the city from the Dutch tyrant had misfired; the victims were the 10,000 Chinese townsmen who had not chosen for one party or the other.

The Dutch sailors of the fleet at the Batavian roadstead, who had little to do with all these problems gave the signal for the massacre that ensued. According to Ary Huysers who presumably was on the scene: "Suddenly we heard to our great consternation nothing but cries of murder and fire, and the curtains were raised for the most abominable scene of unrestrained murder and rapine: Chinese men, women and children were run through with the sword. Neither pregnant women nor babies in arms were saved. Captives in irons, altogether a hundred people, had their throats cut like sheep. Dutch burghers who had provided shelter to many well-to-do Chinese fellow citizens killed them on the same day so that they could partake of their victims' possessions. In short, the Chinese nation was almost totally massacred that day, guilty or innocent, all and sundry." (Huysers 1789:11).

This murderous tempest raging through town is reminiscent of 19th century pogroms in Eastern Europe's cities. People who under normal circumstances would loathe brutality were suddenly swept along. That is the impression one gets from the account by the German carpenter Georg Bernhardt Schwarz: "I myself also had to join. As I knew that my Chinese neighbour had a fat pig, I intended to take it away from him and bring it into my own house. When my boss, the master-carpenter, saw this, he slapped me and told me to kill the Chinese first and then to plunder. I therefore took a rice-pounder and with it beat to death my neighbour with whom I so often had drunk and dined." That was not all: upon discovering a pistol in his neighbour's house, Schwarz went outside "und schosse damit alles todt, was ich nur antraff". He goes on to confess to having killed another two or three Chinese. "I had grown so accustomed to this, that it was the same to me whether I killed a dog or a Chinese" (Schwarz 1751:120).

Conclusion

In the period of 1619-85, the interests of the Company and the Chinese colony of Batavia were evenly balanced: both were engaged in the pursuit of optimal profits from the overseas trade. Because the Batavian inter-archipelago trade depended so much on the Chinese trade, the Chinese colony was given some latitude within the operating structure of the East India Company. What was good for the Batavian Chinese was, at that time, good for Batavia in general. This structure of cooperation, however, was doomed, when the Company and the Chinese simultaneously engaged in developing agricultural pursuits in the Ommelanden without expanding their mode of cooperation into these areas. This rupture within a well-tried system led to fatal consequences when Dutch-Chinese relations were subjected to a heavy strain.

The resulting blow to the prestige of the Chinese captain was bad enough. Infinitely worse, however, was the fact that the Chinese settlements in the Ommelanden were left to their own devices, without the benefit of their own local administration, and were subjected to an inadequate and corrupt system of control by Dutch sheriffs. Bribing and extortion became normal practices. With the all-important and Company-promoted sugar industry growing constantly, an enormous flow of Chinese immigration was attracted, leading to further bribes and extortions.

When market conditions in the sugar trade caused a deep and lasting crisis in the sugar industry, bankruptcy, mass poverty, and mass unemployment ensued. But there was no organized Chinese system to permit authorities to cope with these problems. The final call by the Dutch for help from the Chinese captain whose powers had been systematically eliminated in all matters relating to the Ommelanden and whose authority had been steadily undermined, could only be a futile one.

In the Ommelanden an explosive situation developed in which the despairing Chinese abandoned their "peace-loving" and "cowardly" characteristics. High-handed measures and corruption furnished the spark. And the town-Chinese were the victims of the resulting explosion.

The question finally arises as to whether the Chinese massacre of 1740 was an evil made necessary by inescapable evolution. Parallel developments in Manila where at least six such pogroms occurred would suggest so. Or was it a tragic accident at variance with the normal course of events? I would argue for the latter. In the early years of the town's existence the Dutch and Chinese communities worked out a unique kind of institutionalized cohabitation within the walls of Batavia. An interplay of several factors such as economic depression and gross ineptitude, which can only be properly appraised within the historical context of the expanding city, temporarily spoiled the institutionalized modus vivendi. Soon afterwards it was reinstated in amended and refined form. The Chinese survivors who in 1741 had been relocated in a specially designated Chineesche Kamp at the southern perimeter of the town, soon were again allowed to settle in Batavia itself. Moreover, the Chinese in the Ommelanden were placed under their own chiefs.

Although the Chinese massacre represented a severe crisis in the collaboration, this breakdown was by no means of a lasting nature, not even in the eyes of the Chinese victims themselves. As Michèle Boin argues in a recent paper, the author of "Kai-pa Li-tai Shih-chi" did not attribute the massacre to the system, "but to the bad character or lack of morality among the individuals in charge at that time" (Boin 1984:8). Lin Heng-t'ai, a Cantonese merchant who was interrogated by the Manchu authorities in China after he had escaped the massacre, had the same opinion. According to him, blame for the events should be placed on "the barbarian headman" whose actions even were "thought excessive by the King of Holland" (Cushman 1978:149). In other words, the Chinese of Batavia could live with an administrative and institutional sphere kept seperate from the cultural one, if they only were properly governed. In their esteem, a good and well-functioning "foreign" administration deserved loyalty.

Historians of urban history are still contemplating the need for and the validity of studying the relationship between town and country while studying urban life. In this case, I have tried to give an example of just how powerful and dramatic such a relationship can be.

Chapter VI

THE VOC AND THE JUNK TRADE TO BATAVIA: A PROBLEM IN ADMINISTRATIVE CONTROL

> Les Chinois, disent communement que toutes les nations sont aveugles en matières de commerce, que les seuls Hollandais ont un oeil, mais que, pour eux, ils en ont deux.
> P.D. Huet (1718:140)

China and the Maritime World

Introduction
No historical account of Batavia's Chinese community would be complete without paying proper attention to the history of its own maritime trade network. Such an approach will allow us to look at Batavia in a different perspective, and to study the town as one of the many settlements in Southeast Asia which were served by Chinese shipping. The trade link with China served as an umbilical cord for the town's Chinese citizens but its continuous functioning was also, ironically enough, tolerated by the monopolistic VOC on account of its vital importance to Batavia's economy at large. Junks and wangkangs from Amoy, Canton, Chenhai and Ningpo supplied Batavia every spring with a gamut of Chinese merchandise, ranging from bulk to luxury goods. The most important single "cargo item", however, was quite different: thousands of Chinese were shipped each year to Java's coasts. These sailors, merchants, coolies, and settlers meant prosperity for Batavia, supplying merchandise, expertise and new strength to the community. The passenger traffic defies statistical measurement but it must have been large, considering the long list of ordinances that the Batavian government issued in its continual attempts to control and stem Chinese immigration. The Chinese massacre notwithstanding, at the end of the eighteenth century there were about one hundred thousand Chinese living in Batavia and its direct vicinity.

For all its importance, Batavia's Chinese shipping link has escaped the attention of Western and Asian historians alike. This is not as surprising as it may seem at first glance: Chinese overseas shipping in the seventeenth and eighteenth centuries has only recently caught the fancy of the scholarly community, and it is a telling fact that this interest was provoked by the words of an Indonesian politician, as the following anecdote will demonstrate.

If he were still alive, Ali Sastroamidjojo of Indonesia would probably be astonished to hear that the keynote address he made during his visit to China in 1956 initiated a protracted and vigorous debate in scholarly circles concerning the causes of the decline of China's overseas trade in the eighteenth and nineteenth centuries. If we may believe the eminent Chinese anthropologist and historian, Tien Ju-kang, the following is actually what happened: The Indonesian Prime Minister, who visited the People's Repub-

Chinese trade routes to the Nanyang.

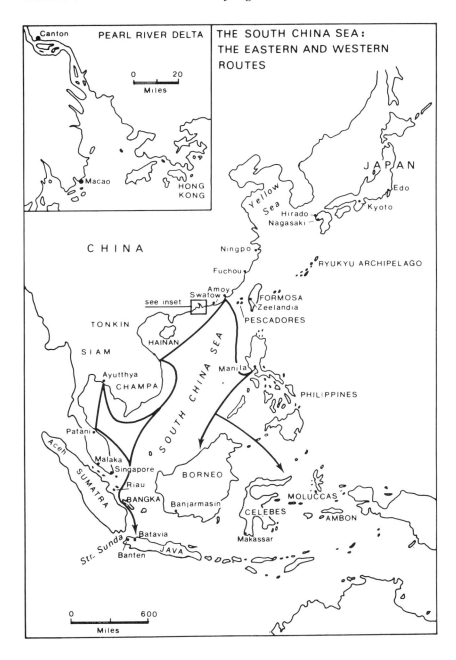

VI The VOC and the Junk Trade to Batavia

lic in the wake of the successful Bandung conference of 1955, referred in his public address to the long-standing friendly relations between the peoples of Indonesia and China, as is usually done at such occasions. In addition, he drew the attention of his hosts to the signal function that the so-called Chinese junk trade had played over the past few centuries in this respect. While the China trade, carried out initially by the East Indiamen of the European trading companies and later by the tea- and opium-clippers, had merely served the interests of the colonialists, the Chinese junks served the basic needs of the native peoples of the archipelago and the Overseas Chinese communities residing in that region.

Tien asserts in his first article on the rise and demise of the Chinese overseas trade in the seventeenth and eighteenth centuries that Sastroamidjojo's words had catalyzed his own thinking on the importance of the junk trade (Tien 1956:1). This may sound a bit too naive to be true, but it is a fact that previously the subject had been overlooked in China. As so often happens, the host was awakened and forced into introspection by the words of his guest.

China's Maritime Past
Previously, Chinese historians had focussed their studies primarily on trade along the maritime silk route during the Sung and Yüan dynasties, or on the spectacular expeditions under the command of admiral Cheng Ho that were sponsored by the Ming emperor on the eve of European expansion overseas. During these expeditions, seven fleets, each carrying more than ten thousand soldiers, sailors and courtiers, sailed to Western Asia, and some of these even reached Africa. These voyages, intended to expand the tribute system, lasted no more than two decades and came to an abrupt halt in 1427 when the Ming court turned its attention to the inner Asia frontier as a result of the resurgence of Mongol power. Shortly afterwards an imperial decree was issued which forbade all Chinese to travel or trade overseas (Mills 1970:1-34). As far as China's historians were concerned, their nation's Golden Age of overseas trade thereby came to an end. They did not fail to notice, however, that during the next hundred and fifty years of maritime prohibitions (which remained in force until 1567), individual merchants from Fukien province secretly fitted out ships to trade with Southeast Asia. Marxist historians have characterized these efforts as "early sprouts of capitalism", which were nipped in the bud by the imperial policies (Feuerwerker 1968:229).

The economic importance of the trading junks, which, after the trade ban was lifted in 1567, were licensed to navigate each year to and from Southeast Asia in the 17th and 18th centuries, was generally disregarded. Ironically, these privately funded enterprises did not spark the imagination of those who were rewriting the history of the Chinese people in the 1950s - that is, with the exception of two scholars, Fu I-ling and Tien Ju-kang. But while Fu focussed mainly on the trade of Fukien province during the last decades of the Ming dynasty (Fu 1956:107-60), Tien demonstrated that in the period between 1600 and 1830, close to a hundred large Chinese vessels accounting for some 20,000 tons of cargo space, sailed year in and year out to the Nanyang, or Southern Seas, providing thousands of people with work in the shipping business and other sectors of the Fukienese economy. Every year, Fukienese junks brought back millions of silver rials from the Philippines, as well as tropical products and huge quantities of rice from other Southeast Asian countries. These imports and the export of handicrafts and locally cultivated cash crops provided an important income to the coastal population of the province, and eventually made it dependent upon trade with the Nanyang.

The Causes of Decline
It was not Tien Ju-kang's intention merely to indicate the importance of the junk trade, however; he also formulated several provocative explanations concerning the nature of Chinese overseas shipping and the causes of its eventual decline. His article of 1956 in China's foremost historical journal, "Li-shih Yen-chiu" (Historical Research), appears a bit dated now due to the stereotypical phraseology of that period, but it remains pertinent because it has set the tone and challenged others to join the debate. The pioneering nature of Tien Ju-kang's work should be stressed, for it tends to be mentioned only in passing, even though the younger generation of historians has borrowed extensively from his writings.

On the assumption that at the beginning of the seventeenth century Chinese shipping was in most respects on a par with Western shipping, Tien Ju-kang proceeded to inquire into the reasons why it gradually declined in the course of the eighteenth century and was eventually crushed by western competition in the first decades of the nineteenth century. He singled out three inherent causes of this decline: a. structural weaknesses in the Chinese organizational sphere, such as inefficient forms of shipowning, cumbersome procedures of capital investment and insurance, and, last but not least, a lack of continuity and unity of command; b. an almost Byzantine maze of prohibitive regulations issued by the government, which stood in the way of a free development of China's maritime sector: e.g., innovation of ship design was forbidden, the number of masts was limited, ships had to return within fixed periods, and so on; c. the unstable political climate and the economic crisis in the southeastern provinces in the last decades of the 18th century, which impaired the further development of Chinese maritime trade.

In a second contribution published one year after the article mentioned above, Tien further illustrated and refined his argument by contrasting the occasional attempts of the Ch'ing imperial government to prohibit or curtail Chinese overseas trade (as it was publicly stated on account of security reasons) to the sympathetic attitude that the European governments displayed towards the development of their own merchant fleets during the seventeenth and eighteenth centuries.

In his early writings, Tien Ju-kang singled out "the poisonous strangling grip of western capitalism" as the culprit at the neck of China's junk trade (Tien 1956:18). He pointed out that by the end of the eighteenth century Spanish and Dutch colonialists had reduced Chinese traders to middlemen in the Philippines and the Indonesian archipelago, although the Chinese retained considerable freedom of movement in Siam and Vietnam which they held until the middle of the nineteenth century, despite the grip of the expanding world market. China's trade with Siam reached its apex in the 1820s and 1830s and then suffered a sudden decline in the following decade. According to Tien, this was not caused by the advance of Western steamships – he asserted that it was too early for that to be the case – rather it was the direct result of the opening up of Canton, Amoy, Foochow, Ningpo and Shanghai to foreign shipping, in accordance with the Nanking treaty of 1842. The Chinese coastal regions soon were turned into a "semi-colonial territory" and the Chinese junk trade thus fell victim to Western capitalism. Even if Tien Ju-kang does not explain in detail why Western capitalism should have been considered such a threat to China's overseas shipping, his assertions on this issue should not be dismissed as idle rhetoric. In bold strokes he provided a setting for further research, leaving room to other scholars in the field to amend and refine his concepts. As mentioned above, the younger generation gladly took up that challenge in the next decade.

The Siamese Connection
In the nineteen-seventies, Jennifer Cushman and Sarasin Viraphol both presented Ph.D. theses on China's trade with Siam. Fortunately the two studies, which were independently conceived, do not completely overlap owing to the differing approaches taken. As the title of his thesis, "Tribute and Profit", suggests, Viraphol has analysed the various means by which the Siamese king succeeded in exploiting his so-called "tributary relationship" with the Chinese Court. Every two years he sent ambassadors to China on junks manned with Chinese crews. These "Royal ships" were required by the king to engage in profitable trade for his own account. According to Viraphol, the major reason for the declining fortunes of this Sino-Siamese junk trade in the middle of the nineteenth century was "the intensification of tax farming as a main alternate source of state revenue and the forfeiture of the king's stakes as merchant king" (Viraphol 1977: 22).

Although in her unpublished Ph.D.thesis, Jennifer Cushman did not ignore the importance of the Siamese Royal Trading Monopoly System, she focussed on the complex mechanism of the Chinese native trade with Siam, which occurred in parallel with the tributary trade (Cushman 1975). She believes, and the evidence strongly supports her argument, that the collapse of the Chinese junk trade to Siam was caused by the demolition of the tariff barriers in China itself. After the treaty ports with their "fair and regular tariff" had been opened to Western shipping, the Chinese administration no longer could protect or favour its own shipping above foreign shipping through the manipulation of import and export tariffs. In other words, Cushman depicts the Ch'ing government's policy towards the overseas trade of its southern seaboard provinces in a more positive light than Tien Ju-kang has done. Even though the imperial government did not encourage native maritime trade in the eighteenth century, she believes it certainly favoured the junk trade above Western trade at Canton, as the Europeans were subjected to outrageous duties and were assessed various illegal fees (Cushman 1975:56-7). For the sake of completeness it should be added that Tien Ju-kang in a recent, almost philosophical, essay on the subject, no longer heaps all the blame on foreign capitalism, but "links the reasons for the slackening of Chinese overseas trade to the long-term stagnation of Chinese traditional society" (Tien 1982:32).

Thus Western aggression is not seen any more as the prime cause of the decline of China's overseas shipping. Rather, it is now generally recognized that changes in the particular institutional context surrounding the Chinese trade were responsible. Along with the tributary trade with the foreign potentates, which Viraphol has studied, China also had her own important overseas trade, which was centered on the southeastern provinces. This trade was indeed occasionally harassed, if not curtailed, by the imperial government, yet the general feeling in court circles existed that it could not be forbidden outright, as the economy of the coastal regions depended upon it - or as Tien Ju-kang has put it: "not daring to grant complete freedom, the government was neither able to enforce prohibitions nor could it administer well" (Viraphol 1977:5).

This ambivalent attitude of the Chinese imperial administration is also quite apparent in Ng Chin-keong's recent study on the coastal trade of Amoy in the period 1685-1735 (Ng 1983). From local gazetteers and encyclopedical collections he has amassed an impressive amount of data which sheds new light on the manner in which Fukien's maritime trade was actually conducted. Ng's prime objective is to analyse and describe this coastal trade within the broad social context of Fukienese society, rather than to deal with such "external" factors as government policy or the challenge posed by western shipping. He shows that the lineage structure so typical of China's southeastern coastal regions was strengthened by the continuous competition among the lineages for such scarce resources as land; and that this competition bestowed upon the tsu or lineage a new feature of inclusiveness by accommodating non-kin members within its structure. The resulting organizational strength of kinship relations not only gave the Fukienese a lead in the domain of coastal and overseas trade, but also enabled them to brave the discriminatory policies of their own and foreign governments.

To sum up, it may be said that Tien Ju-kang's original analysis of China's overseas trade in the seventeenth and eighteenth centuries has been considerably refined and amended over the past ten years. Jennifer Cushman has provided one of the answers to the question of why the ultimate decline occurred; Ng Chin-keong has shown how the organic unity between Fukien's overseas trade activities and the province's particular social conditions may actually have strengthened the organizational sphere, and Sarasin Viraphol has closely examined the Siamese tributary trade in its functional aspects and has put it into a chronological context. One question of chronology posed by Tien Ju-kang has not yet been properly dealt with in detail: did the Western colonial regimes in the Philippines and the Indonesian archipelago indeed reduce the junk trade in those parts to a mere shadow of its former self by the end of the eighteenth century? Tien hastens to add that Singapore constituted an exception to the rule. Founded by Raffles in 1819 with the aim of drawing Chinese Nanyang shipping to its roadstead, this new settlement acted as a powerful stimulus to the junk trade until the 1840s.

But what about the only two large "European" staple markets that existed during the 18th century in the South China sea region? Did the Chinese trade arteries of Manila and Batavia, which ranked among the most important ports of destination within the Fukienese overseas trade organism, gradually dry up as a result of "the poisonous strangling grip of capitalism", or did other factors also play a part in it?

Manila and Batavia
The few publications at my disposal that deal with the Chinese trade to Manila in the seventeenth and eighteenth centuries suggest that this trade link indeed declined by the end of the eighteenth century. Whether this had to do with the strangling grip of Western capitalism or whether it was the result of desperate political measures taken by the Spanish administration to stem the ever-increasing inflow of Chinese immigrants remains somewhat open to question.

The Philippine historian Serafin Quiason has remarked that the heyday of the "sampan" trade with Manila should be placed between 1560 and 1670. According to him, it consisted essentially of the movement of luxury goods and prime commodities from South China to Manila and its subsidiary consumption centres and, hence, to Acapulco on the American continent. It took English merchants trading from India many decades before they were able to gain a share of the Manila market with shipments of cloth from India by the end of the 17th century (Quiason 1966:165). Data collected by the French historian Pierre Chaunu make it clear that these "country traders" from India did not pose a threat to the Chinese ascendancy. In the following decades they never gained more than a 30% share of the market, with the residual 70% remaining in the hands of the Chinese (Chaunu 1960 I:267)

A heavy blow was administered to the Chinese trade with Manila by the Spanish colonial government in 1772. To punish the Chinese for collaboration with the English troops during the occupation of Manila, which lasted from 1762 until 1764, it expelled all non-Christian Chinese. Although when seen in this light, the argument that Chinese traders were reduced to middlemen or gradually shoved out in order to protect capitalist interests would seem to be a bit forced, the American historian William Lytle Schurz insists that this was the case. The Chinese in Manila had so completely monopolized the trades and retail businesses of the colony that Spaniards who wished to enter those occupations clamored for the expulsion and exclusion of the Chinese, eventually finding a responsive listener to their plans in Governor Simon de Anda (Schurz 1939:97).

The case of Batavia, to which we shall presently turn, is much more telling. Even though Chinese economic interests in Batavia were not as dominant as in Manila, the town's continued prosperity was also directly connected with the steady supply of Chinese commodities by junk shipping. One of the first historians to recognize this was, of course, J.C. van Leur, who pointed out that the Chinese fleet trading in Batavia in 1625 had a total tonnage as large or larger than that of the whole return fleet of the Dutch company (Van Leur 1967:198). However, Van Leur was referring to Batavia's early period, and the volume of cargo brought yearly to the archipelago in subsequent years remained by no means constant. As I shall show, Chinese trade to Batavia fluctuated a great deal, both as a result of political turmoil in China itself and as a result of the changing VOC policies towards it.

The data available in the VOC archives at The Hague shed considerable light on the character of the Batavian junk trade, the manner in which it was conducted, and the administrative framework within which it was carried out. This enables us to analyse much more thoroughly than seems to be possible in the case of Manila why and how the Chinese junk trade flourished and finally declined at Batavia in the second half of the eighteenth century.

In a study of this limited scope it would be overambitious to pay equal attention to all aspects of the Batavian junk trade. Here preference is given to the administrative side of the matter over a detailed analysis of the flow of goods.[1] First I shall briefly describe the genesis of the Amoy-Batavia trade link. As the organization and operation of the Batavian junk trade on the Chinese side tally with the system described by Cushman, Viraphol and Ng, a comprehensive survey will do here. Moreover, I will focus on the shipping from Amoy and not touch upon organizational variations at other less important Chinese ports, which at one time or another may also have dispatched ships to Batavia. Having situated Chinese shipping within its structural framework, I will examine the successive administrative measures taken by the Dutch and Chinese governments in a chronological perspective and study their impact on the Batavian trade link.

Structural Framework

The Genesis of the Fukien-Batavia Trade Link

The inhabitants of the southeastern coastal province of Fukien were without doubt China's greatest seafarers. Living on a series of rather infertile coastal plains intersected by swift rivers and cut off from the hinterland by high mountains, the Fukienese were from the earliest times forced to import rice from the neighbouring provinces and to export industrial products like porcelain (crude), ironware and textiles, and cash crops like sugar and tea. During the 15th and 16th centuries, the province suffered under the raids of Japanese and Chinese pirates. As a result, private overseas trade (which could hardly be distinguished from piracy) was forbidden - albeit without much effect. Only formal trade with overseas tributaries of the imperial court, such as that with the nearby Ryukyu islands, was allowed to continue. The gradual suppression of the pirate raids and mounting pressure from Fukienese merchants, who wanted to resume legal private trade to Southeast Asia, led to a new orientation in the Ming government policy. Beginning in 1567, 50 licences per year were handed out to private merchants for overseas trade with Southeast Asia. In the years that followed, the number of these licences varied; e.g., 100 licences were issued in 1575, a number which was restricted to 88 by 1589. The licence system ceased to function around 1620.

The "Tung-Hsi-Yang K'ao", a treatise on Fukien's overseas trade and its administration, was published in 1618 by Chang Hsieh, a customs official at the home port for the licenced trade, Hai-ch'eng. He described how, for administrative reasons, this trade to Southeast Asia was divided by the authorities into the so-called Eastern-Ocean (Tung Yang) and Western-Ocean (Hsi Yang) trade routes (Chang 1981). The eastern route led to Luzon, the Sulu islands, and the Moluccas, while the western trade route reached, via the Indo-Chinese coast and the Malay peninsula, as far as Sunda Kalapa, later known as Jakarta on the coast of Western Java. The most profitable trade took place between the Amoy region and Manila, where great quantities of silver changed hands, imported every year from South America on Spanish galleons. According to Ch'üan Han-sheng, the foremost authority on the subject, two to four million rials-of-eight reached Fukien each year between 1600 and 1729 (Ch'üan 1972:438).

On the western route, the relatively young port of Banten, known to the Chinese as Hsia-kang, gradually replaced nearby Sunda Kalapa as the terminus and became the most important trade market for the Chinese on Java. Its hinterland produced large quantities of pepper, but the town also served as a staple market for traders coming from the Indian Ocean, the Indonesian archipelago and the South China sea. The formalities observed upon arriving in Banten are described in the "Tung-Hsi-Yang K'ao" as follows: "When a Chinese ship arrives here, a chief comes on board to gain information. The captain gives him a basket with oranges and two small umbrellas. The chief reports at once to the king, and upon the ship's entrance into the river, fruits and pieces of silk are sent as presents to the king. The king appoints four Chinese and two natives to act as bookkeepers and other Chinese who speak the local language to act as interpreters, one for every ship. The king has assigned two markets outside the town where market stalls are put up. In the morning everybody goes to the market to trade until noon, when it is closed. The king levies daily market duties." (Chang 1981:48).

It is quite significant how differently the English and Dutch appraised the importance of the junk trade to Banten around 1610. The English merchant John Saris describes in detail in his "Observations of the Eastern Trade" Chinese commodities like silks, porcelain and cloth, while he deliberately fails to mention the others, "because they are not for our country" (Purchas 1903 III:508). The Dutch (who first arrived in Banten in 1596) of course also coveted the exquisite silks and porcelain, but at the same time they became aware of the great importance of the Chinese trade to this staple market precisely because of those "raw commodities" Saris chose to omit. They understood that one day they would have to take the Chinese trade into consideration in their far-reaching plans for the conquest of Asia's trade. For the time being, however, their priorities were elsewhere.

According to Jan Pietersz. Coen, the plan to incorporate the China trade did not originate with the Dutch but was suggested to them at an early date by Chinese merchants residing at Banten. In a letter to the Gentlemen XVII he wrote: "Some time ago, some Chinese, who wish Your Excellencies well, suggested establishing four conditions [monopolies] in all of India: one of nutmeg and mace, one of cloves, one of pepper, and one of silk representing the Chinese trade. The first two monopolies you shall soon acquire, they said, the pepper [monopoly] they believed would be ours upon the occupation of Jambi [...] and with regard to the China trade, they thought it was up to us to take measures." (Coen I:158, letter of 25-12-1615).

When the VOC had eased its main European competitors out of the spice-producing areas of the Moluccas, the Gentlemen XVII decided to select a central location within the Indonesian archipelago where the general bookkeeping in Asia could be carried out and cargoes could be transshipped. It was agreed that this rendezvous would have to be situated either near the Strait of Malaka or the Strait of Sunda, the two thoroughfares between the Indian Ocean and the South China sea, the main theatres of action for the Company's ships. Such a location would render the VOC headquarters easily accessible to the Chinese junks, whose merchandise was needed to attract the native shipping of the inter-archipelago trade.

Attacks on Portuguese-held Malaka miscarried and attempts to gain a grip on the market proceedings in Banten ended in failure. When the Dutch turned their eyes to Jakarta and started to fortify their trade factory at this port, they met with protest and became involved in a protracted struggle with all their competitors in the area: the English, the pangeran of Jakarta, and his suzerain, the ruler of Banten. In May 1619 the matter was decided: the Dutch emerged victorious, razed the quarters of the pangeran and re-baptized the town Batavia. As has been explained in Chapter IV, Chinese merchants from Banten and nearby ports along Java's north coast were cajoled and bullied into establishing a colony at Batavia to supply foodstuffs and other necessities to the Dutch headquarters and to attract the Chinese junk trade to its roadstead. These immigrants had hardly settled before the first junks arrived from China in 1620 carrying rich cargoes and many more settlers. The trade link was established, or, if viewed from a different perspective, the former Sunda Kalapa-Fukien trade was restored.

Ship-Building and Ship-Owning in Fukien
Traditional Chinese technological works give scant information about the ships that sailed to Southeast Asia. Data of this kind can, however, be conveniently found in the local gazetteer of Amoy, the "Hsiamen chih",

which offers detailed descriptions of the vessels which collected at its roadstead: war junks (chan-ch'uan), coastal merchant junks (shang-ch'uan), fishing vessels (yü-ch'uan), smaller craft (hsiao-ch'uan) and finally the largest type of ship, the yang-ch'uan, or ocean vessel with which we are concerned (HMC II:151-81).

The Nanyang trader had three masts, and varied in size from two hundred to eight hundred tons. Armament was strictly regulated (two cannon, eight fowling-pieces, ten swords, ten sets of bows and arrows and thirty catties of gunpowder), for fear of the crew engaging in piracy (HMC II: 178). The junks were mainly built of wood from the mountains in the hinterland or from the neighbouring Chekiang province, but for special parts of the ship, building materials were procured elsewhere. Masts had to be imported from abroad (HMC II:177), and the heavy wood used for the keel block, the rudder and anchors - the so-called t'ieh li (iron strength) wood - could only be found in the Li mountains of Hainan island (Fu Lo-shu 1966:494; CCT:457).

Junks were built not only in China itself. The German missionary Karl Gützlaff wrote in the 1830s that Hainanese sailors en route to Siam cut timber along the coasts of Champa and Cambodia and upon their arrival in Bangkok, built junks in about two months. These vessels were then loaded with cargoes saleable in China, and both the ship and the cargo were sold in China (Gützlaff 1840:99). English visitors to Borneo in 1774 who witnessed the building of a 580-ton junk in Brunei noted that the construction of junks there was considerably cheaper than in China itself: 2,500 taels as compared to 8,000 taels (Purcell 1951:487). Especially were Siamese-built junks highly valued as they were partly constructed of teak. In the 1820s, John Crawfurd compared construction costs of junks at different places and arrived at the following result: Fukien 30:5:8 tael, Kwantung 20:8:3 tael, Vietnam 16:6:6 tael and Siam only 15 tael per ton (Crawfurd 1830 II:159). It therefore is not surprising that shipbuilding activities shifted increasingly to the overseas territories. Tien Ju-kang surmises that Chinese shipwrights started to build junks in Siam at the beginning of the 18th century. An entry dated 1747-4-5 in the "True Records of the Kao tsung period", mentions that since the early 1740s shipbuilders and rice merchants made package deals to import new junks from Siam carrying a full load of rice (CCT:461). From Dutch sources, we know that Chinese junks built in Siam were already considered good value for money a hundred years earlier. Such junks were even used in the service of the Dutch East India Company on the Siam-Japan route in the second decade of the seventeenth century.

Wealthy merchants and members of the Fukienese gentry invested in ship construction, as did groups of small merchants who pooled their capital. John Barrow, a keen contemporary observer, described this phenomenon as follows: "A ship is seldom the concern of one man. Sometimes forty or fifty, or even a hundred, different merchants purchase a vessel, dividing her into as many compartments as there are partners, so that each knows his own particular place in the ship, which he is at liberty to fit up and secure as he pleases. Each owner ships his goods and accompanies them in person, or sends his son or a near relation, for it rarely happens that they will trust each other with property where no family connection exists." (Barrow 1804:42).

The Gazetteer of Amoy confirms this picture. "Whenever people put money together to open a shop or build a ship, they attach the name "Chin" [as a prefix to the name of their partnership]. The character chin

VI The VOC and the Junk Trade to Batavia

[gold] symbolizes cooperation" (HMC V:649). As we shall see, ship-owning was subject to increasingly strict controls in the eighteenth century. In general, the owner himself, the ts'ai tung or financier, remained at home and assigned a supercargo to manage the ship on his behalf (HMC V:652). In VOC sources different kinds of ownership figure. Jan Pietersz. Coen speaks in his early letters of Chinese who came to Batavia as small peddlers, and who grouped together to invest in small craft, in contrast to the great merchants trading with Manila (Coen I:167). In the 1620s, at least one of these wealthy merchants, Wangsan, started to dispatch his vessels to Batavia and even visited the town a few times himself (Van Leur 1967:203, 227). In later years Batavia's Chinese citizens are also mentioned as owners either of western style "yachts" or Chinese junks.[2] After 1727, when the overseas trading guilds or "Yang-hang" were established in Amoy, these bodies assigned a representative, the ch'u-hai (he who goes to sea), who would take charge of the ship and its cargo during the voyage.

The Chinese Junk

Faithfully drawn pictures of the Nanyang traders by contemporary artists are scarce and hard to come by. Audemard notes that A.E. van Braam Houckgeest, one-time Dutch ambassador to the court of Peking (1794-95), is known to have possessed two volumes containing fifty pictures each of Chinese vessels of all sizes (Audemard 1957:16). These designs were lost

A junk from Batavia.

by the time Audemard prepared his study; instead, he had to settle for crude woodblock prints borrowed from Chinese encyclopedic works. Probably the most realistic pictorial representation of the junks used on the route to Batavia can be found on a scroll in the possession of the Matsuura museum of Hirado, which has been described by Oba Osamu (Oba 1972). The Batavian junk, the ship from Kalapa, depicted on that scroll measures 96.08 feet in length, 18.78 feet in width, with a draft of 12.57 feet. It is slightly smaller than the Amoy trader which is also depicted. With their high sterns, bold curves and bluff bows, these ships were a thrilling sight. Just as European vessels of the period, their sterns were decorated with all kinds of pictures and embellishments, but the bow was totally different: on both sides were painted large black oculi, or eyeballs, which stared out over the sea.

We could get no better impression of the general layout of a junk than by listening to what a contemporary Dutch sailor had to say about it. Out of curiosity John Splinter Stavorinus boarded a junk that was lying at anchor next to his own vessel at the roadstead of Makassar in the 1780s: "As soon as I came on board", he writes, "with the company that were with me, we were received with great politeness by the Chinese chiefs, and fruits were set before us, previous to our taking a view of anything. This vessel carried three masts, of which the largest and middlemost was nearly of the same thickness as the mainmast of my ship the Ouwerkerk (a ship one hundred and fifty feet in length) and it was made of one entire piece of timber (contrary to western vessels). The length of the junk, from the exterior of the stern to the extreme point of the bow, was, according to my computation, one hundred and forty feet. The hull was separated into as many divisions as there were merchants aboard, each having a distinct place to stow his commodities. The water was likewise distributed into several reservoirs, and being stored in bulk, was drawn up by buckets through hatches which opened in the deck. The furnace for cooking was near the starboard side of the mainmast upon the deck - for these vessels have but one deck - and we saw the victuals dressed there, in a much cleaner and neater manner than is practised on board European ships. At the stern were several tiers of little cabins, or huts, made of bamboos, for the officers of the vessel as well as for the merchants. Exactly in the middle of these, was the steerage, and in the center of it, was a sort of chapel, in which their joss, or idol, was placed. The rudder is not attached to the vessel by pintles and googings, but it is hung in ropes made of cane, and is very different in shape from those we use. Their anchors are crooked pieces of timber, to which heavy stones are tied in order to make them sink. The whole of their tackle, both cordage and sails, is made of cane." (Stavorinus 1798 II:286-8).

Many different viewpoints exist concerning the seaworthiness of Chinese junks. Most contemporaries, Chinese and European alike, were not very enthusiastic about the qualities of the overcrowded and overloaded Batavian trading junks. John Barrow thought them unfit to contend with tempestuous seas, because of their weak construction (Barrow 1804:10). A Chinese preceptor, Ong Tai-hai, comparing them to European vessels, scornfully reflected: "Looking at our junks from Amoy, slightly formed and fastened with straw, they seem merely children's playthings" (Ong 1849: 60). He was in a position to judge, for he had travelled twice on a junk on his trip to and from Batavia.

Judging from the remarks of another Chinese contemporary scholar, Hsieh Chao-chih, there were comparatively few accidents on the stormy

China sea: "The reason why there is no fear of sinking or drowning on board the overseas trade ships lies in the fact that they do not battle with the wind. When big ships sink, it is mostly due to the fact that they have to beat against the wind. The overseas trade merchants, who are well-acquainted with matters in overseas countries, hoist their sails and let themselves drift in the same direction as the wind blows; therefore they have been able to trade without accident for several years." (Hsieh 1972:86). The English administrator, John Crawfurd, concurs with this opinion: "With all the unskillfulness of their management, I do not imagine, however, that many of the Chinese junks are shipwrecked. This is owing to the facility and security afforded by the monsoons which are so well known to the Chinese pilots that they avoid the tempestuous periods of them. I remember but one example of a junk being lost, during between five and six years that I resided in Java, and of this one all the crew and some of the cargo was saved." (Crawfurd 1820 III:177).

The optimistic picture of Chinese junks safely riding the monsoon winds is, however, not borne out by historical data. Basing themselves on a survey of 180 genealogical records of Fukienese families, staff members of Amoy university have calculated that during the period under study, seven out of eight deaths by drowning at sea actually occurred on the stretch to and from Java (Tien 1985:4). These statistics would probably have been different if the vessels had been properly stowed. An English captain who sailed the Fukienese junk Keying around the Cape of Good Hope in 1846 found it to be a sturdy and seaworthy vessel, although it did not tack very well: when he headed for London from St. Helena, he did not arrive there directly but had first to call at New York! (Chinese jonk Keying 1848:48).

The Crew

"A Chinese junk", John Crawfurd informs us, "is manned with an extraordinary proportion of hands, as compared to European vessels - a circumstance which chiefly arises from the awkwardness of the rudder, the cable and anchor, and the weight and clumsiness of the enormous square sails which are used of. A junk of 8000 piculs or about 500 tons, requires a crew of ninety men, and the proportion of hands is still greater for vessels of smaller size." (Crawfurd 1830 II:160.) A VOC source from 1761 mentions that a junk of 800 tons had a crew of 130 sailors and an additional 130 merchant passengers (Plakaatboek VII:471). Over and above this number, hundreds of emigrants were also transported.

The average junk was manned as follows: The "Ch'u-hai" or "ch'uan-chu", often called nachoda by the Dutch (Malay: nakoda), was in charge of the ship, its cargo and passengers, but this man did not concern himself with the vessel's navigation. He often was a direct relation or, in the Fukienese case, an adopted son of the primary owner (Tien 1956:12; HMC V:652). As payment for his services, he received 100 piculs of free tonnage, cabin accommodation worth 150-200 dollars which he could hire to passengers, and a commission of 10% of the net profits made over the voyage (Crawfurd 1830 II:161). The supercargo also acted as an agent to whom merchandise could be consigned (Ng 1983:157-8). Second in command, but in fact the real captain of the ship, was the "huo-ch'ang" or pilot, who was paid 200 rials and given fifty piculs of cargo space. The pilot, who often was a western sailor, literally lived on deck during the voyage, watching the compass, taking the sun's altitude, observing the passing of promontories, and checking the colour of the sand hauled up from the sea bottom (HFHC X:490). The captains of the steerage and the boatswains of the anchors and the holds received 15 and 9 piculs of cargo space respectively and the sailors 7 piculs. No wages were paid, and everyone carried his own merchandise: crew members of a Chinese junk were merchants first and sailors second, as Jennifer Cushman rightly remarks (Cushman 1975:137). Clerks or "ts'ai fu" assisted the chu-hai in supervising the loading and unloading of the ship and kept accounts. Last but not least, there was a priest, or a cook who functioned as a priest, to perform the different religious ceremonies required during the trip (HMC II:178).

Apart from the crew, there were two kinds of passengers, the merchants or "quewie" (Chinese: ch'i) with their assistants (usually two or more), who rented cabins from the crew, and emigrants or labourers who could be said to have pawned their bodies in order to pay the fee of about ten rixdollars for their passage in the hope of making a fortune overseas. These wretched creatures had nothing to eat and drink but the rice and water that they brought along; moreover, they were forced to sleep on the deck, giving the crowded junks the appearance of African slavers.

How the cargoes of pepper, tin, or cloves, which the Chinese merchants purchased from the VOC in Batavia, were divided amongst them is not easy to determine. The outcome of a judicial investigation into an attempt by a junk skipper named Ongtiko to smuggle illegally purchased cloves out of Batavia lifts a corner of the veil. It was established that the legally exported cargo of black pepper in Ong's junk amounted to 3650 piculs which had been purchased in different shares by 16 travelling merchants: eight of them had bought 50 piculs each, the others 100, 200, 300 (2x), 350, 400, 500 and 1100 (21-6-1713, VOC 1834, f.2533).

Junks entering and clearing China's ports were subject to a vast array of charges, such as measurement dues, pilotage, licensing, and permit fees. Measurement dues were determined by multiplying the length by the width of the junk, the export product being the basis upon which duties were levied (Cushman 1975:54). Because of the difficulty of taking into account all the different merchandise on board, a fixed sum was often demanded. In a detailed analysis of the different charges and dues, Jennifer Cushman concludes that in principle Chinese shipping paid considerably lower rates than Western ships calling at China's ports. Junks, moreover, benefited from privileged exemption percentages, which allowed a fifty percent reduction in fees for those sailing to Java (Cushman 1975:57). Even though these charges were not always levied, their existence left ample opportunity for the local mandarins and the supercargoes to fleece the crews and merchants on board the ships (Chang 1981:136).

Religious Practices on Board
The Chinese did not make a definitive distinction between the natural and the supernatural worlds. In their minds, these worlds existed alongside each other and were closely interrelated. Nowhere did this awareness manifest itself in a more striking manner than at sea or in frontier conditions where physical danger was constantly present. The great importance Fukienese sailors attached to the manipulation of supernatural assistance during their voyages overseas is attested by the omnipresence of pagodas and temples dedicated to tutelary deities along China's coast and throughout Southeast Asia. At the same time as Chinese maritime trade expanded, new temples were raised on foreign shores. The extent of the Lebensraum of the Fukienese could probably best be portrayed on a geographical map by

the locations of the temples devoted to the goddess Matsu.

When, shortly before Chinese New Year, the northern monsoon started to blow steadily, an auspicious day was selected for the departure. The crew and passengers carried on a palanquin a small statue of their goddess, from the joss-house on the poop of the junk to the deity's temple, to take formal leave, and to present offerings in order to ensure that the passage might be made i-lu-ping-an, "swift and without accidents". Often this visit to the temple was accompanied by a theatrical performance. After the ritual was over, the crew partook of the wines and the dishes of pork, fish and vegetables which had been used as offerings; finally they brought the statue of their "Stella Maris" back to the ship, and to the banging of gongs and crackling of fireworks the anchor was lifted, the sails were hoisted, and the overloaded vessel slowly drifted away. For as long as the junk sailed along the Chinese coast, passing by various ports, little sampans brought contraband, last-minute passengers and letter carriers who were on their way to Batavia (Plakaatboek VII:470-1).

Throughout the voyage, the sailors kept the ships as close as possible to the coast so that they easily could determine their position. Offerings were made not only to the winds, but also to sacred promontories that were passed. Father Le Comte, who travelled on a junk from Siam to China in the late 17th century, described the character of these offerings as follows: "Once, passing near a hill on which one of their temples is built, their superstition then out-did itself, for besides the usual ceremonies, consisting of meat offerings, candles and perfume burning, throwing little baubles of gilt paper into the sea, and an infinite number of such fopperies, all hands were at work for five or six hours together in making a little vessel in the likeness of our own, of about four feet in length. It was very artificially wrought, wanting neither masts, tackling, sails or flags; it had its compass, rudder and shalop; its arms, kitchen-stuff, victuals, cargo and book of accompts. Besides, they had daubed as many small pieces of paper as we were men in the ship, which were disposed of in the same place we were in." (Le Comte 1697:8). After much ceremony, the small ship was placed into the water and sent away. The same ritual can already be found in the "Tung-Hsi-Yang K'ao", which prescribes that the crew must set afloat a votive model ("Ts'ai ch'uan" or coloured boat) upon passing a holy mountain, and chant in order to beseech sacred blessings (Chang 1981:186). "This ridiculous entertainment diverted the sailors, while we were struck with a sensible grief of the sight of their blind error, which it was out of our power to cure", sighs the French priest. Le Comte indeed spent a large part of the passage quarreling with the crew on account of "this superstition" and ate only rice during the trip though the captain often invited Le Comte and his fellow passengers to eat some meat with him, "but that being always first offered as a sacrifice to the idol, we looked on it with more horror than appetite", the priest confessed. Another object which was venerated by the crews was the compass. Gutzlaff describes how "some red cloth, which is also tied to the rudder and cable, is put over it. Incense-sticks in great quantities are kindled; and gilt paper made into the shape of a junk is burnt before it." (Gützlaff 1840:85). In this way the Chinese sailors at sea stayed in touch with their gods and tried to master the elements.

The Sea Route

The trajectory followed by Chinese junks along the Western sea route was

A Chinese map of the Nanyang (1844).

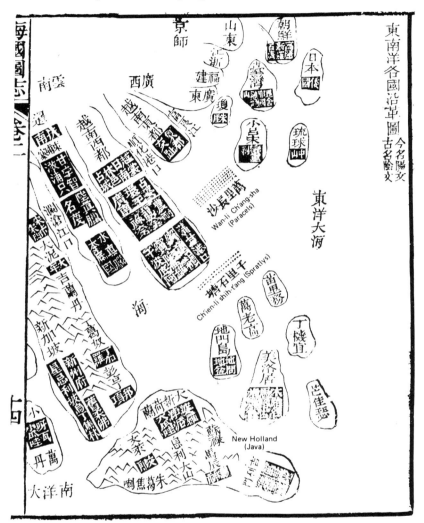

fixed and is neatly described in portulans like the "Tung-Hsi-Yang K'ao", the "Shun-feng Hsiang-sung", and "Chih-nan Cheng-fa".³ These manuals, dating from different periods, prescribe the same route. They employ the traditional standard unit for calculating the length of sea routes, the "keng", which represented about 2.4 hours, one day being divided into ten keng. In terms of distance, one keng was fixed at 40 "li" or 13 nautical miles. The average duration of the voyage to Batavia was, according to Ong Tai-hai who made the voyage in the 1770's, about 280 keng, or in other words, 28 days (Ong 1849:1).

From Amoy, the ship proceeded first to Wu-hsü island at the mouth of

VI   The VOC and the Junk Trade to Batavia   113

the estuary, then it steered southwest along the Chinese coast to the Pearl River delta, where it headed for the coast of Vietnam, keeping the Chichou or Paracels to the left and the island of Hainan to the right. After four or five days the Vietnamese coast was reached at Wai-Lo-shan (Pulau Canton). Via Chan-Pi-Lo-shan (Pulau Cham) and Hué the ship arrived three days later at Hsin-chou (Qui Nhon). Then, after passing Ling-shan or Holy Mountain (Cape Varella), where elaborate ceremonies were performed, it proceeded to Kun Lun (Pulau Condor). The crossing was then made to the island of Tioman, near the Straits of Malaka. Following the coast of Sumatra, the ship passed along Chiu-kang (Palembang) and steered through the straits of Banka before it made the final crossing to Batavia. The most dangerous stretches along the route were, first, along the Vietnamese coast, because of a profusion of reefs in that region, and then the Straits of Banka, a favourite hiding place for pirates. Dutch patrol vessels would often meet the Chinese junks here, to guide them safely to Batavia (VOC 2091, f.4778-9).

Arrival in Batavia
Upon arriving in Batavia, the seafarers were warmly welcomed with "wayang" performances, banquets and fireworks in much the same way as they had been sent off in Amoy. Although the English author, William Blakeney, witnessed the arrival in China of junks returning from Southeast Asia, the scene he nostalgically described at the turn of this century must have been similar to that of Batavia: "One of the interesting sights of the period was the arrival of the great trading junks which sailed hither with

Chinese wayang and masquerade in Batavia seen through the eyes of a Dutch artist.

the fair monsoon. They came into the harbour with a veritable Babel of sounds from tomtoms and horns, their crews massed on high prow and stern, for the purpose of announcing their safe arrival. In all this there was something akin to music; there can be none in the screeching siren, and smoke of coastal and ocean-going steamers, which now daily come and go, and keep the harbour alive with shipping." (Blakeney 1902:26).

Customs formalities at Batavia were not as simple as they had been in the good old days at Banten. A gift of oranges and two umbrellas was not enough to satisfy the officials of the Dutch East India Company. In the early days of the trade, two assistants of the collector of general revenues (ontvanger van de generale inkomsten) and the licence master (licentmeester) boarded the vessels and noted down all merchandise (Plakaatboek I: 210). These time-consuming practices soon gave way to less complex ones in later years. Apart from these import and export duties the captains had to pay for anchor duties, safe conduct passes, gifts for the harbourmaster, the collector of the revenues, the secretaries and the cashier - in all about 1,000 rixdollars (ARA, Alting collection, 67). After the inspection, the merchandise was brought to the Chinese warehouses in front of Batavia castle, where they were put on display and were sold. Until the merchants left again with the southern monsoon in June, only a small number of sailors stayed on board the junk to take care of it and to execute the necessary repairs. The merchants and their assistants took up temporary residence in boarding houses that were specifically let for this purpose by the town's citizens.[4]

Initially, the Chinese newcomers attempted to economize, crowding together, with twenty to forty people within one lodging. But as early as 1626, a stern decree was issued which forbade these practices "which not only cause stench, infection, death and fire among them but also other mischiefs such as improper assembly, indecent intercourse, et cetera" (VOC 1088, f.16; Res GG and C 9-4-1626). During their stay in Batavia the visitors paid - just as the Chinese inhabitants of the city did - a monthly headtax (Plakaatboek II:493). The nachodas of the junks were highly esteemed in town and often took part in discussions on important policy matters while they were present. The selection of a new Chinese captain or headman of the Chinese in Batavia was, for instance, delayed in 1645 until the Chinese junks had arrived and the nachodas could be consulted (Hoetink 1922:14). "Orang baru", or newcomers who stayed behind in Batavia, would often work for those persons who had advanced their passage fee before they could start working for themselves. Other towns along the "Pasisir" also needed Chinese coolies. Semarang even had its own boarding house in Batavia, where the newcomers were lodged until they found ships ready to take them to Semarang. "These, whether of the same or different clans, whether well- or ill-recommended, were all received and recorded; after which every man was employed according to his ability, and placed in the situation best adapted for him" (Ong 1849:24).

A Chronological Approach

Development, Heyday and Decline
The above desultory notes on the structural aspects and the day-to-day operations of the junk trade may serve as an introduction to the chronological treatment of this trade link, to which we shall presently turn. The periodization scheme which I shall apply has been selected on basis of two

yardsticks: the watershed developments that more or less separate each period and the inherent character and continuity which mark each of these periods.

A. The formative phase between 1619 and 1680 was characterized by continuing political unrest in China, which hampered a healthy growth of the trade. The terminus of the trade link had not yet developed into a market with its own territorial hinterland, where large-scale settlement was possible. On average, five junks annually visited Batavia in this period.

B. The phase of burgeoning trade, 1680 to 1740, coincided with a period of peace in China and seemingly unlimited possibilities in Batavia's hinterland. In this section, the several ways in which the Chinese and the Dutch administrations rather ineptly sought to channel the mass movement of men and merchandise and prevent its outgrowth will be studied. With the exception of an interruption lasting four years, about twenty junks visited Batavia yearly.

C. Stagnation and decline typified the last phase, 1740 to 1795, in which the VOC, increasingly beleaguered by the expanding interests of the English in Southeast Asia, resorted to all kinds of exclusive policies, such as the fragmentation of the Chinese trade in order to control and exclude their competitors. The number of junks sailing to Batavia decreased sharply.

A. The Formative Phase, 1619-1680

In the 1620s and 1630s, most of the Chinese commodities carried in the junks were destined for the Javanese market. These consisted of silk fabrics from Chang-chou, sugar, porcelain from the Yung-chun kilns, iron pans, nails and needles, umbrellas, wooden clogs, gilded paper, fresh and dried fruits and a great quantity of coarse textiles.[5] In these early years, about five junks visited Batavia each year, bringing on the average 1,000 new immigrants to the town annually. In 1626, Governor-General Pieter de Carpentier (1623-1627) noted that Chinese shipping profited as much from the proceeds of the transport of passengers as from that of merchandise, adding that the province of Fukien must be both richly populated and needy to send so many thousands of people all over Southeast Asia, "of whom possibly not even a third part returns to China" (2-2-1626, GM I: 192). When the Gentlemen XVII complained that Governor-General Hendrick Brouwer (1632-1636) allowed the Chinese to return with their children to China, he wrote to them in the following way: "China is full of people; the common people are as little valued over there as the farmers in Denmark, Holstein, et cetera. If Chinese junks continue to come, at least a thousand new Chinese will stay behind every year." (4-1-1636, GM I:546).

As the Chinese trade was generally beneficial to the well-being of Batavia's citizenry and did not undermine the Company's monopolies, the arrival of the junks was encouraged as much as possible. In the spring of 1626, the Chinese shipmasters of five junks that were lying at Batavia's roadstead received written certificates stating that half of their harbour dues would be waived the following year if they returned. Five more certificates were given to them, to be transmitted to other nachodas in China (Res GG and C 9-5-1626, VOC 1088, f.26). In addition, the nachodas, accountants, mates, boatswains, and carpenters of the junks received personal presents varying in value from elephant tusks to bags of pepper (Res GG and C 6-6-1626, VOC 1088, f.30). The first junk to appear with the northern monsoon was even declared free of all duties.

Whenever the Company felt its interests threatened, however, it reacted - and quickly. A Chinese junk which had visited Batavia in 1625, but which chose to sail for Japara in 1626, despite a promised exemption from Batavian harbour charges, was caught en route by a Company yacht, escorted to Batavia, and fined 4,000 rials. To stimulate the trade to its headquarters, the Batavian government went so far as to inform the Chinese that it would no longer tolerate Chinese junks sailing to Patani, Jambi, Palembang, Makassar and Bima or Timor (13-7-1626, letter GG to Governor of Formosa, VOC 853). Of course, the Dutch were not yet able to enforce that order, but this action left no doubt about their intentions to get a stronger grip on China's trade with Southeast Asia. Occasionally protective measures were taken against commodities imported by the Chinese. In 1636 a large shipload of "Chinese beer" was, for instance, declared subject to a heavy tax when the sales of locally produced spirits began to decline (Plakaatboek I:401).

During the seventeenth century Chinese junks mainly exported the following items from Batavia: great quantities of silver coins and tropical products like pepper, nutmeg, cloves, sandalwood, buffalo horns, elephant tusks, incense, edible birds' nests, tripang and a variety of drugs. At a later date, around the turn of the century, tin and "vaderlandsche koopmanschappen" (Dutch cloth) also became important export commodities. The export of silver constituted a serious drain on the Batavian treasury. In China, silver was used as the basic form of land tax payment and was therefore in great demand. The Batavian government tried to persuade the Chinese traders to accept payments in kind instead of payments in cash, but this attempt was not very successful. Of the tropical products, pepper was sold in the largest quantities. From 1637 to 1644, 300 to 1000 tons were exported each year to China.[6]

The risks of the trade become apparent from a report which stated that three out of the five junks that had visited Batavia in 1643 were shipwrecked in gales on the way back to China. The loss of the pepper on board these ships and the dearth of other spices in China, due to the fact that Portuguese ships from Goa failed to arrive in Macao, drove up the pepper price in China to the satisfaction of the VOC personnel of the Taiwanese trade factory, which could instantly deliver pepper to China from its stocks (GM II:210). Zeelandia Castle, established in 1624 at Taiwan, was of course much better situated for the Dutch trade with China than far-away Batavia, and it was primarily from these quarters that the Batavian junk trade received stiff competition in the early stage of its existence.

In 1644, eight large junks with a total cargo of 3,200 tons visited Batavia (GM II:254). Difficulties arose as a result of continuous haggling between the nachodas and the collectors of revenues concerning the amount of import taxes that had to be paid for the increasingly varied cargoes from China. Realizing that a new set of regulations was necessary, the authorities decided that all incoming junks - with the exception of the first one, which was traditionally exempt from taxation - would be charged with a "redemption fee" of 550 rials. This charge exempted the ship from all further inspection by the tax collector (Plakaatboek II:85). The increase of this sum in 1654 to 1500 and 1000 reals for large and small junks respectively should be an indication of the increased relative value of the cargoes per ship (Plakaatboek II:192).

After 1645, the number of junks arriving at Batavia decreased sharply as a result of the civil wars in China which blocked trade and supply routes inland (GM II:271). When the Manchus founded the Ch'ing dynasty in 1644 they had by no means conquered all of China's territory. It took them another forty years before they were able to pacify the country. One of the toughest enemies of the new government turned out to be the descendants of the Cheng lineage from the Chin-chiang region in Fukien. Under its young leader, Cheng Ch'eng-kung or Coxinga, this clan had remained loyal to the heir apparent of the Ming dynasty. Cheng Ch'eng-kung gained total control of the Amoy region, the main entrepot of China's trade with Southeast Asia in 1649. In the years that followed, he financed his war efforts from the proceeds of overseas trade, primarily with Japan, the VOC settlement on Taiwan and ports in Indo-China (Yamawaki 1976). The Batavian trade, however, experienced a considerable slump.

As the effects on the Chinese population of the decrease in trade became noticeable, Governor-General Cornelis van der Lijn (1646-1650) permitted his Chinese subjects to trade with Japan (GM II:487). Batavian-Chinese traffic with Taiwan picked up as well, and in 1653, nine Batavian junks sailed into Taiwan's harbor. Uneasy about this increase in the number of Batavian junks, the Governor of Taiwan, Nicolaes Verburg, complained to the Gentlemen XVII that the Batavian Chinese came to buy and sell the same articles in which the Company itself dealt, and they were thus infringing on its monopoly (24-12-1652, GM II:605). The directors in Amsterdam agreed with his views and forbade the continuation of this trade. Governor-General Johan Maetsuijcker (1653-1678) in Batavia initially objected, fearing that this would have a negative effect on the prosperity of the town (GM II:759). But when in 1654 and again the following year, a fleet of eight junks from Fukien unexpectedly appeared at the Batavian roadstead, Maetsuijcker wrote with relief to Amsterdam that these vessels infused new economic life into the town, as much among the Chinese as the other inhabitants (1-4-1655, GM II:823). His feelings of relief did not last for long.

The eight junks that visited Batavia all belonged to the Coxinga faction. The VOC was now facing a formidable trade partner who was not only unwilling to dance to its tune, but even prepared to challenge it. This, at least, became clear from a letter that Maetsuijcker received from the Governor of Malaka, Jan Thijssen Payart. The latter informed him that a junk had arrived from Amoy in Malaka, with a letter from Coxinga in answer to a letter Thijssen had sent the year before to the Chinese warlord. Thijssen's letter had intimated that in the future no more junks should be sent to Malaka; instead they should be directed to Batavia. Coxinga's haughty answer was that as far as he was concerned, Taiwan, Malaka and Batavia all belonged to one and the same country, and he frankly saw no reason why he should be refused admittance to Malaka. The Dutch could live with this answer. From conversations with the nachoda of the same junk, however, it transpired that Coxinga had sent seven more junks to Southeast Asia, three to Siam, and one each to Ligor, Sangora, Patani, and Johore, so that he could choose and purchase whatever commodities he needed from those regions without having to buy anything in Taiwan, Batavia or Malaka (GM II:824).

In 1656 an imperial edict was issued in China "forbidding even a plank to drift to the sea" (Tien 1956:7). By putting a ban on maritime trade, the imperial government tried to undermine Coxinga's main source of income. The latter turned his eyes to Taiwan, severed all trade relations with the Dutch in 1659, and crossed to the island with his troops two years later (GM III:283, 359). He laid siege to the Dutch garrison in Zee-

Chinese junk anchoring at the Nagasaki roadstead.

landia castle, and forced it into surrender ten months later. In an attempt to isolate the Chengs in Taiwan, the K'ang-hsi emperor resorted to even more draconic measures in 1661. He ordered the forced evacuation of the coastal region of China's seaboard provinces, Chekiang, Fukien and Kwangtung. Ng Chin-keong has pointed out that these measures turned out to be counterproductive: they only intensified the hatred of the local population for the Peking government and enabled the Cheng forces to further expand their maritime empire unhampered by serious competition (Ng 1983:53).

From 1664 to 1673, the Ch'ing army and the forces of the Cheng family kept each other in balance until this stalemate came to an end with the eruption of the Revolt of the Three Feudatories. This uprising, commanded by the former Chinese allies of the Manchus, among whom were the viceroys of Kwangtung and Fukien, briefly led to a concentration of forces between them and the Cheng family, but mounting distrust between the leaders of the revolt resulted in the surrender of two of these leaders in 1676 and 1677. By 1680 the Chengs were once again on their own and had to retreat from the mainland to their island base on Taiwan (Leonard 1984: 67-8). For the VOC, the consequences of these political developments were far-reaching: it saw its trade relations with China seriously threatened with severance. Measures were taken at three different levels to prevent this.

When they could no longer sail to Amoy, the Chinese of Batavia fitted out junks for trading expeditions to Japan, an enterprise which the High Government conspired to promote, despite the fact that by so doing, these Chinese traders were encroaching on the Company's monopoly of this route (GM III:112). This trespassing may have been minimal, however, because the Batavian Chinese went to Japan not to purchase Japanese commodities but to engage in trade there with fellow Fukienese who were sailing back and forth from Nagasaki to Fukien under the flag of the Cheng family. As long as Batavia's Chinese brought back Chinese commodities, the Dutch authorities were willing to look the other way, even if this merchandise had been purchased from the followers of the VOC's mortal enemy.

The Gentlemen XVII in the Netherlands anticipated the troubles with Coxinga at an early date. In 1654, they sent an embassy to the imperial court in Peking to offer Dutch assistance in the struggle against the Ming loyalists, in exchange for certain privileges. This mission and those to Fu-chou in northern Fukien, which followed in the 1660s, were aimed at the establishment of free, direct trade with China.[7] This objective was never reached because the Revolt of the Three Feudatories intervened.

The Batavian authorities also pondered the question of how to compensate in some way for the loss of the Chinese junk trade. They decided that it would do no harm to encourage the town's freeburghers to engage in private trade at Portuguese-held Macao, near Canton, while the Company itself was still occupied in "pour-parlers" with the Ch'ing authorities in the capital of Fukien, Fu-chou. The Portuguese of Macao were also involved in a desperate struggle for survival, as their traditional sources of income had gradually dried up due to the evacuation policies of the imperial government. Initially they were threatened with expulsion but by 1668 their situation looked less desperate, and from that year onwards, Batavian citizens were among those engaging in annual smuggling activities in the Pearl River Delta. In this way, Macao functioned as a safety valve to allay the mounting tensions along the China coast (Wills 1984:94-101).

A modern writer on the VOC's relations with China in this particular period, John Wills, draws attention to the fact that "from 1669 to 1675 the only Dutch trade with China was that carried out by the free burghers of Batavia, that is, by Dutchmen settled in Batavia but not in the service of the Company". Starting with one or two ships in 1669 this trade gained importance. By 1674 there were eleven burgher vessels on the China coast whose cargoes represented an investment of about 250,000 guilders. "An important new development" remarks Wills elsewhere, "was the arrival [in 1674] at Batavia of a junk from Canton with a cargo worth about 25,000 guilders, the first junk based in China to be recorded at Batavia in several years." (Wills 1974:150-1.) According to the same author, the free-burgher voyages were completely forbidden in 1678 "as part of a general effort by Company officials to check private trade and prevent other encroachments on the Company's monopoly". A question then arises: had the situation changed to such an extent that the Company could afford to abolish the burgher trade with China? The answer is yes, indeed: the Company sent its own ships. Yet, this is not the whole story.

From Wills' portrayal of the situation, one could get the impression that the Chinese junk trade was not resumed until 1674. This would, however, be a misunderstanding. Marie-Sybille de Vienne, who has made a thorough study of the economic activities of the Overseas Chinese in the archipelago on the basis of the printed "Daghregisters" of Batavia (1624-1682), gives a different presentation of the facts by proving that ships other than burgher yachts sailed to and from Macao.

From 1665 onwards, the Batavian junk trade was hesitantly resumed, most probably with Chinese ports that were not under Cheng control, and continued to rise remarkably in the period from 1670-1674. De Vienne found that twelve burgher voyages versus twenty-six junk voyages were undertaken in these five years, and in the 1675-1679 period, when burgher yachts and junks were found in a proportion of six to fifty, the scale clearly tipped in the favour of the Chinese. By that time, trade with ports other than Macao had been restored. De Vienne concludes that only in the 1665-1674 period had the Batavian junk trade with Macao surpassed the trade with other ports in southern China, as is shown in Table 1 (De Vienne 1979:115). Undoubtedly the Macao connection had played a useful role in tiding over the difficulties.

Table 1.
Junks visiting Batavia (per five year period).

	Macao junks	Chinese junks	total
1665-1669	1	0	1
1670-1674	13	5	18
1675-1679	15	28	43
1680-1683	6	10	16

In 1680 Amoy was finally captured by the Ch'ing forces, and several merchants from that city resumed the junk trade to Batavia in the following year.

In the eyes of the Gentlemen XVII, however, the seemingly whimsical Chinese junk trade to Batavia, which was primarily directed toward the fulfillment of the needs of the Southeast Asian consumer, did not appear to be the system of supply that it was striving for to ensure the regular acquisition of Chinese commodities for the European market. These considerations prompted the Directors of the Company to continue dispatching their own ships to China to engage in trade at Fu-chou, even though this trade was subject to all sorts of restrictions (Stapel 1927-43 II-1:752-67). Important developments in the years that followed dramatically changed the overall situation of the China trade and forced the Dutch to reassess their priorities.

B. The Heyday of the Junk Trade: 1690-1740

A revival of the Amoy junk trade to Batavia occurred in the 1680s, thanks to two important political events which coincided during the first years of this decade.

In 1683, the Batavian Government saw, at long last, the opportunity to bring its nearby rival, Banten (which had, especially in the years just previous, begun to draw a considerable proportion of the junk trade from China as well as Japan) under its dominion. Not only did the Company gain hegemony in Java's coastal areas but it also pacified Batavia's hinterland. This area, the Ommelanden, which had been frequently invaded by bands of brigands from Banten, could now be brought under VOC control and cultivated. The development of the sugar cultivation in particular created a large demand for Chinese agricultural labourers and sugar mill operators.

In China, the coastal evacuation law was gradually rescinded between 1668 and 1681. The conquest of Taiwan by Admiral Shih Lang in 1683 finally put an end to the more than forty years of civil strife which had given China's overseas trade such an inconsistent character. In 1684 the ban on maritime trade was also revoked, and Amoy was entrusted with various administrative functions within the context of the official imperial policy to resume trade relations with the Nanyang (HMC II:178, 193).

How decisive the impact of these political developments was on the further enhancement of the junk trade and the way it was effectuated will become clear if we briefly focus on each of these developments separately and study them within their own institutional context.

a. Amoy. Ever since the Chinese trade was authorized in 1684, the Chinese authorities exerted themselves to promote China's maritime trade and to combat illegal emigration at the same time. Possibly the most succinct conceptual analysis of the political principles that lay at the root of the matter has been provided by Jane Kate Leonard in the introduction to her study of the nineteenth century scholar-official Wei Yuan and his writings on the maritime frontier (Leonard 1984).

According to Leonard, the Manchu authorities departed from the maritime policies of their Ming predecessors to the extent that they treated the junk trade as a key issue, not because of any special interest in the foreign maritime world as such or because of court involvement in trade, but because of the economic argument that the junk trade was the backbone of the coastal economy. The Ch'ing court fully understood that the overseas trade was essential for the economic and political order of China's southeastern coastal region, which had resisted Manchu rule for no less than forty years until finally the last hotbed of sedition was extinguished on Taiwan in 1683. As a result, coastal control and the administration of overseas trade were treated as internal security issues - and not without reason. Even after the coastal area had been subjugated and pacified, anti-Manchu feelings remained very much alive; witness the emergence of the secret societies with their strong Ming revivalist tendencies.

A Chinese ocean-going junk anno 1750.

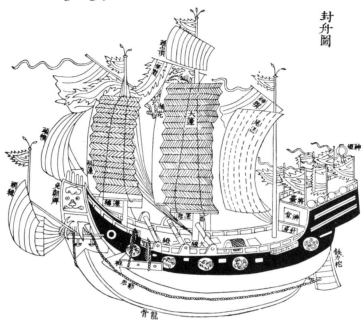

To keep a close eye on the activities of the traders, collectorates of customs duties were established at several ports in the Kwantung, Fukien and Chekiang provinces (Cushman 1975:31; Leonard 1984:60). The personnel of these customs stations collected duties on imports and exports, checked incoming and outgoing cargoes, and registered the vessels engaged in trade. An intricate web of mutual responsibility was woven around those who were involved in trade, and most of the official management functions were actually performed by local traders, licensed merchants who were held responsible for each other's behaviour (Leonard 1984:60-1).

Permits for building junks were only issued to wealthy and trustworthy persons (HMC II:167). For supervisory purposes the bows of the Fukienese junks were painted green and provided with red identification marks; Cantonese junks were painted red with blue characters (HMC II:168). The armament of the junks was strictly regulated. The number of crew members needed was fixed in proportion to the width of the vessel and so on (HMC II:167). Basically, the maritime policies of the central government in Peking were directed at keeping the Southeastern coastal population in check, through ad hoc measures carried out by the local administration and an increasingly refined system of mutual responsibility and self-control. Only when matters appeared nearly out of hand would the imperial court step in with emergency measures, some as all-embracing as the total ban on overseas shipping in 1717. Or at least the court would seriously contemplate repeating this in 1741, as we shall see.

b. Batavia. In 1686, eight junks from Amoy and three junks from other ports in China brought more than 800 coolies and a rich supply of Chinese merchandise to Batavia (8-3-1686, GM V:19, 23). In the next few years, this stream of merchandise and men steadily swelled.

The "Overgekomen Brieven en Papieren series", the collections of letters and papers received from Batavia which were sent every year to the Netherlands as appendices to the "Generale Missiven", contain serial data on Chinese shipping to Batavia. These shipping lists note the date of arrival, name of the nachoda, name of the vessel, the port of origin, lastage, the official number of persons arriving at and departing from Batavia, the date of departure, as well as the port of destination. These quantitative data in combination with the qualitative material derived from resolutions and letters make it possible to follow the evolution of the junk trade in a much more precise manner than is possible for the period before 1683. In the 1685 to 1715 period, the yearly arrivals of Chinese junks at Batavia nearly doubled. The tonnage of the junks differed, but 85 % measured between 150 and 200 tons.

At the same time the junk trade increased, the trade carried out by Company ships along the China coast became singularly unattractive, owing to the ever rising tolls and exactions to which this trade was subject at the hands of greedy officials. In view of this situation, it dawned upon Governor-General Willem van Outhoorn (1691-1704) that the Company might as well stop sending ships to China and employ these vessels instead for the trade with Bengal, where greater profits could be made. The implication, of course, was that the VOC would henceforth rely solely on Chinese junks (and Portuguese ships from Macao) for its supply of Chinese merchandise for the European market.

Table 2.
Number of incoming ships (average per annum).'

	Chinese	Portuguese	Total
1681 - 1690	9.7	1.8	11.5
1691 - 1700	11.5	1.6	13.1
1701 - 1710	11	2.9	13.9
1711 - 1720	13.6	5.9	19.5
1721 - 1730	16.4	9	25.4
1731 - 1740	17.7	4.8	22.5
1741 - 1750	10.9	4.1	15
1751 - 1760	9.1	1.8	10.9
1761 - 1770	7.4	2.4	9.8
1771 - 1780	5.1	3	8.1
1781 - 1790	9.3	3.9	13.2
1791 - 1793	9.5	3	12.5

' Note there were no Chinese arrivals between 1718 and 1721.

Van Outhoorn, very much aware of the prosperity which was brought to Batavia by the Chinese junk trade, did not fail to explain the motives behind his proposal to divert to the Indian Ocean those Company ships which had until then been used for the annual trading expedition to the Chinese coast. His profit-opportunity analysis showed that VOC ships could be employed much more economically in the "Wester Kwartieren" than in Chinese waters, where the profits amounted to as little as 45% of the purchase price (VOC 2219, f.82). He also pointed out that the Chinese junks could operate considerably cheaper than the ships of the Company: "Their sailors are not paid; each of them earns a living from the merchandise that he carries with him. Therefore the freight charge that individuals have to pay to the owners of the junks [...] cannot be much." (31-1-1692, GM V:466). Confronted with this persuasive reasoning, the Gentlemen XVII concurred with his views and decided to abandon direct trade with the Middle Kingdom.

In 1693, 194,891 rixdollars of pepper, textiles and cloves were sold in Batavia to the merchants from China, while 109,923 rixdollars of spelter, silk, textiles, and porcelain, were purchased from them. This was considerably more than the Company ships had bought or sold during their last trips to China in 1689. When twenty junks arrived in 1694, it was calculated that the total amount of merchandise purchased by the Company from them was greater than what would have been the case had 5 VOC ships been sent to the China coast (30-11-1694, GM V:687).

The flourishing junk trade was not without side-effects: the Gentlemen XVII established to their dismay that many Company servants invested heavily in illegal private dealings through the Chinese network, and sent home costly shiploads of porcelain and tea, while the High Government in Batavia grew alarmed at the large numbers of jobless Chinese who were discharged every year on Batavia's shore.

The Bull in the China Closet
The directors in Holland knew from experience that they had little or no leverage with respect to the illegal dealings of their servants in the East, but in the case of tea and porcelain, both destined for the European market, they seized the opportunity to combat the abuses practiced on the shipping route to Europe.

Unlike porcelain, which was in great demand from the earliest days of the junk trade, tea did not become an important commodity until the 1680s. On April 6, 1685 the Gentlemen XVII informed the Batavian government that the illegal import of tea by Company servants was exceeding all bounds. They had decided to earmark tea as valuable merchandise reserved for the Company and therefore issued the order that no one would be allowed to carry tea in his personal belongings any longer (Bierens de Haan 1918:24-5). The order must have yielded little effect, for eight years later, on March 5, 1693, the Gentlemen XVII ordered Governor-General Van Outhoorn to levy stiff surcharges on tea and porcelain in the possession of Company servants returning home on board VOC ships. The Batavian High Government immediately carried the instruction into effect and issued an edict on January 23, 1694. Homeward-bound seamen and passengers were informed that, from that day forth, transport charges would have to be paid for luxury items such as tea and porcelain in their possession: tea was taxed at f 2.10 per pound and porcelain at f 1.00 per pound. All these commodities had to be delivered to and shown in the antechamber of the Governor-General's residence, where they would be weighed, inventoried and packed (Plakaatboek III:359).

The edict caused an outcry from all parties involved. The eight or so requests sent by the Chinese citizens of Batavia to the High Government in connection with the edict are the most interesting to us in terms of content since these letters bared the mechanism of the trade at Batavia in Chinese commodities destined for the European market.

One is tempted to say that a student of a subject like the junk trade, which took place outside the direct surveillance of the VOC authorities, should look for those crucial moments when the colonial administration took heavy-handed or partial decisions. As a direct result of the repercussions

VI The VOC and the Junk Trade to Batavia

caused by such errors in judgement, enquiries were often made into the real nature of matters which had previously remained covered with a veil of discretion, or which had been ignored due to plain lack of interest or cultural misunderstanding.
In this particular case an enquiry was not necessary: the Chinese who were affected by the measures took considerable pains to explain their predicament. First of all, Captain Que Koenqua and Lieutenant Lim Kheequa spoke of "the great sadness and stream of complaints" of their Chinese fellow-men. Feeling themselves responsible for the well-being of the poor and destitute Chinese of Batavia, "who for a long time have peacefully lived under your Excellency's protective wings", they begged the Governor-General to lift the recently issued ordinance as soon as possible. The Chinese officers estimated that each year approximately 1500 "baly" of tea were imported. Five hundred were sold to the Company, five hundred were locally consumed and the remaining five hundred were sold to Dutch sailors and Company servants returning home. The weight of these five hundred baly was equal to 250 piculs. Considering that the freight charges for one pound of tea cost about one rixdollar, the 250 piculs of tea would yield at most 25,000 rixdollars to the Company.
Out of the five hundred baly of porcelain annually supplied by the junks, three hundred were destined for the local market, one hundred were to be sold to the Company and the remaining lot was intended for the informal circuit. One baly of porcelain being equal to two hundred pounds, the freight rate of the porcelain (at 20 pieces per pound) would yield another 8,000 rixdollars. Consequently the new measure would at most realize 33,000 rixdollars for the Company. The Chinese officers pointed out that this amount shrunk into insignificance when considered alongside the losses which the Company would face - and that of its Chinese middlemen, those who levied taxes at the harbour customs, shops, markets, and the weighing house; and those who collected the Chinese headtax and taxes from sellers of tobacco and porkmeat; and finally those who collected from the gambling houses (VOC 1523, f.555-6).
A second petition was presented by nine nachodas. Flowery language embellished their introduction: "for years on end we have commuted between China and Batavia from ports like Fu-chou, Amoy, Chi-lung [on Northern Formosa] and Ning-po, carrying Chinese silks, tea and porcelain. We have always been well-treated, so that words fail to convey our gratefulness for the favours received in the past." The skippers said it was inconceivable to them to contest the Company's sovereign rights to publish and issue edicts and proclamations, but they believed that these edicts should take effect only after a reasonable lapse of time, "as was customary in all commercial treaties among European nations". If the nachodas had been informed of the new measure well in advance, they continued, they would have thought twice "before braving dangers such as attacks by the enemy, gales and thunderstorms, sandbanks and reefs, conflagrations and whatever danger the wild sea harbours for the sailor". Under the present circumstances, they maintained that they were not able to dispose of their cargoes, nor were they able to purchase commodities such as cloth, pepper, cloves et cetera from the Company (VOC 1523, f.557).
The tea sellers joined the chorus of claimants and decried their "imminent ruin" as they were no longer able "to sell the tea as usual to sailors returning home, tea which they had bought on borrowed money". The taxfarmer of the vegetable market and fruit stalls (2260 rixdollars per month) begged to be relieved of his contract. He stated that nearly all tea street

hawkers (of whom there were approximately 200) and a large number of shopkeepers were in arrears with the payment of their monthly taxes of two rixdollars a person. The farmer of the weighing house (530 rixdollars a month) reported that tea was no longer brought to be weighed (VOC 1523, f.561). The porcelain sellers in turn "anticipated their own doom with tear-filled eyes", as they could not sell their merchandise (VOC 1523, f.563). The taxfarmers of the Chinese prahu and tobacco and porkmeat complained that the sources of income were running dry and finally the farmer of the headtax (1400 rixdollars a month) informed the authorities that at least two hundred tea hawkers and another two hundred streetmerchants of porcelain were at the brink of leaving town for the gardens, plantations and sugar mills in the Ommelanden in order to be released from the obligation to pay the headtax and to escape their money lenders (VOC 1523, f.564).

Considering that the money lenders were mainly the town's Dutch burghers, it is clear that the ordinance affected not only the Chinese. The authorities recognized that emergency measures were needed to help out those who had to foot the bill and decided to purchase for the account of the Company the share which originally had been destined for private trade.

In his "Generale Missive" of November 30, 1694, Governor-General Van Outhoorn asked the Gentlemen XVII to change their policies in this respect, for fear that the junks might sail to Johore or Aceh during the next trading season (VOC 1540, f.136v). To support his plea, he provided a balance of the past trading season (VOC 1540, f.130). In 1694 twenty-one junks and one Portuguese vessel had visited Batavia. In all they had purchased and sold the following merchandise:

Table 3.
Balance of the junk trade at Batavia in 1694.

Purchased by the Company:				
119,150	pounds	spelter	9,512	rds
462,309	pounds	assorted porcelain	29,034	rds
93,973	pounds	tea	33,767	rds
6,141	pounds	raw silk	10,921	rds
2,130	pounds	white "gilams" (silk)	4,713	rds
578	pounds	damask	4,846	rds
879	pounds	white "pangsies" (cotton)	1,406	rds
445	pounds	"pelangs" (white damask)	1,876	rds
61,498	pounds	radix China	3,348	rds
19,050	pounds	"galiga" (red paint)	1,053	rds
466,604	pounds	Japanese copper	8,022	rds
			108,498	rds
		sum total in guilders	ƒ 325,533	
Sold by the Company:				
2,323,734	pounds	black pepper	176,184	rds
23,424	pounds	cloves	25,150	rds
976	pounds	nuts	725	rds
2,260	pounds	cinnamon	2,175	rds
4,880	pounds	"catchia" (acacia catechu)	440	rds
66,135	pounds	lead	2,710	rds
		Dutch price goods	23,197	rds
			230,581	rds
		sum total in guilders	ƒ 691,597	

VI   The VOC and the Junk Trade to Batavia

The fact that the sales of the Company had exceeded the purchases from the Chinese junks by ƒ 366,064 served to prove Van Outhoorn's thesis propounded in an earlier letter "that by the frequentations of the Chinese in Batavia, other nations [i.e. Company rivals] did not receive their merchandise and therefore were deprived of the profits made on the sales of these commodities in Europe and Asia" (6-2-1694, GM V:666). In addition to the profits from sales, the junk trade had yielded 17,665 rixdollars in custom fees, headtaxes, safe conduct fees, et cetera (VOC 1540, f.132). The Governor-General added that five VOC ships would have been required to carry the equivalent of what had been purchased from the junks.

The Gentlemen XVII in Patria at long last came to the conclusion that Van Outhoorn was right. March 24, 1695, they formally recognized that the junk trade was a great asset to the well-being of Batavia, and they advised its support by all means necessary (VOC 323). The Batavia High Government noted this official pronouncement with great satisfaction and presumably no longer enforced the "plakaat". At the same time, however, the authorities had their own share of problems with another aspect of the trade.

Stemming the Popular Tide
Fears of the Yellow Peril, of human waves sweeping away the status quo in overseas territories, are as old as colonialism. Those fears not only existed among the colonial authorities but also among the élite of the Chinese residents of Batavia who saw their patronage challenged by the newcomers.

The inflow of "all kinds of rabble from China" was so large that the Chinese Captain and his Lieutenants begged the Governor-General and Council to take action, as they could no longer guarantee for their authority (Plakaatboek III:262). In answer to this request the administration stipulated on May 21, 1690 that all Chinese who had arrived after 1683 had to report within a fortnight at the office of the Chinese Captain, stating their names and occupations as well as the number of their households, slaves included. In all quarters of the town Chinese wardmasters were appointed in addition to the Dutch wardmaster to impose an effective check on illegal immigration.

All resident Chinese were ordered to maintain the traditional hairstyle with a tuft on top of the head. The new "tartar style" with the shaven front and pigtail was banned. This measure undoubtedly was meant to facilitate the differentiation between the resident Chinese and the "orang baru", or newcomers from China, who without exception had shaven foreheads. An unintended result of this order, however, was that Batavia acquired the reputation in China of being a haven for Ming loyalists who refused to wear their hair as stipulated by the Manchu régime.

The nachodas of the junks were informed that they should no longer ship passengers to Batavia; transgressors would pay a penalty of ten rixdollars per person in aid of the Chinese poor relief in town (Plakaatboek III:264-9). This total ban on immigration was a rather unrealistic approach in view of the existing demand for Chinese agricultural labour; moreover, the transport of passengers was the main source of income for the shipowners. For supervisory purposes it was decided that Chinese sailors had to return to their junks each night before six o'clock. Only the nachodas and merchants were allowed to rent houses in town.

These security measures notwithstanding, many sailors and passengers continued to jump ship; the administration then let it be known in 1696 that the departing nachodas would have to pay a fine of 15 rixdollars for every person that was lacking. After some consultation with the Chinese officers in the town, the execution of this order was reversed to the payment of a compensational lump sum of 1200 rixdollars, an amount which gives an indication of the real number of those who stayed behind and who could not be retraced (Plakaatboek III:404).

From 1706 onwards, a limit of one hundred passengers on big junks, or eighty on small ones ("wangkang"), was set (Plakaatboek III:566-7). But this order continually was ignored. The nachodas even landed their passengers along the stretches of the coast that were not sufficiently well patrolled. As a result, sentries were posted near the mouths of the Maronde, Ancol, Ankee and Tangerang rivers in 1707 (Plakaatboek III:578).

This long list of curtailments bears testimony to the fact that the Batavian government faced as many problems as a result of the Fukienese migratory movements as the authorities did in the home province. Push-pull factors affecting the population of that Chinese province proved stronger than the administrative measures taken at either end of the Batavian trade route: to the Fukienese it contributed to the development of an escape route from the rigours of life in "T'ang-shan".

The Advantages and Disadvantages of Indirect Trade
The rash decision made by the Gentlemen XVII to slap a surcharge in 1693 on the transport of tea and porcelain on board their ships was an indication of the growing importance of commodities destined for Europe within the total package of merchandise that the junk trade supplied to Batavia. From this incident we can infer that European demand for luxury items like tea and porcelain stimulated Chinese shipping. As long as the Gentlemen XVII and the Batavian administration were able to agree on the trade's contribution to the prosperity of Batavia and the Company in its totality, the accompanying ills such as illegal trade of Company servants, dependency on Chinese shipping and illegal immigration were accepted on sufferance.

Considering how the Dutch East India Company's commerce throughout Asia was organized around the turn of the century, it becomes apparent that the nature of its link with China ran decidedly counter to the (monopolistic) principles practised elsewhere.

In the Indian Ocean the VOC was reluctant to issue safe conduct passes to Indian ships sailing from the Eastern ports of India to the East Indies. By 1720 Bengal merchants were left only with the coastal trade to South India, Ceylon and the Maldive Islands. K.N. Chaudhuri, the foremost authority on the Indian Ocean trade, does not believe the decline of the market should be advanced as an explanation for this apparent retrenchment in native shipping, but rather that one should blame the growth of "European" shipping and trade in Asia. Bengal traders avoided any embargo which the Dutch might have imposed by shipping their merchandise in vessels flying European colours (Chaudhuri 1978:199). Under these circumstances, the so-called "European country trade" quite understandably could develop quickly and gain the upper hand over native shipping.

Native trade in Southeast Asia was even more seriously affected by the rise of Dutch power. After Malaka and Banten were incorporated in 1641 and 1682 respectively, Aceh and Johore were the only ports left open to Asian and independent European traders in the region. The Dutch policy to exclude foreign shipping from the archipelago continued with one notable exception: the Chinese junks to which safe conduct passes were readily issued. That the VOC thereby became totally dependent upon the Chinese did not seem to bother its directorate.

Batavia's prosperity from the burgeoning junk trade was much envied by the Company's European rivals. Woodes Rogers, who visited the town around the turn of the century, remarked: "The Dutch have all Chinese commodities brought to them cheaper than they can fetch them; and being conveniently situated for the spice trade, they have all in their own hand [...]. Batavia wants no commodities that India affords; it is a pity our East India Company has no settlement to which the Chinese might resort; which I presume would turn to a much better account than our going to China does, where our Traders are but indifferently used. It is about five years since we quitted Banjar [on Borneo] [...] which might have been as serviceable to our East India Company, as Batavia [...] is to the Dutch." (Rogers 1712:407).

Also the French admired the position the Dutch had acquired in the China trade, as the comment of a crew member of the Amphitrite, the first French vessel to visit Canton in 1699 bears witness: "On November 27 Chinese junks stood out to sea [from the mouth of the Pearl River delta] and headed for Batavia. Several among them were flying the Dutch flag, for they were loaded on Dutch account. In this way the Dutch merchants of Batavia trade with all of China through the good offices of Chinese sailors. Thus they obtain the products that are most sought after. They get them cheaply, without being exposed to the exactions which one cannot evade in all the ports of that empire. They also evade the possibility of non-payment, because those articles they have advanced to the Chinese are (if necessary) immediately reimbursed through bills drawn upon Chinese establishments in Batavia or Banten." (Madrolle 1901:49-50).

A wangkang or small size Amoy trader.

In addition to the fact that the Dutch, unlike their European rivals, were not subject to high duties and extortions on the China coast, they could boast of a favourable trade balance with the Chinese. The VOC actually received more income from the sale of tropical products to Chinese merchants than it spent in purchasing merchandise from them. During the first decades of the 18th century the surplus in favour of the Dutch varied between 100,000 and 500,000 guilders (De Hullu 1917:39). An attendant advantage was the fact that the Chinese merchandise did not have to be paid for in silver.

In view of all these advantages and the praise of their competitors, the directorship of the VOC can hardly be blamed for being slow in recognizing that its trade link with China was not as ideal and stable as it seemed. De Hullu has shown in his pioneering study on the China trade of the VOC that as early as in 1702 the Gentlemen XVII had reproached the High Government in Batavia for selling their merchandise under its real market value. Pepper, for instance, was sold at such a low price to the Chinese junk skippers that these would in turn be able to sell it to the English and French in Canton for their return cargo to Europe (De Hullu 1917:39).

Considerations of this kind, however, pale before the much more fundamental question of whether the biggest European trading company in Asia could afford to stay away from the potentially rich market of Canton. By pinning its faith upon the intermediary role of the junk skippers, the VOC assumed a passive stance and thus ran the risk of being too slow in reacting to political developments in the domain of foreign commerce in China, or even to fluctuations in market prices. This in fact happened. The Dutch East India Company literally missed the boat, first by arriving too late in Canton, and second by losing out in the tea trade, the luxury item it actually had introduced to the West.

Changing Perspectives
It would be beyond the scope of this study on Chinese trade to Batavia to deal extensively with the rise of Canton and the sudden emergence of tea as the most important export commodity for the European market. Moreover, the subject has been studied in depth by De Hullu and put in a wider perspective by the Danish scholar Kristof Glamann (1981:212-43). What concerns us here is how the combination of the direct European trade to Canton and the dynamics of the tea trade affected the Chinese junk trade to Batavia during the first decades of the eighteenth century, and how the directorship of the VOC responded to the challenge posed by its European rivals.

The port of Canton was opened to foreign shipping at the same time as Amoy: 1686. While Amoy remained basically the home port for Chinese overseas shipping, Canton played host, as it had done for more than a millennium before, to foreign shipping coming to its roadstead, Whampoa (HMC II:177). The hospitable conditions at Canton did not fail to attract English and French shipping. Already in 1701 the English began to trade along the banks of the Pearl River. Interestingly, their Chinese counterparts in these commercial transactions generally were not local Cantonese merchants but rather traders from Fukien. Like the Europeans, they visited Canton in the trading season, returning afterwards to Amoy. Later in the 18th century, these Fukienese merchants settled permanently at Canton. They were connected to the same network that served the Dutch in Batavia, but their position in Canton was quite different and it showed in the cost price and the quality of the tea which they offered for sale.⁸

Speed and quality control are the two key words in the trade with perishable merchandise, and this is especially true in the case of tea: according to contemporary popular opinion, it should be treated like a delicate young lady, "een fijne joffer" (Bierens de Haan 1918:25). Bohea tea, the best-known brand, was grown in the Wu I mountains of northern Fukien. Picked in summer, the crops reached Canton in early autumn. European vessels at Canton thus had the first choice and could ship the luxury item, well-packed in lead-lined boxes, directly to Europe. The junk merchants would buy what remained, often tea of second quality, pack it in bamboo bundles and sail to Batavia where it was put up for sale at much higher prices than at Canton. Glamann shows that in the pre-1720 period the cost price might have been as much as twice as high in Batavia as in Canton. Indiscriminate handling and packing, as well as a delay of a few more months before the tea could at last be shipped to Europe by special "tea ships" in March put the VOC at a clear disadvantage with its European competitors.⁹

The Chinese Emperor Steps In
Ever since Valentijn, traditional Dutch colonial historiographers have maintained that a hot-headed decision by Governor-General Christoffel van Swoll (1713-1718) brought about the sudden cancellation of Chinese shipping to Batavia in 1718 (Valentijn 1724 IV:348). Troubled by mounting problems with Chinese vagrants in the Ommelanden and the outrageous prices of the tea at Batavia, the Governor-General issued on March 2, 1717 a strong edict which prohibited the illegal entry of immigrants to Batavia and fixed the price of tea.

The extract resolution of January 30, 1717, shows the predicament in which Van Swoll was placed in the trading season of that year. Two junks from Amoy, a small and a large one, arrived with 248 and 440 men on board respectively, although they were only allowed to carry 80 and 100 sailors respectively. From the ensuing discussion regarding the punishment that should be handed out for this transgression, it transpired that although according to the "plakaat" of May 28, 1706, ten rixdollars should be paid for every extra passenger, in reality a maximum fine of 1000 rixdollars had been imposed, regardless of how many illegal immigrants were on board in excess of one hundred. This time the authorities drew the line: the two junk skippers were fined 5280 rials in total, and because the Dutch did not feel disposed to keep the 528 illegal immigrants under custody for a period of five months, their supervision was passed on to the nachodas themselves (VOC 1876, f.2456-9).

On March 2, 1717, the purchase price of three different qualities of tea was unilaterally fixed by the Batavian authorities at forty, sixty and eighty rixdollars respectively, and this after the Chinese had been adamant about lowering their prices.¹⁰ Glamann, who subscribes to the theory that Van Swoll played his cards badly, writes that "the Chinese Emperor answered by prohibiting his subjects to sail to Batavia" (Glamann 1981: 217; De Hullu 1917:42). Chinese sources, however, suggest that these measures had little to do with the avoidance by the junks of the Batavian market as a result of high-handed behaviour by the Dutch: the causes should rather be sought at the Chinese terminus of the trade link. In a proclamation of December 9, 1716, a few months prior to Van Swoll's edict, the Chinese emperor decreed that Chinese commercial ships would no longer be allowed to sail to the Southern Ocean. This new maritime prohibition was a reaction to mounting piracy on the China coast and the illegal export of rice from the Kiangsu and Chekiang provinces. According to the imperial court, "Luzon and Batavia served as asylum for the Chinese outlaws", and "were the headquarters of the Chinese pirates" (Fu Loshu 1966:122).

Careful reading of the data in the VOC archives proves that the Batavian authorities were placed in possession of all the facts at an early date - undoubtedly to their great relief. In the "Generale Missive" of November 30, 1717, they had already informed the Gentlemen XVII that they expected fewer arrivals from China during the approaching trading season. From talks with Chinese nachodas, it became evident "that the Chinese shipping would be restricted on account of the advanced age of the emperor, so that no opportunity would be given for creating disturbances to the detriment of the empire which, according to rumors, is experiencing a period of instability in its public order" (GM VII:323).

These notions were confirmed a few months later: not a single Chinese junk dropped anchor at Batavia. News from Malaka in early February concerning a Chinese prohibition of overseas trade was further specified by information gained from the crew of two English vessels Townsend and Essex, which had left Canton in January and had stopped over at Batavia. The Chinese emperor had indeed issued an edict forbidding all overseas trade to all ports except those in Japan to his subjects: however, after vehement protests from the "wealthy province of Fukien" the trade route to Tonkin and Cochin China was re-opened on October 26, 1717. The extreme security measures which were to accompany this commerce made it virtually impossible for the shipowners to fit out junks, as they feared mass desertion by sailors in Cochin China and they had to guarantee the sailors' return (VOC 1890, f.1716).

Trade expeditions to Manila and Batavia remained out of the question "because the Chinese residing there wear their hair and clothing in the ancient manner"; this mode constituted "lèse majesté" as proclaimed in the translation of the imperial edict which the English sailors had brought along. The same edict made it known that the Fukienese kin of Chinese merchants in Batavia who did not immediately return home would be banished as slaves to Tartary (Edict 10-2-1717, VOC 1890, f.1715v).

The ban on Chinese overseas shipping stayed effectively in force until 1722. But just as had been the case in the years of the maritime prohibition in the preceding century, Portuguese ships from Macao were quick to fill in the void, or at least part of it (De Hullu 1917:44). Consequently, the Batavian trade with China never came to a complete halt; the advance of money for the purchase of tea was, however, transferred to the Portuguese.

In 1719 the Gentlemen XVII instructed the Batavian High Government to buy unlimited quantities of tea at Batavia. Their aim to flood the European market and thus to discourage the competition was achieved within a year or two: tea was hawked in the streets of Amsterdam from wheelbarrows by the end of 1721! (Bierens de Haan 1918:28).

The competition which the Gentlemen XVII were combatting came from the interlopers of the Ostend Company. This Company, situated in the Austrian Netherlands but mainly working with Dutch capital, had received its first cargo of tea from China in 1719. The VOC saw its monopoly threatened and, in addition to the dumping practices mentioned above, began negotiations with the Austrian Emperor to put the Ostend trade to an end. A settlement was finally reached on May 31, 1727 whereby the Emperor committed himself to forbid his subjects any further navigation to the Far East for a period of seven years.

Meanwhile, in Batavia the interruption of the junk trade played havoc with the local economy. In January 1719 the Chinese farmers of local taxes were already 22,352 rixdollars in arrears (GM VII:394). This unhappy situation came to an end in 1722 when maritime prohibitions were lifted at Canton shortly after the K'ang-hsi emperor died. To their great relief the Governor General and Council ascertained that their fears of no Chinese junks coming to Batavia any longer, since so many westerners now sailed to Canton, proved to be unfounded (GM VII:513). In 1722 several junks did show up at the Batavian roadstead, and on March 31 the Governor General wrote that Portuguese assistance would no longer be needed (Opkomst IX:78). Indeed, in the following year, the junk trade to Batavia was resumed as if nothing had ever happened: 21 junks dropped anchor at the Batavian roadstead. Chinese overseas trade from Amoy, however, was only formally opened in 1727 under a series of new regulations. Before we focus on these Chinese administrative measures, we shall briefly assess how the interruption of the Chinese trade affected the policy making of the VOC.

Although the Governor-General and Council were quite content with the fast recovery of the junk trade, the Gentlemen XVII began to have doubts about what seemed to them a Chinese monopoly of the trade. Time and again they exhorted the Batavian Government to send one or more ships to Canton to scout out the local market situation, but all this was to no avail. When the Governor-General and Council met on May 19, 1724, to discuss whether they should follow the orders recently received from the Gentlemen XVII and to send two ships to Canton, they chose to refrain from doing so with the rather lame excuse that it was too late in the monsoon. Their real feelings on the issue can be fathomed from the conclusion they drew: "it would be contradictory to send ships for trading purposes to China and to promote at the same time the frequentation of the junks at the Batavian roadstead" (VOC 2001, f.407).

In 1727 the Gentlemen XVII, weary of so much obstinacy, took decisive action themselves. Even though a settlement with the Austrian emperor was reached, they went through with their plans and sent a ship with a capital of 300,000 guilders' worth of silver on board directly from Amsterdam to China. As a result of this bold move by the directors, Batavia was checkmated and excluded from the direct trade with China. The High Government received, however, the instruction that it should proceed with purchasing tea through the junk trade on the condition that it was reasonably priced and well-packed (Bierens de Haan 1918:29).

The Reorganization of China's Overseas Trade
At about the same time that the Austrian emperor concluded an agreement with the Dutch East India Company whereby he pledged to forbid his subjects in the Southern Netherlands to fit out ships for the China trade, the Yung-cheng emperor in Peking formally granted his Fukienese subjects the right to trade again in Southeast Asia. It will be remembered that his predecessor, the K'ang-hsi emperor, had closed the trade with the Nanyang for such reasons as the illegal export of rice from the Kiangsu and Chekiang provinces and the alleged presence of Ming loyalists and pirates in Batavia and Manila. The exhortations to return within three years time to the Chinese merchants residing abroad when the prohibition was announced in 1717 had scarcely been followed up.

At the behest of the Governor-General of Fukien, Kao Ch'i-cho, the maritime prohibition (which had already been lifted in Kwangtung a few years earlier), was at long last lifted in Yung-cheng 5 (1727). "From that year onwards, trade continued without interruption", states the "Ch'ing-ch'ao Wen-hsien T'ung-k'ao" (CWT:7465). This source also clearly states the new regulations which were introduced to achieve closer government control of trade. These regulations applied to ship-owning; security systems applied among the merchants; the owners and the crews; emigration; limitations on or prohibitions of certain export items, and at a later date also abatement procedures for junks which imported rice from abroad.

No Overseas Chinese residing in Manila and Batavia, however, were allowed to return: "In both places bandits are numerous. Our people from the interior wishing to gain profits usually remain there; we must prevent this", the K'ang-hsi emperor had observed ten years previously. As only two thousand people obeyed the order to return within the stipulated three years, his successor saw no reason to show any leniency for those who now were professing remorse (Fu Lo-shu 1966:158-9).

In Amoy, organized trading bodies, the so-called "Yang-hang", which were responsible for establishing mutual guarantees and for paying customs dues on behalf of the overseas trading vessels, were installed. According to Ng, the Yang-hang were not a completely new institution but a logical development of the existing authorized firms in Amoy dealing with foreign goods, the so-called "Yang-huo-hang" (Ng 1983:168-70). Merchants who intended to send ships to the Nanyang had to report before the fourth month, and those returning before the tenth month. The prospective sailor first had to seek a guarantee from neighbours in his native district. Upon receipt of this guarantee the local authorities issued him a licence with personal details. The port officials at the departure point would check this document and grant a sailing permit. This regulation was relaxed in 1731, when a licence became obtainable in Amoy (Ng 1983:171).

The amount of rice on board was rationed at 250 piculs for a large and 200 piculs for a medium-sized junk Batavia-bound.[11] This was one of the reasons for the "incomprehensible and sudden price increase of the rice" noted at Batavia in 1731. The High Government promptly forbade the export of rice, probably without knowing the real reason for its sudden purchase by the Chinese upon arrival (Plakaatboek IV:283). In 1736 the emperor permitted those who had left China before 1717 and who had remained in Southeast Asia since that time to return to the mother country. Those who had left during the period of maritime prohibition (1717-1727) were still refused entry. In 1741, when the Nanyang trade reached its full bloom (HMC II:179), this prohibition was further relaxed when the censor Wang P'i-lieh presented a report to the throne in which he again explained the reasoning behind the limitations on sojourns abroad. In case a Chinese merchant travelling to the Nanyang was not able to settle his accounts, he would have to stay over until the next year, a practice called "ya-tung" (detained over the winter). If he should stay much longer, this might indicate that he could not be trusted, Wang added. He thought that those who returned after three of four years should be welcomed back, but that they should never be allowed again to leave. His proposals were accepted. This may have been the reason why in 1750 after a many years' stay in Java Ch'en I-lao, a former Chinese lieutenant at Batavia, thought he could safely return to China, but upon his arrival in China, he was arrested and banished.[12]

Finally, the Governor of Fukien, Ch'en Hung-mou, petitioned the court in 1754 that all overseas Chinese emigrants from the Fukien coastal prefectures, "half the population of which depended on navigation for a living", should be allowed to return home even if they had remained a long time in the barbarian lands solely because they had not sold their commodities or cleared their debts. Also the wives and concubines, sons and daughters of those Chinese who had died abroad, he thought, should be allowed to return. The emperor agreed (Fu Lo-shu 1966:193).

Thus the most severe regulations of the K'ang-hsi and Yung-cheng era were gradually relaxed over the years in view of the recognition that an overseas trade network could not function without a more or less permanent presence of Chinese abroad. This shows the imperial policies towards overseas trade to have been much more lenient than is commonly observed.

Dream or Nightmare?
In the 1728-1733 period, the Amsterdam chamber of the VOC fitted out six expeditions to China. These non-stop voyages did not turn out to be the breakthrough the Gentlemen XVII had hoped for. Tea and porcelain had to be purchased in Canton with silver coins for lack of marketable Dutch merchandise, and the crews and merchants of the ships proved to be prone to smuggling. At the same time the High Government at Batavia had managed to bring the cost price at Batavia down to the Canton level (Glamann 1981:236). Even in Amsterdam voices could soon be heard saying that the trade might be better managed and controlled at Batavia than in Holland. Incidental to these main issues was the fact that ships from Batavia could reach China earlier than those of their European rivals, who, when leaving from either Europe or India, would have to await favourable monsoon winds in the Indian Ocean before entering the China Sea (Steur 1984:59). Finally, it was felt that involvement of Batavia Castle would provide the Gentlemen XVII with tropical products such as tin, pepper, and cloves as a means of payment for the Chinese commodities destined for the Dutch market. When informed of these plans, the Batavian High Government was in a quandary: if it were to send ships to China, the junk trade would probably suffer. Finally, the Governor-General and Council relented a bit and wrote to Holland that they consented to take in hand commerce between Batavia and Canton carried out by VOC ships, provided the junk trade would not be impeded. Counterarguments by the Gentlemen XVII, which expressed their intent that curtailment of the junk trade connection would do away once and for all with the problem of the VOC personnel's trade in tea on the shipping route home, met with the High Government's curt reply that they did not agree with such drastic measures. They believed the Company "should act like a good gardener, who will not fell a tree on account of one diseased branch" (De Hullu 1917:138). During the debate held within the Council of the Indies about the ways and means of organizing the China trade, one viewpoint at variance with the others was presented: even though fellow councillors thought his proposals "a simple nightmare", the dissenting voice of the Councillor Extraordinary Wijbrand Blom, a staunch advocate of the junk trade and an opponent of any kind of trade by VOC ships to China, is worth paying attention to, if only because of the precious information his plea provides concerning the character and size of the junk trade in the 1730s. Blom aired his views upon different occasions during the at times fierce debate.

For clarity's sake only the gist of his long-winded remarks will be reproduced here. Blom set himself the task "to enlighten the Gentlemen XVII who never had truly understood the real character of the Chinese trade to Batavia". He warned that disruption of the junk trade as a result of the monopolization by the VOC of the trade between Canton and Batavia would cause considerable damage to the town's economy "as had been observed only a few years earlier" when the Chinese trade came to a halt as a result of the Emperor's maritime prohibitions (VOC 2219, f.38-9).

As an illustration of the size of the Chinese trade Blom computed the total weight of the commodities sold by the Company to the Chinese merchants at Batavia as follows: 3,000,000 pounds of pepper, 1,000,000 pounds of tin, 500,000 pounds of lead, 1,000,000 pounds of sappanwood, and 50,000 pounds of gum-lac.

In all, about 5,550,000 pounds of merchandise (in volume about 7,000,000 pounds) was annually shipped on board Chinese junks to China. Blom figured out that if the Company were to ship these goods to China, seven ships of the 145-foot charter type would have to be fitted out for a period of nine months. On the total VOC sales of the above commodities (which amounted to 565,523 guilders in the preceding trading season) a net profit of 380,538 guilders had been obtained. This 67.25 % profit compared very favourably with the meagre 45 % in the 1680s (VOC 2219, f.82). The total income the Company enjoyed from the sale of tropical products, harbour duties and taxfarms, Blom estimated at 700,000 guilders a year. Turning to the other business dealings of the Chinese in Batavia (those outside the direct sphere of the Company), the Councillor calculated that the Chinese annually purchased and sailed away with about 1,200,000 rixdollars worth of local merchandise; he further stated that they were only able to do this because of the huge quantity of tea they were selling. In 1732 no less than 3,740,000 pounds of this luxury item had been imported by the junks.

If the purchase of tea for the Dutch market was to be limited to Canton and the sale of this commodity to be forbidden in Batavia, as the Gentlemen XVII had suggested, this in Blom's opinion inevitably affected adversely the purchasing power of the junk traders, which meant in turn that the Company would sell less to them and would receive less income from taxes. It would, of course, also imply a smaller turnover in the extra-VOC sectors. Reminding the Directors that the sugar cultivation in the Ommelanden was at an impasse, Blom maintained that the town's economy should not be dealt another blow by curtailing transactions in tea (VOC 2219, f.81v).

The advantages of the junk trade seemed self-evident to Blom for other reasons as well. Just as Van Outhoorn had remarked on an earlier occasion, he pointed out that the running costs of a junk sank into insignificance beside those of the average VOC ship. The Chinese owner had only to fit out the vessel; the crew received hardly any or no wages, and an average of 130 to 200 passengers on each vessel yielded the owner a handsome return in transportation costs (10 rixdollars per person). Blom acknowledged that the Achilles heel of the junk trade was the inefficient way in which orders were placed, but he saw room for improvement. He proposed that every year six complete sets of samples be sent with six different junks to China; in such a way it should be possible to overcome the frightening disincentives of cultural and geographic distance. When his fellow councillors remarked that it would be impossible to check and compare the cost prices in Canton and Batavia if the Company had no representative in China, Blom retorted that this was an academic rather than a real question and added with some malice "that they might know from their own housekeeping", thereby implying that his fellow members of the Council of the Indies had never experienced such problems in their private dealings with the junk skippers (VOC 2218, f.7349, Res GG and C 13-3-1733). These last remarks especially caused ill feeling among his colleagues. Director-General Michiel Westpalm felt called upon to refute Blom's arguments as he feared that their general purport "would be thought of very favourably by anybody who did not know from experience the real character of the Chinese and the sly intrigues of this crafty people, so greedy for gain". Private deals were of a different order than those of the Company, Westpalm countered. Moreover, he denied that the running costs of Chinese shipping were as low as Blom asserted: The Chinese borrowed money at a bottomry of 35 to 45% and in addition had to pay all kinds of tolls and taxes in Batavia. This meant that they would have to make a profit of at least 50% in order to avoid remaining in debt.[13]

In March 1734, the Gentlemen XVII cut the Gordian knot. They decided to keep both options open for the meantime and ordered the High Government to manage the VOC trade with Canton, on the understanding that the tea trade would also continue at Batavia. Under this new arrangement, every year two VOC ships were fitted out in Holland for the voyage to China. Contrary to the former China-bound vessels, these ships were loaded with European merchandise designated for Batavia. These goods were replaced in the Indies by tin, pepper, sappanwood and other tropical products which in turn could be bartered for tea, porcelain and spelter in China.

Under this new policy the shipping links thrived in parallel for the first few years. The junks brought tea in ever greater quantities to Java's shore. The peak was reached in 1738, when the Company purchased at Batavia 15,229 piculs of tea at a price of 412,198 rixdollars (VOC 2425, f.3241-2). From the archival data it becomes clear that the Batavian government promoted the trade at Canton and Batavia at the same time and continuously compared the quality and cost price of tea, silk, and porcelain. This may be an indication that the two shipping links actually were played off against each other.

Table 4.
Tea purchased by the VOC at Batavia (average per annum). (Based on Overgekomen Brieven en Papieren series, VOC archives.)

	quantity (piculs)	value (rixdollars)
1701 - 1710	400	?
1711 - 1720	745	46,215
1721 - 1730	3439	184,003
1731 - 1740	6048	149,023
1741 - 1750	810	16,347
1751 - 1760	0	0
1761 - 1770	0	0
1771 - 1780	3	116
1781 - 1790	4	147
1791 - 1793	0	0

The outcome of these ongoing tests was that the quality of the silk remained roughly the same although the purchase price in Batavia was about 3.5 rixdollars per picul higher, as was to be expected (VOC 2332, f.3457-9, 4-4-1736). Rather striking is the great representation of the Chinese officers in the tea trade. Captain Ni Hoekong, who also possessed several sugar plantations, was the most important merchant in porcelain and tea.[14] The tea was sold through a bargaining process whereby a deal was made after the fourth bid. After the trading season of 1740-41, purchases slumped; the reasons for this are not difficult to find. The aftermath of the Chinese massacre, which occurred in October 1740, once again brought the junk shipping to a halt.

A Debate at the Imperial Court
Governor-General Adriaan Valckenier (1737-1741), whose hands were stained by the bloody Chinese massacre, feared retribution from the Chinese authorities, and therefore sent a letter to the Chien-lung Emperor to place him in possession of all the facts. The contents of his letter were slanted in presentation - to say the least. According to Valckenier, rumours had been spread in Batavia that Chinese vagrants were being dumped in the sea by the Dutch authorities. During the disturbances which ensued, Chinese criminals had set fire to the town "whereupon we had to reciprocate violence with violence, which has resulted in a ghastly carnage in which to our grief some innocent people have been killed". Rather telling are also the motives which Valckenier supplied for the sending of the letter: "We have deemed it necessary to render a true and detailed account to Your Majesty, for fear that other people, jealous of the flourishing trade that the Dutch rejoice in Your Majesty's empire [here he referred to the Canton trade], may depict these incidents in false colours, with the aim to give Your Imperial Majesty the wrong impression of our lawful intervention, so that [eventually] our trade will be hurt and theirs will be favoured" (Huysers 1789:65-72).

In a case study on the deliberations held in Chinese government circles in connection with the Batavian massacre, Jennifer Cushman has focussed on the Governor of Kwangsi and Kwangtung, Duke Ch'ing Fu, whose thoughtful assessment of the situation contributed to the benevolent attitude of the Emperor towards the affair (Cushman 1978). Ch'ing Fu's memorial to the throne was actually an exposé on the contribution of foreign trade to the economic viability of the southeastern coastal provinces and as such fitted in well with the views propounded by many of his predecessors.

Ch'ing Fu's arguments by no means fell on deaf ears in court circles. His views were actually acclaimed by the imperial preceptor Ts'ai Hsin, a native of Fukien province, who opposed a possible maritime prohibition on the following grounds:
"There are more than one hundred ocean vessels in Fukien and Kwangtung. The construction costs of the large ones amount to ten thousand taels; even the small ones cost four to five thousand taels. If prohibition were proclaimed all these vessels would be laid up, and five to six hundred thousand people would lose their jobs.

The stocks of merchandise at seaports like Amoy and Canton present a total value of several million taels. If prohibition were proclaimed bankruptcy would result, and the people's goods would be wasted.

When the ships come and go, there are thousands of families of destitute people who look to this trade for their food. If prohibition were proclaimed the resulting situation would render the people homeless and make them wander from place to place, as there would be no food left for thousands of persons because neither the merchants would have merchandise, nor would the farmers have produce.

This is how distress would show itself in the short term, but after several years the situation would grow even more serious. Fukien and Kwangtung both use foreign [silver] coins, of which annually close to 10 million are imported. To sum up, if prohibition were proclaimed this annual income of some ten million would suddenly disappear and not only the common people's livelihood would be distressed, but the national treasury would also be short of money." (Tien 1956:19).

From the "Ch'ing-ch'ao Wen-hsien T'ung-k'ao", which records the discussion at the Court, it transpires that the debate was really a confrontation between officials who either advocated or opposed unfettered trade. The acting Viceroy of Fukien, Ts'e Leng, wrote that the Chinese who had been massacred had already been residing for a long time in Java and had repeatedly ignored the Emperor's order to return. They all deserved to be punished according to Chinese law, but their ghastly massacre was to be pitied. He believed the Dutch had only dared to perpetrate this murder, because they did not hold the Emperor in sufficient awe because of the great distance of Java from China. He petitioned the crown to forbid the Nanyang trade for fear "that the cruel Barbarians may also agitate against our commercial ships" at Batavia.

A censor from Kwangtung province, Li Ching-fang, countered these arguments by saying that nine out of ten junks sailed to Southeast Asia. The four maritime provinces received such a large income from the taxes levied on this shipping route that the prohibition would incur losses for the administration amounting to several hundred thousands of tael. But considering that the Nanyang trade was a "people's trade", a prohibition would be even more harmful to the traders who all worked according to the principle that they first had to purchase merchandise to sell it overseas: "for the circulation of merchandise, stocks have to be built up". Li Ching-fang therefore proposed to continue the trade with Southeast Asia, but to temporarily stop the trade with Batavia until the Dutch showed remorse. This policy was originally accepted by the Imperial court (CWT:7465).

According to the Imperial Court records of November 1, 1742, Ch'ing Fu in turn pointed out that the Dutch had already shown repentance by sending a letter and actually "pleaded with our junk sailors to do business as usual". Since the Dutch had no intention of disturbing the transactions of the guest merchants at Batavia, he petitioned that trade be permitted again (CCT:460).

The court officials summarized the opinions advanced as follows: "Some officials petition us not to prohibit the southern ocean trade; others petition us to prohibit communication with Java temporarily. Although the opinions are divided, they all share Your Majesty's sublime principle of kindness to foreigners. Now if the king of Java [i.e. the Dutch Governor-General] repents and wishes to reform in order to receive Your Majesty's Universal Grace, then Your servants petition that the various barbarians in the southern ocean be allowed to trade with us as usual." The emperor approved of this proposal (Fu Lo-shu 1966:174).

Was kindness to foreigners or indifference to the plight of the overseas Chinese the main motive for this imperial approval? Cushman believes, and I think rightly so, that the decision was reached on account of less ephemeral grounds: it was based on a clear-sighted recognition of the needs of the maritime border provinces (Cushman 1978:16).

C. *The Decline of the Junk Trade: 1740-1790*

Without doubt the junk trade to Batavia was dealt a staggering blow by the tragic occurrences of 1740. A large part of the infrastructure and the organization of the trade in Batavia simply disappeared because many of

Chinese crude porcelain for the Southeast Asian market from the Geldermalsen wreck, 1750.

the Chinese brokers and key figures had been either killed of banished.[15] The massacre, however, had a transient effect only and cannot be advanced as the main reason why, after its resumption in 1743, the junk trade shrank within a few decades to a shadow of its former self.

It is often suggested that the decision of the Gentlemen XVII to reincorporate the China trade under their own management marked the beginning of the demise of the junk trade. Unhappy with the performance of the High Government at Batavia, who were using part of the profits of the China trade to underwrite the losses incident at the Batavian entrepot, the Gentlemen XVII installed in 1756 the so-called China Committee at Amsterdam, which was charged with the management of direct trade between Holland and China (De Hullu 1923). Batavia was thus side-tracked for the second time and lost its cardinal role in the Dutch China trade definitely. The ships of the China Committee made short calls only at the town on their way to China in order to load pepper, nutmeg, cloves and sappanwood for the Çanton market. In a letter of October 10, 1759, the members of the China Committee advised the High Government "to encourage the junk trade with suitable expedients (bekwame middelen) because it was very profitable to the colony", but stipulated at the same time that the Chinese merchants should not be allowed to ship those goods to Batavia in which the Company itself traded (VOC 4542; Jörg 1982:38).

As Table 4 clearly shows, tea purchases by the Company from the Chinese at Batavia declined in the 1740s and came to an abrupt end in the 1750s. There is no doubt that the junk trade as supplier to the European market declined to insignificance. Yet this is not the whole story; how, for example, should the decline of the junk trade to Batavia as a primary supplier of Chinese merchandise to Southeast Asia be explained? Did the High

VI The VOC and the Junk Trade to Batavia

Government encourage the trade "with suitable expedients" or did it actually hamper it? In other words, was the junk shipping reduced in volume due to "the strangling grip of capitalism" as Tien Ju-kang suggested? These are the far-reaching questions which I shall try to answer in the following pages.

The best way to investigate the policy of the High Government vis à vis the junk shipping is to study over a longer period of time the resolutions that were taken during the Council meetings at Batavia castle. A host of "plakaten" leave no doubt that the Batavian government was anxious to encourage the trade and to preserve it, from the early 1740s onwards. The fact that many plakaten had to be reiterated and adapted would suggest that they were often not heeded. Plakaten, in fact the published resolutions taken by the Governor-General and Council, and therefore comprehensive statements of the aims and methods of the High Government, suffer from obvious defects as a source for historical research. They amount to little more than the expression of the will of the authorities, who trusted that they would be adhered to and carried out upon publication. Whether these edicts were carried out is often hard to establish. Although this definitely shows the weak point of the plakaat as a historical source, it should be added that whenever a plakaat was not heeded, the authorities would be forced to reconsider their standpoint and to contemplate whether to persist or to leave the situation as it was. Deliberations concerning such matters are as a rule summarized and constitute important data in themselves.

Not all the bureaucratic measures taken with regard to the junk trade will be listed here. A piecemeal treatment would obscure any pattern of decision-making which produced these plakaten. If we start from the premise that the policies of the VOC toward junk shipping brought about the decline of that trade (as Tien Ju-kang has suggested) it goes without saying that we should investigate those particular aspects of the junk trade the Dutch authorities focussed on in their decision-making. The interference of the High Government in the junk trade can be listed under the following headings: a. tolls and duties; b. immigration procedures, and c. restriction of navigation by opening and closing certain ports in the archipelago to the junks.

a. Tolls and duties. Great pains were taken by the High Government to simplify and speed up the bureaucratic procedures surrounding the levying of tolls and charges in the 1740s. At times such efforts backfired. One of the first instances in which Governor-General Gustaaf Willem van Imhoff (1742-1750) interfered with the China trade was in institutionalizing the illegal trade in some 250,000 pounds of tea which the homeward bound sailors annually stowed away in their hammocks and trunks. On June 25, 1743, Van Imhoff proclaimed that the following year he would designate one or two vessels to ship this previously illegal freight, and thus "enable the sailors to invest their earnings in such a way that it might not hurt the interests of the Company" (Bierens de Haan 1918:37). On the face of it, the transport fee of four rixdollars per picul was a remarkable improvement on that levied in 1694, which had amounted to one rixdollar per pound, and technically speaking this should have stimulated private purchases. The measure was meant to stimulate the junk trade as well, but the following year it turned out to have had the opposite effect. Scarcity of ready money and fears for a slack market in Holland because of the improvement in techniques for handling private transactions kept the sailors in Batavia from purchasing tea.[16] It may well be that once the excitement of smuggling tea was removed the sailors looked for another item which could impress the "folks at home".

Because the Company had already placed its tea order at Canton, Chinese merchants at Batavia were left with their merchandise and could not even pay the import taxes. To meet them halfway, the authorities lowered these charges by remitting them to 20% of the usual figure (19-6-1744, Plakaatboek V:149). They also agreed to waive the normal entry port duties "as an inducement to the Chinese to continue and enlarge their trade".

Especially in the field of import and export duties, Van Imhoff and his council saw room for experimentation. On December 10, 1743, they had already announced that the junk trade should be exempted from the normal formalities surrounding the levying of import and export duties, the so-called "rechten van de boom". In line with earlier practice at Batavia, the value of their cargoes would be roughly estimated so that the inspection would not have to be so rigorously carried out as would be the case if it were done by a tax farmer. "Thus this shipping will be slightly favoured", it was added (Plakaatboek V:114).

In 1746 all junks were freed from this rough-estimate-upon-arrival procedure, provided they paid a lump sum which was fixed in relation to the size of the ship and its port of origin. This regulation, really a repetition of one applied one hundred years earlier (1644, Plakaatboek II:192) was to be tried out over a period of three years. Charges were as follows:

	Amoy	Canton	Ningpo
large junks	550 rds	750 rds	900 rds
small junks	420 rds	700 rds	750 rds

The tariffs clearly show the difference in value of cargoes brought by the junks from these three ports (Plakaatboek V:430). The relatively high tariff for the Ningpo junks was probably related to the cargoes of Japanese copper and Chinese gold which these vessels used to carry to Batavia (Plakaatboek IX:16).

When the three trial years were over, the authorities gave up the redemption fee arrangement as they believed Chinese shipping no longer needed special treatment. On December 9, 1749 a tax of 6% was fixed on the imports of the Chinese junks and another of 4% on their exports. Chinese trade was now treated on a par with all Indonesian shipping (Plakaatboek V:635, 9-12-1749). Within a fortnight the Governor-General and Council partly changed their minds, instituting a fixed lump sum to be paid on the exported merchandise (Plakaatboek V:639, 23-12-1749).

	Amoy	Canton	Ningpo
large junks	1100 rds	1500 rds	1800 rds
small junks	840 rds	1400 rds	1500 rds

Two years later the 6% import tax was also changed into the fixed payment of a lump sum equal to the redemption fee paid for export merchandise when it was admitted that the junks, which always arrived in the rainy season, had to wait too long for the inspection by the customs. This prolonged delay was harmful to the merchandise, which often got soaked during the tedious inspections (26-6-1751, Plakaatboek VI:68). Consequently, the import and export duties of the junk trade were fixed as follows:

VI The VOC and the Junk Trade to Batavia

	Amoy	Canton	Ningpo
large junks	2200 rds	3000 rds	3600 rds
small junks	1680 rds	2800 rds	3000 rds

These figures were maintained until the early 1790's when the decay of the trade made a reduction desirable.

Among other positive measures that were taken in later years to modify existing regulations and speed up the operation of the trade was the decision to institute a lump sum payment at the weighing house, at the request of the Chinese nachodas on May 24, 1774. These pointed out that they paid a fixed redemption fee of 2200 rixdollars for a large, and 1680 rixdollars for a small junk, which theoretically amounted to about 6% of the total value of the cargo. As the tolls of the weighing house were equal to 1% of the cargo, they proposed to pay a fixed sum of 336:32 rixdollars for a large, and 280 rixdollars for a small junk. This simple calculation would imply that the average cargo of a large junk was valued at about 33,600 rixdollars (Plakaatboek VIII:864). The Governor-General approved the proposal but valued the junk cargoes somewhat higher and fixed a redemption fee of 600 rixdollars for large and 500 for small Ningpo junks. Cantonese junks were valued at 500 and 400 rixdollars and the Amoy junks at 400 and 300 respectively (Plakaatboek VIII:897). The relatively low value of the Amoy cargoes can be explained by the fact that these junks were primarily used as passenger vessels, transporting in addition cheap merchandise like pots, porcelain and pans for the Java market. Finally the decision of the High Government to cease permitting the detention of junks by last-minute legal proceedings should be noted. All legal claims had to be put forward before the first of June.[17]

Having focussed on several positive measures that were taken by the High Government to promote the Chinese junk trade within the limits of their own interests, we shall now investigate whether any obstacles were raised which impeded the proper functioning of the Chinese junk trade.

First of all it should once again be pointed out that there may exist a considerable gap between the aim and the execution of ordinances. There is little doubt, however, that trade procedures and port formalities at Batavia functioned less effectively than they should have. In the personal papers of Governor-General Willem Arnold Alting (1780-1797) there is some telling evidence that Chinese captain Oeij Hingko (1775-1784) fleeced the junk skippers at their departure. Upon one occasion, he made them pay no fewer than sixteen different fees and charges under the following headings:

		Cantonese junk	Amoy junk
1	Anchorage	100 rds	100 rds
2	Pass	100 rds	100 rds
3	"Tjunia" (boat fee for visiting the junk)	8.24 rds	8.24 rds
4	The servant at Custom house ("de Boom")	3.12 rds	3.12 rds
5	"Bitio" (tax on sale of rice?) at custom house	6.24 rds	6.24 rds
6	The Chinese secretary who noted down 499 and 401 passengers and crew respectively	212 rds	122.36 rds
7	The secretary of the High Government	954 rds	552.18 rds
8	The watchmen at Custom house who recorded the export cargo on the pass	358.06 rds	695.30 rds

The Batavian roadstead, second half 18th century.

VI The VOC and the Junk Trade to Batavia

		Cantonese junk	Amoy junk
9	The VOC	212 rds	122.36 rds
10	The harbourmaster	150 rds	150 rds
11	The general tax collector who signed the papers	65 rds	65 rds
12	Special import and export fees	40 rds	30 rds
13	The cashier of the tax collector for preparing the pass	3.12 rds	3.12 rds
14	The carrier of the pass	20 rds	20 rds
15	The watchmen	10 rds	10 rds
16	The "mata mata" or spies at Custom house	20 rds	20 rds
	total	2262.30 rds	2010 rds

Of these fees, it was found that items 4 and 5 were either imaginary or unnecessary, 6 and 7 should be paid in connection with the issue of exit visas to the passengers (1.25 rixdollars per person with the exclusion of the crew), 8 and 9 were unknown, 10 should be fixed at 65 rixdollars, 12 at 20 rixdollars, 14, 15 and 16 were unknown. According to the regulations, the nachodas of the junk of Amoy should have paid 824 rixdollars to the Chinese Captain, instead of the 2,010 rixdollars levied (ARA, eerste afdeling, Alting collection, 67).

An example like this one provides today's researcher with an incidental glance into the day-to-day formalities around the clearance of Chinese junks at Batavia. Although it has little more than impressionistic value as a piece of evidence, it does show that the procedures did not always function as well as the Plakaatboek would suggest.

b. Immigration procedures. The score of plakaten issued between 1740 and 1790 in connection with the immigration of Chinese once more underlines the above remarks on the nature of the plakaat: insofar as they were of a restrictive nature they seem to have been hardly heeded at all. As early as July, 1743, the nachodas were exhorted to bring "honest agricultural workers, sugarmill workers, gardeners and merchants" on their next voyage (Plakaatboek V:50). As a follow-up another edict was issued in 1745 which permitted each junk to transport 50 to 70 passengers in addition to the crew and the merchants (Plakaatboek V:238). The authorities explained their decision by stating that too strict a limitation on the number of sailors on board might endanger navigation and that passage fees constituted an important source of income to the shipowners. Further, they established "that many Chinese at Batavia had died or moved elsewhere in recent years". To all intents and purposes, immigration soon filled the void left by the massacre, for within ten years complaints could again be overheard about "unchecked immigration".

On 13 May, 1754, the High Government announced that all Chinese merchants who came to trade during the northern monsoon had to collect a "permissie" ticket (costing 13.5 stuiver), while those who intended to stay had to pay one rixdollar for a "domicilie" ticket (Plakaatboek VI:666). Two weeks later a special body of regulations aimed at keeping law and order among the Chinese was issued (Plakaatboek VI:673-5).

The "Overgekomen Brieven en Papieren" series in the VOC archives contain annual lists in which neat figures are provided of the numbers of Chinese that arrived at or left from Batavia. For the first time indications of a few women also appear among those thousands of immigrants. These figures on the passengers traffic were compiled by Chinese officers who were charged with the task of counting them and making sure that as many people left as arrived. The passenger lists have no statistical value whatsoever as gross excesses are frequently mentioned in the Resolutions of Governor-General and Council. In 1754, for instance, seven junks from Amoy brought 4608 persons, of whom only 1928 figured on the lists (Plakaatboek VI:666). A few years later, in 1760, a fraud committed by the Chinese officers was discovered, in which 220 people had been reported on board a junk which was in reality carrying more than 700 (Plakaatboek VII:409).

When the High Government adopted a more rigorous policy and wanted to confiscate the cargo and fine the nachodas of the junks, they met with vehement protests as had happened before, but this time the message was different. The nachodas said that if they were fined they would be completely ruined and would not dare to return to the Yang-hang in Amoy (31-4-1761, Plakaatboek VII:469). Moreover, they explained that with the money procured from the transport of passengers they were able to pay only part of the expenses. They drew their greatest profits from goods transported for private merchants, each of whom travelled with one or two assistants on the ship, thus comprising a considerable part of the crew. If goods were confiscated, merchants who had nothing to do with the transport of illegal passengers would also suffer. Furthermore, the nachodas pointed out that a considerable number of their passengers consisted of letter carriers who would return upon having delivered their letters in Batavia. The upshot of it was that the total number of crew members and passengers permitted was increased to 250 on large, and 200 on small junks. This liberal regulation was acceptable to the Chinese and therefore heeded, for in next decades there were only a few complaints about excessive numbers of "orang baru" coming to Batavia from China.

Table 5.
Number of junks visiting Batavia, with ports of origin (per five year period). (Based on Overgekomen Brieven en Papieren series, VOC archives.)

	total	Amoy	Ningpo	Canton	others
1721 - 1725	46	21	16	2	7
1726 - 1730	79	43	17	8	11
1731 - 1735	88	46	12	23	7
1736 - 1740	82	55	6	15	6
1741 - 1745	41	27	4	8	2
1746 - 1750[1]	37	27	2	8	-
1751 - 1755	37	26	4	6	1
1756 - 1760	39	33	1	5	-
1760 - 1765[2]	34	23	2	9	-
1766 - 1770	33	27	1	5	-
1771 - 1775[3]	21	20	1	-	-
1776 - 1780	25	25	-	-	-
1781 - 1785	33	22	-	11	-
1786 - 1790	52	13	-	11	28

[1] 1746 and 1747 are missing
[2] 1763 is missing
[3] 1772 is missing

The authorities were now quite conscious that too many restrictions might cause the Chinese to emigrate elsewhere in the archipelago; at the same time they attempted to stimulate and control the trade by fixing a quota for passengers. The relative importance of the passenger traffic explains why the number of junks from Amoy calling at Batavia remained stable for a long period of time while junks from other ports in China virtually stopped calling at Batavia, even though extra measures were taken to favour them with low prices for pepper. Over this period only the junks from Amoy were allowed to bring newcomers, probably because the Fukienese were found to be more easy-going than the Hakka or the Cantonese. At any rate, even in contemporary Chinese sources, it is stated that most Chinese people living at Batavia were from the Tung-an district, the hinterland of Amoy (HFHC X:490).

c. Restriction of Shipping Routes. There are data available which point to more permanent factors which impeded operations, such as attempts by the High Government to regiment and confine the junk trade to a few routes and ports and to concentrate it at Batavia. Ironically, these measures were not primarily aimed at the Chinese junks themselves; they should be explained as defensive measures aimed against the penetration of the English into the Indonesian archipelago and the South China sea during this period. Thus the effort to confine the Chinese junk trade was symptomatic of another process that was going on, the breakdown of VOC hegemony in Southeast Asia's waters.

The American historian Holden Furber describes in detail the steady rise in English country trade tonnage and the VOC failure to formulate an effective answer to this challenge from the 1730s onwards. Instead of relaxing the restrictions which prevented the development of a privately owned Dutch country trade fleet in addition to its own VOC ships, the High Government clung to its monopolies. As early as 1739, the Dutch realized that the winds were changing when "free trade of all sorts of nations" at Canton produced a sharp decline in profits (Furber 1976:279). Country traders, as the name implies, increasingly purchased regional products in Southeast Asia which they sold on the Chinese market, thus becoming a redoubtable competition to the VOC (which had dominated the sales in these commodities at Canton for a long time). Governor-General Van Imhoff and his successor Jacob Mossel (1750-1761) tried to stem the British penetration of Southeast Asia through negotiation but to no avail: In the spring of 1751, the British actually announced that they would consider every port in the archipelago where a Dutch flag was not flying "free and neutral" and thus open to their trading vessels (Furber 1976: 281).

The country traders represented only part of the problems that were looming ahead. The English East India Company was also looking for ways and means to use Southeast Asian products as an alternative form of payment for the shipments of silver that it sent to Canton annually to purchase silks and tea. At the same time, the British planned to establish an entrepot in Southeast Asia to attract Chinese shipping on favourable terms. The Seven Years' War (1756-1763) forestalled the rapid execution of these plans, but as soon as the war was over, a marked expansion of the English trade occurred from Madras and Calcutta to Aceh, Kedah, Kuala Selangor and Riau (Basset 1971:12).

The challenge of the country traders to the VOC did not fail to affect Chinese shipping to Southeast Asia. Junk merchants met with the country traders sailing under the British flag on the Southeast coast of Borneo or procuring pepper and tin in Sumatra without calling at Batavia, when it dawned upon them that there were large holes in the net that the VOC had spread over the archipelago. The VOC tried to stem this evasion with all the means it had at its disposal: control of strategic thoroughfares by patrol vessels and the application of strict rules applying to the shipping routes and ports of call to Chinese shipping. In 1753 the High Government passed a resolution barring free navigation of the Chinese to combat the - in the Dutch view - illegal trade by junks from Amoy to Palembang and the Southeast coast of Borneo (15-5-1753, Plakaatboek VI:350). Via this route, great quantities of tin and pepper slipped through the net. The Governor-General and Council decided that they would allow junk traffic to Batavia and Malaka only and would issue special licences to three junks for the trade with Makassar and Palembang. A year later, this resolution was elaborated. All junk trade was "once and for all" forbidden to Ambon, Banda, Ternate, Celebes, the east coast and the south coast of Borneo (Sukadana included), Java, Sumatra and the Malay peninsula. One junk was permitted to travel to Makassar while two licences were issued each year for the navigation to Banjarmasin (9-7-1754, Plakaatboek VI:688-9). In the following years, several attempts were made to stop the trade to all ports other than Batavia, but the Chinese network proved too firmly woven to abolish it completely. Malaka, Banjarmasin and Makassar could not flourish without their Chinese trade, and all these ports were eventually reopened. Figures concerning these trade links are scarce, but in 1765 it was calculated that the trade to Makassar yielded the Chinese an average annual profit of some 3600 rixdollars (Plakaatboek VI:352). The licence for this was originally sold each year to the highest bidder; later, however, it was given as an extra emolument to the Chinese Captain in Batavia, who sold it for a considerable sum to the Chinese merchants.[18]

In spite of, or perhaps we should say due to, all this meddling with the trading routes the decline of the junk trade to Batavia became more and more apparent. In 1766 the Governor-General and Council convened a secret meeting to discuss the situation. It was calculated that the year before, some 10,000 piculs of tin from the Malay peninsula had reached Canton via channels not related to the VOC while in Amoy no less than 18,000 piculs had been discharged; in all, this was about equal to the quantities the Company itself was selling on an annual basis (VOC 500, Secret Res GG and C 21-2-1766). This leakage of Southeast Asian products constituted a major problem for the Company because the proceeds from sales of tin and pepper (about 700,000 guilders) were used to purchase tea at Canton (Steur 1984:56). The High Government therefore decided to thwart these "smuggling activities" by sending Company vessels to patrol the Banka Straits, which all China-bound shipping had to pass. Two years later, it was acknowledged that these patrols were futile, and consequently they were abandoned (VOC 500, Secret Res GG and C 7-4-1767 and 31-3-1768).

Attempts to resuscitate the trade with Ningpo through the shipment of 2,000 piculs of pepper and 1,000 piculs of Banka tin on the junk of the Batavian Chinese lieutenant Kouw Hong-liang also ended in failure. This junk, which had been fitted out by the High Government and the lieutenant on a shared risk basis simply disappeared, never bringing back the cargo of Chinese gold for which the High Government had been hoping.[19]

In a letter of 20 June, 1776, addressed to the supercargoes of the Dutch trade factory at Canton, Governor-General Jeremias van Riemsdijk (1775-1777) wrote that the Chinese no longer brought valuable goods to town, adding that "the consequences for this colony are most detrimental, much to our regret" (VOC 4414; Jörg 1982:35). The nachodas of the junks sent by the Yang-hang of Amoy were of the same mind and they presented a petition to Van Riemsdijk in which they requested that stronger measures be taken to call a halt to the transport of Chinese goods to Java via the "Buitenkantoren" (outer factories) of the VOC. The number of junks visiting Batavia yearly had by then decreased from ten in 1755 to as few as four. According to the nachodas this was caused primarily by the Chinese trade with Johore which yearly received five junks without levying tolls or taxes on them. Because the Chinese merchandise sold at Johore was distributed at a low price throughout the archipelago, it became virtually impossible for the nachodas trading at Batavia to compete. They showed that they had to invest about 10,000 rixdollars in every Java passage to pay redemption fees, housing and so on in Batavia. Van Riemsdijk complied with their request, further curtailing Chinese navigation in the archipelago and imposing a double tax on all Chinese merchandise that was not directly brought in from China to Batavia (Plakaatboek X:81).

Striving to please the nachodas further, in the following trading season the High Government promised them 200 picul of tin at bargain prices and as much pepper as the Company stocks at Batavia allowed. Clearly the Company was trying to accommodate the merchants and to make up for the declining profits in their transactions outside the Company sphere as a result of the relatively high tolls and taxes in town.[20]

It is rather ironic that the Yang-hang of Amoy, which had been forced to regulate shipping in accordance with the dictates of the VOC, now implored the High Government to tighten up its regulations even further for fear that they could not survive competition with junk owners who sent their ships to other ports in Southeast Asia where no or few charges were levied. As a result of these restrictions and constraints taken by the Batavian authorities, the Chinese trade within the archipelago lost its vitality. When it was realized that Chinese junks sailed to Johore mainly because it had grown into one of the main centres of junk construction and repair in the area due to the availability of cheap and durable timber, the Yang-hang had to reconsider their standpoint.

As early as the spring of 1780, they were imploring the High Government to leave the junk shipping to Johore unmolested. This petition was granted by the Dutch authorities "trusting that as a result of this permission, the navigation of the junks to other 'unpermitted ports' would be halted as much as possible and the navigation to Batavia would be enlarged" (Realia II:81, 14-7-1780). The High Government may initially have cherished the hope that it could revive Chinese navigation within the archipelago and create feeder routes to its headquarters, but the Chinese communities living in the outer ports which had lost direct contact with China soon showed signs of decline. The testimony of the Chinese officers of Malaka, a port which was denied further direct shipping links with China in 1778 (Plakaatboek X:309), is noteworthy because it not only shows the signal position of the Chinese trade in the region but also illustrates some of this trade's peculiar aspects.

The Chinese officers wrote a letter to Governor-General Willem Arnold Alting (1780-1797) in early 1781 and explained that as a result of the recent curtailment of the junk trade, this town, which served as a regional centre for the VOC on the Malay peninsula, now faced a severe shortage of tea, porcelain, sugar, silk, candied fruits, yarn, needles, preserved greens, dried fish, paper lanterns, sacrificial wicks and other such Chinese objects. These items could indeed be purchased via Batavia but only at very high prices, because shipments passed through the hands of many middlemen and were subjected to a double toll, once upon arrival in Batavia and once more upon arrival in Malaka. It was, moreover, unbearable for the letter writers, they stated, that they could no longer send money to their parents and relations in China. According to them, this constituted a very grave and most irresponsible issue, "because a Chinese who does not remember his parents and friends will be cursed for being an ungrateful person, unworthy of his life. As a result, the remittance of funds has grown from an old custom into an iron rule to which everyone should adhere, no matter how destitute he may be, for fear of being without luck or blessing in his later life."

In Malaka, the severance of trade relations with China brought about the departure of two-thirds of the Chinese water porters, ginger bakers and gardeners for the nearby Riau archipelago, which under its Bugis ruler, Raja Haji, was emerging as a new meeting point for British country traders, Chinese junks and local shipping. Malaka now risked losing its position as staple market for the native shipping in the area, the Chinese officers maintained, "for Chinese merchandise is needed to attract the natives who never come with money to the market, but are used to bring elephant tusks, aguil wood, bezoin, dragon blood and home-made textiles to barter for Chinese merchandise". They concluded their letter by pointing out that the twenty or thirty vessels from Aceh which used to visit Malaka in previous years now all called at Riau, with the result that the Company lost no less than 22,000 rixdollars on its tolls and taxes (ARA, eerste afdeling, Alting collection, 67).

In this case, the negative effects of the fragmentation of the junk trade were particularly telling and Governor-General Alting lost no time in lifting the ban on navigation (Plakaatboek XI:379, 27-2-1781). The problems with Riau were settled three years later by Admiral J.P. van Braam who defeated the Bugis in 1784, thus foiling a British plan to establish an entrepot on these islands. For want of a better place, the English then acquired Penang in 1786.

Even the fourth Anglo-Dutch war (1780-1784), which for some time made Dutch shipping to China almost impossible, did not bring about an upswing of note. The number of junks once more increased, as did the diversity in the ports of origin. The Company enlarged its purchases somewhat, amongst others in tea, but the transactions of the traders outside the VOC sphere remained meagre, as the High Government found out when it attempted to fine several nachodas for having brought more than the permitted number of passengers. High Government officials discovered that "the trade from the Chinese empire with our principal town had declined to such an extent that the value of the junks together with their cargo would not even have been sufficient to pay the fines that we intended to mete out" (15-6-1787, Plakaatboek X:924).

A subsequent decision in 1791 to take some tax measures "aimed at the revival of the trade of the Amoy junks which has so clearly declined and even threatens to perish" and the permission granted to Dutch sailors to transport tea home in their luggage, "because the so seriously ailing trade of the junks would otherwise decrease even more" were taken a day after the fair: the once important emporium at Batavia had declined beyond recovery (Plakaatboek XI:381, 428).

Reasons of Decline
Commissioner General S.C. Nederburgh was cited in Chapter II for his

VI The VOC and the Junk Trade to Batavia

comment concerning the slowed pace of business transactions at Batavia during the 1780s. The venality of the local officials (which he pointed out), coupled with interference by the Dutch authorities with shipping routes, did not fail to have their effects on the decline of the junk trade. In addition, one more negative measure should be mentioned: the export of silver coins was severely curtailed in the 1790s and allowed only to individuals who supported their relations in China. In 1796 the total amount allowed was fixed at 30,000 rials (Plakaatboek XII:281), but in 1799 the export of gold and silver was completely prohibited (Plakaatboek XII:983). What impact this prohibition had (it actually far predated of the 1790s insofar as the sales and purchases of the Chinese merchants were concerned[21]) may be gleaned from the explanation given for the decline of Chinese shipping in contemporary Chinese writing. In the appendix to Ong Tai-hai's account of his sojourn in Java (dating from 1813), the arguments advanced clearly lay the blame on the Dutch:
"We of the flowery nation, coming from a distance to traffic at Batavia, were formerly allowed to take the proceeds of our commerce, and either to lay in a new stock or to carry back the money to our native land, as we found it convenient. But after a time, it was strictly forbidden to export silver from Batavia, and we were compelled to expend our profits in the purchase of goods, before we could spread our sails and return. Moreover, it took some time to bring the return cargoes [often the product of other places] to Batavia, so that our junks had to wait many days until the monsoon was over and were unable to reach Amoy; or they were delayed until the end of summer when typhoons were frequent, so that vessels and marines perished together. This has been the case for a series of years, until the inhabitants of the seacoast, who are devoted to this branch of commerce, burst into incessant lamentations, and the revenues of our country [China] suffered, while no remedy could be discovered." (Ong 1849:20).

So far the question has been posed concerning the extent to which interference by the VOC in the junk trade to Batavia may have contributed to its demise. In addition we may pose the question of whether any developments occurred in China itself which may also have helped bring about this decay. Most decisions pertaining to the Nanyang trade that were taken at the Chinese court from the 1750s onwards do not seem to have been particularly prohibitive in nature. As I have shown above, the prohibition on long term overseas residence was relaxed. A prohibition against the export of silk was proclaimed in 1759 because it was feared that export drove market prices up in China, but after the Dutch petitioned for its relaxation it was permitted again under a strict quota of 1,000 bolts of silk per ship (CCT:463-66, Fu Lo-shu 166:227, 235-237).

It will be remembered that Tien Ju-kang singled out the economic crisis and the upsurge of piracy in the last decade of the eighteenth century as the primary factors which impaired the development of shipping in China itself. Most writers on the subject would agree on this point, and one of them even asserts that the junk trade was disrupted for nearly thirty years until piracy was crushed in 1809 (Leonard 1984:81). The most comprehensive statement illustrating Chinese aims and methods in combatting piracy and of the predominant attitude taken by Chinese officials is contained in the essay "A discussion of the Seaport situation" written by the Governor of Fukien, Wang Chih-i in 1799. Wang maintained that prohibition of trade should be avoided at all costs, as too many people depended upon it (Cushman 1975:171). In 1806 the size of Fukien junks was limited by the

A Chinese junk amidst Southeast Asian and European vessels. Note the passenger cabins at the stern of the junk.

authorities, but it would seem that this limitation was directed at coastal shipping only, for the Plakaatboek of 1808 still differentiates for junks calling at Batavia between those with one and two decks, the latter type measuring some 800 tons (Plakaatboek XV:41).

The "Hsia-men chih" mentions that of the many Yang-hang which were established after 1727, there still were eight functioning at the beginning of the Chia-ch'ing era (1796). This is actually one more than thirty years earlier when there had been seven (Viraphol 1977:109). Together with the coastal shipping firms (Shang-hang), another thirty in total, these firms owned a thousand seaworthy trading vessels. Eighteen years later, only one Yang-hang, the Ho-ho-ch'eng Yang-hang, remained, the others having all gone bankrupt due to poor management and competition from the coastal shipping companies which engaged in illicit overseas trading without paying the necessary duties (HMC II:180). Whether the junk trade to Batavia suffered great losses during the raids by pirates in this period is not mentioned in the local gazetteer, although it is stated that the Yang-hang had to contribute 20,000 taels yearly to fund the coastal patrols (HMC II:179).

These bits and pieces of information chosen at random suggest that the decline in maritime shipping activities in Fukien due to local factors occurred later and for different reasons than the decay of the Amoy-Batavia shipping link. In summary it can now be safely affirmed that the decay of the Chinese junk trade was indeed not of its own making. Instead, it was due largely to the nature of the VOC policies which cannot, however, be explained only by pointing to the changing strategies of the Gentlemen XVII vis-à-vis the China trade, as has often been suggested. This should rather be seen within a larger perspective which leaves room for issues like the weakening grip of the VOC on the archipelago or the infiltration of British interests in the South China sea.

P.T. Couperus, assistant collector of import and export duties at Batavia, wrote in 1815: "the trade of the Chinese to Batavia is very much declined. Every year a few junks still arrive with porcelain, tea, silks, paper and lacquer from Canton and Amoy, but their number decreases with the years." (ARA, eerste afdeling, Couperus collection, no. 44). He would have been surprised to hear that this same trade was to experience a dramatic upsurge in Singapore a few years later, when Raffles at long last succeeded in establishing the Southeast Asian duty-free entrepot the English had been dreaming of for so many years.

Conclusion

So much for the story of Chinese junk trade to Batavia, which perhaps can best be summarized as the story of a network of private entrepreneurs wedged between two widely diverging political systems. Constants would seem to be the desire of the Gentlemen XVII to engage in trade with China, and the necessity of the Fukienese for trading abroad; variables were the changing means by which the VOC could achieve its aims and the manner in which the Chinese government sought to regulate the trade without danger to the realm. The nature of the documentary materials has made it difficult to deal with the subject as comprehensively as one would have liked. The operators of the trade did not leave behind any material to speak of, and one can only hope for discovery of such important materials as those of the Cairo Genizah merchants. As a result, the student of the subject must turn to the Dutch and Chinese sources produced by bureaucratic systems which tried to restrain this enterprise and to tailor it to their own socio-economic order. These efforts by public authorities to gain control have provided the central thread which ties together the various parts of my mainly chronological narrative.

Such an approach which follows the official policy line harbours certain defects: it tends to provide the Chinese and Dutch policy-making groups with a deceptive sense of unity of thought, and the interests of the Batavian urban community are pushed into the background to the extent that one wonders whether this is a study of the VOC and the junk trade alone.

This is a far-reaching question which has not yet been wholly answered in the preceding pages, but which seems worthwhile to pose both because it throws extra light on the untenable position of Batavia as an urban community at the end of the eighteenth century (a theme which has been dealt with in Chapter II), and because it also will enable us to further specify the character of the "strangling grip" Tien Ju-kang complained of. It may be possible to give the term a connotation totally different from that which he originally intended.

First of all, it should be pointed out once again that the apparent unity of approach within both the Chinese and Dutch bureaucratic systems turns out to have been a welter of various opinions, conflicting interests and organizational jealousies. This shows up in reports of the endless discussions at the imperial court concerning the pros and cons of the Chinese Nanyang trade network: "the prohibition of which will not only harm the livelihood of the common people, but may in the long term even injure the national treasury", as Ts'ai Hsin gloomily put it. It emerges even more in the correspondence between the different levels of decision-makers in that economic empire par excellence, the VOC.

At an early date, the Directors in the Netherlands, who strove for a maximum return on their investments, observed with distress the capital-consuming character of their headquarters in Asia and the independent course that was followed by their proxies in Asia, the Governor-General and Council of the Indies. It is exactly in this respect that the paradox of the biggest European trading company in Asia, which had to be served by a foreign shipping link, presents itself in a most arresting manner. As has been shown throughout this chapter - and throughout this book - this dependence stemmed from the fact that Batavia owed its entrepot position within the archipelago to the presence of its large population of Chinese entrepreneurs.

By 1756 the Gentlemen XVII felt that most of the profits from the China trade were disappearing into the upkeep of Batavia. They decided to deal with the China trade themselves and left it to the Batavian High Government to solve the town's economic woes in an Asian trading world that was being transformed into a more open international market. They did not leave much freedom of action to the Governor-General and Council in this respect, and this in turn speeded up the transformation of Batavia from its position as a maritime trade entrepot into the position of capital to a territorial hinterland. As the "heart of the general constitution of the Company", as Valentijn once put it, Batavia ceased beating. When Commissioner General Nederburgh arrived in the town from Holland in 1793 he found a community in decay, governed by a local élite who possessed the keys to warehouses filled with the Javanese cash crops with which they had lined their pockets. He described the sitation as follows: [Among those in command] "one meets with unbounded lust for power, combined with an unrestrainable precipitation towards manoeuvring their own considerably extended families into the best positions, and to discharging into [the

VI The VOC and the Junk Trade to Batavia

pockets of] those family members immense amounts of money" (G.J. Schutte 1974:153).

First the Gentlemen XVII withdrew their stakes from Batavia, then the High Government gave up Batavia intramuros and established themselves at Weltevreden, as has been described in chapter II. These steps which ultimately symbolized Batavia's decline as an entrepot were not taken overnight but were considered for many years; nonetheless, they considerably affected the conditions under which the junk trade operated. It may be wise to consider these different stages before quoting the famous saying that "the monopoly which first served as the Company's couch finally turned into its deathbed", "Het monopolie is eerst het rustbed, daarna de doodssponde der Compagnie geworden" (De Haan 1935 I:720). In the case of Batavia, this saying runs particularly true. Seen in this light it was not the strangling grip of an expanding world economy which killed the junk trade, but rather the stiffening grip of a worn-out colonial trading system which dragged the Batavian junk trade into the throes of its own death struggle.

Chapter VII

THE CARYATIDS OF 17TH CENTURY BATAVIA: REPRODUCTION, RELIGION AND ACCULTURATION UNDER THE VOC*

Introduction

It is often claimed that the absence, or bias, of sources makes the writing of a balanced history of women impossible. This kind of reasoning is not new. The same has been said of the writing of the history of the proletariat, colonized peoples and other downtrodden groups. Upon setting out to write this chapter on the women of ancien régime Batavia I was strongly aware of this complaint. Travel accounts that have come down to us in printed sources yield quite substantial information, because generations of visitors to early Batavia have witnessed and described with astonishment the behaviour of the dark-skinned Portuguese-speaking consorts that comprised the female side of Dutch colonial society in Batavia. Without exception, their verdict was harsh: chewing betel nuts, associating with their slave-girls and apparently incapable of intelligent conversation, and still less, of acceptable table manners, the daughters of Batavia were regarded with derision by European writers. Nothing would be easier than to present an anthology of these often quite entertaining anecdotes. The dilemma of course is that such an account would be one-sided if based upon descriptions and explanations by males only, outsiders who obviously did not share the world of women that we intend to study.

What about the archives of the Dutch East India Company, that treasure-trove for the colonial historian? The judicial and notarial archives in Jakarta constitute a potential source of information on the inhabitants of Oud-Batavia, but these are at present not accessible to me. To search for information regarding women in the business correspondence of the Dutch East India company - almost exclusively an employer of men - would be like looking for a needle in a haystack. It is therefore tempting to say that it is almost impossible to come up with substantial data about Batavian women.

How did it happen that Portuguese-speaking women of Indian origin were selected by Dutch colonizers as their spouses? If the question is raised we touch upon such subjects as colonization policy (why Asian and not European women?) and acculturation (how were these women prepared for their role in Dutch colonial society?).

It is within this larger context that the archives of the Dutch Reformed Church community in Batavia and the Acta of the Church Council, in particular, yield interesting material about the role and position of women in early seventeenth century Batavian society. Consequently this contribution is not a study of women as such, but a study of colonization, missionary efforts and acculturation: three themes that in combination contributed to the emergence of the much maligned and misunderstood Batavian woman, who supported the Batavian colony.

VII The Caryatids of 17th Century Batavia

A Batavian belle going to church.

Dutch Colonization Schemes

"Belligerent merchants with unlimited power": this is the brief but striking epithet of the Dutch East India Company. Armed with a charter to navigate, trade and colonize in Asia (which excluded all other Dutchmen), the agents of this vast mercantile enterprise established in the first decades of the 17th century a strong net of trade settlements and fortresses which were scattered along the coasts of the Indian Ocean and the South China sea, and on the islands of the Indonesian archipelago, linking Yemen in the west with Japan in the northeast. Most of these settlements were nothing more than trade factories, staffed with a minimum of Company personnel, with or without dependants. Only at a few nodes of activity was it decided to support the organization, the maintenance and the defence of VOC monopoly by creating real volksplantingen or Dutch settler colonies. Batavia, the headquarters of all the Company's activities in Asia - often called the rendez-vous - was the most important of these Dutch tradecolonies.

If the Dutch were no conquerors or proselytizers in the Iberian style, it was due primarily to their working premise that commercial activities should be engaged in to the benefit of the balance sheet and not for the Glory of God or his champion, the Portuguese king. If the Dutch were not successful colonizers, it was - over and above the circumstances which will be dealt with below - due to the almost paranoid distrust with which the Company monitored private enterprise within its precincts.

Such questions as what white colonies should be like, how they should be populated, how they should be advertised to emigrants in spe were hotly discussed in a remarkably open and straightforward manner in the 17th century Dutch Republic. It is nonetheless striking that these discussions on colonization were almost totally centred upon the Dutch possessions in the West - and not without reason.

The West India Company (WIC), on account of the accessibility of the South American continent, the character of the trade items and the local conditions in these regions, encouraged private enterprise. However, the East India Company (VOC), with its monopoly on the trade routes to Asia, made it clear that all those sailing on its vessels to the East were its servants. In those rare cases that men or women were intentionally sent to bolster the ranks of the freeburgher society, it was clear to all parties concerned that these freeburghers were needed to serve the Company and not the other way around. In the Orient monopolies were scrupulously guarded.

Why did the Company nonetheless at an early date permit and encourage its servants to resign their positions and establish themselves as freeburghers, and why did it even attempt to provide these bachelors with Dutch wives, brought all the way from Holland? To speak of freeburghers in this context seems almost a contradiction in terms. It would lead us too far afield to digress upon the efforts to create white colonies in the Moluccas before Governor-General Jan Pieterszoon Coen, the founder of Batavia, systematically revealed his ideas upon this matter in the early 1620s. Suffice it to say that as early as 1607 Admiral Cornelis Matelieff permitted some of his soldiers and sailors to marry local women in Ambon (Opkomst III:55). Upon his arrival in the East Indies in 1610, the first Governor-General, Pieter Both, was accompanied by clerics, artisans, their families, and 36 spinsters, the last turning out to be mainly of ill repute (Opkomst III:135).

Coen unfolded his ideas about the peopling of Batavia in several letters written to the directorate in Amsterdam. He made it clear that he had already been forced to take temporary measures and had purchased slave women from the coast of India, because the directors did not seem interested in establishing a colony. "Who does not know that the human race cannot exist without women?" he demanded. Soon his irate letters produced results. In the following years, a considerable number of young Dutch girls were shipped to the East. It was not until 1623 that Coen finally presented a master plan to the Gentlemen XVII.[1] His advice was of a confidential nature on account of its potentially disturbing nature, and consequently this discussion took place behind closed doors, in contrast to how the gospel of West-Indian colonization was spread by Willem Usselinx through public tracts and pamphlets. It is worth noting that Coen, who had reformed and centralized the administration and bookkeeping of the Company to such a degree that it became possible to supervise its activities everywhere in Asia, seemed to favour the revival of private enterprise. Firmly in the saddle - the rendez-vous Batavia having been founded, the population of the Moluccas having "felt

VII The Caryatids of 17th Century Batavia

his spurs" and having submitted to the spice monopoly - Coen could afford to slacken the reins a bit. His pet-idea was to turn the new rendez-vous of the company into the biggest trade and staple market of the native trade in the archipelago as well. To achieve this goal he proposed that a strong class of free Dutch citizens should be given the freedom to trade within the archipelago from Batavia, while the Company should maintain its monopoly over a limited number of commodities and trade routes only. His ideal type of colony approached in many respects the Portuguese and Spanish towns in the Orient and in scattered references he grudgingly acknowledges this.

In Manila, a large community of perioeci (largely consisting of Chinese farmers and traders) supplied the Spanish garrison of the intramuros with all the necessary food supplies so that they did not have to be imported from elsewhere at high cost. Failed attempts to take Macao and Malacca had taught the Dutch that the Portuguese colonies showed remarkable military strength and resilience. Even while cut off by Dutch fleets from assistance from the Portuguese fatherland, the local populations of these colonies faithfully rallied around the Portuguese flag and succeeded in keeping the Dutch assailants at bay. Without doubt, this was due to the composition of the Portuguese social system of soldados and casados, bachelor soldiers and married settlers, which was geared to military conquest and defence. Diogo do Couto decried the inner decay of the system in Goa but it held out all the same against foreign aggression (Winius 1985). Pivotal institutions like the Church, the city councils and the Casa de Misericordia, contributed to this strength. The Dutch were well aware that they had a lot to learn from the Portuguese in matters of colonization.

Portuguese colonies did have a reputation for corruption and vice. Concubinage which was a dominant feature in Portuguese colonial society, was an abomination to Coen. All the same, it was a sine qua non as very few Portuguese women emigrated to the Orient. Germano da Silva Correia may have argued to the contrary, but C.R. Boxer has proved him wrong in this respect (Boxer 1975:63-4). In an outpost like Macao, concubinage grew into a major preoccupation for some, as Portuguese merchants created veritable harems of female slaves, most of whom originated from Malacca and Japan. Only when the Jesuits moved in and issued heavy sanctions, such as excommunication, was this custom pushed back to less offensive proportions.

It cannot be denied that the Portuguese authorities made earnest attempts to solve the chronic shortage of manpower in Asia by encouraging the "Romulus and Remus" approach. Marriages of soldiers (who were thereupon released as casados) with local belles were already encouraged between 1505 and 1515 by Viceroy Dom Francisco de Almeida and his successor Alfonso de Albuquerque. The latter even offered privileges and financial rewards. To no avail however: in Goa the caste system proved to be an unsurmountable barrier for marriage with girls from reputable local families. Another method of promoting marriage and the growth of population in the East was more to Coen's fancy, as we shall see. The Portuguese crown sent young girls of marriageable age from the orphanages of Lisbon to India. These so-called Orfas del Rei were provided with dowries in the form of awarding minor government posts for their future husbands. But as Boxer has shown, more than fifty a year were never sent and five to fifteen seems to have been the average, not really a major contribution to the population of the colony.

When Coen presented his colonization plans, all these facts were known to him.

First of all, he made it clear that, contrary to the Portuguese example, he cherished no high expectations of Dutch soldiers and sailors. They were not "of the right kidney". In most cases all those who applied for release from service were totally unfit for the establishment of a colony.

In a letter dated November 16, 1621, Coen complained as follows: "Some behave themselves worse than animals and cause abominations and scandal towards us among the Indians. As the latter have not seen other or better men, they think all our nation is so godless, unreasonable and unmannered. What good may one expect from this scum? Soldiers and sailors are of use against the enemy (they seem to have been created by the Lord for this goal) but what else can we do with them, as long as your Lordships do not sent honest people? Released from service, it is for some too much effort to gape and catch the air in the mouth, nay, they are even too lazy to chew whatever is blown into their mouths!" (Coen I:644).

According to Coen, women were the precondition for trade: "the fundament of the state in India. If there were women here, the staple of the Indian trade would be yours" he wrote to the Gentlemen XVII (Opkomst IV:xxxiv). But rather than just asking for girls, he proposed that a large number of respectable Dutch families should emigrate to Batavia and that these families with their children should be accompanied by four to five hundred boys and girls between 10 and 12 years of age from all the orphanages of the United Provinces; he suggested a boy-girl ratio of 2:1. The girls were either to be placed in families or in a special Company-financed school "where they will be brought up, clothed, taught and educated by some of the most able women until - coming of age - they can be married to good honest husbands, in order that honourable families may originate from these alliances".[2] The governing idea of this scheme was that all the virtues of the Dutch family, and of Dutch women in particular - modesty, cleanliness and piety - should be transmitted to this godforsaken place and that it would somehow rub off on the female consorts of Asian or mixed ancestry who were already there.

Coen, not a man to leave it at that, was willing to shoulder personally responsibility for the consequences of his project. In early 1625 the Gentlemen XVII wrote to his successor in the Indies that "to set a good example and as encouragement to many other honest people here [in Holland], as well as the most important officers in India, the honourable [Coen] has got married here in order to travel with his wife thither" (Van de Wall 1923:40). Coen's zeal notwithstanding, the project came to naught.

First of all, he did not receive the kind of innocent virgins he had requested. At the arrival of the ship 't Wapen van Hoorn in Batavia, just before his departure to Holland (he stayed there from 1623 until 1627), he beheld with dismay the disembarking female passengers. "Here [in the archipelago] neither free women nor female slaves are so unfit and ill-mannered as some of the [Dutch] daughters who have arrived by this ship. It is almost as if they originate from the wilderness instead of having been brought up among people." (Coen I:731-2.) In this respect he was more critical than his subordinates, because Valentijn tells us that the men of the garrison welcomed the women "like roasted pears" - a delicacy at the time, I suppose (Valentijn 1724-26 IV-1:248).

Secondly, marriages of Dutch couples in the Indies often turned out to be barren ones. Miscarriages and infant deaths were frequent: "Experiundo cognitum est, prolem ex patre et matre belgis in Orientalis-India natum haud esse vitalem, vitamque brevi cum morte commutare".[3]

Although Coen had married Eva Ment, a young lady of impeccable conduct, he was not even able to set an example in giving proper education to other people's daughters. Supercargo Jacques Specx entrusted his daughter (born from concubinage with a Japanese woman) to Coen's guardianship when he was called home. Set to work as one of Eva's ladies-in-waiting, the twelve-year-old girl was caught in flagrante delicto with her seventeen-year-old lover in Coen's own living quarters. The guardian's revenge was terrible: the boy was sentenced to be shot and the girl was exposed and chastised nude in public.[4]

If the practical and moral feasibility of the population project had to be reassessed, the Gentlemen XVII added an observation of their own. It dawned upon them that, seen from the economic standpoint of assets and liabilities - and to them that was the crux of the whole question, the transportation of marriageable orphan girls simply did not pay. Furthermore, the presence of women on board the ships was bad for discipline. To the argument that Dutch women were found to be barren they added: "We have found on the other hand, that when our men marry native women, strong robust children are produced, who stay alive". All sponsoring of women as migrants to Dutch factories east of Africa was halted. In 1632, the school for the putative virgins was closed. By that time there were no more than eleven boarded in the school, and twenty-four others lodged with Dutch families (VOC 1105, f.333). Thus after a mere decade, the VOC ended its experiments in dabbling with provision of women, or should we say wombs? The number of women on its payroll was reduced to one. There is a touch of irony hidden in the job of that one remaining Company servant: she was a midwife.

The Portuguese Example

I have shown how the attempt to colonize Batavia with white settlers failed for social, biological and, in last resort, economic reasons (if only because the transportation and housing of white spinsters meant a high investment). But what was the investment intended to yield? Not just families as biological units, but families as economic units within a free independent burgher class. If this is so, a more fundamental question has to be raised. Did a class of Dutch independent merchant families - as Coen had proposed - have any viability in a town created and administered by a trading company? In the VOC-dominated trade economy, almost everyone in Batavia was in a dependent position. Capital, political influence, means of communication, instruments of administration, all were centralized in the hands of the Governor-General and his council.

Just a few citations from the correspondence between the Gentlemen XVII and Coen's successors will suffice to demonstrate this. Out of the dialectics of this exchange of letters, a new "colonial policy" was born. In a letter of 23 November 1631 the Gentlemen XVII wrote: "It is certain that we may expect more service and security from the Chinese than from our own people as long as the latter do not find better ways to earn a living" (the implication was that the burghers were either profiting from or obstructing the Company's affairs) (VOC 315, unfoliated). Governor-General Jacques Specx was ordered to curtail the freedom of commerce which had been conferred on the Dutch burghers only a few years earlier: "If Your Lordship feels that the citizenry cannot hold its own without this trade, then it is preferable that such citizenry be absent from Batavia. Because if one of the two must suffer - the Company or the Dutch citizenry - then it is better that the citizenry cuts, contrives and suffers." (Opkomst V:cii). Specx's successor Hendrick Brouwer could not agree more. He wrote his directors in Amsterdam in 1634: "The planting of the Dutch colony in India will not produce anything fruitful. The inborn Dutch free disposition cannot suffer such strict exclusion of action or limiting regulation as is imposed by the prerogatives of the Company's charter." (Opkomst V:219). This letter was crossed by one from Holland in which the Gentlemen XVII were decisive: "We shall never more realize our plan to stabilize a Batavian colony with Dutch families. We must aim at attracting several Indian nations who may in course of time choose to settle on a permanent basis [...] and Dutchmen (Company servants or freeburghers) who want to marry Indian women instead of Dutch women."[5]

Brouwer's successor, Anthony van Diemen, noted in the autumn of 1640 that the Portuguese were marrying local women: "It is certain that the Portuguese have governed these nations better than we can; let us hope that time will make us wiser, so that we may gather the fruits from the Batavian natives who increase in reasonable numbers" (Opkomst V:245). Then the last word on colonization was spoken by the Gentlemen XVII in 1643: "The Indian colonies must be promoted with native nations on the Portuguese example. [...] The Indian world is too big for us to possess for ourselves alone, and our country is too small to dispatch such a force as is needed for the stabilization of a colony".[6]

In other words, the white colonization scheme, for all its grandiose plans, had never been more than a means to the Company, certainly not an end in itself.

Church and State

The new realistic colonization policy found its legal expression in the Bataviasche Statuten, issued in 1642. This body of regulations and laws for the administration of Batavia, compiled under Van Diemen's supervision, conforms at first sight to that of many Dutch institutions. In practice, however, they were closer to those behind the comparable Portuguese institutions in Asia. For instance, the manner in which the Weeskamer (orphan chamber) was run as a money-lending institution for local Christians did not differ much from the function performed by the Casa de Misericordia. This phenomenon becomes even more apparent in religious matters. It was stipulated for the first time that henceforth no religion other than the Dutch Reformed faith was to be practised in town. This reminds us of the Portuguese colonies where it was understood that "the good Catholic answers completely to the social ideal [...] the transmission of the Catholic religion suffices by itself to transform the ideas and customs of a man, whatever his race, his colour, his traditions. Converted, the native is civilized, without having to submit him to any intellectual formation." (De Lannoy and Vanderlinden 1907:172). Moreover, in the Indonesian archipelago, religious and political goals coincided. The government regulation of 1650 actually dictated that "justice and police should be backed up with the Christian Reformed religion" (Van Deventer 1886 I:211). The Company used the church for its administration and the church used the worldly expediency of the Company. Nevertheless, it would be a serious misunderstanding to think that these two bodies cooperated as equals.

The Dutch Reformed Church in the East Indies was not a daughter church of the Dutch Reformed Church in the Republic. It was a sister church and therefore was not legally bound by it. On the other hand, it had to submit to the worldly authority of the Governor-General and his council. Even at church-council meetings, political emissaries of the Company were present. The right to read through all correspondence between the clerics in the East and their colleagues in Patria was reserved for them. It should come as no surprise that all regulations that were issued concerning religion tended equally to the further edification of the church and the benefit of the Company.

As with the Portuguese colonial government, the Company made a sharp distinction between those who had perceived the one and only truth (here there was a difference of taste between the Dutch and Portuguese), and everyone else, who were commonly called "blind heathens".

But alongside these parallels, some remarkable differences can also be discerned between the Dutch and Portuguese colonies. The Dutch language never made an inroad among the native populations in Asia. The Company as an entity continued to live its own life in isolation. These two factors impeded any further acculturation or assimilation outside the religious sphere. The profession of religion was really a sign of political allegiance, a trait d'union on the macro level between the Company and a few population groups. Women played this same role on a micro level. Although higher Company servants, beginning with the rank of merchant, were allowed to be accompanied by their wives from Holland, all others were forced to live as bachelors (with or without concubines) or to marry local women. How these girls were incorporated into Batavian society, and from which population groups they originated, can only be understood if we briefly review the different roles of the population groups which together constituted the Batavian colony.

The Role of Religion

Now that white colonization seemed out of the question, the envisaged functions of the burgher class - to draw the inter-archipelago trade to Batavia's harbour and to provide defence - were related to two population groups who seemed particularly suited to fulfill these roles: the Chinese and the Mardijkers. Why these two groups were the appropriate ones becomes clear if we dissect the social order of Batavia into five types of institutions, characterizing the political, economic, military and religious, kinship and educational endeavours. Then it becomes clear that, as far as the white population was concerned, the VOC monopolized nearly all these institutions and therefore held everyone in an iron grip. But, of course, there were population groups other than the Dutch in Batavia. Arranged in order of numerical strength the town population was composed of Chinese, Mardijkers, mestizos, several min-

Mardijker husband and wife.

VII The Caryatids of 17th Century Batavia

ority groups of Indonesian origin like the Bandanese, Malays and Balinese; and finally the slaves, who made up roughly half of the total population. In the first half of the 17th century, these slaves were mostly of Indian and Ceylonese origin; their lingua franca was Portuguese.

The Chinese population of Batavia was part of a large Chinese trade diaspora that had already spread over the whole archipelago before the Dutch arrived in the East. Batavia was directly connected to the Middle Kingdom by Chinese shipping; at the same time, the economic activities of the Chinese were partly integrated into the Company sphere and supplemented VOC activities. As such, the Chinese came to play the economic role par excellence among the Batavian citizenry. The Company "particularly paid attention to accommodating the Chinese" but at the same time it managed through taxes and tolls to take some of the cream off the shared porridge, thus deriving considerable benefits from the Chinese. In the military, religious and educational spheres of the colonial order, the Chinese had few contributions to make. They were actually excluded from the citizen soldiery, and were a potential threat on account of their great number and resistance to assimilation.

The mestizos and especially the Portuguese-speaking Mardijkers (or native Christians) became the population groups upon whom the VOC chose to rely in political and military affairs. These were the only population groups large enough to keep the Chinese in check; if necessary, in combination with the local garrison of Batavia castle. They were mostly wage labourers, horticulturalists, artisans, clerks or soldiers in the service of the Company. Ethnically, the Mardijkers formed a curious group. Originally the word "orang merdeka" or "free man" was used in Ambon for free Moluccans who had been baptized and educated by the Portuguese. This remarkably assimilated group of people had adopted the language and life style of their colonial masters. In Batavia the term Mardijker was used as a collective noun for Asians of varying social status and origin, whose common characteristics were the Christian religion and the Portuguese language. Most of them were freed slaves from the Coromandel and Malabar coasts or from Ceylon; some had been captured by the Dutch on board of Portuguese vessels; and others had come on their own initiative from formerly Portuguese settlements like Pulicat and Malacca after these had been taken by the Dutch. More or less pious in their adherence to the Roman Catholic Church, this Portuguese-speaking group was gradually incorporated into the Dutch Reformed church in Batavia. As their numbers increased in the 1630s, they acquired their own clergymen and church services in Portuguese. The first "Portuguese" church building established strictly for their own use dated from 1670.[7] For the 1620-1670 period, population figures are rare, but the fast increase of this population group may be gleaned from the fact that between 1630 and 1680 the number of Mardijker citizen-soldiery companies increased from two to six. All attempts by the authorities to spread the use of the Dutch language and stem the flood of the Portuguese language notwithstanding, Portuguese became the lingua franca of Batavia. Dutch remained restricted to the company servants of higher status, and Malay was only spoken by the Bandanese and Ambonese in town.

Christianity formed a trait d'union in colonial society. The VOC administration desired a docile population that conformed to the same Christian norms as the Dutch population in the Republic. The tasks of the church were quite complex: the recording of birth, marriage, death, the provision of education and welfare were all comprised within its responsibilities. Consequently the church was much deeper rooted in society than a twentieth century observer might imagine.

Many benefits could be reaped from conversion to the Reformed Church in Batavia. Native converts would receive a small monetary allowance, but, more important, native Christians could not be sold into slavery for debts, and Christian slaves could not be sold to non-christian owners. Only after conversion could native women marry Dutchmen. Having studied on a macro-level how a large population group was tied into the Dutch colonial administration, it is now time to analyse on the micro-level how those native women who originated from this group of freed slaves were taught to adapt to the tastes of the Dutch males.

The Taming of the Shrew, or the Socializing Function of the Church

The title of this section is not mere facetiousness. It is based on historical reality. In Japan, a few Dutch words of the Company period have survived into today's colloquial vocabulary. Among those words otemba is probably the most interesting one. It means "unmanageable lass" and is derived from the Dutch word ontembaar (untamable). It was an exclamation that the Japanese must have overheard when the Dutch sailors in Nagasaki decried the intractability of the local women. Japanese women have the reputation of being among "the meekest and most submissive in the world", but this reputation is based upon the context of their position within their own culture. Put into unusual situations or isolated from her own cultural background while staying with the Dutch on the tiny island of Deshima in Nagasaki, Madame Butterfly turned into a cornered cat.

From the earliest days of the settlement of Batavia, the VOC authorities attempted to eradicate the lawlessness and immorality that reigned in this frontier society. Crude punishments and severe rules were standard practice. Coen's ordinances against concubinage, and several legal cases against female poison-mixers, who had been duped in a relationship, bear witness of the terrible tensions that existed.[8]

A particularly salient example is the lawsuit against Catrina Casembroot and her friends of Asian origin in 1639. The resolution of the Batavian council is worth citing in extenso:
"The lawsuits against Catrina Casembroot, widow of Nicolaes Casembroot, a late free merchant of this town, on account of the committed fornication with several persons while her husband was alive, as well as afterwards; who by various impermissible and ghastly means of witchcraft, charms, and administered potions has constrained and tried to force persons to her uncouth desires, yes, to such an extent that she has also ordered, permitted and consented to poison two people, one of whom, Jan Scholten, the late town barber, has died, while the other, a Dutch woman called Grietgen Bartholomeus, wife of Andries Cramers, messenger of the Bench of Aldermen, after having swallowed the prepared poison, was in grave danger of dying, but now due to the Lord's succour and medicine has nearly regained her health. Apart from this, Catharina has also for some time gained a living by stealing goods belonging to others, using her own female slaves for this goal.

Item, Lucia de Coenja, Indian wife of Anthonij de Coenja, mardijker in his town, on account of her efforts to poison the above named Griet-

je Bartholomeus with permission of Catrina Casembroot, with the intention to make Grietgen's husband Andries Cramers fall in love with Catrina through the use of magic and love potions.
Item, Paula da Silva alias Brouwa, also an Indian wife of Aernout Leenderts, a Papanger[9], on account of the procurement and transmission of the aforesaid poison, as well on account of the fact that she has offered her service to a certain woman to bring her husband to a peaceful life through the use of magic herb and other kinds of black arts.
Item, Annika da Silva, like the above-named a native of these regions, the wife of Leendert Jacobs, a soldier, on account of the adultery committed with diverse persons while her husband was still alive, whom she has forced into uncouthness through several malignant means of magic and love potions. In addition to this, she has tried to murder her husband through poisoning. In order to rouse feelings of love she has transmitted love potions to Catrina Casembroot and her sister, Elsgen Jansz., as well as certain black women so that they might withhold their lovers, who wanted to marry someone else, from the intended marriage. In addition to this, she has prepared the poison to murder the wife of Andries Cramers and given it to Paula da Silva on the request of Lucia de Coenja, who, with the privity of Catrina Casembroot, has administered it mixed with cooked vegetables to Grietje Bartholomeus.
Having taken well into consideration the papers and the strong evidence submitted at this meeting, but above all on evidence presented by the Bench of Aldermen, it has been decided to sentence the delinquents for their godless demeanour, fornication, thieving, devilish practices, and empoisonments, to execution at the place normally designated for criminal sentences. Catrina will be drowned in a barrel with water, the other three Indian women, will be strangled one by one attached to a pole, and thereupon be branded in their face, under confiscation of all their goods."[10]
Excesses of a society in turmoil, they represented the eruption of a smouldering volcano. The problem was that Dutch norms and customs could not be imposed by legal measures, they had to be internalized. Quid leges sine moribus? Especially in this respect, the Dutch Reformed church assisted Justice and Police, and it is this aspect that I should like to examine.
Religious discipline differed in goal and character from penal justice. The aim of religious discipline, first of all, was to educate the flock in the profession of religion and in good behaviour. It always aimed at the promotion of the purity, harmony and happiness of the flock by bringing lost sheep back to the bosom of the Church. Sinners had to be brought to repentance towards themselves as well as God. The second aim was to reconcile the sinners with their victims through their public confession of guilt.
Four times a year, the Holy Communion was held. Prior to the Lord's supper, all the parish members were visited at home by the clergymen or representatives of the elders and deacons. Complaints among the parishioners were smoothed over where possible, the more serious cases were dealt with when the Church Council met on Thursdays. On that day the elders and deacons held the censura morum. There and then it was decided who should be refused admittance to the following Lord's supper.
Because of its role as a welfare institution but also due to its sanc-

tioning and moralizing functions, the church has produced a large body of records which are of considerable interest to the social historian. Some of these records, like the Acta of the Batavian Consistory, or Church Council, have been published by Reverend J. Mooy (Bouwstoffen). In the Acta, one encounters many women in action or in distress as a result of the developments I have sketched above. Here it may suffice to give a few examples of the colonial situation when we deal with the welfare sectors. Finally we shall attempt to analyse how native women were acculturized to such a degree that the church discipline could effectively exercise social control over them.

Nearly all applicants for alms were women. As early as April 1627 the complaint was heard that too many women had to be supported (Bouwstoffen I:284). Some of them may have been elderly slaves who had been manumitted by their masters in order to relieve their own responsibility for them. This motive I have not been able to verify. Most frequently the applicants appear to have been widows who alone were not able to provide for the livelihood of their families; for instance, Martje Alberts and her child, who had survived a massacre by mutineers after the Batavia was wrecked on the Australian coast (Bouwstoffen I:319).

In colonial society polygamy was no exception. Chinese traders, for instance, often had wives and families at both ends of their trade routes. The church was very strict in its measures against this "heathen institution". Occasionally the Acta record complaints from women like Maria Mesquita or Anna van Succadana, whose husbands had deserted them and crossed over to the devil. Anna quite cleverly mentioned that since her husband had had himself circumcised and had converted to Islam she henceforth felt herself discharged from the Holy Oath of marriage and felt justified in asking for permission to remarry (Bouwstoffen I:277). Rather exceptional is the case of Catalina Charles of Haarlem who remarried after she had been told that her first husband had died in the Indies. When she arrived in Batavia with her second husband, she found her first spouse in excellent health (Bouwstoffen I:320).

Prostitution was also rampant in Batavia, as is common in societies with uneven man-to-woman ratios. On August 13, 1625 "a native women Maria presents herself to the council 'complaining about her husband, Manuel, who forces her and her female slave to daily earn dishonest money by calling in the Dutch and receiving a whore's wage from them'" (Bouwstoffen I:215-6). In August 1631, it was established that several Christian women had committed adultery with Chinese and Islamic Bandanese, "while Valdero, head of the blacks [Mardijkers], and some others keep female slaves whom they daily dispatch to prostitute themselves. He earns about half a riall or at least 3/8 riall from them." (Bouwstoffen I:425). Rather comic is the sheepish apology offered by the Church Council to Mr. and Mrs. Minne (literally meaning lovemaking) in response to their complaint that the Reverend Joannes Stertemius had explained the 10th commandment in church by exclaiming that "the coconutpalms, trees, pavements, porches, verandahs, and interiors would bear witness of the fornication that Batavian women engage in" (Bouwstoffen I:604). Such an accusation the couple refused to tolerate! This is a clear indication that the Batavian population had developed enough healthy self-respect to protest against such outbursts by their spiritual guides from the pulpit. Without doubt brothels led a thriving existence in town. They were mainly located in front of Batavia castle, a location which allowed soldiers who could not bring women into the barracks to pay occasional visits to the ladies of pleasure.

Jan Pieterszoon Coen had stipulated that concubinage should be eradicated at all costs. According to him (and here he based his opinion upon empirical facts), it resulted in abortion, infanticide and sometimes in the poisoning of the master by a jealous concubine. In any case, it almost inevitably led to illegitimate offspring. To expect that concubinage could be eradicated was a vain hope: time after time in the Acta, reports can be found of investigations carried out by the Church Council, in which as many as 95 or 110 couples were said to live in this temporary union.[11]

René Maunier in his "Sociologie coloniale" has written: "La même où le concubinage n'était point régnant, c'était souvent par l'esclavage qu'avait lieu l'union de fait entre dominateurs et dominés. Concubinage, ou l'esclavage: c'ont été là, pendant des siècles, les moyens par lesquels s'est opérée l'union sexuelle entre les conquérants et les conquis. Ces 'petites épouses' ont été fréquemment contre leur gré ou bien à leur insu, agents de relation d'ordre moral entre sauvages et civilisés." (1932:183). It would be imprudent to portray this phenomenon literally in such black and white terms in Batavia. Not among the Dutch, but among other groups, especially the Mardijkers, who thereby acted according to the Indo-Lusitanian tradition, concubinage was most rampant.

In 1652 the Church Council requested its scriba, Secretary Johan Roman, to inquire into the backgrounds of concubinage. Roman reported that it would be very difficult to generalize. He found that every couple had its own reasons. Some couples were made up of free people, or Christians "who could only produce frivolous excuses like poverty, debts or that they really should not live together". Other couples were made up of free men and slave girls, or Christians and Muslims, heathens or unbaptized girls. Some of these people stated that they were willing to marry but "unable to do so as the laws and constitution of this republic impeded their union; one woman had given birth to two children while living with a married man, another woman had left her blind and poor husband and was now living with another man" (Bouwstoffen II:264). All couples who had been caught were instructed to marry forthwith.

Were these "petites épouses" prepared for marriage? Originally they were not, but were baptized right away. Out of this custom grew the greatest religious dispute that the Dutch Reformed church has known in the Indies: the question of whether the sacraments should be separated. Children of Christian fathers had to be baptized: the government needed them. However, they could only be baptized if the mother was also Christian. In the early pioneer days, mothers of illegitimate children, therefore, had been baptized in the Moluccas with little objection. These Jesuit-style water-baptisms came to an end in Batavia.

When in 1620 the first Holy Communion was held in Batavia, the Church Council found itself saddled with a problem. The censura morum board would not permit unmarried but baptized mothers to receive communion. These women were sinners. About their male partners we find nothing. Soon the argument could be heard that other native women who were not well-versed in the testaments should be prohibited from sharing in the communion. It was argued that many of them had asked to be baptized with worldly aims in mind, such as in order to marry, or to be released from slavery, "like the dipped sow these people go back to roll in the mud [...] pearls cast before swine, who tread them with their feet [...]" (Enklaar 1947:36). According to this line of thought it was better to keep baptism and communion separated, and permit baptized people only to receive Holy Communion after they had sufficiently proved their earnest religious zeal. In the outer church provinces of the archipelago like Ambon and Banda this practice of separating the sacraments became the rule.

In Batavia, which was the only really sizeable church community in the archipelago, it was decided after much bickering that the old Dutch custom should be maintained and the sacraments combined. No one was to be baptized unless she or he were able to demonstrate some knowledge of the catechism. Religious as well as political principles underlay this decision. It was said that if people would be baptized without question, concubinage and fornication would be openly sanctioned. "Whoremongers already openly rejoice in the separation of the sacraments, as they can easily get their concubines baptized" (Enklaar 1947: 53).

A population of Christian subjects, who were Christians in name only, did not fit in with the political interests of the administration, which especially in the case of the "Portuguese-colonial-style" policy for which it had chosen, needed a faithful flock of co-religionists. Consequently, as time passed by, the government and the church accommodated the Portuguese- and Malay-speaking population groups by special measures. Each group acquired its own clergymen and church and from 1664 onwards the "Portuguese church" celebrated its own Communion with the accompanying censura morum. In other words, from that year onwards the Mardijker community started to exercise its own social and religious control. As a source of information on Mardijker and mestizo women, the Acta of the Dutch-language main church consequently become a bit less comprehensive in nature. The Acta of the Portuguese church do not seem to have been preserved.

The path to baptism that native women had to tread was a thorny one - that is, in the period that antedated the measures described here above. Of course, we should not overestimate the religious education to which they were submitted, or judge it by today's standards, but it was often the first (moral) education that they received and was consequently of importance. As early as 1625 it was decided that native brides or wives of Dutch men had to be present at confirmation classes whether they were baptized or not, "to learn the fundaments of the Christian religion and the answers to some questions in order that they may not only be Christian in name but also in fact" (Bouwstoffen I: 227). Also the young native girls who had been purchased by the Company to be prepared for marriage with Dutch personnel had to follow special preparatory courses every Monday afternoon. These were not empty formalities. Regularly the Acta report that women like Natalia van Batavia, Paulinha van Tayouan, Monica van Bengalen or Ursula van Palliacatte present themselves to be examined.

After surmounting the hurdle of baptism these native girls were ready for marriage. In the early years they did not yet fully realize that once they expressed their willingness to marry, they had to fulfill their promises. In the Acta of the 1620s we often find it recorded that women changed their minds and wanted to back out of the agreement a few days before the marriage ceremony was to take place. As the marriage

Sirih box, eighteenth century.

had already been announced on three consecutive Sundays from the pulpit, this vascillating behaviour of the ladies elicited stern rebuffs from the Church Council. They were forced to marry.

The final test of whether Batavian women really came to behave as prudent wives is reflected in the censura morum that was held every third month. It cannot be without significance that during the first two decades of the town's history, two-thirds of the people who were refused admittance to the Holy Communion were women. Thereafter the number of censured women started to decrease while the number of men remained the same. Sexual licence became less and less the reason for refusal. In the end we hear only of quarrels with husbands or squabbles with the neighbours. There is no doubt about it: the ideal of the satisfactory wife had been achieved!

The Daughters of Batavia Take Revenge

In conclusion, it can be claimed that the church was the only Dutch institution which was genuinely able to influence the lives of Batavia's women. It reformed them, imposing a certain morality on their behaviour, and it provided them with a veneer of metropolitan norms. Paradoxically, once these ladies felt at home in the church, they transformed it into an arena in which they competed with their sisters in pomp and splendour.

In 1669 the Church Council felt obliged to employ Company slaves during the church services to silence the domestic slaves who were sitting near the pulpit, and to post military personnel at the church doors to keep out other slaves. After the service was over, it was the habit of these slaves to rush into the church to assist their mistresses in collecting Bibles, betel-boxes and other ornaments which the latter used to demonstrate their wealth. Visitors from Europe were appalled at the sight of "these burgher daughters dressed up like princesses" who ran the public worship service on Sunday like a show, apparently without the slightest fear of retribution from the pulpit. On the contrary, the clergymen, who should have rebuked them and should have preached humility, instead tacitly acknowledged their own wives and daughters as masters of the church, and let them display their dresses and diamonds to their hearts' content (De Graaff 1930:17). Cuius regio, eius religio?

Chapter VIII

BUTTERFLY OR MANTIS?
THE LIFE AND TIMES OF CORNELIA VAN NIJENROODE

"De vrouw is onbekwaam"
(Roman Dutch Law)

The Social World of the Batavian Widow

Introduction
Batavia, the headquarters of the VOC in Asia with her "va et vient" of fortune hunters from Asia and Europe, constituted a "frontier-society" in which power found its expression in family ties and wealth. David van Lennep, to whom we soon shall turn again, summarized this situation as follows: "[...] to scrape together money is the principle here, in such a manner that it is openly confessed, to deny this is held to be ridiculous. Look how one argues in Batavia: 'the voyage hither is long and dangerous, the climate is unhealthy and fatiguing, these sacrifices and dangers must be compensated for! Only a genius can make an (honest) fortune. It would be foolish to display more consideration in behaviour and action than others, and consequently fail to reach the objectives for which we have come.' Real life proves this disgusting theory."[1]

In Holland, young men of better families went East to make that period's equivalent of "a fast buck" so that they might return home and spend the remainder of their lives in leisure. Due to institutional as well as to physical limitations, only a few actually were able to achieve these objectives, as I shall presently show.

During the ancien régime only males embarked for the Orient with work contracts in hand, for the Dutch East India Company did not hire female employees. To Governor-General Jan Pieterszoon Coen (the founder of Batavia), however, it was eminently obvious that mankind could not survive without women; and indeed, the Gentlemen XVII at an early date faced up to the necessity of providing their servants in the East with Dutch "nubile daughters". In the preceding chapter I have described why these attempts miscarried. The supply of girls remained qualitatively and quantitatively substandard, and in the tropical regions the majority of Dutch women tended to wither away. After 1635 the directors changed tactics and opted for the Portuguese mode of colonization. Henceforth marriages with Asian women were encouraged so that ultimately a loyal mestizo population in Batavia might be created. Portuguese-speaking slave girls from the Coromandel and Malabar coasts of Southern India were in particular demand. The mothers of the "black nobility" of Batavia, the characteristic housewives who spoke Portuguese at home and double Dutch in public, were the result.

The Batavian woman and the role and function she fulfilled in the colonial society of Batavia in the days of the VOC regime have drawn comments from many writers. Nicolaus de Graaff, a VOC physician, con-

VIII Butterfly or Mantis?

demned her for being stupid and indolent. The archivist and historian Frederik de Haan typified her as the ostentatious element of urban society. The novelist, V.I. van de Wall, caricatured her in a gallery of portraits, "Vrouwen uit de Compagnie's tijd". The American historian, Jean Gelman Taylor, recently depicted her as a typical representative of mestizo society in general.[2] Personally I have called her the pillar, the caryatid, of Batavian society and have analysed which forces of colonial society contributed to this particular function.

It was not an attractive proposition for a man who had married a "native black woman" to return to the Low Countries, as regulations did not permit his wife and children to accompany him. It is not surprising that many a Company servant preferred to live in concubinage: whenever he chose to repatriate he could buy off his commitments to his mistress and children and select in his own country the wife of his dreams with whom he wished to live out his life. This functional system of concubinage, which actually was in vogue among Asian and Portuguese merchants long before the Dutch showed up in Asia (Boxer 1963:85), was vehemently battled against as an abuse by the clerical authorities in Batavia, since marriage and baptism were the bridles of social control of the urban population.

Much more crippling than all these rules and prohibitions by church and state were, however, the extraordinarily unhealthy way of living of the average Company servant and the rigours to which the tropical climate subjected him. The majority fell victim in the prime of their lives to the ever-recurring epidemics, not in the least because excessive drinking had ruined their constitution. It has been calculated that only 30% of those who came to the East in Company service returned to Patria, allowing, of course, for those who chose to remain (Bruijn 1976: 233).

And what about the Batavian housewives of these gentlemen? In charge of a comfortable slave household, this lady, often born and raised in Asia, generally led a less strenuous life than her male partner. Only during or shortly after her pregnancies would she have run a higher risk and been more prone to infections or illnesses. That was the most critical time of her life. Although it is impossible to assemble hard statistics, it may be surmised that women had on average a longer lifespan than their husbands. Boxer, speaking about the Portuguese, draws attention to the fact that the death rate among men, due to the combination of continual warfare, over-indulgence, and tropical disease, was higher than among women (Boxer 1975:77). Antonia Frazer, speaking about 17th century England, stated that "men appear to have been more prone to disease" (Frazer 1984:82).

One authority on the subject takes exception to this thesis. According to the American historian Holden Furber, the death rate among European women in the East was much higher than among men. "It was a rare company servant who did not marry twice", he remarks (Furber 1976:310). He bases this argument on the genealogical research of Wijnaendts van Resandt on 375 high-level Company servants. However, the fact that many of these men married several times does not show that men in general lived longer than women. The group from which Furber drew his sample was evidently in no way representative of Company servants in Batavia in general. Only those who survived the rigours of the tropics for many years became high officials, and, because of this relative longevity, they were, it may be assumed, much more likely to remarry than others. The argument can also be turned around. Many women married several times, although for obvious reasons a widow past the first flush of youth and without a steady income must have had more difficulty in finding a partner than an elderly male with a steady income. Indeed, one frequently finds documentary evidence in the VOC archives about the large number of widows of deceased Company servants forced to eke out a living on tiny pensions, not to mention the records of the Church which was often at a loss regarding what to do for the destitute widows of the free population. But not all widows faced such a sorry plight.

Contemporary sources also indicate the pivotal position held by wealthy widows of the upper echelon of VOC servants in Batavian society (Taylor 1983:35). Evidence produced by Furber indeed confirms this line of reasoning. Quoting Wijnaendts van Resandt's findings once more he asserts that many established Batavian families in the 18th and 19th centuries descended from second or third marriages of high ranking officials in the period 1680-1730. "The second or third marriage was normally made with young widows, either country born or survivors of two or three years' exposure to the danger of the tropics. Such widows outlived their new husbands." (Furber 1976:311.)

In the East, all Dutch men, the "freeburghers" excepted, served the East India Company. Although the monthly allowance they received was quite modest, this caused no financial hardships, for considerable sums of money could often be drawn from job-related emoluments and side interests. Certain positions like those of head-cashier of Batavia castle, boss of the Company's wharf on Onrust island, or chief of such distant factories as Deshima in Japan, were much coveted for the opportunities they offered to line the pockets of the incumbent. The VOC physician, Nicolaus de Graaff, provides an ironical illustration of these practices in the "Oost-Indise spiegel". When chief-factor Hendrick Cansius returned from Japan in 1683 and greeted his old comrade, Governor-General Speelman, at the Batavian roadstead he boasted that over the past year there had been more private trade than Company trade in Japan. According to De Graaff, "Speelman answered: 'Enough, who inquires after the private trade in Japan?', but all the same what he said can be easily believed for after the private merchandise had been unloaded from Goudenstein [Cansius' ship], the vessel had risen three and a half feet!" (De Graaff 1930:30).

Company servants usually entered a clause in their wills that relations in Patria should be provided for with the savings of uncollected income in the Company pay-office. The local, often illegally acquired, possessions in the Indies were left to those of their kin who were living there. Little surprise that in this way many a widow accumulated a large fortune from the proceeds of her deceased husband(s). Women who "used up" three or four husbands were no exception in Batavia. Consequently, mature widows were more highly valued by ambitious young men than the young daughters of the local VOC élite, because the former were attractive propositions for investment.

Women played more than passive roles in accumulating of fortunes. Private trade in Japan was condoned because supervision of the personnel stationed there was well-nigh impossible. In Batavia, the Company's regulations which forbade the personnel to engage in private trade (the so-called spillover trade, "morshandel") were better adhered to. That is where the wives actively appeared on the scene. "Distinguished ladies", as De Graaff sarcastically calls them, not only were directly involved in trading, they also acted as brokers in real estate or as moneylenders to the local Chinese (De Graaff 1930:29). In his short study on the Armenian wives of Company servants in Suratte, Kolff has indicated that the wheelings and dealings of these housewives may have been an essential part of the Company's trade over there as they provided access to the overland trade networks (Kolff 1984:7-16). In a less open but still conspicuous enough manner, Batavian housewives were also involved in all kinds of trafficking. The French contemporary traveller and gem dealer, Jean Baptiste Tavernier, credited Batavian housewives with a lot of influence: "Generally they take advantage of the goodwill of their husbands in such a way, that they abuse the favours received, that they goad them [the husbands] on to serious iniquities, and finally, commit malpractice under the cover of their husbands' prestige" (Tavernier 1682 II:262).

If one takes these remarks at face value, the following questions may seem a bit naive, but they should be posed nonetheless : Was the mature, wealthy "Batavian widow" conscious of her relatively strong starting position vis-à-vis a possible suitor? Did she make use of her comfortable financial status or her financial dealings to make demands on those who were courting her? Did these "lustige Witwen" use their wedlock with an established VOC servant or a young, fast-rising star as a steppingstone for a quick ascent on the hierarchical social ladder? Or was the contrary the case and was she forced to suffer passively and resignedly the advances of cavaliers, doomed to fall victim to those who were after her wealth?

The English historian John Crawfurd had the following to say about the subject: "As soon as a woman becomes a widow, and the body of her husband is interred, which is generally done the day after his decease, if she be but rich, she has immediately a number of suitors. A certain lady, who lost her husband while I was at Batavia, had, in the fourth week of her widowhood, a fourth lover, and, at the end of three months, she married again, and would have done it sooner, if the laws had allowed of it." (Crawfurd 1820 I:147).

I have touched upon the personal side of the question; but what about the institutional arrangements within Batavian society: did, for instance, the juridical system en vigueur enable or permit an unattached widow to steer an independent course and to engage in business deals without the protection of a husband? And if she did marry her suitor, could she continue to trade without his interference? The historian who would like to suggest an answer to these questions must attempt to locate in the existing archives personal observations made by the women concerned, and look for juridical cases.

What men had in mind in these matters is easy to establish, witness the ebullitions under David van Lennep's pen. This not altogether unscrupulous bachelor embarked for the Orient at the end of the eighteenth century in order "to repair the damages which the errors of my youth have committed and to repay my financial debts". After his arrival he was so shocked by the greed and graft of the local élite that he did not aspire to any profitable position and contented himself with the rank of member of the Court of Justice (Lubberhuizen-van Gelder 1945:98). This did not mean that he had given up all hope of settling his debts.

In a bundle of gloomy letters he informed members of his family in

Holland about his plan to hook a well-off widow (good for 800,000 guilders). As the current laws of marriage provided that all property of the wife, even if she herself had earned or inherited it, automatically also belonged to the husband, this implied that this wedlock eventually might help him to alleviate the burden of his 270,000 guilder debt. "It is not quite possible to pay off a large debt from property of this size all at once, without resorting to alienating many stocks and shares to the detriment of her financial position, and without embittering her - in short without losing her trust - if one would manage her possessions in such a way", he wrote in one of these letters. It was not just the technical aspect of it all which oppressed him - he supposed that the payment of his debt would not be too obvious if paid off in four yearly instalments - he also displayed some compassion: "I am quite willing to sacrifice myself to obtain this goal [she clearly was not that attractive in other respects] but it would be evil to sacrifice a fellow human being, and would be even more wicked to cheat or ruin a woman, who is willing to share her own brilliant destiny with mine." (MMPH, Van Lennep, 20-11-1803.) The victim concerned must have realized this in time, for from later correspondence it becomes clear that Van Lennep was turned down.

While we have gained some insight into the mentality of the hunter from this piece of information, we remain in the dark regarding the line of thought of the prey. As long as pertinent evidence is lacking we can only offer some assumptions. In short, the question has been posed, but it remains impossible to answer - unless a lucky find is made in the archives.

The Quest for a Role Model
Ten years ago I was given the opportunity to tour the southern coast of Japan aboard the sailing yacht of a friend. Only much later I realized that the yacht's name, Minerva, foreshadowed the academic nature of this pleasure trip. One of the ports of call was the sleepy fishing harbour of Hirado island, facing the west coast of Kyushu. Notorious in medieval times on account of the wo-k'ou pirates whom it served as a haunt, Hirado gained some respectability in the early seventeenth century when it was selected by the VOC as a suitable location for a trade factory. The Dutch establishment in Hirado was, however, not allotted a long existence, for in 1640 the VOC merchants were ordered out by the shogunate under the newly promulgated maritime prohibition laws. They were subsequently relocated on the man-made islet of Deshima in Nagasaki Bay.

The local situation in Hirado still reminds today's visitor of these days. On the left side of the narrow entrance, high on a rock which rises steeply from the sea, the white castle of lord Matsuura, the former local daimyo, perches like a large sea-bird. Halfway up the hill on the other side, one sees through the treetops the roof tiles of the yashiki or lordly mansion. Along the inner harbour, a few remnants of the old Dutch factory can be found. In addition to a water-well, the stone sheet-piling of the quay, and the ruins of a former lighthouse near the waterfront, remnants from the past include a remarkably wellkept flagstone path which runs up a hill: in Japanese it is called the Oranda ishidatami, the Dutch stone pavement. The path once led to an observation post on the top of the hill.

An exhibition of the treasures of the former daimyo is held in the

VIII Butterfly or Mantis?

Hirado castle.

yashiki of the Matsuura family, a large but elegant wooden building, once deprecatively described by Jan Compagnie as "a simple piece of carpentry, covered with thin planks" (Montanus 1669:27). Halfway along the "Dutch path", another museum, "the Historical Tourist Museum", is situated with a somewhat moth-eaten collection of curiosa of local importance. In one of the showcases of this small museum, I came across several paraphernalia of Surishia, a local belle, who was a concubine of Cornelis van Nijenroode, the head of the Dutch factory between 1623 and 1633. Most striking among these curiosa were the two letters written in the 1660s by Cornelia, the child born of this alliance, who was by then living in Batavia. A miniature screen depicting a woman (according to the local tradition, Cornelia herself) is testimony to the daughter's filial piety towards her mother.

It is evident that the Japanese people respect this kind of attitude. In 1682, Cornelia's relatives in Hirado erected a miniature stone pagoda in the Honsei temple in memory of this paragon of oya koko (filial piety) since she never forgot her old mother and continued to send her letters and presents from faraway Batavia.[3]

During my stay in Hirado I resolved to make further inquiries in the VOC archives about Cornelia, but soon this turned out to be unnecessary. A fascinating article about the girl was published not long afterwards by Iwao Seiichi, who is well known for his historical studies of Japanese overseas expansion to Southeast Asia prior to the proclamation of the maritime prohibitions in 1636 (Iwao 1978:142-55). Iwao tells us that during his research into the Batavian archives almost fifty years ago, he encountered a remarkable number of notarial papers, baptism registers and marriage documents concerning Japanese residents of this town in its early years. Among these sources he found evidence on

The small pagoda erected in honour of Cornelia van Nijenroode.

Cornelia's life in Batavia. Basing his research on these data and the letters in Hirado referred to above, Iwao succeeded in "bringing home" the prodigal daughter of a Dutch father and a Japanese mother. As the life story of Cornelia unfolded, my curiosity raised by the letters was fully satisfied.

To my astonishment I recently encountered Cornelia's name once more as I was ploughing through the Acta of the Batavian church council. From these sources, however, she does not appear to be a kind and scrupulous daughter but rather an irritable housewife, whose quarrels with her second husband, the barrister Johan Bitter, escalated to such a degree that both were denied admission to the Holy Communion. At the end of his article Iwao indeed briefly refers to an unhappy second marriage, but he does not commit himself further by drawing any conclusions. The Batavian chronicler Van de Wall (not consulted by Iwao) has on the contrary turned this episode of Cornelia's life into a tragicomic sketch. One citation may suffice to indicate the tone of his account: "Neel had a tongue of her own. Experience had shown that a thunderstorm was about to break out whenever Neel planted her heavy arms on her bulky hips and narrowed down her little eyes into slits, while a torrent of well chosen Japanese expletives escaped from her lips." (Van de Wall 1923:65). Romanticizing may have been Van de Wall's strong point but note how stereotyped his picture is! Did the quarrels between Cornelia and her second husband originate in nothing more than an incomptabilité d'humeur, or Cornelia's bad temper? The Acta, but moreover the judicial evidence that eventually was traced back in the archives of the Dutch East India Company and the Supreme Court of Justice of Holland, show that the story is not as simple as that.

They point in another direction, demonstrating the characteristics of a classical drama in which the second husband attempts to loot the total inheritance his wife received from her first husband. So intimate a picture of the way of thinking and inner motives of the unfortunate wife arises from this unexploited source material that a renewed attempt at a biography seems quite justified; this time it suggests the life story of a woman who may represent with all her strengths and weaknesses the prototype of "the Batavian widow".

Happy Times

A Snapshot of Colonial Family Life
One of the more elaborate paintings in the exhibition on Dutch overseas history in the Rijksmuseum of Amsterdam is without doubt the Cnoll family portrait.[4] Jacob Jansz. Coeman has depicted chief-merchant Pieter Cnoll, his wife Cornelia - with her exotic eyes - and their two young daughters. "Both children are a delight to the beholder", the art-historian De Loos-Haaxman writes, "posing gracefully, both pretty faces adorned with the same coiffure. Affluence presents itself in many ways around the parents and the girls: pearls, golden buttons, a precious little box, textiles and lace, a spread fan and two toy-dogs. The composition is well-balanced, the colours attractive and closely tallying with the composition in all its parts." (De Loos-Haaxman 1968:10.) Catharina, the eldest daughter, must have been about eleven years old, and her little sister, Hester, six or seven. Strangely enough, De Loos does not say anything about the two slaves in the shadowy background. Had they not been inserted, one would hardly have realized that one was looking at a tropical scene.

Little is known about Coeman, the artist. In 1663 this native of Amsterdam sailed for the Indies as a so-called "visitor of the sick". Generally these ziekentroosters were assigned to the clergy; they were not allowed to preach, only to read a text written by ordained clergymen. Even if they did not have an academic education, ziekentroosters were on the whole relatively well-read people. In Ambon and Formosa, their aid was often invoked in educational matters whenever a shortage of schoolmasters arose.[5]

More is known about the highly successful professional career of Cornelia's stoutly built husband, Pieter Cnoll of Delft. In 1647, he disembarked at Batavia as a young assistant with a monthly allowance of 18 guilders. His zeal and intelligence soon caught the eyes of his superiors. He was placed at the disposal of the Councillor of the Indies Willem Verstegen, who was responsible for the bookkeeping of the Company's treasury in Batavia castle. Cnoll lived up to the expectations, for in 1651 his salary almost doubled, to 30 guilders, and in the following year he was promoted to the rank of junior-merchant (earning 45 guilders). In 1657 this fast-rising star was appointed cashier "under special mortgage of his real estate". Four years later, on June 12, 1662, it is stated that he was to temporarily replace Balthazar Bort during the latter's absence as the commander of the expedition to China in the capacity of second head-merchant of Batavia castle. On July 16, 1663 he got himself appointed to one of the most coveted positions in the VOC hierarchy: first head-merchant of Batavia castle.[6] His official income was not spectacular, about 120 guilders, but as the head-mer-

Pieter Cnoll and his family.

chant he held the key to the Company's treasury and most of the cash collected and issued at the Company's headquarters passed through his hands. It will not come as a surprise that he soon became one of Batavia's richest citizens. At the zenith of his career, Cnoll commissioned the newly arrived Coeman to paint the family portrait. We shall now focus on the frail-looking lady at his side, the heroine of this study. She never joined the Company - but, in a sense, she was sired by it. Therefore, let us first study her "roots" and her colonial parentage.

Anak Kompenie
Cornelia's father, Cornelis van Nijenroode van Delft, was a member of the early VOC generation of Jan Pieterszoon Coen.[7] In his lifetime he was known equally for his ability and his arrogance. Nobody was secure from either his sharp tongue or his acid pen. The good-natured skipper Willem IJsbrandtzoon Bontekoe - writer of the famous travel book - was one of his victims (Bontekoe 1952). Van Nijenroode, who sailed as a head-merchant and squadron-commander on Bontekoe's vessel during the China expedition of 1622, severely scolded him for being a sloppy sailor and a haughty fellow, just because the skipper occasionally dared to disagree with him (Groeneveldt 1898:131). Van Nijenroode was also often at odds with his own direct chief, Admiral Cornelis Reyersen. He always thought he knew better than his superior and, embarrassingly, he usually did. Nobody would deny that Van Nijenroode, apart from being a source of annoyance to those closely associated with him, was all the same a very able Company servant. Reyersen even saw him as his eventual successor (Groeneveldt 1898:469).

Events took charge in this case, however. While Van Nijenroode was visiting Hirado to stock in provisions for the China fleet, the local head-factor, Leonard Camps, suddenly died in November 1623. Being the highest in rank, Van Nijenroode was elected his successor. This choice pleased the Japanese. As difficult as he was to get along with for his Dutch colleagues, he seems to have been easy and compliant to his Japanese hosts. His early years in the Orient had taught him how to behave abroad. Few Company servants could actually boast of wider experience in dealing with Asian potentates than Van Nijenroode himself as the following information concerning his career will show.

In 1607 Van Nijenroode had arrived in the Indies as a diamond specialist aboard the ship Delft, which had been fitted out by the VOC chamber of his native city. Between 1610 and 1622, he stayed almost continuously in or around Siam, the first two years in the capital Ayutthya; then from 1612 until 1615, he resided in the port of Pattani on the northeast coast of the Malay peninsula, and thereafter for two years in Sangora (today's Sonkhla), about one hundred kilometres to the north. In 1617 he was back again in the important factory of Ayutthaya, this time as head factor. He remained on this post until 1622. After this, he served the above mentioned short stint as squadron commander to the China fleet, which resulted in his appointment in Hirado on November 21, 1623. The experience he had acquired in his dealings with the proud Siamese was soon tested in Japan.

After initial attempts to open a trade factory in China had failed, Reyersen's successor, Martinus Sonck, moved his troops from the Pescadores archipelago to nearby Formosa in the autumn of 1624. He built a fortress and, in order to alleviate the financial burden of its construction, he began to levy tolls on all foreign shipping, Japanese traders included. When Van Nijenroode heard about this, he ventured to expose the unjust nature of this measure in a letter to his colleague in Formosa: the Japanese had been trading on this island for many years prior to the Dutch arrival and saw no reason why they should suddenly have to pay taxes (GM I:187, 3-2-1626). Van Nijenroode's warnings were not heeded and after many minor incidents, the situation culminated in an outburst in 1628. Furious Japanese merchants who had once more been thwarted by the Dutch in their attempts to trade with the Chinese took the local governor, Pieter Nuyts, hostage in his own office. Nuyts eventually gained his freedom under very humiliating conditions. He was to surrender five Dutch hostages to the Japanese merchants who were to accompany them as safeguards. Among the hostages was his ten-year-old son. In addition, a compensation for all the losses the Japanese claimed they had suffered was to be paid out to them. Upon returning home, the Japanese merchants reported the affair to the shogun, who promptly imprisoned not only the five Dutch hostages, but also the crew members of all VOC ships that happened to be in Japanese waters at the time. The ships themselves were unrigged and put under embargo. Significantly Van Nijenroode and his staff in Hirado were not restricted in their movements, although the go-downs of the factory were sealed. Shortly before the "Formosan incident" took place, Van Nijenroode had written to Batavia, asking to be relieved from his post (GM I:232, 13-12-1626). Under the circumstances, this was no longer possible. He had to remain at his post to act as a mediator, and to do all he could to alleviate the suffering of the prisoners. The incident was only closed four years later when Pieter Nuyts, by then dismissed from his post of governor of Formosa, was sent to Japan by Governor-General Jacques Specx to atone for his reckless behaviour.[8]

Realizing that under these circumstances there was no chance of his returning to Batavia in the near future, Van Nijenroode made himself comfortable and continued to lead a merry life with two Japanese concubines, Tokeshio and Surishia, each of whom presented him with a daughter. This way of life, combined with an excess of alcohol, evidently put too much strain on his constitution, for halfway into 1631 his health failed and thereafter continued to deteriorate. Pieter Nuyts, who visited him upon his arrival in September 1632, wrote: "Nijenroode is so feeble (I won't say due to what kind of disease) that he has not left his room for more than a year; moreover he has been struck by God's hand, so that he cannot use one half of his body nor has he any feeling left in his limbs".[9] That same autumn he became so weak that, fearing he could not live much longer, he started to hand out presents to those close to him. A document in the Hirado papers shows that his elder daughter, Hester, received a large golden chain weighing 10 taels and a golden Japanese couban weighing 4 taels and 3 maces; the youngest daughter, Cornelia, was also presented with a couban weighing 4 taels and 3 maces and a golden chain weighing 5 taels, 5 maces and 4 condrins.[10]

After Nuyts' arrival in Japan, Dutch-Japanese relations were restored to their former cordial state. The arrest was reversed, the crews freed, and the ships rerigged. It looked as though at last the debilitated Van Nijenroode could be sent home. On January 19, 1633 all his belongings were packed into 39 cases and trunks and shipped on board Heusden, which was ready to sail. The cases were crammed with all kinds of bric-a-brac, including Indonesian keris, silver condiment

The VOC factory at Hirado.

sets, silverware, satins, diamonds – in all, three hundred different kinds of artefacts.[11] Twelve days later, one more case was added: Van Nijenroode's coffin. He had passed away just before boarding on January 31, "beaten and completely worn out, full of diseases and miseries". The large number of boxes in his inventory already suggested considerable wealth and his testament, which was opened on February 3, proved this supposition. Two nieces in Holland received two thousand guilders each; a nephew was bestowed with "all his weapons without exception"; Hester's mother, Tokeshio, was made a present of 300 taels of schuyt silver; Cornelia's mother, Surishia, was bestowed with 200 taels; and furthermore "he, the testator, willed his daughters together (and, in case of the demise of one of them, to the surviving one) all the golden chains and other small ornaments that may be found in his closets after the Honorable's death". Silver ewers, cups, candelabra "with the accompanying snuffers" were bequeathed to friends in Batavia.[12] But neither the value of all goods, which had already been put on board, nor the total amount of outstanding debts could be estimated at that time. Only after the arrival of the Heusden in Batavia was it established how much Van Nijenroode had saved up during his ten years' tenure in Japan. It forced Governor-General Hendrick Brouwer to devote one separate paragraph to this case in his Generale Missive to the Gentlemen XVII in Holland: "The chief merchant Cornelis van Nijenroode, who had lapsed into a virulent illness and phrenesia a considerable time before his death, and who had forsaken in Christ Our Saviour his final days, died in January 1633 in Firando, leaving behind two little daughters from two different women. He has enriched himself during his life with unfaithful actions or illicit and private trade to such an extent that apart from his monthly allowances (whose net amount free of taxes amount to ƒ 32,316.17.2), his inheritance has fetched ƒ 23,604.14.4 at a public auction here. Because Nijenroode through the amassment of such considerable fortunes has acted in defiance of the regulations, the complete inheritance has been seized by the fiscal authorities for the Court of Justice and has been declared confiscated."[13]

If Nijenroode's possessions had not been dispatched to Batavia, and if they had not been so neatly packed at the time of his death, the authorities would certainly not have been able to seize his entire estate. Such a severe punishment for a man who had died, leaving no heirs in the Indies, apart from two illegitimate infants, can only have been issued to serve as a warning to other Company servants.

Van Nijenroode's provisional successor in Hirado, Pieter van Santen, wrote the Governor-General that he had sequestered 1000 taels to carry out the last wish of the deceased, who had stated that he wanted his daughters to be brought up according to the Gospel. This act of sequestering such a considerable sum was, according to Brouwer, "truly quite an impertinent thing to do". He calculated that the girls could be put out to a nurse for less than twenty taels a year, and considering that 1000 taels "at the usual rate can fetch a yearly interest of 180 taels", the Governor-General was under the impression that Van Santen, who had himself sired two children in Edo and Hirado, was seeking means to eventually provide his own children with a considerable amount of money as well.[14] Consequently, Van Santen was called back to Batavia. He was thought to be "too young, too proud and too impulsive, qualities which run totally contrary to the Japanese temperament and conditions" (Hirado Diaries I:310). Later on, the Governor-General and the council regretted this rash action and decided to offer Van Santen the presidency of the VOC settlement in Quinam. Van Santen indeed exhibited a considerable amount of pride, for he rejected this proposition indignantly and chose to return, accompanied by one of his daughters, to Patria (VOC 1112, 15-7-1634).

When Nicolaes Couckebacker of Delft was appointed successor to Van Santen, he was ordered to send the two Van Nijenroode girls to Batavia. His orders were accompanied by some moralizing observations about intercourse with Japanese women: "the procreation of bastards degenerates the pious nature of the Dutch" (Hirado Diaries I:330). That he turned a deaf ear to these warnings is illustrated by the fact that, like Van Nijenroode and Van Santen, he also begot two daughters from two women during his six years' stay in Japan.[15]

Upon his arrival in Japan, Couckebacker reported on the above-mentioned 1000 taels. He claimed that Pieter van Santen had entered this amount into the Company's books, though not before having deducted the very high sum of 442:1:14 taels, i.e. the total already spent on the girls' upbringing. He also pointed out that the girls would not yet be sent to Batavia because their mothers were not willing to part with their children, unless they received 300 and 200 taels respectively, according to the terms of the testament.[16] From transmitted evidence it had become clear to Couckebacker that the factory council had given guarantees that this clause would indeed be carried out. Awaiting further instructions, he therefore decided to keep the children in Japan for the time being and to reserve, as agreed, thirty taels for each girl.

On September 24, 1636, the diarist of the Hirado factory notes that on that day the council finally decided "to pay out to the mothers of Nijenroode's daughters the sum designated in the legacy, 300 and 200 taels respectively, to take the children from their mothers, and to send them to Batavia this year" (Hirado Diaries II:127). However, it was not known whether a special exit permit from the Japanese authorities was needed and therefore it took one more year before Couckebacker could at last inform the Governor-General on November 20, 1637 that Hester and Cornelia had embarked on the Company yacht, Galjas. The 500 taels, in all 1425 guilders, had been passed on to the debit of the Company cash in Batavia.[17]

Neither of the girls would ever see their "mothercountry" again. Only one year earlier (June 1636) the shogun had decreed that all Japanese residing overseas should be barred from entering Japan again, and a few months later (in September) all Portuguese were ordered to leave with their Japanese wives and children. Finally on June 16, 1639, all Japanese women who had borne children of Dutchmen and Englishmen were banished to Batavia with their offspring. Japanese women, furthermore, were no longer allowed to live with Dutchmen or to associate with them.[18] It was not very difficult for the Japanese authorities to enforce these severe regulations, for the Dutch were totally isolated from the local population after their removal from Hirado to Deshima in Nagasaki Bay in 1641. In addition, the Dutch personnel were forbidden to remain longer than one year at a stretch in Japan. Only prostitutes continued to visit the factory personnel at fixed hours in order to "prepare hot tea at night" as it was discreetly put.[19] The Batavian authorities never affirmed whether these measures indeed improved "the pious nature" of the Company servants in Japan.

A Floating Life of Motherhood
The main sources of information on the adventures of the Van Nijenroode sisters after their arrival in Batavia are the birth and marriage registers of the Dutch Reformed Church and the thorough research carried out before the war by Iwao Seiichi into the notarial archives of the Landsarchief at Batavia. The children must have entered the orphanage upon arrival, but no evidence of this can be found in the archives. The Orphan Board or Weeskamer, which ran the orphanage, played a very important role in Batavia. Witness the motivation for the establishment of the Weeskamer as expressed in the resolution of August 23, 1625: "as we notice and daily are told that these orphans after the death of their parents are tremendously fleeced, either by the negligence of their guardians on account of the insufficient legitimation of the goods inherited or due to other reasons".[20] At the time that Cornelia and Hester were staying in the orphanage, the tasks of the Weeskamer were further specified by the "Bataviasche Statuten"; they provided for the making of inventories, the guardianship of minors, and the administration of their possessions until they reached maturity at 24

The orphanage of Batavia.

years of age (Plakaatboek I:518). In the case of the two sisters, all inherited goods, apart from the jewelry, had been confiscated.

We encounter Hester again in the baptism registers of the Portuguese Church of Batavia. In 1643 she acted on two occasions as godmother to children of intimate friends. The social circles she moved in can be established from the baptismal registers. Both godchildren were of Japanese or partly Japanese origin (Iwao 1978:149). The Japanese community of Batavia was quite small; its basis had been laid by mercenaries who had entered the service of the VOC in the early 1620s, and its last addition consisted of the group of women and children who had been banished from Japan in 1639. After 1636, the shogunate allowed no Japanese to travel abroad. Consequently, this Japanese community was doomed to lose its identity within the melting-pot of the colonial town.

Iwao has established that 95 marriages relating to Japanese immigrants were registered between 1618 and 1659. Among the 106 Japanese who were involved in these marriages, 73 were males and 33 females. There were only 11 marriages between Japanese men and women, so that the vast majority of these marriages was of a multi-racial nature (Iwao 1970:3). The total of Japanese immigrants at its peak was between three and four hundred people.

Hester married twice. The first time she married an English lieutenant, Michael Tresoir, on March 8, 1644. No children were born of this marriage. Her husband had his will drawn up on March 8, 1655, but did not expire until four years later. Iwao has established that Hester remarried a few years later a certain Abelis Benting, to whom she bore one son, called Johan (Iwao 1978:149-50).

In 1652, eight years after her sister, Cornelia escaped from the supervision of the "most pious, most qualified and richest townsmen" (who constituted the orphanage board) by marrying Pieter Cnoll, whose successful professional career we have already briefly examined. One year after the wedding party, the first child, Catharina, was born and in the following years, nine more appeared at intervals of 1.5 to 2 years. She must have been almost continually pregnant for no less than 18 years. The birth dates of her children were as follows:

28 August 1653	- Catharina
1 November 1654	- Jacob
22 June 1656	- Pieter
27 December 1657	- Cornelis
26 December 1658	- Hester
20 August 1662	- Johannes
4 October 1663	- Anna
24 June 1666	- Martha
29 August 1668	- Maria
7 September 1670	- Elisabeth Catharina[21]

Writing about women in 17th century England, Frazer has pointed out that this "floating life of motherhood" was not merely a life full of joyful occasions; it was a cycle of virtually unceasing pregnancy, childbearing and child-burying (Frazer 1984:61). Young mothers did not easily resign themselves to the inevitable blows, witness mrs. Thrale who wrote one hundred years later of this process of "forever bringing and losing babies which tears the body and the mind so terribly" (Robinson 1970:91). The same was the case with Cornelia. By 1671, the year in which Cornelia wrote her second letter to her mother, only four of her children were still alive. Cornelis (14), Hester (12), Martha (6) and Elisabeth Catharina (8 months). Only Cornelis lived to adulthood.

Social Circles
With regard to Cornelia's social circle, again the birth registers have something to tell to us. We are dealing here with baptisms performed in the Dutch Reformed Church and not in the Portuguese Church as had been the case with Hester's godchildren. The names of the godfathers and the godmothers indicate the social circuit in which the Cnoll family moved. Susanna Schemon, who attended the baptism of Cornelis, was the daughter of Nicolaes Couckebacker. She had married the Japanese Captain, Nicolaes Schemon (De Haan 1910 I:197). There also seems to be a Japanese connection in the case of Hester's baptism (26 December 1658). Both the godmothers, Mrs. Frisius and Mrs. Hartsinck were married to "old Japan hands". Frisius had served as an ambassador to the shogunal court in 1649. Carel Hartsinck had lived in Hirado between 1633 and 1637 before he was transferred to Tonkin and thus was an old friend of Cornelia. She had ridden on his knee as a child. Hartsinck had sired two boys from a local woman. Both sons later rose to influential positions. Pieter (born in Hirado on October 15, 1633) obtained a doctorate at Leiden University and became a counsellor of the Duke of Brunswick. Willem Carel (born in Hirado, July 12, 1638) rose in VOC service to the office of Governor of the Coromandel coast.[22] This case, as well as the one of the "Hirado" children of François Caron - not to speak of Cornelia and her sister - indicates that nothing seems to have stood in the way of these "natural" children being fully accepted within Dutch society, either in the Indies or in Holland. The Mrs. Hartsinck present at the baptism was not the Japanese mother of Hartsinck's boys but Sarah de Solemne, whom he had married in Formosa in 1641. Mrs. Frisius, Femmetje ten Broecke, was the wife of Andries Frisius of the Hague, a member of the Dutch emissary to Japan of 1649, at that time secretary to the Council of the Indies, president of the Board of Marital Affairs (Commissie van Huwelijkse en Kleine Zaken), and Captain of the militia of the administrative personnel outside Batavia castle. In short, the godfathers and godmothers belonged to the upper echelon of the VOC hierarchy, a few having some past experience with Japan, others merely being colleagues and comrades of Pieter Cnoll.

The link with Frisius in particular gives us some indication of Cnoll's sociability in Batavia - or perhaps better said - of his popularity. In 1658 he was appointed, probably with Frisius' help, Ensign to the militia of the Company administrative personnel within Batavia castle. His promotion to lieutenant followed on June 17, 1661. By this time, the position was already titular rather than strategic in character since the recent feuds between Banten and Batavia had been settled in favour of the latter at the conclusion of the peace treaty of 1659. Rather than martial prowess, healthy financial resources and a sense of camaraderie were needed if one desired to occupy a leading position within the citizens' soldiery. Batavian militia ensigns used to vie with each other in regaling their troops on the commemoration day of the town's baptism (August 28, 1621). A. Bogaert, who published a memoir of his travel adventures in 1711, recollected with relish the days when he used to participate in these annual parades. "In the early morning we collected at the home of the eldest sergeant of the troops. Then we proceeded under his command to the house of the ensign, where a splendid overloaded table was awaiting us [...]. Late at night we halted again at the ensign's home, after having paraded all day long. After having fired a couple of volleys of congratulations, we would set the weapons aside, and spend the whole night dining and carousing." (Bogaert 1711:180.)

Another indication of Cnoll's rising status within the Company hierarchy was the location of his home. He moved out of the cramped quarters in Batavia castle and had a house built, large enough to shelter his family and a retinue of fifty slaves, along Batavia's most beautiful canal, the Tijgergracht. When the new line of defence works, ranging from Antjol via Jacatra to Tangerang, had reached completion, the countryside became much safer. Wealthy burghers - and Cnoll was among them - started to purchase large tracts of land outside the city walls. The chief merchant soon discovered that he was too busy to supervise the work in his garden along the Jacatra road, so he leased it out in 1660 at a rent of 12 rials a month, but kept the "wooden house, some flowers, rosemary's, et cetera in pots or in wooden greenhouses, for the pleasure and amusement of his family and himself" (De Haan 1935 I:108). The move out of the city brought new life to a debate that had been going on for years: whether or not to allow carriages in town.

In the early thirties, Governor-General Brouwer had ordered a total ban on these status symbols, but his successor Van Diemen wrote to the Gentlemen XVII on December 9, 1637, that he would allow them to be used under certain circumstances. From his words it is clear that the group lobbying for the reintroduction of the carriages in this case consisted of women. "Because our partners or adored female companions in this melancholical climate lack the coziness of their parents and relations much to their regret, and because the exigencies of the Company's service do not permit us to share much free time with them, I have permitted - in order to ease their life and render some recreation and diversion possible for them, as well as to shun the intolerable heat of the sunshine when they go to church on Sunday - putting the horses again to the carriages, which now for several years have stood idle, and to let them roll at the service of the ladies. I shall be pleased to hear sooner or later, what your lordships think about this disposition contrary to your order. In the meantime I shall take care that these measures will not result in evil or costly outcome." (GM I:640.) The ostentatiousness of the Batavian nouveaux riches élite emerged clearly at an early date, but little could be done to combat it. The battle against "joy-riding" was lost when the surroundings or Ommelanden of Batavia were opened up. Because of the distance that had to be covered on outings to his retreat, Cnoll purchased a splendid carriage with four horses. On both sides a coat of arms with a turnip (Knol) was mounted. This carriage was to play a crucial role in Cornelia's later life.

With the Cnoll family, as depicted by Coeman, away from the hectic life in Batavia at their country-retreat, the question arises how this newly acquired status reflected itself in the letters that Cornelia wrote to her mother.

Meaningful On-shin
As we have seen above, all Dutchmen and Englishmen who had married and settled down in Japan were expelled in 1639. In October 1641, this measure was followed up by an even more draconian one. All further

correspondence between those who had been "repatriated" and their relatives who had remained behind was strictly forbidden. In 1656 the Japanese authorities relented on this last measure and again permitted some exchange of family greetings by letter, the so-called on-shin. A certain Murakami Buzaemon, representing the Japanese burghers of Batavia, sent that year through the good office of the Dutch head-merchant on Deshima, a communication to the Nagasaki bugyo or regent Kainosho Kizaemon, in which he reported about the conditions in Batavia (Iwao 1978:150). A few specimens of these reports can still be found in the Nagasaki prefectural library (Murakami 1917:21-7). Two letters from Cornelia written in 1663 and 1671 are part of this genre. They were discovered in private property by the Hirado scholar, Sato Dokusho, about seventy-five years ago (Sato 1910). These letters, which now are on display in the Hirado Historical Tourist Museum were addressed to the wife of Handa Goeimon, Cornelia's mother Surishia, who married Handa after the death of Van Nijenroode. Although the information given in the letters is rather meagre, all the same it tells us what Cornelia's main concerns were. The first one reads:
"Thanks to the charity of the office of the two governors (ryomandokoro) of Nagasaki that I receive every year, I received Your letter of the 21st of the ninth month (1662) with the presents without fail. I understand that you both are in good health. This is the list of the presents that I send you:
1. One piece of cloth with Chinese pattern for grandmother.
2. Two kin of refined first quality Borneo camphor.
3. Three pieces of Gingan cotton cloth.
4. One piece of pepper-and-salt coloured chintz.
The above-named lot of three items is meant for Handa Goeimon.
One Gingan for Hester's mother.
One salt-and-peper coloured chintz for the wet nurse of Cornelia.[23]
Hamada Sukeeimon and his daughters are in good health and are very grateful for the many presents that you have sent. Please do not worry about me. My husband Cnoll is a good fellow, and he rises ever higher. Although it is only a trifle, I send one piece of Chintz to Yoshitsugi Kuzaeimon.[24] Please do receive it. I have a favour to ask you: Please purchase for me 6 pieces of lacquered incense plates and a comb of boxwood. Respectfully yours, 1663, 21st of the fifth moon, Cornelia Cnoll."

One of Cornelia's letters.

VIII Butterfly or Mantis?   191

Short as it is, the letter nevertheless draws our attention to several issues. There seems to have been a regular exchange of these "family news" letters accompanied by an exchange of local products. The amount would seem too small to suggest any private trade. The information we have about the Cnoll's family life in Batavia is meagre indeed.
The second letter dated by Iwao as to have been written on April 21, 1671, is almost completely written in kana.[25] Other letters may have been exchanged in between 1662 and 1671 but, if so, these have not been preserved. In reality the letter opens with a postscriptum - a Japanese letter is rolled up towards the beginning - here, in translation, it will be added where it should be, that is at the end:
"To Hirado addressed to Handa Goeimon.
Every year I receive almost too much charity of the office of the two governors of Nagasaki. The letter of 11th of the ninth month of 1668 as well as the presents and the requested goods I have received the 27th of the 10th month. I have duly delivered them to all parties concerned. Everybody rejoiced and said that it was too much to accept. We are especially in good health, and last year (1670) in the fourth month I gave birth to a baby girl. Now we have four children; they are all in good health; please do not worry.
I send you the following piece-goods as a present.
best quality Salempoori cotton   1 piece
best quality Canequine (calico) cotton   1 piece
best quality small Canequine (calico) cotton   1 piece
Salempoori cotton   25 pieces
Palcalle cotton   20 pieces
batik   2 pieces[26]
Will you please transmit these goods to Handa Goeimon?
One piece of white cotton of 4 tan length for Hester's mother.
One tan of Palcalle cotton for my wet nurse.
Over the last two years nothing has been sent by me; you may have worried about me. But nothing special has occurred. I am in good health so you do not have to worry about me. I have become a mother of ten children; six have been lost, four are in good health. Elder brother is fourteen, his sister twelve, followed by a little sister of six and the little baby who is eight months old. All are in good health. Especially the eldest son and the second daughter send grandfather and grandmother their warmest greetings. That you are still in good health makes me happy time and time again. From the contents of the letter you have sent me from Japan I have understood your situation and this gives me the feeling that I have seen you. I sadly wipe away the tears with my sleeve.
To Handa Goeimon and his wife, Murakami Buzaeimon transmits the following message:
'I have received the presents from you every year according to the list. I feel very indebted to you. Here in Batavia, Dai-feitor[27] Cnoll, his wife and children are in excellent health. But because for two years on end husband and wife Cnoll did not send you any letter you were worried, which is quite understandable. Since he has risen to the position [of opperkoopman] he has no leisure. On the one hand he [one sentence deleted]; on the other hand the sale of all goods is handled by the feitor alone. It is a small gesture, but I send one tan of white figured silk.'
The widow of Hamada Sukeeimon says that she has received presents

every year according to the list. She is most grateful. Mr. and Mrs. Cnoll and their children are in good health here. The details you can hear from Murakami Buzaeimondonne[28]; therefore I do not expand any further in this letter. As a sign of my good health, I send you a white piece of Palcalle cotton, although it does not amount to anything. I understand that grandmother has died from sickness on the 26th of the eighth month of 1668 at the age of 75. I believe she has passed away in peace. I am waiting for news about your good health, I remain sincerely yours, the 21st of the fourth month, Cornelia Cnoll.
P.S. I forgot to write what I wished to say first! To grandmother and grandfather I send 2 tan of Dutch linen presented by elder brother and his little sister. It is a small sign of kindness. Would you please have this white crepe cotton of two tan dyed in a dark red colour? Sincerely yours."

The main concern of these letters is the good health of Cornelia's relatives; yet, presents, all of which are Indian cotton fabrics, play an important role too. The question arises why cotton cloth was so highly valued in Japan? Part of the answer is found in the stern edict that was issued by Governor-General Maetsuycker in 1669. The Regents of the empire of Japan, it states, had transmitted in 1668 to the Dutch opperhoofd in Deshima a list of proscribed items which should not be imported, "but the crews of the VOC ships that had arrived in the following years had flouted all warnings and had infringed the prohibitions". Fortunately the Japanese authorities had not yet meted out severe penalties, but in order to protect the well-being of the Company and its servants in particular, Maetsuycker "now saw himself forced to attend to this matter and therefore he forbade everyone, whether merchant, skipper, undermerchant, mate or below that rank, without exception, to transport under whatever name or pretext the following items to Japan". Thereupon follows an extremely detailed list of what one might summarize as exotica (in the eyes of the Japanese authorities): woolen cloth (i.e. "Dutch cloth"), Chinese silk in all its varieties, foreign animals, dogs, monkeys and birds (the ship's cat excluded), wood for medicinal use, glass, music instruments, children's toys, Spanish flies (!), Chinese utensils, medical instruments, Dutch money, weapons, not to mention all objects connected with the Christian religion, the Bible included (Plakaatboek II:509, 18-4-1670).

Two considerations of the Bakufu government underlie these prohibitions: On the one hand, by barring certain imports from the Japanese market, the government could maintain a monopoly on exotic items, reserving them for exclusive use by the élite. On the other hand the authorities also sought to stimulate a home industry in certain sectors in this way, so that the dependence on import could be lessened. The closing of the country was after all as much a political decision as an economic one: the Bakufu attempted to render Japanese society autarkic and thus create its own separate "world system". Porcelain and silk products, which had been mainly imported from China before the 1640s, were soon produced in Japan, in such quantities that the country was self-sufficient in this respect by the end of the century.

Cotton was not prohibited by the authorities, because cottonseed had been reintroduced into Japan a hundred years earlier by the Portuguese and Spaniards and was no longer thought of as a foreign item. Since the Keicho period (1596-1614) cotton fabrics had been woven all over

Japan for everyday use, and this industry did not need to be protected against foreign imports (Yokoi 1927:115). When Cornelia wanted to send a gift to her relatives she had few choices.

In the same vein, could the prohibition against sending "paintings or any kind of print, with or without Chinese characters, wherever they may have been made" also offer an explanation for the curious way in which Cornelia sent her mother an image of herself? As prints or pictures were forbidden, she sent a miniature wooden screen with the figure of a woman carved into it. Today this screen is treasured in the Hirado museum, as are Cornelia's letters.

Another point in her letters worth closer attention is Cornelia's description of her husband and his business dealings. Our full understanding of what she has to say is marred by the unfortunate fact that one sentence has become unreadable, exactly that sentence where she explains about his purchasing and selling. The workload of the first head-merchant (opperkoopman) of Batavia castle was indeed as heavy as she tells her mother, as one can judge by the various instructions in the Plakaatboek aimed at lightening this official's burden.[29] Officially the Director-General was responsible for the administrative affairs of the Batavia headquarters, but in face of mounting political tasks he soon delegated the total business administration of Batavia castle to the first head-merchant. This official was supposed to share his responsibilities with the second head-merchant (as is repeatedly emphasized by the instructions) by the simple means of taking the responsibility for the sale of all goods himself and leaving it to his colleague to purchase all merchandise. Each was to check the other's bookkeeping. It goes without saying that the first supercargo was the more responsible; he kept the keys "to have access day and night, as the occasion requires, to the offices of the administration and the go-downs" (Plakaatboek II: 380).

In consideration of all these responsibilities, it is no surprise that Cornelia's husband was a busy man. Yet he still found time to preside over the Commissariat for Marital Affairs, being a paragon of those virtues characterizing the decent husband.[30] Considering how his career progressed, Pieter Cnoll was probably well on his way to occupying a seat in the Council of the Indies, but before he could reach this apex his health failed him.

The Last Will
On February 15, 1672, at eight o'clock in the morning, notary Anthony Huysman was summoned to the sickbed of head-merchant Pieter Cnoll. After having endured horrible pains and fever for an entire night, the weakened patient told him that "he realized the inevitability of death". While he was still compos mentis, Cnoll asked the notary to draw up a testament in the presence of his wife and two colleagues and friends, Pieter Pauw and Constantijn Nobel, who had also been sent for. The will shows that the couple wanted to make sure that the entire estate would come to the surviving partner without interference from outsiders. Cornelia, by now about 42 years old, was no longer a sweet young thing who could be pushed around.

It was recorded by the notary that "all possessions, personal property as well as real estate, shares, credits, debts and income received et cetera, nothing in the world excepted, wherever it may be or from whomever it may have been received" would be delegated to the surviving partner (as it is clear that Cornelia was meant, we shall from now on refer strictly to her). She was to take care of the children "feed them, quench their thirst and cloth them until they reach adulthood or get married" and should "teach them to read and write and prepare them for an honest profession, by which they could make a living". Marriage or adulthood would entitle each of them to an equal share of the considerable sum of forty thousand rixdollars.

Huysman was thereupon enlightened by Cnoll concerning the considerable fortunes of the family which were more than sufficient to provide for these gifts in cash. After having established that this was indeed the case, the notary entered a special clause into the will to the effect that neither the directors of the Orphan Board nor anyone else who might attempt to interfere in the execution of the inheritance would be allowed to do so. Cnoll had expressly recorded that he forbade the transmission of any list or inventory to third parties.[31] Cornelia in particular was aware that all sorts of entanglements could result if a neat inventory ended up in the hands of the authorities. Consequently the terms of the will stated that she was appointed "the absolute managing administrating guardian of the children, even if this would run counter to existing laws or certain ordinances of the orphanage board". She was, however, free to call in help from one or more guardians (by some irony of fate Constantijn Nobel himself was one of the directors of the Orphan Board). If any children should die before having received their legal portion, this share would automatically revert to the surviving brothers and sisters. If by any chance all children would die prematurely the inheritance would revert to the surviving parent.

In Dutch 17th century law the legal position of married women was practically non-existent: de vrouw is onbekwaam, i.e. the (married) woman had no legal competency to enter into and be bound by a contract. We shall return to this point again below; for now suffice it to say that Cnoll's will was formulated in such a way that no male guardians were appointed (there were no adult male relatives), but Cornelia was appointed by him the legal guardian of his children. He alone possessed legal right over them, and he took the opportunity to delegate this authority to her. After his demise, their children were to become her children in legal terms.[32]

A special donation of two hundred rixdollars was set aside to provide for the poor and destitute of the town. Cnoll's sisters, Sophia Cnoll and Maria Spillebout, both residing in Leiden, were also mentioned. If still alive they were to receive five hundred dollars each. The debt of one hundred rixdollars that ensign Joan van Schrieck owed to the testator - the man most likely had not been able to carry the financial burdens of that position - was remitted. Cnoll, ill and exhausted, faced certain death, yet it was further stated that if in extremis Cornelia should precede him, he would pay to the son of his wife's sister a sum of five hundred rixdollars in his aunt's memory.[33]

These were the main points that were drawn up on that early February morning. Huysman asked the patient, his wife and the witnesses to sign the document and collected a fee of two rixdollars to which was added an allowance of 20 stuivers for the transport to and fro the Cnoll estate (Plakaatboek II:453). As he was shown out, dark clouds gathered, covering the sun and Huysman had to hurry home to escape the torrential rain that was about to pour down.

The testament was made none too soon; that same day the patient

VIII Butterfly or Mantis?

was assailed by even more virulent fevers, and only two days later, between eleven and twelve at night, Pieter Cnoll passed away. But business still had to go on. In the afternoon of February 20, the Governor-General called the Council of the Indies to an extraordinary meeting to provide for a successor to the vacant position of first opperkoopman of Batavia castle (Daghregister 1672:53). Cnoll was succeeded by the second in command of the cash, Gerrit Vrieslandt; his position was in turn filled by no one other than Constantijn Nobel.[34]

The moment had arrived to execute the terms of the will, which was unusual in its utter simplicity. The total absence of inventories has already been mentioned. This implied, among other things, that any instruction as to how the household of forty slaves should be dealt with was lacking. As in Portuguese colonial society, Batavian slave owners would often insert a clause in their testaments to the effect that those slaves who had been closest to their master would be manumitted, while others would receive a small sum. This omission was to be avenged later.

Pieter Cnoll's favourite attendant and payong-bearer, Oentoeng (it is possible that this was the impish slave depicted on the family portrait in his master's shadow as he steals an orange from a fruit dish, the standard of the militia lightly on his shoulders) was passed on to young Cornelis when he came of age. The slave was treated so badly by his new master, a freeburgher, who was not even allowed the privilege of using the payong, that the former escaped to the Ommelanden where he eventually became a formidable robber chief and nuisance to the Company: the famous Surapati.[35]

If the Cnoll's had shown better judgement and more magnanimity towards this slave, they might have saved the East India Company army the necessity of undertaking a number of expeditions. They might have prevented the deaths of hundreds of its soldiers; and they might have saved hundreds of thousands of guilders expended over the next twenty years on the campaigns in pursuit of the runaway Surapati, who ultimately established his own kingdom in Eastern Java. One year later,

The Gentlemen XVII.

the Gentlemen XVII also committed an imprudence; it will, however, have escaped their notice that by doing so they paid the Cnoll's back in their own coin.

Second Life

Valckenier's Grudge

In the autumn of 1673 the directors of the East India Company held a series of board meetings in Middelburg. These meetings, which were normally held in Amsterdam, took place in Zeeland for two years at six year intervals to please the members of that proud province (Stapel 1927-1943 I:244). During the two months of deliberations, important issues were dealt with, such as the seizure of Dutch ships and their crews by the English, the distribution of the bills of exchange received from the Indies and the assessment of the demands for goods to be sent from India to the Republic in the year 1675. On the last two days the weary board dealt with some remaining minor topics. A few people who had been introduced by the directors were appointed to certain positions, with the notable exception of one person, the lawyer Johan Bitter of Amsterdam. Bitter had requested to be nominated as a candidate for the Council of Justice in Batavia. His influential patron, Gillis Valckenier, Company director and burgomaster of Amsterdam, was not present at the meeting, and it is clear that this absence enabled some of the other board members to speak out freely and to express some doubts. On account of "what had been said and heard about him [Bitter] two or three years ago", these spokesmen wondered whether he was the right man for such a position. As no conclusion could be reached, Bitter was advised to apply to the Amsterdam chamber directly, with the understanding that this chamber would be authorized to appoint him if he was deemed capable after some further investigation into these rumours (VOC 107, 3-11-1673). Nobody wanted to press the issue, but the message was clear. Whether the Gentlemen were right or wrong in their premonitions about Bitter's qualities should become clear from his subsequent actions. It seems appropriate to say something first regarding his family, his personality and the way it shaped his career.

Johan Bitter was born in 1638 of well-established parentage in the town of Arnhem. In 1660, at twenty-two, while still a student of law at the now defunct Harderwijk University, he married his cousin Bartha Eygels.[36] Two years later, he received his doctorate.[37] Thereupon the young barrister, a man of detail to whom legal matters were the staple of life, took leave of his Alma Mater to carve himself a niche among his colleagues in Amsterdam. Confronted in the metropolis with a wide variety of human beings and their legal problems under all sorts of circumstances, he soon became aware of the disparity between legal theory and practice. Although he may not have been ungifted as a legal scholar, he appeared unable to separate important matters from trifling personal ones and to remain aloof. This perhaps indicates a dominant trait in his character and one that provides the clue to the development of his entire career: whenever he felt even a little slighted, he would resort to legal defence to such an extent, that he incited offence and antipathy among his colleagues. His career as a practising lawyer was nothing short of a failure. Life at home seems to have been more tolerable for him. On July 10, 1661, Bartha Eygels gave birth to her first baby, a girl who was named after her mother. Eight more children were

VIII Butterfly or Mantis?

to follow over the next ten years, five of whom died prematurely - a pattern quite similar to that of the Cnoll family.[38]

With his failure as an independent barrister and the pressing financial burden of sustaining a family, Bitter decided to embark upon a legal career in the service of the VOC.

The Court of Justice of Batavia, the Raad van Justitie, at which he was aiming can perhaps be best described as the Higher Court of the Indies. It may be helpful to insert a brief historical sketch of the position and function of this legal institution within the Batavian administration in order to have a better understanding of the complex narrative that follows.

In the early days of the Company, the administration of law had been carried out in the manner of VOC shipboard, i.e. by the highest commanding authorities, the Governor-General and Council. Separation of political and legal authority was brought about in principle in 1620 when Jan Pietersz. Coen installed "a board of eight commissioners or legal specialists" by whom all civil and criminal cases of soldiers and Company servants could be heard (La Bree 1951:54). Administration of justice over the vrijburgers (freeburghers), and "foreigners" - including, of course, the native people - was carried out by the Schepenbank, the Bench of Aldermen in town. In some cases the Court of Justice within Batavia castle acted as a court of appeal for sentences passed by the Schepenbank. Although in theory the Court of Justice was an independent organ from the 1620s onwards, this turned out to be different in practice. Not only did the political authorities often interfere directly with legal matters, but also some structural ties remained between the two groups. The President of the Court of Justice, for instance, had to be a member of the Council of the Indies. Studies by La Bree (1951:54-84) and Van Kan (1943) on the functioning of the legal institutions in Batavia are full of references to continuous adjustments and amendments that were made over the years to buttress and guarantee a certain independence of action to the Court of Justice. This trend can also be discerned from the qualitative evolution of the Council's composition of personnel. Despite the fact that the Council initially consisted of "the most capable and aged Company servants" (who were also accused of being "all idiots and blockheads" by one of the first law educated members), by 1656 the majority was comprised of people with legal backgrounds. It does not seem incongruous that a man with Bitter's legal experience and influential connections should choose to embark upon a colonial career in the hope of improving his financial plight. Unfortunately some of the Gentlemen XVII seemed disinclined to help him.

Valckenier was outraged when he heard about the treatment Bitter had received in Middelburg. He felt personally slighted by this lack of confidence and he called for a special meeting of the board of the Amsterdam chamber as soon as his representative at that meeting, Tulp, had returned (VOC 239, 15-11-1673). On Wednesday afternoon, November 15th, after some trifles had been dealt with, Valckenier addressed the same question to each person: "can you or do you want to charge Bitter with past indiscretions which could prevent his appointment to the Council of Justice in Batavia?" At this time no one dared to raise any objections and it was decided to invite the candidate to enter the meeting hall and state his views on the affair. Bitter had prepared himself well, presenting three pieces of evidence which might clear him of any suggested lack of abilities. The first letter he produced was signed by six of the oldest and most prominent legists in town, plus two attorneys. They not only thought him "well versed in the fundaments and knowledge of the laws" but also deemed him to be "modest, peaceful, honest and ambitious" in his private and public life. The two other letters shown by Bitter throw some light on the origins of the rumours that had been spread about him. It turns out that he had quarrelled with a medical doctor, Hendrick Houtappel, about "a certain invoice", but that this case had eventually been resolved when it was established by two aldermen, Schaep and Ranst (who had been called upon as mediators), that the quarrel was the result of mistakes and misunderstandings. Even the physician concerned had been willing to testify in the presence of a notary that everything stemmed from misunderstandings; he had added that he thought Bitter to be "an honest and faithful lawyer". After the letters had been read, the directors deemed the matter closed and appointed Bitter without delay at a salary of one hundred guilders a month (VOC 239, 15-11-1673). His path into the Company was thus smoothed by Valckenier's patronage and the lawyer prepared himself for the rigours of the passage to the Indies.

Life Begins at Forty
Early in January, 1675, Johan Bitter, his wife and five children braved the cold winter weather to board a small boeier yacht which was to transport them to the Texel roadstead. There the outgoing fleet of eight sails was riding at anchor, awaiting a favourable Eastern wind that would provide a safe passage along the Haaks shoals to the open sea. The Councillor of Justice and his family boarded the largest East Indiaman, Ceylon, which measured 776 tons and carried 110 soldiers for service in the East and 13 passengers as well as a crew of 177 sailors. After the Strait of Dover was passed, strong southwesterly winds were encountered which caused the fleet to seek shelter along the English south coast. The ships cast anchor in the Solent near Portsmouth. During a fortnight spent in idle anticipation, several soldiers and sailors seized the opportunity to desert. From England onwards, the voyage progressed without too much hardship, and four months later, on June 22, the Ceylon reached Cape Town, where fresh victuals were taken on board. No lives had been lost to disease or accidents (Bruijn, Gaastra and Schöffer 1979 II:184). The two-months passage between South Africa and Batavia, however, turned out to be harrowing: thirteen sailors, fourteen soldiers and two passengers died due to illness and accidents, among them Bitter's wife, Bartha Eygels, and one of the children. On September 12, 1675, the mourning widower and his four children arrived in Batavia and moved into the living quarters for Company personnel within the compound of Batavia castle. Facing a new career, if not a new life in the East, Bitter was now 38 years old, almost the age of retirement in the tropics.

At the time of Bitter's entry, the Council consisted of nine members, the president included. Most of them already had another function within the Company hierarchy and all without exception enjoyed income from emoluments. The reader will remember that other penurious member of the Council of Justice, David van Lennep, who was so shocked upon arrival in the Indies by the greed and graft of the local élite. In his young days he had played in a cavalier way with other people's money. In the Indies out of the reach of his creditors, he became reconciled with the idea that he should content himself with his meagre income. He chose for decent poverty, which as a bachelor, he could afford to do.³⁹

With four young children to care for, matters stood differently for Bitter. It did not take long for the newcomer to discover that the 100 guilders a month he received were totally insufficient to provide for himself and the upbringing of his four children. It was quite a shock to discover that the cost of living was about double what he was used to in Holland. A contemporary of his summed this all up: "A Company servant can make ends meet with 900-1000 rixdollars a year, that is 80 rixdollars a month, if he does not eat Dutch food. A chicken costs 6-8 stuivers, one stuiver will only buy you three or four eggs, a pound of fish or meat costs about 4-5 stuivers. [...] Sixty rixdollars a month amounts to such a sobre kitchen in Batavia that forty rixdollars in Holland can buy you a better dish and most of all a better drink (Van der Burg 1677:14). As we have seen, Bitter only made about forty rixdollars. His future would have looked bleak indeed if one of his colleagues had not drawn his attention to an elderly widow, "with a house of her own, large, magnificent, well-furnished and amply provided with silverware, served by about forty male and female slaves, and moreover in the possession of a carriage with horses". It is not difficult to guess who was the subject of this description (HR 783:63).

Middle-Aged Courtship
What followed next has been so vividly described at a later date by Cornelia, through her lawyer, that it would be a shame to refrain from quoting part of it, even if much of the original fervour is lost in the translation: "And having seen how well off this lady was, and realizing that in his position he would need a large treasury (large cassa), and that an opulent household might serve him uncommonly well, he fell in love with the claimant's [Cornelia's] means. Through the good offices of friends he got himself introduced into her company and set out to court her. Finally he succeeded in persuading her to such a degree with sweet words and promises that she resolved to marry him." (HR 783: 63).

Was it just infatuation that made this 46-year-old widow, who had in the meantime lost all her children but one son, take this decision or was there more to it? Judging from all the stipulations she made in the marriage settlement, to which we shall soon turn, it was strictly a marriage de raison. Bitter's academic background and his high status as Councillor of Justice strongly attracted her. The man was as poor as a church mouse, yet his high office would offer opportunities that were denied to her as a widow; furthermore it would keep the doors to the parlours of the Company élite open. Perhaps most important, Bitter's membership in the Court of Justice could provide Cornelia with the necessary legal backing in her business dealings; people would think twice before cheating her.

The likelihood of these assumptions, which seem self-evident, is buttressed if one looks at similar examples in other colonial societies of the same period. According to Boxer, in Spanish America Creole ladies of good family were usually keen to marry judges. This was beneficial to their social status and "it afforded all kinds of opportunities for using their husbands' influence" (Boxer 1975:48). This same trend could be discerned in Portuguese India where ouvidores (judges) and senior magistrates tended to marry Eurasian heiresses with property, even

Batavian street scene.

though this was repeatedly prohibited by royal decree (Boxer 1975:78).

Cornelia took a deliberate risk by consenting to marry Johan Bitter, for although she may not have understood all the legal implications, she must have known that, legally speaking, she placed herself in an inferior position. As elsewhere in Europe, Dutch law conferred upon the husband total dominance over his wife. In Holland this legal subjugation was only brought to an end in 1956, when the handelingsonbekwaamheid, the legal inability of the wife to take action in private dealings, was at long last abolished. Handelingsonbekwaam implied that without the authorization, assistance or consent of her husband (or in case he refuses, without authorization by the Court of Justice) the wife may not carry out any legal action concerning her assets, nor may she conclude any contract (Asser 1957:141). Cornelia thus placed herself under the guardianship of her husband, and in his role of guardian the husband possessed complete authority over her person as well as her possessions. This authority over assets had two important aspects: on the one hand, only the husband could make contracts or engage in legal action, as we have seen; on the other hand, he was to administer his wife's fortunes. In practice this enabled the husband to dispose of his wife's property as he liked without having to obtain her consent to do so. It is understandable that under these conditions safeguards had to be erected in the shape of a marriage contract whenever a wealthy woman got married.

The middle-aged bride-to-be took no chances. She called in the help of legal advisers to draw up a watertight marriage contract "even though he [Bitter] had declared to her that if she would marry him, she would remain complete legal guardian, mistress and administrator of all her means and properties, at present as well as in the future, with nothing excluded, so that she could freely dispose over them, purchase and sell, invest, mortgage and alienate them at her own liking" (HR 783:63). In his declaration, Bitter must have referred to the condition of explicit permission to become an openbare koopvrouw (lit. public trades woman), permission which he could give her only after the marriage (De Blécourt and Fischer 1967:70).

The conditions of the marriage settlement - which, as usual, had to be concluded prior to the marriage ceremony itself were extremely restrictive for Cornelia's new spouse-to-be. Cornelia reserved the considerable sum of 25,000 rixdollars for Bitter in case she would die before him. If he should meet an earlier death than she, she would bestow 12,500 rixdollars upon his children. The groom received no money in cash at all, according to the terms of this agreement. The interest from the 25,000 dollars Cornelia reserved for Bitter, augmented with an additional sum she also had deposited, would be appropriated to the maintainance of the married couple and their household. Bitter was to add 5,000 rixdollars of his own as well as his monthly income (all emoluments included) to this pool. If this were not sufficient to provide for daily expenses, Cornelia would make up the deficiency with extra money derived from other sources.

Cornelia still did not believe that this was a sufficient guarantee of her full authority over her own means, and therefore she rather pathetically demanded that her future husband had to swear "that his intentions to marry her had nothing to do with her means, but originated only from pure and sincere feelings of love towards her and from his concern to provide his children of his first marriage with a good upbringing (HR 783:64). On March 7, 1676, the matter was settled: in the presence of notary Davidt Disponteyn the marriage settlement was signed in perfect harmony, the only sour note being the fact that Bitter had not been able to raise more than 3,759 rixdollars. They married on March 26, only six months after Bitter's arrival (RU, Van Boetzelaer Archives, no.16).

It has already been stated that whatever conditions were stipulated and agreements made, these only were designed to limit a possible mismanagement by her future husband. They amounted to no more than a defence mechanism to be used in extremity and should not be seen as legal documents that bestowed authority on the wife, which she per definition could not have. As the old saying goes, the proof of the pudding is in the eating, and so was the case with this marriage. The first taste was enough to tell Cornelia van Nijenroode that she was in for an experience, for which, if nothing else, the name of her husband should have warned her.

Portrait of a Marriage
Shortly after the two partners had settled down to enjoy marital bliss, Cornelia revealed a plan to invest 3,000 rixdollars in a house that was under construction for a Chinese doctor near the Nieuwe Poort of Batavia. She wished the contract to be executed under her own name, so that the interest could be paid directly to her and not to the common account. The Bench of Aldermen which had to legalize the contract, refused to accept this, and here the opportunity presented itself for Bitter to state that he allowed her to act as an openbare koopvrouw (HR 783:84). Unfortunately, he did not do so. He said he had not been consulted about the deal, and furthermore flatly informed his wife that, though she perhaps did not realize this, it had never been stated in the settlement that he should leave the administration of her properties to her. He told her that the only freedom she enjoyed in this respect was the freedom of inheritance. That, of course, was small comfort.

It soon dawned upon Cornelia "that her person had been the object of his words and promises and her means and effects had been the object of his inner contemplations". Indeed, "the outward caresses and the obliged meetings began to abate, and within a short time came to a total halt. Shortly afterwards, their relation turned into displeasure and gruffness, and finally exploded into harsh and insufferable treatment." (HR 783:65). According to Bitter, she in turn took her displeasure out on him, complaining about his children, whom she could not tolerate, even ordering them out of the house, although the youngest was only 5 years old (HR 783:85). A terrible row broke out which could not be mended by the newlyweds themselves. Help was called in from outside. Through the mediation of Cornelis Speelman and Constantijn Ranst, both Bitter's colleagues in the Council of Justice, a new agreement was reached. Ranst, a distant relative of Gillis Valckenier (Bitter's patron), was married to Hester Hartsinck, which may have endeared him to Cornelia. Cornelis Speelman was a personal friend of Cornelia's. These two consultants must have agreed that Cornelia had indeed tried to keep Bitter on too short a leash and therefore persuaded her "in order to mollify and smother further troubles" to hand over to Bitter the 25,000 rixdollars in cash and in debentures which he originally would have received after her death. If he were to die prematurely it was specified that she would receive half of it back. Thus Bitter was enabled to administer at least that part of the property which had been promised to him. Regarding the other possessions under discussion, it was agreed that Cornelia could keep them to herself and administer, invest and redeem them as she liked. Bitter's children were put out to board with "honest people". The boarding fee was to be paid out of the household account. On September 15, 1676, only six months and eight days after the conclusion of the marriage settlement, this new agreement was signed by both partners. To make sure that neither would reconsider the decision the following clause was inserted: "We the undersigned have devised this contract in affection and friendship to improve concord and avoid ghastly troubles" (HR 783:65).

On September 19th, 1676, 13,000 rixdollars in 37 sealed bags as well as 12,000 rixdollars in obligations were handed over to Bitter. Cornelia believed that she had bought peace with this arrangement. Indeed, at first it looked that way, as that same week Bitter had written excited letters to his friends, stating "that he had remarried and was living in comfortable circumstances, that he had won himself a rich wife, a widow with a son, that he possessed money, property and rank in sufficient quantity, that he had remarried in such a way that he was satisfied with his worldly means, that he had married with the Lord's benediction. If his friends had not already understood these things from his earlier correspondence, they surely must have done so from what others must have written them." He went on to say, "that he was firmly established in a magnificent house, he possessed money like shells, horses like iron, worthy of a prince, and many other extravagances which were not fitting a gentleman of his rank and age" (HR 783:66). What he did not tell is that his wife had given him a rapier and whip ornamented with gold. This might have given his friends the impression that he was treated as a schoolboy. When he was confronted much later with the contents of the letters, Bitter did not deny having written them, nonetheless remarking "that even the most distinguished gentlemen used to write litteras jocasas, or jocular letters" (HR 783:94). That may have been true but his ambitions and his urge to brag about his swift success to his friends in Patria could not be disguised.

When the agreement had been signed, Cornelia took up business again: she gave out an obligation amounting to 500 rixdollars debited to the account of a certain skipper Verbeek and provided the Chinese doctor with a mortgage of 3,000 rixdollars to build his house.[40] The new accord with her husband proved to be little more than an armistice: soon new quarrels of a more domestic nature broke out. Bitter used offensive language to Cornelia's sister, Hester, mocking and abusing her, and he chased his stepson Cornelis out of the house, shouting he would run the lad through with his rapier if he did not immediately hand over his horse to his stepfather. He threw a fit of conspicuous waste, during which he broke bottles and candelabra, and he threatened to chop up the coach.

The above evidence has been derived from juridical documents containing indictment and defence (HR 783:66-7). For the purposes of entertainment, if nothing else, one is tempted to quote the picturesque 17th century Dutch exchanges of insults that have been noted down almost verbatim. However much invective language may have changed over time, the message relayed remains quite the same. A word-for-word quotation (albeit translated) of Bitter's lines might appear to serve little purpose, apart from the following consideration: on closer

The townhall of Batavia.

VIII Butterfly or Mantis?

scrutiny, one realizes that Bitter's tirades are not only a long, monotonous litany of insults, but also, if observed within the larger context of a multi-racial colonial society with its hierarchical structure, a rather telling indication of the values of contemporary Batavia. The lawyer who summed up all the insults at random before the Court of Holland only intended to show how despicable a person Bitter was; the historian tries to reestablish why Bitter's behaviour was so insulting and what tactics he followed.

"He daily scolded her as hoerendop (whore-madam), beast, devil-face and whatever was ugly, and then he would suddenly relent and say 'come on, mammy (maatje), let us make peace again'." He would immediately start all over, if he received no positive reply and would shout "beast", et cetera and reach for the sjambok (the slave lash) to beat her. He would shout at her, jumping up and down in front of the domestics, and tell them to "neither listen to their juffrouw, nor obey her, adding that she would not dare spank them, and if she dared to do so, they should then come to see me at the townhall or wherever I may be, I shall protect you against her!" (HR 783:67).

By calling his wife devil-face, Bitter was clearly referring to her mongoloid features: he frequently referred to how she looked. To threaten his wife with a slave whip, humiliating her in front of the domestics, and provoking the slaves to disobey her were of course deadly tactics when used against a mistress who was in charge of forty domestics. On September 29, Cornelia ran away from the chamber of horrors which once had been her home and went to Cornelis, who had already moved out (HR 783:85). The following day she was alleged to have been beaten up so thoroughly that her arm was dislocated. To prove this she presented an attestation by her doctor, a certain Mr. Jan, to Reverend Pays. Two supposedly independent doctors, who were immediately hired by Bitter, presented a diagnosis in which it was claimed that they were unable to find a bruise on her (Van Alphen 1683 II:314). Whatever the truth, the scandal had now burst into the open.

Two days later the court of morality took action. If it was the role of the Court of Justice to mete out harsh punishment whenever wrongs had been committed, it was the role of the Church to soothe ruffled tempers and prevent wrongdoing. During a preparatory meeting of the Church Council prior to the Holy Communion, Reverend Pays reported that he had paid a visit to Johan Bitter on account of complaints against him by his wife. This effort to alleviate the discord between the couple was in vain, for Bitter had icily refused all mediation.

Pays had hardly finished his report when the door of the vestry was flung open and in came the devil upon whose tail he had trod. Bitter was enraged, protesting furiously against the pretensions of the Reverend and his company in this marital feud. "How could an honest arbiter discuss a case like this without even giving the defendant any further hearing?"[41] he demanded. He then challenged any member of the council present to prove himself a man and to dare speak out against him. After the intruder was shoved outside, so that the councillors could deliberate about an answer, they resolved to deny both Bitter and his wife access to the Holy Communion. The gentlemen agreed that they would tolerate no more of his provocations. Bitter was called in, and told this. He was not impressed at all, but rather challenged them before the Judgement of Heaven. Muttering that he could not understand how one could be suspended in such an unjust and illegal way, he finally stalked out (Bouwstoffen III:303-4).

Now that war had been declared upon the Church Council, Bitter threw open all his registers and no longer hesitated to draw other people into the feud. At the Court of Justice he cursed his wife, "making all kinds of grimaces, squinting and sticking out his tongue". He probed into Cornelia's background and found much that pleased him in the archives of the secretary of Governor-General and Council. Waving the documents exhumed, he told whoever was interested that Cornelia's "father had given his God-forsaken soul to the devil" just before his miserable death and that his assets had been confiscated afterwards (HR 783:67).

At home he apparently no longer felt safe. He barricaded his room, fortifying it with a "heavy paving-beetle, a rice-pounder and a large wooden maul". In early October, after Cornelia had returned to the house he hired a bodyguard whom he even brought to the dinner table, probably to taste his food. Having ruined the atmosphere at home, Bitter turned his attention to the extra-mural social ties of his wife.

His rude behaviour discouraged visits of her friends and, on one occasion, he barged into the drawing room where she was receiving those who came to comfort her, holding out a mirror in front of her face and exclaiming "look, what a beautiful gem!" One night he ran in "with a rapier in his hands, in underwear and on bare feet, without shoes or slippers" (only slaves walked on bare feet), under the mistaken impression that she was receiving a male visitor. Finally he simply closed the door to all visitors. One November afternoon, Cornelia, who had invited some friends home for a cup of tea, found Bitter blocking the front door. "Ladies, please come in, I have invited you for a cup of tea in my home", the hostess begged as she saw that her friends were hesitating. "Your house? It's my house, I have already sold it, and I will also deliver it", her demonic husband snarled. The ladies beat a hasty retreat (HR 783:68).

Humiliated in front of her domestics to the extent that they scarcely listened to her, Cornelia was then the victim of Bitter's brutality before Batavian society. The questionable conduct of her father was raked up, her looks were ridiculed, and she was publicly disowned of her possessions. The mercurial Bitter further refined his schizophrenic tactics, promising her a divorce if she would pay him 50,000 rixdollars cash. "Then he would go to the fatherland and live off that gratuity (geltje) with his little ones (kindertjes) like a prince." The last days of November found the couple involved in a fight that was at last settled only by Cornelia's strategic retreat from the house.

Withdrawal from her home did not mean that Cornelia had surrendered, however. She called in help from friends and prepared to attack her husband anew. She discovered that Bitter had spent part of his newly acquired wealth on diamonds. These were shipped home on the East-Indiaman, Europa, which had left Batavia on November 11. Probably via her former husband's ex-subordinates she was told that Bitter had also sent home 3,000 rixdollars by a bill of exchange in the name of his friend, Jacob Does. The worst of her suspicions were now affirmed: Bitter was simply draining her fortune and channelling the money to Holland. Fortunately, Cornelia had been informed of this just before the last ships of the fleet weighed anchor so she was able to send a letter addressed to an acquaintance in Holland, requesting him to inform the directors of the Company.

VIII Butterfly or Mantis?

On February 15, 1677 the irate wife summoned her husband before the Court of Justice, charging him with the theft of her possessions and with brutal treatment. The Governor-General and Council had permitted her to do so on December 22, 1676 (Daghregister 1676:356). She demanded divorce from Bitter's bed and board, the restitution of the 25,000 rixdollars and the vacating of the house by her husband, as well as the return of several slaves who had been manumitted by their new master iustia et invita domina. Above all she requested the court to cancel the prerogatives the marriage settlement had awarded to her evil husband (HR 783:69).

Bitter reacted instantly by gathering evidence which he could use against Cornelia. He visited the Church Council which happened to meet that day, complaining that he had been cited by the Court of Justice in causa divortii. As this was a blot on his reputation, he asked the Church Council "for a declaration based on the Acta of the Council", concerning his past behaviour towards his wife (Bouwstoffen III:326). This request was granted. Inserted into the acts of the ordinary meeting of March 1, we find the complete text of the attestation Bitter had requested. Its contents make it clear why he had asked for it: as soon as the marriage took an ugly turn, Bitter made sure that he steered a safe course within the law, while his frustrated wife let her emotions run free.

The attestation stated that, after the Church Council resolution of September 17, Bitter had earnestly asked the council to visit his wife once more and to admonish her to reconcile herself with him. On December 26, trying to bring about some peace, two parsons and one elder made a final attempt to reconcile the couple. On January, 2 they reported that this peace mission had failed and they had encountered in Bitter's wife's "stubborn implacability even after they had done everything in their power to soften her high-running feelings" (Bouwstoffen III:329).

Armed with this testimony, Bitter felt strong enough to mount a counterattack and he requested the Court of Justice to order Cornelia to "return to her husband and live in peace and fear of God". He also made it clear that no matter whether there was a marriage settlement or not, the law entitled him to the administration and alienation of Cornelia's assets as well as to half the income, interests and usufruct derived from it.

At Loggerheads with the Church

As we have seen, apart from being an ingenious handler of the law, Bitter's main problem was his impetuous temper. Shortly afterwards this brought about an imbroglio worthy of an opera buffa. On April 1 - and we cannot ascertain anymore whether or not someone played a prank on the clergyman - the Reverend Zas called the attention of his fellow council members to an embarrassing incident. Six days before, three members of the Council of Justice had served a summons to Bitter in the company of the Secretary of the Council of the Indies, Jacob Over't Water, his assistant Vuijrborn, the bailiff, a certain njonja, Judith, and Bitter's wife. Judging from the composition of her company, Cornelia must have visited her house to collect some of her belongings. On that occasion, the rumor went, those present had overheard Bitter saying "that the Reverend Zas was not worthy of occupying the pulpit". More abusive language followed. Zas took offence at these provocations, as Bitter seemed to imply that Zas, as the mediator in the marital discord, had chosen the side of Cornelia for dishonest reasons. This was intolerable to Zas, and he felt that his fellow members should also understand that the affront was not directed at him alone, but at the Church Council in its totality. In his opinion, action should be undertaken immediately. The Church Council members complied and an investigation was begun, but to the dismay of Zas none of those present at the locus delicti was willing to bear testimony (Bouwstoffen III:333). Bitter may have been jesting, so it is possible that no one had taken his remarks seriously. After a lot of wrangling, one of the witnesses was willing to say that what had been noted down in the minutes of the April 1 meeting was basically right.

Called to account for his behaviour, Bitter was asked whether he stood by the insinuations he had supposedly made. He looked surprised and asked the committee whether the Reverend Zas could leave the room. It is not hard to imagine the anger of the clergyman when his fellow-members complied with the request. Facing the committee-members not without defiance, Bitter asked them to repeat in specie what he was supposed to have Zas accused of; only then was he willing to explain himself, although not verbally but by way of a written testimony as this was a "matter of great weight". After they had complied with his request, Zas was called in again. The Council thereupon resolved to grant Bitter eight days to produce a written statement. He had been playing for time and he got it (Bouwstoffen III:333). In the weeks that followed, one imagines Zas exhorting his colleagues to do something quickly, but it was two and a half months later before Bitter was again summoned before the Council. Asked why he had not replied as promised, he apologized for not yet having been able to produce evidence in probata forma. He stated that he would try once more to gather it (Bouwstoffen III:340). Conscious that he could no longer fend off their demands, Bitter changed strategy and complained in a letter to the Governor-General about the way in which he was bothered, if not persecuted, by the Church Council. His "doleantie" was heard, and on June 21 a letter from Governor-General Maetsuycker was read to the Church Council, gently recommending the pious gentlemen to take their time and not to press their case with one of his Company servants who had been described by his own secretary, Over't Water, as "a diligent lawyer" (Bouwstoffen III:341).

The Council relented and gave Bitter eight more days to produce his evidence. Seeing no way out, he handed over a bill from Notary Keysers concerning certain business dealings in which Zas was involved. According to Bitter, this document proved that the reverend was conspiring with Cornelia. When the notary was asked whether this was true, he denied the allegation (Bouwstoffen III:342). Again Bitter was given eight days to bring forward real evidence. The Church Council was running out of patience and firmly decided that the case should be brought to an end. Meanwhile, Zas, of course, regretted having brought up the matter at all, as it appeared to have stirred rumours rather than resolving anything.

If the Council members thought that Bitter's bag of tricks was exhausted with this, they were mistaken. One week later he appeared empty-handed at the vestry. Professing to be very sorry, he said that the evidence the Church Council was asking for could no longer be shown as he had deposited it with the Court of Justice. He had started legal proceedings against Notary Keysers. Seeing no other way out of this mess, the Church Council now passed its final judgement. Because he had failed to produce any evidence in support of his allegations, Bitter was accorded the following chastisement. First he should apologize in front of the Church Council for his provocative behaviour; then he should ask forgiveness from Reverend Zas, who in turn should pardon him. Thereafter, both gentlemen should honour and respect each other. Bitter's suspension from the Holy Communion was to remain in force until this penitential exercise was carried out (Bouwstoffen III: 344).

Informed of the judgement on July 1, Bitter merely shrugged his shoulders. On second thought, he did inform the Council via the elder who came to visit him "that he apologized for having challenged them to appear in front of the tribunal of heaven; it had been a slip-of-the-tongue". However, he was not willing to assent to the second paragraph of the verdict and apologize to Zas. When on October 25 Bitter was again summoned to appear, he referred to a verdict pronounced by the Court of Justice nine days earlier concerning his quarrels (Bouwstoffen III:358). This must have been his lawsuit against Notary Keyser; unfortunately the archives yield no further information in this respect. The Church Council was not rebuffed and did not accept the lame "slip-of-the-tongue" apology that he was willing to make to them either. On November 1 Bitter was told this and invited once more to do penance. His written reply was as follows: "The Hon. Gentlemen Brelius and Van Dam have cited me to give satisfaction to the ecclesiastical resolution on next Monday. This is my reply: I stick to the answer which I have given on October 25. I thank [these two] gentlemen for all the pains they have taken, and recommend the gentlemen of the Church Council to practise some prudence along with their wisdom." (Bouwstoffen III: 361v).

Not quite able to believe that this was his final answer in the case, the Church Council decided to summon him a third time. This time, it was the verger's turn to transmit the message. On November 26, it was reported that Bitter did not comment. Consequently the Council gave up all hopes and declared him contumax - refractory. From then on, Bitter was denied the opportunity to defend himself. Four days later one of the members wondered what should be done next with this recalcitrant person. No one knew. It was therefore suggested to take a wait-and-see attitude and in the meantime to send someone to admonish him and warn him "of the difficulties that were awaiting him" (Bouwstoffen III: 363). The church elder Van Dam was willing to act as doomesday sayer. On December 6 he reported that his efforts had been successful: Bitter would write another letter (Bouwstoffen III:365). Although on December 13th a soiled epistle was indeed received, its contents were such that it was hastily put aside (Bouwstoffen III:366).

On January 3, 1678, the Reverend Zas asked for "an act of justification" concerning the case that had been going on between Johan Bitter and himself for nearly one year. This ecclesiastical act was read aloud to the Council on January 17, 1678. There is no need to reproduce it verbatim; by now the case should have been clearcut. This was, however, not quite so, for it turned out that the Church Council had not ignored the demand from the Governor-General and Council to calm down a bit. It had notified Governor-General Maetsuycker of the ways in which it planned to pursue the case and even had tried to make it palatable (tragtede 'tselve smaeckelick te maken). Maetsuycker was quite pleased and had added in his reply to the Church Council that, contrary to what Bitter asserted, Zas "had never complained about the marital feud between the couple, but had only transmitted to him [the Governor-General] the complaints by Bitter's wife" (Bouwstoffen III: 375).

Stepping away from our narrative for the moment, we can review all the tricks by which Bitter had tried to escape ecclesiastical jurisdiction: he used bluff, vague promises, arm twisting, and finally the initiation of a parallel case before the Council of Justice, in the belief that it was highly unlikely that an ecclesiastical judgement would be meted out before the verdict of the Court of Justice had been served (Van Boetzelaer 1947:72). It is not improbable that this blown-up farce in the end amounted to a greater pain to the Council itself than to the defendant, as the last lines of the justification suggest: "Bitter until today has not been willing to conform to our sentence, although this Church Council has in season and out of season tried to admonish him in a stern manner". Indeed Bitter could not have cared less and, as if nothing had happened, attempted a few months later, to exact from the Church Council a declaration that his wife had asserted that he intended to murder her. Understandably this request met with stony silence (Bouwstoffen III:386).

One might ask what the use is of sifting out and presenting so detailed an account of what amounted to an ecclesiastical airbubble? Would it not have been sufficient to refer to the above case in a few lines instead of interrupting the long tale of the complex marital feud? This account represents an attempt to examine the background of the story; moreover, through this particular case we learn something about Bitter's strategy in particular and about the drawn-out legal proceedings of the 17th century in general. Last but not least, it may explain why in the end Bitters contemporaries quite understandably chose to stay away from this troublemaker. Bitter was continuously collecting evidence either for his own defence or to prepare an attack on his opponents. To this man of detail, legal procedure was a non-stop boxing match of throwing teasing punches at the opponent. Whenever he felt cornered, he did not hesitate to call for assistance. He manipulated proceedings in such a way that his opponents ultimately ran out of steam.

Social control through ecclesiastical discipline was one of the cornerstones of early Batavian colonial society, as I have shown in the preceding chapter on the Caryatids. The Church Council in the Indies had become an odd echo from the fatherland, shaped and changed by local circumstances. It was totally subservient to the Governor-General and the Council, who in turn employed it as a means for keeping society in check. It is rather ironic that in this respect Company servants could quite successfully ignore the fulminations of the Church Council if they felt properly backed by their superiors, whom they really feared. That is the reason why Bitter, albeit somewhat ruffled, emerged unscathed out of this prolonged struggle with the ecclesiastical authorities. The only punishment that could truly frighten him was disciplinary action taken by his direct superiors.

A Clash with the Worldly Authorities
Still, there was another matter which did disturb Bitter: he had not quite succeeded in gaining control over all of Cornelia's assets. Even

worse, it looked as if she was progressively spiriting away money via all kinds of furtive plots, and in this way succeeded in keeping it out of his reach. These suspicions were verified when he found out about one case in particular. Cornelia had managed to get a close friend, Adriaen van Becom, to transfer 3,000 rixdollars, that were deposited with the Company on Cornelia's name, to his own account. At the bottom of the receipt which Company cashier, Baukes, who also was involved in the complot, had written out, Van Becom entered a notice that the money was not his, but in reality belonged to juffrouw Cnoll. He left this receipt with Baukes, who in turn gave it to Cornelia. Van Becom and Baukes were both members of the Church Council and will undoubtedly have rejoiced in playing this nasty trick on Bitter (VOC 1431, f.766). When Cornelia fell out with Bitter, she needed money to live apart from him, so on the order of the Director-General Rijckloff van Goens (probably also an old friend of her first husband) Baukes paid her the money without Van Becom's knowledge.

Having somehow found out about the 3,000 rixdollars on Van Becom's name, Bitter started legal proceedings to distrain upon the latter's goods. He triumphed, for the Court of Justice ordered Van Becom to pay out the sum to Bitter, and fined Van Becom another 50 rixdollars. Van Becom quite understandably felt aggrieved by the sentence and asked for a revision with the Governor-General and Council so that he could tell all those aspects of the case which had until then been covered up. "These, recognizing that this verdict never could be maintained as one could see the palpable iniquity of it", begged Van Becom to desist from applying for revision of the sentence. Of course they had reasons for doing so, for Rijckloff van Goens had not acted according to the regulations, and having just been elected Governor-General in January 1678, he preferred to hush everything up. On the other hand, it was presumed that Bitter would not like the public at large to know how his wife had outwitted him either: "he preferred to have triumphed in name, rather than to submit himself to a precarious revision procedure". He indeed asked Van Becom not to apply for revision on the condition that he would never have the verdict executed. At long last Van Becom, who was quite sick and tired of the case and who had furthermore been assured by the members of the Council of the Indies that he would not be cheated, relented and told Johan Bitter that he would not press for revision if given "a written act of non-execution of the verdict". A rendezvous was chosen near the Malay church and in the presence of a councillor of the Indies, Willem van Outhoorn, the document was handed over (VOC 1431, f.766v).

The "brains" behind this operation was another councillor, Cornelis Speelman, who also had intermediated in September 1676. This old acquaintance of Cornelia - for many years he had served under Pieter Cnoll at the bookkeeping department - was not quite a gentleman in his private business dealings, as De Haan has clearly shown.[42] That made him perhaps the right person to deal with the slippery Bitter, who was frightened to death of Speelman. This fits in well with Valentijn's characterization of Speelman: "He was a man sparkling with fire and brains, uncommonly bold in his speech, inspiring great awe, generally so much feared that he made everybody tremble; but he was a great supporter of his friends" (Valentijn 1721 IV-1:311). Five years later, when Speelman had died, Bitter rather spitefully complained that he had been forced into abandoning his personal interests "by a big fart (een blaas met bonen), out of fear for a man who at the time possessed neither high rank nor power" (VOC 1431, f.770). Not only was that remark beside the point - Speelman had rank and power, having succeeded Van Goens as Director-General - but more important, Bitter does not mention that by the time the case was settled in early 1679, his own position in Batavia had become rather precarious. As a matter of fact, the trump card that Cornelia had played in Holland started to yield results.

A Smuggling Racket Unmasked
In the Resolutie-boek of the Amsterdam chamber of the Dutch East India Company we find on July 29, 1677 the first reference to the collection of diamonds Bitter had stealthily sent to Holland. The mate of the ship Europa, a character named Jan Hay ("Jack Shark") appeared at the Tuesday-morning session and was submitted to cross-examination by the directors, Tulp and Backer, as well as by the advocaat (managing director) of the Company, Pieter van Dam, who happened to be in Amsterdam at the time. On the table before these gentlemen, Hay placed a small piece of cloth containing the 24 diamonds which Johan Bitter had entrusted to him in Batavia - and which had been purchased with money he had embezzled from Cornelia. A notary was present to note down his affidavit. In exchange for the promise that he would be granted freedom from prosecution, the sailor testified that there was a collection of letters and a bill of lading that might provide further information. He did not know their whereabouts (VOC 240, unfoliated). This riddle was solved two weeks later when one of the directors, Isaacq Hochepied, handed over to the chamber authorities a personal letter he had received from Bitter, as well as a collection of letters addressed to other people.[43]

The Amsterdam chamber of the VOC.

The gentlemen were in for a big surprise, for among letters in which Bitter bragged about the big fish he had hooked, a bill of exchange was found belonging to the Batavian alderman, Jacob Does, which was addressed to the Amsterdam merchant, Pieter van Wicquevoort, entitling him to 3,000 rixdollars to be paid out of the Company treasury. From the correspondence, it was clear that the money did not originate with Does but with Bitter. A complete inventory of the diamonds was found with a letter addressed to another merchant in Amsterdam, Eghbert Munter. According to the minutes of this particular meeting, it was discovered that "Bitter asked Munter to send him a receipt, but under a false name, out of fear that the true facts might be brought to light, although this could not be conclusively proved due to the obscure

VIII Butterfly or Mantis?

wording employed in the letter". Yet another letter addressed to Isaacq Staets left little doubt about Bitter's real intentions: he apologized for not having been able to send the rarities Staets had asked for (VOC 240, 28-7-, 12-8-, 26-8-1677).

Chagrined that the original misgivings about Bitter's suitability for service in the East had been confirmed, the Amsterdam directors reported their findings at the next general meeting of the Gentlemen XVII and proposed to recall the culprit "buyten qualiteyt en gage" - demoted without pay.

The directors were angry at Bitter for reasons which had nothing to do with the divorce case or the fact that he had embezzled his wife's money. For the time being, they were vexed that nota bene a member of the Court of Justice directly appointed by themselves had been caught in the act of diamond smuggling. Diamonds were traditionally esteemed as objects of investment due to their small size and relative high value: the owner could easily hide and transport them without drawing attention. Understandably, the management of the East India Company feared that large capital sums derived from private illegal trade in the Indies were being continuously smuggled out and shipped home without their knowledge. A host of edicts and regulations in the Realia and the Plakaatboek meant to control the trading or polishing of diamonds bears witness to this.[44]

Willem van Alphen, secretary to the Court of Justice in Holland from 1631 till 1684, has done posterity a great service by publishing legal documents that he thought to be exemplary or unique in character. In his "Papegay ofte formulier-boek van allerhande requesten, mandamenten, conclusien, als anders, in de dagelijcksche practijcke dienende voor de respective Hoven van Justitie in Hollandt" he has published the text of a request that the board of the East India Company submitted to the Law Court of Holland in 1675.[45] It concerns a case of diamond

Title page of the "Parrot book".

smuggling which had come to the attention of the Company directors because the parties involved in the smuggling disputed the rightful possession of the gems and were foolish enough to ask the court to step in to arbitrate. The Company did not hesitate to claim all evidence brought forth by both parties about these diamonds as they had been illegally imported, and indeed this position was accepted (Van Alphen 1683:10-4). Bitter may not have been familiar with this particular precedent as the verdict was pronounced shortly after he had left Holland, but it serves to prove that the Company very strictly enforced its prohibitions in this respect.

On September 8, 1677 the diamond smuggling case in which Bitter was involved was presented at the general assembly of the Gentlemen XVII (VOC 108, Res.XVII). The Amsterdam chamber had prepared the case well so that it could be dealt with and resolved that same morning. The diamonds were confiscated on the grounds of the terms of article 23 and it was decided that the bill of exchange would not be paid to Van Wicquevoort for the time being.[46] The total value of the diamonds and the bill of exchange amounted to 16,450 guilders. A resolution was passed to write Governor-General Maetsuycker to request him to exhort the Council of Justice to see justice done in this case, and finally to administer vigorous justice as an example and detriment for the others. All of Bitter's letters were to be sent back to the Indies to serve as evidence. A curious note was added to this order: "It is the opinion and the intention of this board that, whatever the issue of the sentence of the court may be, the above-mentioned Mr. Johan Bitter should be sent back home without delay as a servant useless to the Company" (VOC 108, 8-9-1677). This time the Gentlemen XVII, even including Valckenier, unanimously agreed upon the way the man should be dealt with.

The Punishment
On June 6, 1678, the China and Land van Schouwen dropped anchor at the Batavian roadstead after a voyage of nine months and nineteen days. That same afternoon the letters of the Gentlemen XVII were given a cursory first reading. Bitter was summoned from his office at the town hall, confronted with the accusations of private trade and dismissed forthwith (Daghregister 1678:291-5). How exactly he was called to account for his behaviour during the following months is not clear. We do know that Bitter had to borrow money, 4,300 rixdollars in all, so it is most likely that the law court had forbidden him to touch the assets of Cornelia, pending the divorce case. However, he secretly mortgaged Cornelia's house to alderman Jacob Does, one week before the sentence was due (HR 783:70).

The separation case was handled under peculiar circumstances. Some members of the Court may have declared themselves unwilling or not competent to decide upon the case because they had been involved in it themselves. Consequently, they were replaced by outsiders. Furthermore, a member of the Council of the Indies, Dirk Blom, was added to the Court of Justice with the special order of swiftly expediting two verdicts which had been delayed and procrastinated: a law suit by the public prosecutor, Gualtherus Zeeman, vs. the former director of the Surat Factory, Andries Bogaert, and the lawsuit Van Nijenroode vs. Bitter. In both these cases the president of the Court, Balthazar Bort, had to cede his ranking and his right of the first vote to Blom. Thus matters were steered into the direction desired by the political authorities (Daghregister 1679:419).

By now everybody knew that the Gentlemen XVII wanted to draw blood in the separate case on diamond smuggling which was also pending, and, realizing that Bitter was a free target, the "most capable and aged Company-servants" decided to punish this "orang baru", who had so awkwardly attempted to rob one of the local hens of her golden eggs. Cornelia's request to be divorced from bed and board was provisionally granted on November 4, 1679. Without doubt, that was the most she could get. Divorce from table and bed in principle had a temporary character at that time; the judge was only allowed to grant it in the hopes of a conciliation (Van Apeldoorn 1925:197). But there was more to the verdict: the defendant was to be excluded from all advantages accruing from the two "marriage-settlements": he had to restore 25,000 rixdollars as well as the house and the manumitted slaves. All costs of the legal proceedings were to be borne by him (HR 783:70, 86). The Church Council must have taken heart at this verdict, for two days later it admonished Bitter once more "to reflect upon his position and to carry out his Christian duties" (Bouwstoffen III:436).

The sentence on the diamond smuggling followed one week later, on November 11, 1679. Bitter was found guilty, deprived of his rank, and ordered to return home (Daghregister 1679:509). His written defence, "that he had sent some diamonds to Holland to have them made into jewellery for his daughters", had not been taken seriously by the court (HR 783:87).

In a last desperate attempt to undo his victorious wife, Bitter sent a request to Governor-General and Council on January 2, 1680, asking either to be granted revision of the divorce case at Batavia (this implied a postponement of his return to Holland) or to be provided with a warrant to order his wife to accompany him on his voyage home. The request was declined, with the remark that upon arrival in Patria, he could address himself to such tribunal as he saw fit. Bitter then submitted a "further elucidation" on January 16. This was all to no avail, for the highest authorities unrelentingly repudiated his demands and advised him to read once more the terse text they had sent him on December 19: "By order of the Heeren Mayores, the suppliant is instructed to leave for Patria with the last ship of this season" (Daghregister 1679:579). The ecclesiastical authorities were a bit more accommodating. Upon his request, Bitter was provided with copies of all the resolutions that had been passed in connection with his marital quarrels. He was wise enough not to ask for any references to his collisions with the pious gentlemen themselves.

At the last moment a hitch almost occurred. Jacob Does and Mattheus Luchtenburgh, who had lent Bitter considerable sums of money over the preceding months, requested that Bitter should be kept under arrest until he had repaid them. This request was rejected "as it ran counter to the orders of the Heeren Mayores", the Gentlemen XVII (Daghregister 1680:108). When the fleet raised anchor on March 15, 1680, the troublesome lawyer on board, Batavian society could finally sit back and heave a deep sigh of relief.

Dutch Interlude

Second Round Against Cornelia
On the long voyage home Johan Bitter had ample time to ponder the reception he would receive from the Gentlemen XVII and the possibility of his turning the tables on his triumphant spouse.

Cynical directors who had encountered many cases of diamond smuggling would view with great scepticism a defence maintaining that the diamonds had been entrusted to the mate of the Europa not for smuggling purposes but rather to be set into jewelry for his daughters. Valckenier's protection would indeed be necessary if he were to prevail; it was clear that plans could not be made: this would be a wait-and-see matter.

On the other hand, nothing prevented him from opening proceedings against Cornelia before the Court of Holland, provided the Court would be competent to sit on the matter. Here was the snag: in view of the provisional separation decree pronounced in Batavia, it could be argued that the defendant, Cornelia, had obtained a domicile of her own in the East Indies, outside the territory covered by the Court of Holland and that therefore this Court was not competent to hear a claim against her. Bitter found his own legal solution to the problem.

Arriving in Amsterdam, Bitter was shocked to hear of the recent death of his mighty patron, Gillis Valckenier. Fortunately for him, members of his faction such as Louis Trip and Dirk Tulp were still sitting on the board of the Amsterdam Chamber and it can be assumed that Bitter obtained useful information and advice from them.[47] In the matter of diamond smuggling, there was something in the wind which might turn out to be favourable for him. The directors were realizing that the "illegal" import of diamonds was a disease of the time that could not be isolated but could perhaps be remedied. A possible cure would be to channel the diamond trade into legal channels, and discussions were in progress regarding the ways in which this could be carried out. Consequently, Bitter kept a low profile in this respect.

However, he lost no time starting proceedings against Cornelia before the Provincial Court of Holland. To render the court competent in this case, he had to employ a few legal strategems. Bitter intended to bring about the competency of the court by effecting an arrest under the hands of the VOC on all assets belonging to Cornelia van Nijenroode that were deposited with the Amsterdam Chamber of the East India Company. Through this arrest, the VOC (which fell under the jurisdiction of the Court of Holland) was tied up in a process between Bitter and Cornelia, and the competency of the Court as regards the VOC automatically entailed competency vis-à-vis Cornelia. This, in short, was Bitter's plan d'attaque.

And so, probably in February 1681 – the exact date has not been published – Bitter handed in a petition for Mandate of Arrest to the Court of Holland, and fired the opening shot in the battle which was to follow.

Thanks to the same Willem van Alphen who has already provided us with such valuable information about diamond smuggling in his "Papegay" we can reconstruct the case (Van Alphen 1683 II:313-27). The "Papegay" not only provides us with the text of the request but also reproduces the more important documents bearing on the formal side of this case, plus the sentence pronounced at the end. Van Alphen pub-

VIII Butterfly or Mantis?

lished all this as an example of a "Request in order to obtain Mandate of Arrest on goods in the hands of the East India Company belonging to a Juffrouw, domiciled at Batavia in the East Indies". Looking at the documentary evidence one wonders about Van Alphen's motives: did he simply want to treat his readers to an interesting juridical titbit or was his intention to give them a glimpse of how the law was clumsily upheld in the Far East.

The request had a dual purpose. It not only aimed at obtaining an arrest in order to ensure Bitter's claim against Cornelia, but also contained the claim itself, with the intention that it would be decided upon in due course by the Court. Introducing the matter in his request, Bitter gave his description of the material facts. A short summary of the main points will suffice to show that "decent, pious but ill-treated" Bitter was running true to form.

He explained that as a widower, he had remarried a Batavian widow Cornelia van Nijenroode, after having concluded a marriage settlement (huwelijkse voorwaarden) with her on March 7, 1676. He had been excluded from the community of goods, yet certain conditions had been stipulated, among which was preferential treatment for the longest living partner. After the marriage had been concluded, he had behaved himself as a pious, Christian, peace-loving husband. However, influenced by others, his wife started a dispute about the administration of her possessions and the investment of certain sums of money. In spite of the provisions of the law which entitled him to dispose of these affairs as he liked, he had drawn up a certain accoord or reglement to avoid future disputes and to foster an atmosphere of marital love and concord. Those commodities he was to administer and those which fell outside his responsibility, were carefully noted down and registered. He had even agreed to board out his own four children "at high cost" because his new wife could not stand their presence in the house. Sadly enough, however, all this had been to no avail, for his wife had once more created domestic squabbles and eventually had moved out, separating herself from her husband's bed and board. She ignored admonishments from the Church Council, ordered her slave personnel and domestics to ignore her husband and disobey him, spirited away money and had possessions removed from the house. She had accused him of maltreatment (Bitter here of course refers to the "dislocated-arm-incident") and, only after all these ploys had misfired, had she seemed to relent. She came back, only to move out again a few weeks later and institute legal proceedings against him, demanding a separation from bed and board. Because of the intervention in the Court of Justice by persons who were not qualified to administer the law, a provisional sentence, totally to her advantage, had been enacted: separation from bed and board and, along with this, a strong prohibition forbidding her husband from engaging in any further administration of her assets.

Having presented the antecedents, Bitter then proceeded to state his case. It should be emphasized that a provisional separation reached in this way was not at all the same thing as a divorce. Bitter maintained that the marriage had not been broken up by malicious desertion or adultery on his side; the bond of marriage remained and therefore the separation was only of a temporal nature. Bitter wanted to make it very clear that all attempts to make his wife accompany him either on the same ship or on another, in case she should not be able to tolerate his company yet, not only had misfired, they even had been thwarted. The

Batavian authorities had ventured to advise him that he should depart without delay and had added that if he did not agree with the way things were being handled, he should seek redress at any court of justice of his liking after his return in Patria. This meant that the jurisdiction of the court would be based on the domicile of the petitioner and not, as would have been correct, the court of the domicile of the defendant. The petitioner had followed the advice of the Batavian authorities by placing his present domicile under the jurisdiction of the Provincial Court of Holland.

Substantiating his claim, Bitter further argued that it was not Christian, nor could it be suffered from a Christian government, for his wife to persist in absenting herself from her husband, while he, the petitioner, was prepared to do everything in order to bring about a reconciliation and to live with his wife, whom he did not know how he had offended, as he wished to cherish her as a pious Christian husband.

As to the competency of the Court - the legal snag - Bitter argued that the domicile of his wife should not be considered as separate from the domicile of her husband; if this were not considered acceptable, in any event, the jurisdiction of the Court should be based on the arrest of the effects of his wife.

Subsequently, Bitter humbly petitioned the Court to issue a Mandament authorizing the First Bailiff to arrest such goods, charters, and other effects as the petitioner could indicate to belong to Cornelia van Nijenroode, his wife, with the understanding that the Court would also order those persons who held her effects to allow and to suffer the arrest. Last but not least, he begged the Court to order Cornelia van Nijenroode to reconcile herself with the petitioner, to return to the connubial household, to live with the petitioner as behoved a pious and Christian wife and to continue in this until death should part them, with the understanding that he, the petitioner, would from his side render her all due love and obligations and would continue to do so as a Christian and peaceful husband observing the conditions of the marriage settlement.

A harsh punishment should befall Cornelia if she ignored or refused to obey such an order. She would be declared a malicious deserter, and lose all advantages of the marriage settlement. If this were to happen, the petitioner would obtain the advantages stipulated in case of his wife's death.

Bitter also made an effort to repair his current financial position: pendente lite, he applied for a provisional "sortabel", reasonable, part of the receipts of the goods under arrest.

By arrest of February 26, 1681 the Court issued the Mandate of Arrest as petitioned. Van Alphen does not furnish the text of the Court's judgement which should contain the date on which the case would come up for a hearing before the Court. This date, as shown elsewhere, was the first Monday of October, 1682. It is obvious that the Court, in fixing this date so far ahead, kept in mind the time needed for a summons to reach Cornelia in Batavia and for instructions from her side to reach the Hague. Normally, a period of two or three weeks - the latter in Zeeland on account of the difficult communications between the islands - would have been observed.[48]

Five Angry Men
A curious document related to this case is published by Van Alphen in

the "Papegay". It is a Consultatie, a counsel's opinion, given at the Hague on February 21, 1681 by the following, evidently learned, barristers: Martin van der Goes, Adriaen Coetenburgh, Johan Stepel, Zegher ten Holte and M. de Hertoge.

The date is five days anterior to the date of the Mandate of Arrest. Could the Court of Holland, puzzled by Bitter's petition, have felt the necessity to seek learned advice before making up its mind? This hardly seems likely. An arrest in order to safeguard a claim, as applied for here, does not raise any difficulty provided that the claim, on the face of it, seems to be justified, and Bitter's petition did not fail to meet this requirement. Furthermore, the fact that the arrest is permitted does not prejudice in any way the question whether or not the claim really does stand. The decision in that matter is reached only after due deliberation in court. Consequently, as granting a Mandate of Arrest was a routine matter which had to be, and normally was, handled expeditiously in order to prevent the disappearance of the goods to be seized, it would be very odd indeed if the capable Court of Holland had been in such a quandary as to what to do, that it considered it necessary to await the findings of five advisers.

There is more reason to presume that in this document we encounter another of those ingenious collections of favourable evidence the far-seeing Bitter was so specialized in preparing.

In the beginning of the document, the advisers list the documentation put before them. It mentions the marriage settlement with subsequent agreement, documents of the Batavia Court, the proclamation granting a separation from bed and board included, the relevant exchange of requests and resolutions between Bitter and the High Government at Batavia, the Baukes rescription and also a number of testimonials to Bitter's personality by the Church Council, by five parsons, by a previous President of the Batavian Court of Justice and even by the Governor-General himself.[49] They depict Bitter as vigilant and industrious in his profession, obedient, well-mannered and easy-going in social contacts, open to and striving for reconciliation, all of this in contrast to his wife. It is clear that such a file can only have been assembled by Bitter himself. The texts of these testimonials indicate proficient doctoring. From the consultation, it is clear that the advisers were well-informed about Bitter's assertion that he feared there was no justice for him in the Indies.

Therefore it is hardly surprising that the advisers, passing over the question whether the separation had been pronounced rightly or not, opened fire upon the Batavian Court of Justice which had considerably wronged Bitter. According to the advisers, it had wrongfully allowed a member who had testified under oath in the same case, to take part in the decision making, and finally it had denied Bitter's plea for a reconciliation, notwithstanding every judge's duty to try to bring about reconciliation ex officiis.[50] The High Government at Batavia (the Governor-General and Council) also did not escape a broadside. They had insulted Bitter in summo gradu by ordering him home without his wife and children while the case from which reconciliation could be expected to result was still open. All this had been suffered by a man whose sterling qualities had been so amply praised by the highest worldly and ecclesiastical authorities.

So far, the Consultation fitted in closely with Bitter's argumentation in his petition and constituted a useful support for his contentions. On the face of it, the advisers were quite right in expressing the opinion that Bitter had been badly and unjustly treated. Surprisingly, in their final conclusion the advisers did not touch upon Bitter's claim before the Court. They left it open whether such claim would be admissible. They may have had their doubts about it, for their advice was that Bitter, having been mistreated in the Indies, should address himself to the Sovereign Power in the Country: the States-General. This body had the authority to mediate the complaints of anyone who felt to have been insulted in the Indies. He should "in order to obtain that their High Mightinesses would use their benevolence in hoc casu extraordinario, etiam extraordinario remedio to have the aforesaid Bitter examined by whatever Court by way of revision, or assisted and supported" (Van Alphen 1683 II:327).

Reading between the lines, Bitter would have been able to find that the learned advisers saw no chances for a direct claim for revision of the Batavian sentence before the Law Court of Holland. Was it for this reason that his petition appears to carefully steer clear of that word?

If we can explain the Consultatie as an example of Bitter's typical scheming manoeuvres, the question still remains of when and how it reached the Court. That it did so is evident. Could this have occurred during the pleadings when the case came up in Court?

The Arrest
On February 27, 1681 the First Bailiff of the Hague Chamber of the Court of Holland, L. Versluys, bearing his bailiff-stick decorated with the coat of arms of the province of Holland, proceeded to the Plein-square where he knocked at the door of the logement of the East India Company in which the Commissioners of the Haagsche Besogne were meeting. Acting at the request of Johan Bitter, former Member of the Court of Justice of the Indies, and in the name of the Government, he arrested under the hands of the Commissioners a capital of 34,000 rixdollars deposited in the Company's treasury by Cornelia van Nijenroode, wife of his impetrator, as well as a capital of 12,000 rixdollars deposited by his impetrator in the Company's treasury. Furthermore all such capitals and effects belonging to Cornelia van Nijenroode deposited with the same Company together with the already accrued and still accruing interests on those capitals were to be arrested. Versluys ordered the Commisioners to allow and to suffer (gedogen en gehengen) this arrest and summoned them to appear before the Court on the first Monday of October 1682; at the same time, he presented copies of the mandate and of his protocol of arrest.

Pieter van Dam, attorney of the Company, whom we best remember on account of his masterful "Beschrijvinge", received the unexpected visitor.[51] He accepted the documents and said only: "We shall straighten this out and take note". With that, Versluys could leave and the Commissioners could get on with more important matters. Little could they know that this intrusion into their affairs was only the beginning of a very protracted case which eventually would demand considerably more of their precious time (Van Alphen 1683 II:317).

In the same way, two weeks later, V. Poelenburg, a colleague of Versluys from Amsterdam, visited two other citizens of the capital, Nicolaes de Roy and Gijsbrecht David Strantwijck, in order to effect arrests and summons, as it was believed by Bitter that both were keeping charters, papers and other effects belonging to Cornelia. With

The subpoena.

Strantwijck he had definitely come to the wrong address. This gentleman said curtly: "I have no papers"; however, De Roy affirmed that he acted as her proxy (Van Alphen 1683 II:318).

Arrest having been effected in so far as it was possible, it was time to inform Cornelia about the arrest and to summon her.

With Cornelia living in Batavia, Versluys, acting again at the request of Bitter, did so by Edict in the Hague on March 14.[52] First, the bell at the city hall of the Hague was rung; then Versluys charged and ordered Cornelia van Nijenroode to allow and to suffer the arrests, and ordered her to reconcile with, and by consequence join, her husband in the connubial abode. Finally, he summoned her to appear before the Court in person or by proxy on the first Monday of October 1682. He gave notification of his activities in a sealed Missive, enclosing copies of the mandate and the protocol of summons. It was now up to Bitter to see to it that the sealed letter was handed over to Cornelia, and so he did, as is described below.

With the wheels of Justice in motion, Bitter could only sit back and speculate on further developments. Would his endeavours to steer around the Batavian sentence succeed, and would Cornelia's actions offer the possibility of her being branded a malicious desertrix, with all

The bone of contention.

the financial benefits he would gain from such a development? It was hardly likely that she would not fight back - and then the question would become one of where that might lead. If worst came to the worst and his case miscarried, there would be no other recourse left but a revision at Batavia. However Bitter's return to Batavia would only be possible after the accusation of diamond smuggling had been refuted, as he hoped. And so Bitter could do little but wait.

The Lost Sheep Retrieved
Meanwhile in Batavia, Cornelia van Nijenroode, unaware of all these activities, was coming into her own. She believed that she was finally rid of her husband. She had obtained the provisional separation and he had been recalled without being able to drag her along. Apart from being concerned about the legal aftermath of Bitter's last-minute borrowing-spree, which still had to be settled with the creditors, Cornelia felt relieved.[53] Justice was at her side, and although the financial damage sustained was considerable, enough capital remained to enable her to take part in Batavia's costly social activities, which she had missed over the past years as a result of all the squabbling.

When the wet monsoon season was over, she ordered the horses to be put to the carriage. François Valentijn has provided us with the following anecdote: the couple had fallen out over this carriage because, against his wife's will, Bitter had ordered the turnips (Knollen) painted on both doors to be removed in order to replace them with his own coat of arms: "Doch die KNOL brak haar zeer BITTER op" ("but that turnip smarted her bitterly") the author smugly remarks (Valentijn 1726 IV-1: 385). In this coach, defiantly decorated with turnips, Cornelia went out and showed herself again in public. Her pleasure in this was not to last for long, for the authorities, alarmed by the opulent behaviour of the Batavian townspeople, issued a ban on keeping "coaches or covered calashes". Once more the wheels of that fateful means of transportation came to a halt (Plakaatboek III:47).

Nonetheless, Cornelia had at last emerged into Society again and invitations started to come her way as the higher circles welcomed her back. By the end of June 1680, she felt sure enough of herself to send a letter to the Church Council, humbly begging to be admitted to Holy Communion again (Bouwstoffen III:456). The deacons did not meet her demand with a stern rebuff but neither did they show themselves to be in a forgiving mood. They desired that juffrouw Van Nijenroode provide more information about her feelings towards her absent husband. The committee also suggested that it might help if she expressed some willingness eventually to be reconciled with her husband.

As a matter of fact, no Church Council was authorized to welcome married people living in discord at the Holy Communion. Consequently, the gentlemen desired better information about the background and the stipulations of the bed-and-board separation. That July, Cornelia was still not among the communicants. Not daunted, she went to see the Reverend Zas just before the council met on September 30 to select new candidates for the next communion. Her answers still did not satisfy the inquirers and she was again passed over (Bouwstoffen III:463).

To be denied access to the Holy Communion meant that she was denied full membership in the Christian community, which was a blot on one's reputation. Yet it did not prohibit Cornelia from fulfilling important functions in Batavian society. When Petronella Wonderaer, the wife of her old friend Director-General Cornelis Speelman, died on April 2, 1681, Cornelia was present to give a hand to the family, and on the following day she helped to receive the mourners at Petronella's home after the funeral ceremony (Daghregister 1681:223).

On July 3, the Church Council held its usual meeting to decide about the admission or refusal of communicants. This time the nihil obstat was pronounced in Cornelia's case. On the request of the council, she had stated that she was in principle willing to seek reconciliation with her husband whenever the opportunity presented itself (Daghregister 1681:483). Had she known that her husband was doing all he could to steer in that same direction she might have let the wine cup of the communion pass from her. In Batavia, however, everything seemed to be forgiven and forgotten. The lost sheep had been brought back to the fold. But she was granted only one summer to live in peace.

A Letter from Holland
On November 6, 1681 the president of the Court of Justice of Batavia, Willem van Outhoorn, summoned all members for an extraordinary meeting at Batavia castle. Having welcomed the gentlemen, he stated the reasons for the gathering. A few days after the fleet from Holland had arrived, Jan Blieck had applied to him in the capacity of attorney (procureur) on behalf of Johan Bitter. Blieck's intention was to hand over two letters sent by Bitter. One glance at the name of the sender was sufficient to arouse his fear that there might be a snake hiding in the

grass; that was why he had convened this special meeting. Blieck, who was waiting outside, was called in and presented the documents, one sealed letter addressed to Cornelia van Nijenroode and one short accompanying message by Bitter addressed to the Court. The sealed letter was Versluys' missive of March 14; in his own letter Bitter demanded that the document in the sealed envelope not only be handed over to his wife by the Court's bailiff, but also that the latter would exact an answer from her. Bitter's request was not that excessive, but the gentlemen of the Batavian Court were not willing to offer any assistance to their erstwhile colleague. They had clearly had their fill of him, and consequently they told Johan Blieck to deliver the letter himself. Knowing Cornelia, the latter realized that this was easier said than done.[54]

In consultation with Pieter Kettingh, who was also acting as Bitter's proxy, he enlisted the help of a local notary, Christoffel van Outgers, who was to apply to Cornelia and deliver the sealed letter to her. After a few days, Van Outgers returned with the letter still in his hands. He had not been able to find Cornelia. In order not to lose any more time, Blieck and Kettingh now ordered Van Outgers to hand the letter over to one of the domestics in her house and, in case they refused to accept it, to leave it behind in the vestibule. In Holland in such a case the arrest would have been nailed to the front door. The large overhang of Cornelia's house made necessary another, and as we shall see less satisfactory, working method. The unfortunate notary at least knew what he could expect. Arriving again at the Nijenroode estate, he happened to meet the same domestic he had met on earlier occasions. To his question of whether juffrouw was at home, the maid replied: "no". What about her son (Cornelis)? "No!" "So I cannot speak to either of them?" the notary, a bit superfluously, said. "No" again was the answer. "Will you then be so kind as to transmit this letter to juffrouw" he asked, going on to explain what was in the envelope. "I am not permitted to accept any documents", the girl replied. Thereupon, the notary realized he had to resort to the ultimate expedient and he posted the letter on a nearby chair. "Don't you do that", the girl shrieked, "I shall throw it onto the street". Seeing that he was no match for this vixen, Van Outgers started backing out the door, not forgetting to utter formal protestations of the costs, damage and interests a usu. Looking back over his shoulder as he headed home, he saw the papers land with a splash on the pavement of the Tijgergracht. The notary's adventures were duly reported by Van Outgers by protocol as published in the "Papegay", where a statement legitimizing his actions, given by the President of the Aldermen Bench, Anthoni Hurdt, dated December 16th, 1681, may also be found (Van Alphen 1683 II:320-1).

The Church Council, ever vigilant regarding the behaviour and wellbeing of its flock, did not miss the opportunity to utter disapproval about the rash behaviour of the lady, who only six months before had shown such a repentent attitude towards the church and her husband and who was on basis of this allowed to participate in the Communion. The diligent vice-secretary, P. Wijtens, was ordered to make a summary of Cornelia's written promise received in July, so that Johan Bitter in Holland could take cognizance of it (Bouwstoffen III:489).

Cornered from all sides, Cornelia van Nijenroode could no longer ignore the arrest. She must have had her misgivings about a lawsuit in Holland, a country completely unknown to her, where, in contrast to her wily husband with his host of legal friends, she had few or no supporters. Her case would be handled by a Court she had no experience of, composed of judges who had no insight in or experience of local conditions or social relations at Batavia. But it was also clear, - or made clear to her - that she had no choice. So she appointed the Hague solicitor Adriaen van Sterrevelt to act for her before the Court of Holland.

Bitter Refuted
On the first Monday of October 1682 the case was introduced in Court. Adriaen van Sterrevelt acted for Cornelia, George Roosenboom for Bitter and Cornelis Vinck for the East India Company. The defendant, Cornelia, declared obedience to the Court at the request of claimant, who probably wanted to ensure that she would not be able to wriggle out of any unfavourable judgements. Subsequently the parties handed in their conclusions (Van Alphen 1683 II:322-3).

As may be expected, Roosenboom's conclusions closely follow the formulation of the petition for the Mandate of Arrest. They enlarge, however, on one point that if Cornelia were to be declared a malicious desertrix the original terms specified a community of goods. This time, if such were the case, Bitter would not only be entitled to half of the

Consulting a lawyer.

community property but also to a quarter of Cornelia's half by way of forfeit. Further, the "sortabel" part of the preceipts on the goods seized, provisionally indicated in the petition to be enjoyed by Bitter, was in this statement to be five percent of 46,000 Reals, which calculated over three years, would represent 8,280 Rixdollars.

Van Sterrevelt's conclusions were short and to the point: Bitter's claims could not be admitted in court as they were obstructed by the fact that the case had already been decided by a binding judgement of the Court of Justice at Batavia, the exceptio rei judicatae.

Vinck declared on behalf of the East India Company that it was unlikely that it could be proved that Cornelia van Nijenroode had any money or goods at any Chamber of the Company in Holland and that despite the fact that she might have money or effects deposited with one or another Comptoir in the Indies, these were not "arrestabel".

The case proceeded in the usual way, Van Sterrevelt's exceptio was pleaded and the Court retired.

On December 22, 1682, sentence was pronounced. The arrest effected was confirmed, but only in relation to Bitter's application for reconciliation. In this respect Van Sterrevelt's exceptio was rejected, but on all other points Bitter's claims were declared non-admissable and the arrest requested on basis of these arguments was declared void and unjustified because of the binding Batavian judgement (Van Alphen 1683 II:323). What do the proceedings suggest about the private feelings of the Court of Holland? The very shortness of its judgement and its readiness to apply the exceptio convey a hint; it might quite well be that the Gentlemen behind the table did not feel inclined to open this Batavian Pandora's box.

Van Sterrevelt had achieved what was possible. His client could be content. He must have realized that a serious endeavour aimed at reconciliation could not be blocked by his purely technical exception. For Bitter the judgement was a setback and had serious implications: he had no chance of steering a course around the Batavian judgement and of triumphing over Cornelia on his home territory in Holland. Revision at Batavia then was the only possibility left. Did the judgement upset Bitter? Apparently not at all. Months before the case came up in Court he was already working on a revision at Batavia.

A Volte Face
Had Bitter's position vis-à-vis the Gentlemen XVII improved in the meantime to such an extent that he could resort to this ultimate course of action? Indeed, through the good offices of the Valckenier faction matters had taken a definite turn for the better for him.

F.S. Gaastra in his forthcoming study on the management of the financial position of the Dutch East India Company throws some light on the dispute concerning the payment of the bills of exchange.[55] Because the bills of exchange Bitter had sent from Batavia had been accepted by the cashier of Batavia castle, the authorities decided that there was no legal argument to block the payment in Holland. Of crucial importance, however, was the fact that the charge of private trade was dropped. Not only was it discovered that it was difficult to prove that Bitter had been lying when he asserted that the diamonds had been sent to Patria only in order to have them cut and polished for his daughters, but also the directors suddenly made a volte face and decided to legalize the trade in diamonds. Members of the Valckenier faction, like

Louis Trip and Johan Hudde, continued to reign supreme within the directorate. Judging from what happened on Monday, June 15th, 1682, they must have kept Johan Bitter posted in all the developments behind this decision.

On that day an important discussion took place about the possible conditions under which diamond smuggling might be turned into a legal operation. It was suggested that anyone who henceforth wished to send diamonds from the Orient to Europe would be free to do so provided he paid a recognitie, a tax of 3%, on the estimated value. Upon delivery, the transporter would receive 1/8% of the estimated value of the diamonds as compensation for delivering them. The Company itself would reserve the right to acquire those diamonds it wished to purchase at a price at least 25% above the estimated value. After it had been decided to use this plan as a basis for further elaboration, one of the Heren produced a document by Johan Bitter addressed to those present.

In this document Bitter complained about several issues: "first of all about the fact that he had been recalled from the Indies, where he had been defending himself against the accusations; secondly that he had been unjustly and wrongly separated from his wife; and thirdly about the detrimental sentence served by the Council of Justice in Batavia. He finally asked either to be allowed to continue his legal proceedings in Holland or to be permitted to do so in India." (Res. XVII, VOC 109, 15-6-1682).

Surprised by this unexpected action, the assembly decided to postpone this matter until a later meeting, during which Bitter would be allowed to present his request once more and to furnish further explanation. In the resolutions of the next meetings, there is no reference to the case, so it may be concluded that on second thought the Gentlemen XVII decided to await the decision of the Court of Holland in the autumn.

As we have seen, this sentence, served just before Christmas (on December 12), was a setback to Johan Bitter; of course, the battle was not really lost, as the bond of marriage was acknowledged. Yet it was evident by now that he would have to return to the Orient to continue his efforts. Consequently, he drew up a request to the Gentlemen XVII to be employed once more in a suitable function, onder sortabel en convenibel employ, and started to prepare himself for the great voyage.

Bitter's wishes were granted. He was re-appointed to the Court of Justice, just as nothing had ever happened, and so persuasively did he state his unfortunate marital position that the Gentlemen XVII decided "to write to Governor-General and Council and recommend them to do all they could to mend and solve the problems that had been raised between him and his wife in the past, problems which were linked up with the unfavourable sentence that the Court had served him. If they might not succeed in bringing about a reconciliation, a revision might as yet be granted to him. Pending the proceedings, he should not be employed outside Batavia." (VOC 109, 8-3-1683). The next day, the legalization of the diamond trade was formally authorized and effected.

Revision, a Legal Last Resort
Revision was a legal reversal, which had to be obtained at the Council of Justice of Batavia castle. It has been described as "the ultimate remedy aimed at proving that mistakes - erreur en misslag - had been made in the sentence of the court" (Van Kan 1943:13). It was applied

for only when all other possible legal remedies had been attempted in vain. Its exceptional nature notwithstanding, revision was often resorted to in the Indies. Pieter van Dam, who has devoted a special paragraph to revisie, counted in his time several hundred cases (Stapel 1927-1943 III:96). It is worthwhile to examine this institution more closely here because as a result of its "exceptional" nature it throws considerable light on the peculiar ways in which the legal and administrative authorities rubbed shoulders or came into conflict as a result of their respective interests. The Governor-General and Council often overstepped the limits of their responsibilities and meddled in the juridical sphere - but not always successfully, as is demonstrated below.

It occasionally happened that the administration of the colony would be ordered by its directors in Patria to interfere in judicial proceedings; the Bitter-Van Nijenroode case provides us with a perfect example of this. We have seen how the Governor-General and Council were directed by the Gentlemen XVII to send home one of their servants without delay, on account of gross misdemeanour. Thereupon, the Court of Justice of the Company headquarters pronounced a sentence in a divorce case which was clearly prejudicial to the interests of the Company servant in question. Although it is quite likely that it did so because it felt the hot breath of the directors on its neck, this of course cannot be proved. The Company servant concerned, ironically a member of the Court of Justice, was denied the opportunity to ask in situ for revision (on account of the order of the Gentlemen XVII that he must return immediately); instead, he was given the advice to seek redress in Holland if it would suit him to do so. Should one understand that revision can only be applied for with the Sovereign, i.e. the States General in the Dutch Republic, "because the sovereignty in the East Indies over the countries and places, as well as the inhabitants that are possessed by the Company, depend upon their High and Mighty, de Hoogmogende Staten Generaal?" Van Dam gamely asks in his "Beschrijvinge", "or are the Governor-General and Council authorized to do so?" He immediately provides the answer to this question by explaining that from the beginning, the States General always advised people who complained about having been harmed by the administration of justice in the Indies to return and ask for redress by applying for revision in Batavia. Revision of a sentence pronounced in the Indies was never allowed in the Republic.

Not entirely satisfied with the rather succinct treatment that Van Dam gives to revision, the legal historian Van Kan has provided a very detailed analytical description of the historical development of this colonial "emergency brake". It is interesting how the interaction between administrative and legal organs plays the leading part in his exposé, which can be summed up as follows:

Right from the earliest days in the colonies, people who felt themselves wronged by the Indian jurisdiction tried to appeal in Holland. This was always refused. To whom could they then appeal in India - to the Council of Justice? No, they had to address themselves to the Governor-General and Council, a custom which was codified by Johan Maetsuycker when he drew up the Statuten van Batavia (Plakaatboek I:512). Although the revision itself was carried out by the Council of Justice, the admission to the revision procedure, the prologue to re-trial, was decided upon by the Governor-General and Council. According to Van Kan, this original prescription constituted the germ of what eventually

VIII Butterfly or Mantis?

developed into active meddling by the administration with jurisprudence (1943:27). Around 1662, an amplification was added by the Gentlemen XVII which deprived the Governor-General and Council of the power to deal with the admission to the revision procedure. From then on, this right was also given into the hands of the judicature. In practice, however, the Governor-General and Council continued to "accord revision" until the end of the century, when at long last the Gentlemen XVII intervened and forced the Governor-General and Council to give up these prerogatives. How then did the procedure work in Bitter's time? Within two years after the sentence had been passed the person who felt wronged could present a request directly to the Governor-General and Council to be accorded revision. This request would be granted or refused. If it were granted, a tribunal would be installed ad hoc, consisting of the Council of Justice supplemented with adjunct-revisors (appointed by the administration). Thereupon the case would be settled by this reinforced Council of Justice.

Let us now look at how Van Kan discusses the way in which Bitter's case was dealt with by the legal authorities and the Gentlemen XVII in Holland. He establishes that they did not wish to embark on a discussion regarding the wisdom of the Batavia sentence and therefore told Bitter that no legal remedy remained other than a request for revision in Batavia. The reason they did not relegate him to the Council of Justice, Van Kan says, is simply because they condoned the existing situation in the Indies. Consequently the case was remitted to the Governor-General and Council. As shown above (Van Kan never saw the evidence of the case in its totality), we know that the real story was more complex. The Gentlemen XVII had to draw the Governor-General and Council into this matter because on an earlier occasion the directors had ordered the Indian administration to interfere in the legal process that was being meted out to Bitter. They had thus willingly trampled upon their own rules in every possible way, and they had therefore to do something to make up for it.

This long interlude is intended to serve as an introduction to the strange situation that developed slowly after Bitter's return to Batavia. Soon the legal and administrative organs in Batavia got so mixed up with the case and with each other that matters veered out of control. To get back to the story we must return to the ominous autumn of 1683 which saw the return of Johan Bitter in Batavia.

The Talk of the Town

Appeasement and Accommodation
In the summer of 1679, a little ahead of Johan Bitter, Nicolaus de Graaff, a travel-minded ship's surgeon and writer, returned from his fifteenth voyage at sea. He was 57 years old and deemed it time to retire. In his home, Egmond aan Zee, a windswept fishing village in the dunes of the North Holland coast, the old tar was received with great respect and was duly appointed sheriff. But, hearing the sea only a stone's throw away day in and day out was too much for him: he at last yielded to its call and decided to embark upon yet another voyage to the East. In the spring of 1683, he entered the service of the East India Company at Amsterdam and was appointed chief-surgeon on Ridderschap van Holland, a brand-new East Indiaman of 36 canons with a

Batavia around 1670.

total of 300 men on board. De Graaff tells us that the fleet consisted of five ships: "We on Ridderschap flew the admiral's flag from the main's top, having on board the Hon. Johan Bitter, a wise and modest gentleman, who served as the admiral of the fleet".[56] After an uneventful trip, the fleet arrived in Batavia on November 27. "Thank Heavens, only five men were lost, two died in their bunks, and three were lost overboard and drowned", he wrote. De Graaff's job was now over; he could hand over the care of the sick to the local practitioners. Bitter, the admiral, still had some matters to attend to: a report concerning the voyage had to be made to the Governor-General and Council and thereafter the funeral of his personal steward, Adriaan van Antwerpen, who had died a few days after arrival, had to be arranged. Having completed all these tasks, he could take up his own personal affairs (De Graaff 1930:168-70). He certainly visited his daughter, Bartha, who had married Constantijn Nobel Junior during his absence (on June 6, 1680). She would have informed him of Cornelia's behaviour during the two years which had gone by since he left. We shall now see how "wisely and modestly" he approached Cornelia.

To say that Cornelia van Nijenroode watched with mixed feelings the disembarkation of her estranged husband would undoubtedly amount to a gross understatement. The fact that he had been restored to his for-

VIII Butterfly or Mantis?

mer rank was a bad sign; moreover, the rumour that the Gentlemen XVII had granted him the right to seek revision of the November 4, 1679 verdict suggested that the victor could easily become the victim. Her only solace was the knowledge that Cornelis Speelman had assumed the office of Governor-General (November 2, 1681) while Balthazar Bort had succeeded him as Director-General: two of her old friends were at the helm of government.

Contrary to her expectations it was not Bitter who knocked at her door three weeks later; it was the president of the Church Council, accompanied by an elder. They came to tell her that her husband had visited the Church Council on December 9 to ask for mediation, as it had come to his ears that his wife had been readmitted to the Communion. Had she really professed the desire to be reconciled with him, Bitter had asked. The evidence he had received pointed indeed in that direction. He said he wished to know what her inner feelings were like at present; furthermore he would very much appreciate the intercession of some delegates of the Council (Bouwstoffen III:569). Bloated with moral purpose, the two gentlemen stated the reason of their visit: they had come to inquire after her present intentions.

Because Christmas Eve was only two days away and Cornelia did not want to miss that celebration, she stalled, fretting and refusing to make up her mind, and finally asked for some time to think "until after the next communion". The two delegates thought that this non-committal answer would not be well received, but nevertheless they were willing to transmit it to their brothers (Bouwstoffen III:573). As they expected, the Church Council indeed took exception and requested an immediate reply. They received it the next morning in written form.

"I do not quite recall", Cornelia wrote, "that I stated in writing about three years ago that I was reconciled with the Hon. Bitter. If the Church Council concludes from the use of the word 'conciliation' that I am willing and desirous to live with the above-mentioned Bitter, then I must tell you this: it was not my intention at the time, neither is it now. [...] I believe that I have reconciled myself with him to the extent that I do not see him as my husband but as my fellow-man and fellow-Christian. I have put aside all uncordial feelings of the past, I wish him all the best in health and mind, but I do not waive the rights of separation from bed and board granted to me by the highest legal authority in this country." She would not have him back under any conditions was her message to Bitter. The council concluded that if this had always been her explanation of the term "conciliation", it had been duped for three years; therefore it sternly denied Cornelia van Nijenroode further access to the Holy Communion "so that we do not participate in her sins" (Bouwstoffen III:575).

Persistent as a horsefly, and still very much the lawyer, Bitter asked for and received from the Church Council all the relevant documentation concerning this brief episode. He needed it to show the government of the Indies that revision was unavoidable since his wife refused to demonstrate an accommodating mood. His request was granted. Once more the legal machinery started to grind into action. Afraid that he might soon lay his hands on her assets, Cornelia succeeded in spiriting away 10,000 rixdollars before it might be too late (HR 783:88).

Everything now seemed to conspire to bring about Cornelia's ruin. Speelman, who suffered from occasional bouts of dropsy and chronic pain as a result of kidney-stones - painful reminders of his merry youth - visibly declined in health. He failed to show up in public in the last week of December. When the Councillors of the Indies - except for Bort who also had fallen ill - went to the residence of the Governor-General to wish him a happy new year and drink to his health, the strength of the old lion had declined so much that he could not receive his friends (Stapel 1936:138). Four days later, Speelman "ill but still standing and walking about his room" dictated a testament or procuratie. His best friends, such as Balthazar Bort, Jacob van Dam, his secretary, and Andries Cleyer (the famous doctor and "Japan watcher") were appointed executors of his considerable estate. To help out these gentlemen in sorting out the household affairs "in which they might commit errors due to their ignorance", Speelman asked assistance from three of his best lady friends: the widow Aletta Hinlopen, Cornelia van Nijenroode en Cleyer's wife Catharina. On January 11, 1684, Speelman passed away, and two hours later so did Balthazar Bort "who also weakened by a long illness, walked the way of all flesh to eternal bliss, at the age of 58 years" (Stapel 1936:141-2).

An incredibly opulent funeral followed which cost not less than 13,790 rixdollars. Valentijn in his "Oud en Nieuw Oost-Indien", produced a fine description and, just as at Petronella Wonderaer's burial, Cornelia van Nijenroode, together with the two above-named ladies, received the protestations of condolence (Valentijn 1724-26 IV-1:315). It was to be her last public appearance. With the demise of these two friends and patrons, a new generation took over.

Protection from above was thinning out; this was clear from the revised sentence that was pronounced on May 9, 1684. The sentence of 1679 was declared erroneous; Cornelia was ordered to open the door of her house to her husband and to live in peace and fear of God. Her spouse was given full authorization of the administration and alienation of her assets and was entitled to half of the interests and the proceeds (HR 783:88).

Not without some tears, she gave in and prepared for the worst. But, lo and behold, in came a friendly, courteous Bitter who did not seem to bear any grudge. One may imagine him telling her that he had sown his wild oats; they were too old to carry on quarrelling, and they had better square accounts with the past. If one continues with this imaginary encounter, one cannot help but think that Bitter's use of the word "account" may have caused his wife's pulse to race for a moment, but she would have restrained herself; she had also grown wiser, if not sadder. To everybody's surprise, their own included, the couple worked out a modus vivendi, and they progressively developed into paragons of decent Christian living, visiting the Church in perfect harmony every Sunday.

On September 25, 1684, only three months after they had started this second honeymoon, the now exemplary couple humbly begged to be re-admitted to the Holy Communion (Bouwstoffen III:611). Abrim with latent edification the council enfolded the lost sheep in its arms; Cornelia was admitted directly, and Bitter was told that his presence would be greatly appreciated but there were problems. A glance at Reverend Zas may have told Bitter enough. He said he would gladly apologize to the Council for his rude behaviour seven years ago, and if Reverend Zas would also be so kind as to accept his sincere apologies he would be a happy, thankful man. Once more the pious gentlemen must have felt relief and thanked the Good Lord for having granted grace to these

VIII Butterfly or Mantis?   233

penitents (Bouwstoffen III:612). To make the happy ending complete, Bitter's children who were still boarded out with the Couper family were welcomed back in the Tijgergracht mansion (HR 783:71). Cornelis Cnoll, his wife and children, had already taken up residence next door. The only jarring note in this symphony was struck by Bitter, who commenced to square old debts out of his wife's assets. Cornelia appeared to take it in good humour. Her husband needed some freedom of movement, and she was willing to give it on the basis of reciprocity. Debts were bad for the family's reputation. "And thus they lived in reasonable concord", Bitter asserted, "except for an occasional fit of temper on her side." (HR 783:88.)

The Tijgergracht.

All of this sounds too good to be true, one might exclaim, and indeed it was. They might have succeeded relatively well in ignoring each other if the children had not been there. Children, and perhaps even more so daughters-in-law, have the unfortunate habit of saying aloud what parents only dare to think and may indeed prefer to leave unspoken. This proved to be the undoing of the couple's solidarity. In August 1685, after one-and-a-half years of apparent peace with only an occasional rumble, the volcano erupted once more.
    A few days earlier, through his peaceful coexistence with the Cnoll

family, or whatever one might call his policy of "appeasement and accommodation", Bitter had finally achieved his objective. Having slowly and carefully discovered how much money Cornelia had deposited with the Company treasury, he transferred twenty thousand rixdollars (until then entered under the name of the late Pieter Cnoll), to his own account. His explanation that he did so to facilitate the administration of the money met understandably with incredulous faces at home. It began to dawn on his family that Bitter had only been marking time to achieve his aims. Now the monster was rearing its ugly head again. The first to say so openly was Cornelia's daughter-in-law.

Hostilities Break Out Again
On the afternoon of August 25, Cornelia, two lady friends, and her daughter-in-law, were having a cup of tea when Bitter entered the room. We don't know whether he once more held a mirror in front of his wife, but his behaviour was such that his daughter-in-law became furious and called him "beast". This, in turn, elicited the reply labbekakster (milksop). In the twinkling of an eye, punches were exchanged, accompanied by shrieks of "mijn dochter, mijn kind" from Cornelia. The room was quickly transformed into an arena wherein mother and daughter "pulled the husband's hair and submitted him to a fierce beating, until at long last he succeeded in getting rid of these two malicious wenches", as Bitter's lawyer later noted with apparent relish (HR 783:89). This family clash did not remain an isolated incident. An escalation of hostilities soon occurred; and forsaking all his good intentions Bitter once more exploded.

Dusk was already deepening on January 5, 1686, when three sailmakers, who happened to return to the Embankment pier via the Tijgergracht, were confronted by the rather unusual sight of a middle-aged gentleman chasing an elderly lady. He caught hold of her hair at the steps before the entrance of her house. The sailors intervened; as they checked the damage done to the unfortunate woman, who was bleeding from the mouth, the aggressor slipped away. A notary was hastily summoned to note down this brutal incident, and the three old salts testified what they had seen and heard: "You whore, beast, bitch, come here and I shall trample you under my feet until the blood spills from your gullet" (HR 783:72).

Hardly had they uttered these words when the culprit reappeared with the sheriff and his runners in his wake. Bitter identified himself as a member of the Court of Justice, shouting: "Bought dogs, tell me how much she has paid you for the testimony! What have you to do with her? If I wish to scold my wife all day long, that is none of your business", he gesticulated and urged the sheriff to arrest them. Handcuffed like criminals, the three witnesses were escorted to the "geweldiger", where Bitter submitted them to a cross-examination.[57] "Come on, lads (vrijers), change your testimony and I shall let you go without harm", he said, but he met with a stony refusal. "I shall make you pay, on my honour", the interrogator continued, and he kept his promise. The three sailors were put in irons in the dungeon - with remarkable result (HR 783:73). One night of cockroaches, musty walls, stench and hunger was enough to change the minds of the three cavaliers. They gave in and signed another attestation, declaring the first null and void and thus regained their freedom at last. Bitter, ever attentive to details, gave them each a quarter to appease their appetite.

VIII Butterfly or Mantis?

When the real story of these events filtered through to Bitter's colleagues, they criticized his unlawful behaviour, but no immediate disciplinary action was taken. They may have felt that he was after all a diligent fellow who treated his work with exemplary seriousness, and moreover was quite decent as long as one did not bring up his marital woes.

Soon the opportunity presented itself to Cornelia to find out whether the authorities were still willing or able to deal with her complaints. She discovered that without her knowledge her husband had remitted 12,765 rixdollars in bills of exchange to his friends in Holland. The ships had already left so she could do little about it and had to write it off as a loss. To place in safety the 8,000 rixdollars still remaining in Cnoll's name with the Company, she sent a petition to the Governor-General and Council, informing them that Bitter was now trying to transfer the sum to the account of freeburgher Frans Gade. Her request that this money should not be touched was granted (VOC 701, 1-5-1686).

Precedent and Prejudice
We now interrupt this narrative of the fencing match to reflect on the development of the case and its background. The preceding anecdotes may contribute to sustaining the reader's interest as the complex narrative is unfolded. To the historian this extended excercise in cacophony presents the opportunity to make audible the voices of members of Batavian society and to demonstrate how individuals representing different interest groups within colonial society interacted. Still, in addition to offering role models that may be relevant in the analysis of the legal and political decision-making concerning the position of women in Batavia, there is another important consideration. I opened this study with the remark that the exact sciences provide the student with an instrument of which his colleagues from the social sciences can only dream about: the possibility of repeating experiments to prove general laws. Per definition, the historian can never repeat an experiment; the closest he can come to this when he is puzzling out certain connections is to keep several factors constant as he tries to analyse the issue.

As I see it, at this point in the narrative, the Cornelia van Nijenroode case does offer one of those rare instances where the ceteris paribus condition is nearly accomplished. Several important factors remain constant: the two main actors in the drama as well as others in the cast - the Church Council, the Court of Justice and the Council of the Indies. I should say "almost" constant, for the institutional organs as well as the persons themselves may have changed inherently over time. The battlefield and the issues remained the same, however. What had changed in the meantime were the external events that influenced the processes of decision-making. Here we are provided with a case in which the same people face the same problems twice under almost the same conditions. With this in mind we can pose questions and examine the evidence regarding whether, as the law would suggest, women in extremis had no right of say over their own assets, or whether society in fact did provide certain safety valves.

When the legal scholar speaks of precedent, he cites a case that has happened in the past, upon which one may reflect, or to which one might appeal for a solution or judicial decision. Legal precedence was Cornelia's main problem. The law court, which constituted her last resort, denied her the provisional separation she had been fighting for. From then on, legally speaking she was condemned to provisional measures and therefore continuously looking for safeguards which could set right the moral wrongs done to her. Due to the female-inequality clause built into coeval law, she could expect little from legal quarters. I stress this last point as one might otherwise have the impression from what follows and from the way in which Cornelia puts her objections into words, that in ultimo only the partiality of the members of the Court of Justice obstructed a final resolution of the discord. It was not as simple as that. We are not dealing here with a feminist agitator avant la lettre who brought forward her own programme of protest. Under the reigning circumstances it was not given to her to expose the unfair position of women as such. What, however, she did believe in was that justice could ultimately be had if one fought for it. We shall now look into her subsequent strategy to establish whether she was right in assuming that justice would triumph.

The High Government of the Indies
It has been stated above that through the direct intervention of the Governor-General and Council, 8,000 rixdollars were frozen in the Company's accounts. This was in the most literal sense of the word a stopgap solution. Apparently buoyed up by the thought that she had not been entirely abandoned, Cornelia revealed her inner feelings in another letter to the highest authorities. She asked to be allowed to live separately so that her husband could not mistreat her, and she requested safeguards that would prohibit her husband from gaining access to her goods and slaves while her request was pending. This appeal was not allowed, the Council of the Indies deemed the contents to be outside its cognizance and re-forwarded it to the Court of Justice.

The High Government.

Le Conseil Souverain ou d Etat

If one looks at the minutes of the May 1, 1686 meeting, when this resolution was passed, however, attention is drawn to a short note by Governor-General Camphuys in the margin. He concurred with the decision taken but could not help remarking that "this council should dispose in such a way as it thinks necessary to prevent calamities or to justify its actions. Whenever a particular case harbours some kind of danger, the government most certainly is entitled to take provisional measures in such a manner that it leaves the further elaboration of the principles of

VIII Butterfly or Mantis?

the case to the judge." (Res GG and C, VOC 701). In other words, he was saying that the government should not desist from taking provisional measures for the sake of public peace and order, pending final settlement of the case in question by the competent authorities. His remarks would not have reached Cornelia van Nijenroode in exactly these words, but it is likely that the gist of it was transmitted. Perhaps the contents of her own letter, which we do not know verbatim, elicited these remarks from Camphuys. Whatever the case may have been, the text of a second request by Cornelia van Nijenroode has been preserved in full, and here she picks up the lifeline thrown to her.

Cornelia first expresses her disappointment that the Governor-General and Council have remitted her request to the Court of Justice. She had expected on account of the moderate tone and the reasonableness of her demands that "it would not have been hard for Your Lordships to take political measures which might result in the prompt prevention of disasters and further troubles". She intentionally had not asked for a legal separation from bed and board with the concomitant provisions that each of the partners would live off his of her own means. She might have done so, she stated, if she had directed her request directly to the judge. Instead she had simply asked for some safeguards for her personal security and her means. If these had been granted, no one would have felt that legal proceedings had been instituted, nor would it have been suggested that the Council had taken on the authority of the judge. Political action would have been taken to advance the public order.

Now that she had bared the outlines of her strategy, Cornelia ventured to explain why she had wished to avoid appealing to the Court of Justice. Originally she had not felt like doing so, but realizing that the political authorities had remitted her case to the Court, she felt there were points that required an explanation. "There were quite a lot of reasons why the claimant wished to shun the Court of Justice. She preferred to maintain silence out of respect for this institution as well as her husband. Her words might be taken for an offence brought against them." Therefore she remained silent for the time being.

The supplicant once more beseeched the Governor-General and Council to take political action, in view of these points, in order to prevent further mishaps and to reserve her already greatly diminished assets for her own use, either by mediation or by an outright order, "but under such stipulation that later no exception can be furthered which renders the settlement an illusionary one, like the last one, which to everybody's surprise had occurred after the solemn ratification of the second contract". (Here she is referring to the mediation by Speelman and Ranst in September 1676.) If the authorities should deny her this political step, she requested that she be allowed to clarify the objections she felt towards the Court of Justice (VOC 701, 14-6-1686, f.276-7v).

The Council of the Indies was in a quandary. We already know Camphuys' views. Willem van Outhoorn, who also presided over the Court of Justice, asked to be excused from taking part in this debate. The resolution finally adopted was a pusillanimous one: the two bantams were once more to work out a self-imposed separation from bed and board. Two members, Director-General Anthony Hurdt and Gerard de Bevere, were asked to bring this about. Strictly considered, this solution went directly contrary to everything that Bitter had been fighting for; it was an unrealistic approach and one which furthermore served to prove the embarrassment of the authorities.

Over the next few months, very little was achieved in settling what by now had become the talk of the town. The first reference we meet is a request by Johan Bitter that was discussed at the August 20, 1686 meeting of Governor-General and Council. Introducing himself as the husband "who since his wedding day has been so much swung about and pestered by his wife that everybody in town is pitying him", he recounts how he has fared since his reappearance in Batavia. Initially he was relegated to a small shack in the compound, later on he could reinstall himself in the house, thanks to the revised sentence of the Batavian court. Unfortunately, life had been made progressively harsher for him by his wife "who continuously reared her malignant head, vilifying her husband and drubbing his children out of the house, yes, throwing mud at him, reproaching him with stories of a vicious way of living". As a man of honour, he requested the authorities to delegate two gentlemen who might stop his wife from slandering him with offensive language because all this back-biting did not agree with his social position as a member of the Court of Justice (VOC 701, 20-8-1686).

Bitter had immediate cause to send this letter: only shortly before the couple had once again treated Batavian society to a dramatic performance. At the end of July, one of their nightly family quarrels had spilled over from the parlour into the street. Around midnight, the Councillor of Justice himself had been both heard and seen dragging his wife along the street as she shouted "Murder, murder!" Concerned about the gossip that might result from such barbarous behaviour, that same night he had rung the doorbell of his neighbour, the Reverend Vosmaer, and complained as the door was opened: "Look what a shrew I have married, she has thrown sand in my eyes. Prithee, look at me!" which met with the retort from Vosmaer's wife, "I have nothing to do with either you or your wife's quarrels" (HR 783:74). And although Bitter had muttered about her lack of neighbourly spirit, he may not have realized, as we can with the wisdom of hindsight, that this was one of the first indications that the urban community at large was getting fed up with the disruptions, which were undermining all standards of decency (built up with so much effort) in this colonial community. It would be hasty to draw the conclusion, on the basis of the attitude displayed by the wife of one of the religious officers, that the church was hereby announcing its withdrawal from the battlefield. Nonetheless, it is startling to see that from the spring of 1686 onwards, the Church Council no longer refers to the couple and seems to have given up all hope of bringing them together once more. The above incident as well as the news that Bitter had quartered a soldier with his wife to check up on her activities, and that he was further accused of sleeping with one of her Lady's maids, the slave Lucretia, will not have heightened the respect of the Governor-General and Council for him (HR 783:74). His request was declined.

On November 25, 1686, Director-General Anthony Hurdt and Gerard de Bevere reported on their attempts to bring about a reconciliation. They confirmed their colleagues' presentiment; their mission had been a total failure. Conclusions were drawn five days later, after the councillors had been given some time to reflect on further action. Cornelia's request for "a political separation from her husband" was declined. Yet she was allowed to reveal the scruples she harboured against the Court

VIII Butterfly or Mantis?

of Justice. Unfortunately, it is not known what her objections finally were, but it is not unlikely that she stated that her husband's colleagues were birds of a feather, or something in that vein.

By the end of 1686, Cornelia was even denied access to her own house - "on daddy's orders" - as her slaves shouted in Portuguese from behind the closed door (HR 783:75). The family feud had by then taken such dimensions that Governor-General Camphuys felt obliged to devote one complete paragraph to it in the Generale Missive of December 13. Referring to the consecutive resolutions that had been passed on May 1, July 11, August 20 and 21, he no longer was interested in establishing which of the two was the culprit, and he concluded: "We do not know who is the true originator of this feud, but are quite willing to concur with the old adage that 'where two people are quarrelling, both are to blame'" (VOC 1418, f.452).

Neither Christmas nor New Year's Eve brought about a reflective or a repentant mood in either Bitter or Cornelia. Bitter actually used these days of leisure to look back and add up all the grievances he had suffered so far. Notary van Es' first official transaction in the year 1687 was to note down word for word Bitter's long litany of complaints against his wife: she had been unfaithful to him since their wedding day, she was full of "malice, peevishness, sinister implacability, guile and lies". Appended to this attestation was a copy of an affidavit by the notary himself that he had entered Cornelia's bedroom one night to order her to lie with her husband as a proper wife, and that this order had met with a terse refusal. Both documents were handed over to the Court. Informed of their contents, Cornelia immediately challenged her husband to prove the allegations.[58] Bitter thereupon complained to the Governor-General and Council, alleging that day after day his wife robbed the house of objects of value, to the vexation of himself and his children. Having been barred from legal proceedings by the Court itself, he now demanded permission from the Governor-General and Council to bring an action against his wife "as the president of the Court (Willem van Outhoorn) seemed to renege on his obligations". "If need be, then appoint another president", he suggested. And then he asked to be provided with copies of all the letters his wife had written to the authorities.

The breaking point had been reached. Agreeing that they were through with the couple, the executive council reached an extraordinary decision: the couple would be served notice that, failing a swift settlement of their differences, they were to depart for Patria with the autumn fleet (VOC 702, 15-1-1687). So threatening, so time-consuming, and so disturbing had the case become to public order, that the authorities saw no other way of dealing with the problem than to encapsulate it and ship it to Holland. To put it in medical terms: after preventive measures had failed, and curative medicine proved futile, it was decided to remove the ulcer by means of surgery.

The Last Round
It took Governor-General Camphuys in the Generale Missive of December 23, 1687, no fewer than 11 pages to cover Batavia's talk of the town. For further particulars, he had to refer to the 22 resolutions taken by his council and himself between January 15, 1687 until the day of the couple's departure on December 15, 1687. Camphuys had some cause for complaint since this case had continually bothered him over the past

A Batavian mistress and her backscratching slaves.

twelve months. Yet, it should be admitted that the legal tangle was partly of his own making. Having agreed that Bitter and his wife should be denied further access to the Court of Justice, it soon dawned upon him that "nobody is safe, if there is no judge". Consequently he had grudgingly taken the necessary measures to safeguard Cornelia's position. Johan Bitter had been denied recourse to the law only insofar as the divorce case was concerned; in other matters he still had access to the court. With his special talent for ferreting out legal loopholes he relentlessly made use of them until his embarkation.

On Cornelia van Nijenroode's side, the usual dogged perseverance can be discerned, but at the same time the first signs of exhaustion and old age appeared. She still spoke out clearly on a few occasions, but increasingly she leaned on the shoulder of her by then twenty-nine-year old son. Because Cornelis Cnoll has been referred to above only in passing, it now seems appropriate to comment briefly upon his career.

The entire 40,000 rixdollars that Pieter Cnoll had left to his children had come Cornelis' way, instantly turning him into a wealthy man when he reached adulthood. This enabled him to request the Governor-General and Council that he be discharged from the rank of sergeant in the army, as he desired to spend his life as a freeburgher of independent means (VOC 693, 11-10-1678). Although he did not specify this in his request, another reason why he wished to leave life in the barracks was his imminent marriage to Hillegonda Dubbeldekop. Three children were born from this union: Pieter in 1679 (Cornelis Speelman attended his baptism as godfather), Anna in 1682 and Jacobus Wijbrant in 1687.[59] Apart from the earlier mentioned quarrel with his step-father about the use of his horse, we do not find any reference about open clashes between the two men until 1686. Cornelis had by then taken a seat in the recently reformed polder-board, the so-called office of Heemraden (Stapel 1936:203). He was living in a house adjoining the backyard of his parents' compound, and it probably was with his mother's connivance that he removed an iron railing, which Bitter had installed at the back of the house to keep his stepson out. Cornelis Cnoll was summoned by the Bench of Aldermen and fined 125 guilders for this uncivil behaviour (HR 783:89). Futile though his action may have been, it serves to show that young Cornelis had grown into a man

VIII Butterfly or Mantis?

and was willing to take the kinds of action which were not wholeheartedly welcomed by his stepfather.

Glad to have her son at her side, Cornelia secretly channelled part of her possessions (and therefore per definition also Bitter's) to her son's estate. This did not go unnoticed by her jealous husband, who promptly started proceedings against his stepson before the Bench of Aldermen in order to force him to disclose his mother's assets that he had acquired in this way. Cornelia gave expression to her feelings on March 18, 1687, in a long request to the Governor-General and Council, and sent her son to act as her spokesman.

She pathetically informed the authorities that she had made up her mind and resigned herself to her fate. "Having heard that I and my husband Johan Bitter must depart for Patria, I comply with the order, though with regret, due to my old age and weak constitution." She was not pleased by the idea of embarking on a perilous voyage to a country totally foreign to her. "The only means to avert this departure would be to give up my claims against my spouse. If all this concerned only my property, I would gladly relinquish it. But the thought of having to endure blows, scorn, indignities and further maltreatment at my husband's hands, keeps me from doing so, and I suppose that it would not be in accordance with Your Lordship's intentions either if I were submitted to such treatment. Therefore I cannot but embark on the passage to Holland and await the verdict of the judge there."

She beseeched the authorities to grant at least a few privileges to her:
- that she be allowed to live separately from bed and board and thus be saved from molestation by her husband;
- that she might sail on a ship other than her husband's "to prevent further tragedy";
- that until the day of departure she be allowed to retain as many slaves of the thirty-odd still serving in the large house as she needed for her personal upkeep (at the time of the request she was served by one male and 4 female slaves; Bitter was attended by 16 male and 9 female slaves);
- that it be decided who should live in the house, or whether it should be sold immediately;
- that she be allowed to fetch the clothing, which was now locked up by her husband, "lest she would have to go to church in a black kebaya";
- that an inventory be made of all personal belongings left in the house over which she might be designated as the owner;
- that all proceeds from the sale of the house, furniture and slaves be put on her account;
- that the Orphan Board take over the administration of the 8,000 rixdollars belonging to her, but kept in the treasury of the Company, as well as the 12,765 rixdollars that her husband now claimed to have still in his possession[60];
- that her husband be denied the right to conclude any contract with the money on her account;
- that she be paid a daily allowance from the administered assets;
- that testimonies made in the earlier stages of the procedure be reaffirmed for later use (VOC 702, Res GG and C 18-3-1687).

As already mentioned, Cornelis took on the job of explaining the contents of the letter to the Council of the Indies. Little passed unnoticed in Batavia. Three days later, on March 18, Bitter, who in the meantime had got wind of the visit, submitted a request stating that he surmised his stepson "had once more undertaken something for his troublesome mother against his person". Consequently, he asked for a written testimony of all that had been discussed. "Not only the law of nature but also the law of all peoples teaches us that both parties should be informed about each other's statements", he asserted (VOC 702, f.208). The request was refused. Seeing that he did not make much headway in this manner, he made a last desperate grasp into his bag of tricks: he accused his wife of black magic.

On March 26th, Bitter summoned five "Moorish priests" to his house and showed them a jug covered with a black substance. This Corpus Delicti had been discovered hidden in his house; apparently someone intended to harm the master of the house with magic spells. The exorcism-specialists were invited to examine the object closely. Notary Van Es was present to note down their findings. First the black substance was removed, then the underside of the jug was examined. Attached to it was a square piece of paper with Arab letters. Inside the jug, on the bottom, the exorcists found a small doll or image of devilish appearance. They expressed their judgement in no uncertain terms: this jug harboured evil designs directed at inflicting an enduring illness. Yet, the "priests" confessed that it was hard to say on basis of the characters or other signs, at whom this magic was directed, who might have ordered it, or who might have written the inscriptions.

Today's observer will identify a witch as a displaced person who by use of supernatural means tries to impose herself on a community, and thus challenges public order with her actions. As long as she directs her activities against individuals only, her presence is generally condoned. The principal risk a witch runs is that someone may denounce her as a danger to the community. These social conditions were totally absent in this case. Black magic was a common occurrence in Batavia, but it seems somewhat far-fetched that Cornelia, a woman with a background quite different from the Indian and Indonesian women who commonly practised it, should have made use of it. In any case, the accusation was not taken seriously and only produced a bit of commotion, not least from Cornelia, who felt greatly offended by this insult.

When he made no progress by witch-hunting, Bitter again directed his legal arrows at Cornelia's son. It will be recalled that Cnoll had been acquitted by the Bench of Aldermen of the distress his stepfather had levied on his property under a charge of embezzlement. Bitter appealed to the Court of Justice and this time the verdict went in his favour (April 5, 1687). Cornelis Cnoll was now sentenced to divulge those assets belonging to his mother which he was keeping in his possession. However, he did not do so, but rather applied to the Council of the Indies on April 15 for admission to the revision procedure, a request which was granted. Bitter was not in the least impressed by this decree and continued to press his stepson to declare under oath "what assets of his mother were in his possessions at the time of the arrest" (VOC 702, f.235). Feeling cornered, Cornelis once more approached the Governor-General and Council with a request that Bitter be ordered to give up these attempts until the revision procedure had occurred.

This was a cunning argument, for Cnoll intended to use the full fatalia of two years, the period allotted to the preparation of the case; he said further that he would send all the legal documents to legal

VIII Butterfly or Mantis?

scholars in Holland "as is usually practised here in India; without their advice one would not have much hope to win a legal battle in revision, as those adjoined to the Court in case of revision hardly ever are trained barristers" (VOC 702, f.254).

The Council of the Indies deliberately procrastinated in the case and decided to ask for the comments of the Governor-General, who had been absent when the request was read. One month later they still had not made up their minds. Livid with anger at these delaying tactics, Bitter requested on July 22 that the revision be declared "sub- en obreptyf", sly and underhand. The date of his departure was approaching and these delays ran counter to his interests (VOC 702, f.367). One week later the Council agreed to give Cornelis Cnoll the full two-year period he had asked for, and hereby Bitter's last attempt to get hold of Cornelia's assets were effectively blocked (VOC 702, f.381).

Cornelia did not make much headway either. Much to her chagrin, the Council of the Indies never answered her request, and on August 15 she complained in another request that her early misgivings had been confirmed: Bitter was progressively disowning her of whatever there was left of her estate. She called for immediate action, and to underline her plight she enclosed a testimony drawn up by her notary Frederik Michault, who had attempted two days earlier to intrude into her boudoir. This had been sealed off by Bitter a year before, after she had left the house to reside elsewhere.

Michault had been summoned by his colleague Van Es to the Bitter estate at three o'clock in the afternoon, but he was kept waiting for several hours until he was given the opportunity to unseal the door. When he tried to do so, he discovered that the seal already had been broken. Bitter feigned great surprise and worked himself into a frenzy at being caught in a lie. Finally, Michault was thrown out with much tumult (HR 783:78; VOC 702, f.410-3).

Seven days later, the still-angry Johan Bitter knocked at the door of the Council of the Indies and demanded in a loud voice that "his wife, with all her sly blackbiting and villaneous talk to the detriment of her husband and guardian, should no longer obtain any hearing until she had divulged the real extent of the assets in her possession since their wedding day". Only if she complied with this order, would he open the books of her administration (22-8-1687, VOC 702, f.421).

The Authorities Lose Patience
The Governor-General and Council considered both requests and decided it was time to deal with the matter once and for all. The hopes for reconciliation had not been brought about, so they felt that one might as well cut the Gordian knot immediately: two curators would be appointed to take care of the property and the affairs of the former Cnoll estate until the day of embarkation. They would keep under sequestration the money that Cornelia van Nijenroode had deposited in the Company treasury and supervise the sale of all her property. The proceeds from the sales and the deposited money would be entrusted to the judge in Holland, who could see to it that the money was paid after the final judicial sentence to the rightful owner (VOC 702, f.429).

The political decision had been taken: the wife of the Councillor of Justice was placed under legal control.

One of the members of the Council of the Indies, Gerard de Bevere, a barrister by profession, took exception to this extraordinary step and on August 26 he submitted an advice of his own. He professed that he could neither understand nor condone the fact that Bitter should be stripped of his marital authority "as a result of his wife's specious argumentation that he was deliberately ruining her means, something which never could be proved by her". He explained his point of view as follows: The revised sentence of May 9, 1684 had entitled Bitter to half the profits derived from his wife's property as well as the administration and the alienation of her means. Much earlier, even before the provisional separation had been granted, Cornelia had been sentenced to communicate to her husband all documentation concerning her means, as well as to divulge how much the profits and fruits enjoyed since the wedding day had amounted to.[61] According to De Bevere, Cornelia had never obeyed this sentence, though she should have done so. "Bitter possesses legal authority to rule over his wife as guardian and husband, a fact which has been strongly confirmed by the sentence." De Bevere therefore concluded that the Governor-General and Council should not grant Cornelia's request to be put under the protection of trustees, "an outrageous demand, to the detriment of the interests of her husband" (VOC 702, f.429).

Although legally speaking he was right in pointing this out, his colleagues nonetheless did not accept his arguments; instead, they stuck to their decision, with the notable exception of the president of the Court of Justice, Willem van Outhoorn. His motives were not as profound as De Bevere's: he simply refused to have anything to do with the case now, just as he had refused to do so since June 14, 1685. Born in the Moluccas and an Indischman at heart, Van Outhoorn had only stayed briefly in the Republic to finish his studies at Leiden. He wholeheartedly loathed the contentious "orang baru", Bitter, who was not and never would be "one of us". Ever since he had acted as a witness when Bitter stealthily handed his written promise to Van Becom in front of the Malay church in 1679, he had not liked this fickle character; and these feelings had deepened during the many meetings that he had presided over at the Court of Justice. He emphasized once more that he refused to preside over the case "because of the rebuffs he had endured from Mr. Johan Bitter, on account of which Bitter himself also had professed that he would rather not see him preside over this case" (VOC 702, f.596).

On August 29, Johan Bitter was summoned by the Governor-General, who informed him of the Council's deliberations. As was to be expected, Bitter objected to the proposal to appoint curators of the estate. Since his wife was willing to submit herself to this decision - after all, she had asked for it - the Councillors Willem ten Rhijne and Daniël van der Bolk were appointed to sequestrate and administer both Cornelia's assets and the disputed capital which was being held in the Company's treasury on Johan Bitter's account (VOC 702, 29-8-1687).

As a result of this new turn, Cornelis Cnoll now felt obliged to ask for permission to accompany his mother to Holland, together with his family, so that he could assist her during the legal proceedings (VOC 702, 5-9-1687). Time was running out for Bitter. He had only a few months left to wind up his affairs. Because the authorities had shown their hand and had imposed their will, he was no longer wary of stirring up tumult, and this he did, with a vengeance.

Rear-Guard Action
First of all, Bitter liberally poured oil on the flames of his old feud with Van Becom. Speelman had probably attempted to smother these flames in an interview with the Councillor of Justice eight years previously, but now the latter showed he was not mollified at all. He said that he had been forced under threat to hand over the written act of non-execution of the court's verdict. The fact that Speelman, the bully in his version of the story, had died in the meantime, did not hamper Bitter in the least. He addressed himself to the trustees of the Speelman estate, Marten Pit and Nicolaas Schagen, and claimed an indemnity equal to the amount he had forfeited in 1679. This caprice was dictated by the fact that the liquidation of Speelman's inheritance turned out to be a long, drawn-out affair. The late Governor-General had soiled his hands in shady affairs and three years after his death the executors of his will were still besieged by people claiming to be entitled to the repayment of debts. An additional complication was the fact that there were still large amounts of money that had to be collected.[62] In this particular case there were no doubts about the factual background of the claim. The people involved, with the exception of Speelman, were still present; the president of the Court of Justice, Willem van Outhoorn had been witness to the affair himself, although he did not like this to be widely known.

The stir caused by Bitter's claim should not be underestimated. But for a small inner circle, no one had known about the affair. Bitter himself wisely had kept the deal secret to avoid losing face. He had even used the Baukes rescription as evidence in Holland to support his case against his wife.

On September 9, 1687, the curators Pit and Schagen struck back and presented a memorandum to the Governor-General. After telling their version of what had really happened, they expressed surprise that Bitter had waited no fewer than eight years before asking for remedial action, whereas he should have done so within four years. As a barrister he knew that relief is offered by the authorities only if the claimant can buttress his allegations with new evidence. Bitter had failed to do so, they stressed. It also was beyond their comprehension why a person, who to all intents and purposes had concluded a contract in a town governed by a well-established administration, should never have complained shortly afterwards if he felt to have been wronged. They added that if Bitter were to be allowed relief, Van Becom would certainly ask for a revision, which again would dramatically alter the whole case. Their final words suggested that one should be very careful with Bitter. They feared that he might further embroider this case after returning home if his demands were met, even if only half-way.

It may suffice to let Schagen and Pit speak for themselves: "We should like to see that the calumnies Bitter has imputed in such an insolent and bold manner at the address of an illustrious person like the late Governor-General, will be totally expurgated by our memorandum. Otherwise it is to be feared that Mr. Bitter (we are well acquainted with his temper and character) will welcome the opportunity to spread at will in Patria or elsewhere these unfounded and unopposed idle stories of having been forced and threatened by a man who cannot call him to account anymore." (VOC 1431, f.766-71). The Council of the Indies was not carried away by these fears but showed itself imperturbable. It promised Bitter remedial action, even though the fatalia had expired, provided he produced fresh evidence to support his allegation. However, he was of course never able to produce any hard evidence.

If the administrative élite hit back - not without having lost face in the process - so did Bitter's colleagues from the Court of Justice. The public prosecutor, Gualterus Zeeman, summoned Johan Bitter on account of the illegal arrest and coercion of the three sailors who had witnessed him fighting with his wife in the street. As only a few of the documents of the Batavian Court of Justice are available in the Algemeen Rijksarchief at the Hague, we cannot sort out all the details of this particular case. From several resolutions taken by the Governor-General and his Council, it appears that though two of the witnesses were present, the third one had left for Ternate, reason enough for the Court to pronounce an interlocutory sentence that the prosecution should continue. Bitter - at this time he was trying to drag out the trial - tried to obtain a revision against this interlocutory sentence with the claim that all witnesses should be summoned. When this request was declined on November 18, the defendant raised objections against the participation of Councillor Willem ten Rhijne in the legal decision-making.

According to Bitter, Ten Rhijne should not sit on the bench in the Public Prosecutor vs. Bitter case, because he was a drunkard. "At least that is what my colleague, Nicolaas Schagen, has told me in a confidential mood", he added. Governor-General Camphuys, whose relations with his councillors were rather strained, replied not without irony that if Ten Rhijne, a member, really was defective in this respect, he would not only be incapable of serving in the Court of Justice but also anywhere else. Confronted with the Governor-General's words, Schagen promptly had to tone down his accusation in public and muttered: "When I alleged that Ten Rhijne is continuously drunk, I just meant to say that he is fond of liquor, and often grasps for the bottle in public, and thus exposes himself to everybody's mockery. All Batavia knows this well enough!" Although Bitter finally was served a reproach, he meanwhile had made the Court look perfectly silly, and had without a doubt also exposed it to the mockery of everyone.

While Johan Bitter was involved in opening old wounds and applying salt to them, at least one event went on as scheduled: the preparation of the home-bound fleet. In September the first five ships were selected: 's Lands Welvaren, Waalstroom, Zallant, Sion and Goudestein. On October 31, these were declared seaworthy: "safe and sound of wood, watertight and well-structured without the least defect".[63] The only problem which hampered preparations for the passage home was a structural one: as the tropics claimed their toll of Dutch lives, there was a chronic dearth of sailors to man the returning ships. On November 18, Cornelis Cnoll was allowed at his request a cook and a wet-nurse for his baby as far as the Cape. A few days later his mother was allowed a maid to attend to her weak constitution. Bitter received permission to take along two slaves, also as far as Cape Town.[64]

It was high time for the sequestrators Willem ten Rhijne and Daniël van der Bolk to take action. Bitter had initially protested against the choice of Van der Bolk "because he was younger than himself", but that argument had met with little sympathy from the authorities. On December 2, a public sale was held of all the sequestered goods and within a few days everything had been sold: the furniture, the coach, the horses and the slaves. A few days earlier Bitter had secretly sold the house to his old friend Jacob Does for 6,500 rixdollars.

A Dutch East India man at anchor.

This ran counter to earlier agreements between Bitter and his stepson, Cornelis, who was to purchase the house from his parents. When Cnoll demanded to know why he had sold the house to Does, Bitter replied that he did not quite see why he should not have done so. His stepson had, after all, let it be known that he would accompany his mother to Patria and as far as Bitter was concerned this released him from any obligation. Protests by Cnoll to the administration were of no avail; he was told to fight it out with Does by himself. When he did so, the latter countered with the statement that Cornelia was still 1,000 rixdollars in debt with him: then he added that he did not want to discuss with a third party agreements in which the latter was not involved: he had bought the house from Bitter and he was not willing to sell it again. Considering that the estimated value of the house was much higher than the price for which it had been purchased, this answer was not surprising. Even if Cornelis threw a tantrum, it made little difference: he had been checkmated. His original intention had been to accompany his mother and to support her in the lawcase in Holland, and then to return to his own native town afterwards. Understandably, mother and son were so full of resentment that they refused to pay back the loan, but on the request of Does this sum was ultimately deducted by the authorities from the 1,265 rixdollars realized at the auction.[65]

Johan Bitter was not conscious of these last-minute developments. On December 7 he left for Banten where the fleet was awaiting its last passengers. As vice-admiral, he travelled in the company of the admiral, Jacob Couper, on board the ship Waalstroom of the Amsterdam chamber. These two gentlemen, attentive to the custom that travellers should bring presents for family, and friends at home, had chosen for rather exotic gifts. Couper took along the Javanese dwarf, Alexander van Passigan, whom he had received as a personal gift from the susuhunan Amangkurat II of the Surakarta court "with the intention to give him away in Holland" (VOC 702, 5-12-1687), while Bitter brought along a cassowary, a ratite bird from Ceram.[66]

A freak accident almost forestalled the execution of the banishment order. At the Bantam roadstead, a sudden squall caused havoc among the fleet, tearing Waalstroom from her mooring and sending her into the nearby Goudestein. In the process, the latter lost her bowsprit and part of the forecastle, forcing this ship to return to Batavia. Waalstroom, however, sustained little damage and left forthwith with the other vessels.

Cornelia, "in a very weak condition accompanied by her son, burgher Cornelis Cnoll, and his family" left Batavia on December 15, 1687 on board Eenhoorn, a ship which was to sail alone to Cape Town, and to join the others there (Bruijn, Gaastra and Schöffer 1979 III:127). During the passage, the unexpected happened. Cornelia's health was a matter of continuous concern to the family; this was another reason for her son to accompany her: if she died at sea he had to salvage the inheritance before Bitter could lay his hands on it. Despite this, however, life at sea agreed with Cornelia. On the other hand Cornelis fell gravely ill en route; he eventually died in sight of the Table Mountain, where his body was buried (HR 783:100). Left behind with a daughter-in-law and two grandchildren, Cornelia had no strong shoulder left to lean on. She must have been grief-stricken. After a halt of one month at the Cape, the fleet raised anchor and headed northwards. Upon reaching European waters, it was decided to try to avoid the Dunkirk privateers by making a large detour and circumsailing Ireland and Scotland. Eenhoorn arrived at the Maas-estuary on August 10; it took Waalstroom and the other Amsterdam vessels ten more days to reach Texel. Consequently Cornelia had a slight lead over her husband and she did not fail to make use of it.

Final Years

Judgement
Immediately upon arrival, Cornelia van Nijenroode went to see Adriaen van Sterrevelt, the lawyer who had defended her case at the Provincial Court of Holland in 1682. Following the advice she had received from the Batavian authorities before departure, she lodged a Request for a Mandate of Arrest and applied for immediate judgement at the same Court. Johan Bitter was surprised by this fast action, but parried the

Detention at the sponging house.

blow by moving to his native province of Gelderland, where he in turn initiated proceedings against his wife. Undoubtedly he reckoned on the partiality of the local court. For once he made a serious miscalculation: when he was so careless as to show up in the province of Holland to settle some transaction, he was promptly arrested on the request of Van Sterrevelt and lodged at the Castellenije, the quite luxurious sponging house of the provincial Court at the Hague (Fockema Andreae 1969: 142). Van Sterrevelt was able to do so because according to Dutch law, a debtor, whose residence is outside the jurisdiction of the Court, may be arrested upon entering the territory under its jurisdiction (Van Alphen 1683 II:324-5). Normally the defendant would be freed on bail almost immediately, but Bitter, obstinate as always, refused to raise one. He protested that he was illegally detained as he himself had already asked for and received an appointment, a judicial disposal, from the Gelderland court. He proposed "exceptie van nonqualificatie, incompetentie ende renvoy" or, to put it briefly, remittance of the case to Gelderland, as it was at the same time pending overthere. Thus he forced the Court to pass a judgement. Having done so, he paid the bail and left the Castellenije. On November 11, the Court sat, rejected the defendant's grounds for exception and sentenced him to answer the questions of the Court, and to compensate for the expenses incurred so far.

As this did not coincide with Bitter's ideas, he appealed to the High Court of Holland and produced the same arguments he had used at the provincial court (HR 783:83).

Appalled at all this legal bickering and warned by the letters from the Indies, the High Court appointed two commissioners, Thomas Hope and Vincent Bronckhorst, to assuage the ruffled tempers of the two contending parties in order to establish some understanding that might lead to a mutually agreeable form of further legal action. This objective was reached surprisingly soon. Both parties agreed "te cesseren en afzijn", to withdraw and terminate, all exceptions they had raised at the provincial courts of Holland and Gelderland and "to submit all their problems and disputes with their consequent outcome, with nothing in the world excepted, to the High Court of Holland". Each party was free to take such legal action as it wished before the High Court, with the understanding that Bitter's arrest at the provincial court of Holland remained in force.

Both parties summoned each other. Adriaen van Sterrevelt, attorney for the "prosecutrix in convention and defendant in reconvention", Cornelia van Nijenroode, requested separation from bed and board, quo ad thorum et mensam, and demanded the restitution to his client of 45,500 rixdollars and two stuivers, the proceeds of the public auction of the gold, silver, moveables, furniture, male and female slaves plus interests, and the 8,000 dollars still remaining in the treasury of the Company.

George Roosenboom, attorney for Johan Bitter, "defendant in convention and prosecutor in reconvention", requested that his client's wife resume living with her husband, that she disclose all her assets, with nothing excluded, and that his client be declared her guardian and thus entitled to the interests on half her income as well as the administration and alienation of all her possessions. In case she did not agree to live with her husband, Bitter's lawyer asked the court
- to brand her "a malicious desertrix";
- to award Bitter one-fourth of all her goods, in addition to the right of administration, et cetera, as mentioned above;
- to assess a "moderate" allowance which the husband should pay her out of these funds for living expenses.

He also asked that his client be compensated for all the losses incurred due to this case, such as the costs of the long voyage he had been forced to undertake to the Indies to ask for the revision of the sentence of November 4, 1679 (HR 783:84-91).

For clarity's sake the respective claims have been recorded here first. In reality the order of the proceedings, of course, was different. We can be very brief about them, for Van Sterrevelt in his opening statement told the dramatic story of the marriage, the marital quarrels and the consecutive legal action. The reader has already been informed on these points. Thereupon, George Roosenboom countered and gave Bitter's version of it all. After Roosenboom had done so, it was Van Sterrevelt's turn to answer. He deemed the prosecution in reconvention and defence in convention "upholstered with so many lies, impertinences and malicious insinuations derived from such untrue and impertinent arbitrariness that it truly would be vexatious to point them out on paper and argue about them". The only issue he liked to draw Their Lordships' attention to was the final paragraph of the opponent's claim, "who so much indulges in his passionate and impetuous temper that he contends absolution of the marriage, so that he can marry somebody else" (HR 783:92).

Roosenboom also made a final plea, and for convenience's sake divided up Cornelia's allegations into one thousand articles, some of which he now singled out for further comment.
- On the reproach that Bitter had only married for her money, he replied: Bitter "has even made love to her in order to live with her as a Christian husband".
- On the boastful letters written to friends, he commented "This Cato cersorius should consider herself whether she has never engaged in droll propositions or discourses with her friends or has written droll or jocular phrases in a familiar way".
- On the so-called dissipation of her fortunes: he retorted that Bitter indeed had spent quite a lot of money after his wife had run away "as she had a large and troublesome household of forty or sometimes even more slaves, and furthermore a state-coach and horses; consequently this ménage had been costly indeed".
- On their respective tempers, he remarked that Bitter was "pious, decent, and peace-loving and no squanderer or spendthrift", while his wife was "very cantankerous, malicious and vicious" (HR 783: 93-4).

The Court pronounced sentence on July 4, 1691. After all these years of strife, the verdict comes as an anticlimax to today's observer: Cornelia was ordered to join her husband and live with him in peace and in fear of God; Bitter was declared entitled to half the income and the usufruct of the defendant's assets; both partners were sentenced to divulge to each other the inventories of all their respective possessions, if necessary confirmed by an oath. All further claims were rejected by the Court. Both partners were ordered to appear within a fortnight in front of the commissioners to obey the orders, and to expedite them (Dictum, HR 904, 29-6-1691).

From a Dictum dated December 1 of the same year, it appears that the headstrong woman's spirit was not yet broken. Cornelia had not complied with the sentence of the High Court, and now it was her turn to be detained at the Castellenije until she would give in (HR 904, 1-12-1691). Shortly afterwards she was released on bail upon having transmitted inventories of her property, but another Dictum of July 24, 1692 shows that the commissioners and her husband still believed that she had not divulged everything.

The High Court declared, in pursuance of the sentences of May 9, 1684, and July 4, 1691, the prosecutor in reconvention to be entitled to the administration and alienation of his wife's property owing to his position as guardian and husband. Nevertheless it still was not yet able to decide upon the couple's differences concerning the lists and inventories produced by each of them after the July 4, 1691 sentence: it declared the arrests valid and allowed the claimant in reconvention to take up the 8,000 rixdollars (that still remained in the Company's treasury) and all other arrested goods. Both parties were ordered to appear once more after the summer recess of August before the commissioners, to iron out their last disagreements, and so that the court could finally administer the law in convention (HR 904, 24-7-1692).

The meeting in September never took place; that summer Cornelia must have passed away. Investigations in the municipal archives of Amsterdam and the Hague have yielded nothing. But perhaps, after the

The High Court of Holland.

long, lonely fight, it is appropriate that this courageous woman-warrior does not appear to die but rather to fade away.

A Man of Independent Means
Before an attempt is made to draw some final conclusions out of this colonial drama, a few loose ends remain to be picked up. For what became of Bitter, did he live happily afterwards, paying tribute to the saying that one man's death is another man's breath? Administrative and family documents kept at the Rijksarchief in Utrecht, and especially an unpublished master's thesis written by Leon Cortenraede on the Regents of Wijk bij Duurstede have provided information on Johan Bitter's further course of life (Cortenraede 1983). As it would not be in line with the general tenor of this study on the position of women in colonial society to study in depth the activities of a 17th century regent in a Dutch provincial town, a brief sketch may suffice.

On June 27, 1692, the book of churchmembers of the Dutch Reformed Church of Wijk bij Duurstede mentions three new members: Mr. Johan Bitter and his daughters, Aletta and Eva.[67] At that time, four of Bitter's children were still alive: Bartha, the eldest (1661), was living in Batavia and was married to Constantijn Nobel Jr; Arnolt (1664), who was practising law elsewhere in Holland, was confirmed as a church member at Wijk bij Duurstede in 1696; Aletta (1668) and Eva (1670), who had returned with their father on Waalstroom, were still unmarried and were taking care of him. From Cortenraede we know that immediately after his arrival in Wijk bij Duurstede, Bitter bought a house in the Oeverstraat for 1,438 guilders together with an orchard of 1.5 morgen (about 3 acres) with a garden-house estimated at 1,081 guilders outside town near the Leutergate (Cortenraede 1983:105-7).

The visitor to this charming little town east of Utrecht, situated along the northern bank of the river Lek, will agree that Bitter could hardly have chosen a more agreeable place to spend his last years. Of course, a great deal has changed over the past three hundred years. Duurstede castle, once the residence of the bishops, David and Philip of Burgundy (1459-1524), was already in disrepair in Bitter's time. Now only its ruins remain. The orchards that encircled the town and gave it "seen from the other side of the river a particularly enchanting aspect", have been replaced by an unused terrain intended for local industry.

The exact location of Bitter's house can no longer be ascertained, but a few stately houses remain and give cachet to the Oeverstraat which crosses the town in a North-South direction. Close to the southern tip of the street is the former Leutergate, now called Runmolengate, with a mill on top. Upon passing the city gate, one faces the wide outlook over the river with its outer marches, where Bitter must once have spent many a summer afternoon in his orchard. The market square is situated in the centre of the town, two minutes from the Oeverstraat. A large imposing church with a truncated spire looms over the town hall built in 1662. According to the archival data (Cortenraede 1983:115) Bitter's coat of arms should decorate the walls of the church, but it has disappeared.

If these vestiges were once the centre of Bitter's activities, the notarial, administrative, and church archives enable us to trace the footsteps of this man of independent means. But before we do so, one question remains: Why did Bitter, who came from Arnhem and who had

Town hall and church of Wijk bij Duurstede.

no close relations living in the Wijk bij Duurstede neighbourhood, move to this little town? Nicolaas Schagen, the vice-president of the Council of Justice in Batavia, was a scion of a well-established Wijk bij Duurstede family and it is quite conceivable that Bitter was introduced to this town at the intercession of his former colleague (Wijnaendts van Resandt 1944:33).

Judging from his first steps upon his arrival at Wijk bij Duurstede, everything points to his firm intention to live a quiet and secluded life from the proceeds of his marriage to Cornelia van Nijenroode. The intention may have been there, but matters turned out differently. Within three years, the 60-year-old pensioner joined the town council, where he managed to play a most prominent role for another twenty years. He died on March 17, 1714.[68]

On four different occasions he sat on the Bench of Aldermen and twice he served as burgomaster. This pattern corresponds well with the general trend at the time. As D.J. Roorda has pointed out, from the 1650s onward, rentiers increasingly figured in the town governments. In a city like Hoorn, a capital of 20,000 guilders was sufficient to provide for an oligarch's lifestyle (Roorda 1983:124). The 8,500 rixdollars Bitter had reaped from his legal proceedings put him in a fair way to achieve success.

We have seen that Bitter was not the possessor of natural tact. He was in fact considerably below average in this respect, and judging from several references made to him in Cortenraede's study he never mellowed, but rather kept his irascible temper until the end. On one occasion, fellow members of the City Council even transmitted to the States of Utrecht a list that was meant to show "with how much disdain the regents in town are treated by Bitter".[69]

On their way to becoming spinsters, both daughters were married off just in time to well-established regent-families in other towns. Eva married Hendrick Both, a burgomaster of Amersfoort and a descendant of one of the first Governors-General of the Indies.[70] Aletta married Albert van Lidth de Jeude of Tiel in 1707, but she died one year later.[71] Arnolt left in 1698 for the Indies where he rose to the office of Advocaat-fiscaal (public prosecutor).[72]

Johan Bitter did not remarry but he was by no means in want of a comfortable family life. As we have seen, his daughters lived with him for many years; later, he found another source of comfort in Bartha's sons, Jan and Dirk Nobel, who were entrusted to the care of their grandfather in 1696 and 1699 respectively (Van Schouwenburg 1986:23). In the Utrecht provincial archives, a few letters sent by Bartha and her brother Arnold to their father remain to bear witness to the bond of affection between the father and his children. If they do not counterbalance, they at least broaden our view of Johan Bitter (RU, Van Boetzelaer Archives, No.483).

Bartha's letter of November 20, 1701 is mainly of human interest. She informs her father of the death of her husband and reveals to him her fears about remaining alone as a widow in Batavia. That anguish turned out to be a bit premature, for in 1704 she married Andries Leendersz. We shall not go into her fond comments regarding the portraits of her two young sons that her father had sent her, but we shall dwell briefly on her remarks concerning the financial situation of the family. Bartha's late husband, Constantijn Nobel, had lost a considerable sum of money in a business venture shortly before his death, but she still had sufficient assets and earned some income from renting out houses. There are also some references in the letter about money bills forwarded to her father in Holland, evidence which is further supported by notarial documents in the archives of Wijk bij Duurstede and Amsterdam.[73] Van Schouwenburg has made a very detailed study of the financial state of Bartha's children in his genealogical contribution on the Nobel family. He comes to the surprising conclusion that by 1711, Johan Bitter was 25,325 rixdollars in debt to them (Van Schouwenburg 1986: 18-21). Does this mean that the old man was still squandering money?

One cannot help having the feeling that Bitter, administering funds for his children and his grandchildren, may have put them to his own use. If so, the old fox evidently had not lost his penchant for administrative tricks. Apart from the money bills referred to above, the papers of notary Nicolaes Keppel yield evidence that Bitter indeed was administering the assets of his son Arnolt. On July 30, 1698 he was appointed his son's proxy in all his business affairs.[74]

On balance, it may be that Bitter did not have as much money left from his marriage with Cornelia van Nijenroode as we might imagine and as he may have wished. Lawsuits and lawyers have their price and of course Cornelia's grandchildren were her inheritors in loco parentis.

This surmise is borne out by the evidence exhumed from the Amsterdam municipal archives. Although there was a possibility that the Cornelis Cnoll estate had been dealt with during the stay at the Cape, the register of the guardianships (register van voogdijen) of the Amsterdam

Orphan Board record that on January 25, 1689 a certain Abraham van Uylenbroeck was appointed legal guardian for Anna and Jacobus Wijbrant Cnoll, six and two and a half years old respectively. By means of the inbrengregister (record of capital brought in) of the Orphan Board it can be established that Cornelis Cnoll left 56,700 rixdollars in money bills to his wife and children as well as many curios and other possessions. In the spring of 1690 Hillegonda Dubbeldecop purchased her children's share of the inherited porcelain and jewelry for ƒ 15,734. Consequently the Cornelis Cnoll estate must have amounted to at least 200,000 guilders. Two years later Hillegonda appeared again at the Orphan Board, accompanied by her husband-to-be Alexander Henderson to whom she had transmitted her guardianship the day before in the presence of notary Jacobus van Uylenbroeck.[75]

This information provides the full explanation of the only reference uncovered to date in the Wijk bij Duurstede notarial archives in connection with the Cornelia van Nijenroode estate: "Johan Bitter declares to have reached, an agreement with the hon. Alexander Henderson and Abraham van Uylenbroeck in connection with their disputes about the estate belonging to him and his deceased wife. On the strength of the agreement reached, a certain money bill transmitted from the Indies amounting to 6,104 rixdollars will fall to the share of the above named gentlemen [...]".[76] It is clear that Bitter felt the hot breath of the Cnoll children's guardians on his neck. Jacobus Wijbrant Cnoll was not to rejoice in the considerable inheritance. He died, 17 years old, in September 1703 at Vianen, leaving to his sister Anna and her husband Christiaan van Schellebeecq 122,000 guilders.[77] The wills of Cornelis Cnoll and his mother Cornelia van Nijenroode have not been traceable. Yet, we can nonetheless establish that the lion's share of the original Cnoll estate did not come into Bitter's hands, so that he had to be content with the sums plundered while his wife was still alive - quod erat demonstrandum.

In her letter of 1701, Bartha expressed the wish to return home; ten years later she and her second husband decided to do so. All their property was shipped on board but before she herself could even set foot on the ship, Bartha Bitter fell ill and died. This tragic incident is the main message of the letter Arnolt Bitter wrote to his father on November 30, 1711. As in his sister's letter, we find the usual information about people coming and going, asking favours, bringing presents, a tangle of human relationships based on dependence and mediation, so typical of ancien régime colonial society.

Arnolt Bitter was more sober than his father, and was even not devoid of a touch of irony, to witness the following lines in which he attempts to dissuade his younger sister Eva and her husband, Hendrick Both, from coming to the Indies. Would it be wrong to read between his closing lines a scarcely veiled reproach of his father?
"India is not the place of plenty as imagined. Promotion is always very slowly gained; the lesser ones may only whistle for a windfall. [...] If I were so lucky to possess such an important employment in Patria as brother-in-law Both [a burgomaster], I would never leave it, even less so if I weighed 220 pounds and my wife 180 pounds. Such fat people are not fit for the Indies! Even I, who has never achieved even as much as 180 pounds, feel this bodily. To make the passage [to the Indies] for the sake of [marrying off] one's daughters is foolish, because here daughters are as much a source of embarrassment as in Holland.

Anyhow, everyone may do as he sees fit, but he who wears the shoes, knows where it pinches.

I would like to repatriate in about three years. By that time I think I can afford to live in Amsterdam as a 'generous burgher'. This past December I celebrated my 48th birthday, so that I shall be 51 by then.

To attach myself at this age to a marriage and risk my peace of mind with the fickle temper of a wife I do not (I beg your pardon) deem expedient; even more so as a marriage would place me once more on the centre stage of worldly life. If I resolved to do so, I would throw in my lot with a wife who could give birth to children. Then I would not be able to decide when to return to my dear old Patria but would run the risk of being forced to remain here all my life and slave away until my last day. Nowadays money cannot be married anymore, all must be contributed by the vigilance of the husband in order to support his family." (RU, Van Boetzelaer Archives, no.483.)

Conclusion

Of the preceeding story, the moralist would comment that crime does not pay, although the victim tends to suffer more than its perpetrator. The question is whether this contribution has something more to offer to the historian, so that he may be able to draw conclusions with a more abiding value concerning the period he is studying. The biographical approach has enabled us to trace processes of social control and legal practice related to the position of married women in Batavia during the second half of the seventeenth century. The case is emphatically delineated by date, as the situation changed after the turn of the century, when local interests tended to become progressively centred in the hands of a number of established families who came to constitute the Batavian élite. Under those conditions male relatives could exercise pressure whenever they felt that the interests of one of their wealthy female family members, and consequently their own interests, were threatened by an over-covetous husband. The crux of this story is that it constitutes a test case in which both actors have fought over the whole scala of juridical institutions until the bitter end with little or no interference of family interests. It is often said that the administration of justice is based on such accepted maxims as "fair play" and "even-handedness". This biographical essay has shown that these axiomata were evidently disregarded in 17th century Batavia.

It would be wrong to attribute thought processes and values of our contemporary era to the world of our 17th century ancestors. As remarked earlier, the historian is concerned with events occurring and people living within a certain society, and his task is to explain them in terms of that society. Before we review the way in which the administration of justice in this particular case took place, it might be interesting to quote from several prominent legal and social historians on this period to see how they characterized its administration of justice. Fockema Andreae defines the period as "a paradise for lawyers" (1953: 80). Indeed the formal procedures we have encountered must have constituted a happy hunting ground for legal chicaneurs. Van Deursen has well demonstrated how common people were supposed to restrain themselves from legal action against authorities (1979 III:14-23). He thereby quotes Roorda who states that "it was virtually meaningless for the average burgher to start legal proceedings against regents at the Bench of Aldermen or at a higher judicial body" (Roorda 1978:49). In view of these considerations, it goes without saying that under a matrimonial law which stipulated that all property of the wife, even if she herself earned or inherited it, belonged automatically to her husband too, an indignant wife stood little chance against her husband, especially if he was a judge himself: they were one person in law.

In his treatise "The Subjection of Women", John Stuart Mill has well described the issue of property-rights between married people. "She can acquire no property but for him; the instant it becomes hers, even if by inheritance, it becomes ipso facto his. [...] By means of settlement, the rich usually contrive to withdraw the whole or part of the inherited property of the wife from the absolute control of the husband: but they do not succeed in keeping it under her own control; the utmost they can do only prevents the husband from squandering it, at the same time debarring the rightful owner from its use." (Mill 1981: 31.) The strict marriage settlement Mill is referring to only came into use in England after 1700, to the extent that this device really could prevent alienation by the husband's administration as Bonfield has recently shown (Bonfield 1983). So far these remarks have concerned the woman's legal position, but what about her actual treatment? Let us return to our case study.

Cornelia van Nijenroode had a marriage settlement made according to the custom of the time. Only the preclusions from disclosure of all the assets in her possession may have been exceptional. When seriously put to test, the agreement proved to be as leaky as a sieve, as the law entitled her husband to administer her estate. After the abortive intervention of mutual friends, the first organ of social control the feuding couple met with was the Church. However, the juridical procedure of the clericals was directed at the safekeeping and purity of the community of communicants rather than toward the administration of law.

Against all odds, Cornelia initially gained the upper hand in the marital strife and actually obtained the provisional separation from her husband at the Batavian Court of Justice. Let us briefly review what happened. From the legal annotations by the Councillor of the Indies, De Bevere, written in the autumn of 1687, we know that in the first instance, Cornelia was ordered on September 10, 1678 to divulge the size of her assets. This decision ran counter to her late husband's will and thus constituted a serious drawback for Cornelia. Shortly afterwards, however, the case took an abrupt turn for the better for her. This was probably the result of the letter received from the Gentlemen XVII in which the authorities were ordered to administer vigorous justice to Johan Bitter in connection with inculpation on account of private trade, and "to send him back home without delay as a servant useless to the Company" (Res.XVII, VOC 108, 8-9-1677). In other words, Bitter was all but outlawed by the authorities in Holland. Only under these circumstances could the judges in Batavia muster up the courage to give Cornelia her rights after first having passed judgement on Bitter in the diamond smuggling case. Altogether, a clear example that at the time, legislature, the administration of law and government was still hand in glove; Montesquieu had not yet been born. Back in Holland, Johan Bitter played a game of bluff poker and won. He succeeded in making the directors of the Company admit that the severe punitive measures meted out to him in connection with his behaviour as a Company servant had been prejudicial to his personal interests. The Gentlemen XVII later repented their blunt intervention in the juridical procedure between Bitter and his wife and advised the Governor-General in Batavia to allow him revision if necessary, thereby breaking their own rules and the theory that the legal historian Van Kan has propounded in such detail in this respect. Once put in the rights in Batavia, Bitter soon so scandalously misused his prerogatives as a Counciller of Justice that the Council itself could no longer function as a medium of mediation in the case. This prompted Governor-General Camphuys to declare the case a threat to public order. From then on the marital feud was treated as a political matter. This kind of procedure, sometimes called "evoceren", was resorted to more often in later years and legitimized by the Gentlemen XVII (Coen II:214). Even this last resort could not bring about a lasting peace. Batavian society was not able to bring its own house in order.

The further course of this legal case in Holland speaks for itself, although I cannot help but comment that the formality, and, most of all, the rigidity with which the rules were enforced, make one think rather more of the relentless Fatal Sisters in a Greek drama than of the judges of a country which at the time could boast of a degree of broad-mindedness envied even by its severest critics.

Finally to return to the question reflected in the title of this chapter: was Cornelia a Black Mantis or Butterfly? I would say neither. This woman warrior's stubborn struggle against all odds - reminiscent of a valiant samurai fighting for a lost cause - suggests the choice of that particular term coined by the Dutch in Nagasaki to describe the character of their unmanageable female companions: otemba.

NOTES

CHAPTER I
1   The contents of the five articles which have appeared in print elsewhere, have been thoroughly revised for the present publication. The original date and place of publication are mentioned in the first note of each article.

CHAPTER II
*   First published under the title "An insane administration and an unsanitary town", in: Robert J. Ross and Gerard J. Telkamp (eds), Colonial cities, pp. 65-85. Leiden, 1985.
1   "Minuut verhaal van de toestand van Batavia", ARA, eerste afdeling, Couperus collection, no. 44.
2   Aristotle, Politics (1330a, 34 ff) cited by Finley 1977:305.
3   Couperus, "Minuut verhaal van de toestand van Batavia", ARA, eerste afdeling, Couperus collection, no. 44. For a detailed analysis of Batavia's annual census see: Leonard Blussé and Albertine Bollemeijer, The population of Batavia, Intercontinenta series, Centre for the History of European Expansion, Leiden University, to appear in 1987.
4   Sombart 1916 I:142-3. I was put on this track by Moses Finley's devastating but stimulating critique (1977:305) of Gideon Sjoberg's "The pre-industrial city; Past and present" (1960).
5   For a discussion on the desirability of establishing Dutch colonies in 17th century Java, see Opkomst VI:vii-xxvi.
6   VOC 317. "Patriasche missiven" of September 21, 1649 and October 14, 1651.
7   See Bataviasche statuten 1862:393-518 and Plakaatboek V. See also the New Statutes of 1766 in Plakaatboek IX.
8   "Van de ongesondheyd van Batavia en 't redres om dezelve voor te komen", published in Semmelink 1885:348-68.
9   This interesting name, literally meaning nine-o'clock-flowers, stems from the city regulation that dung should not be thrown into the canals until nine in the evening.
10 Witness the remarks of the resident of Cirebon, Godfried Carel Gockinga in a letter to his father-in-law, Governor-General Alting in Batavia that: "both princes of Ceribon asked politely that the number [of modder-Javanen] be decreased. The common man can only be pressed into this work with difficulty and the gathering of these people results into their migration elsewhere." Letter of January 18, 1788, VOC 3814.
11 "Notul 1e maart 1776". ARA, eerste afdeling, Radermacher collection, no. 481.
12 "Bijlage L.", Notulen Bataviaasch Genootschap 10(1872):xlvii: "The mortality in Batavia is large beyond imagination. It is not exceptional to have a good friend over there, in whose company one has been only a few days ago, whose door one finds closed shortly afterwards, while he, his wife and children already have been buried." (Haafner 1820:187-8.)
13 ARA, eerste afdeling, Nederburgh collection, no. 299.
14 ARA, eerste afdeling, Meerman van der Goes collection, no. 212: "Voorstel de zetel der Hoge Regering van Batavia naar Semarang te verplaatsen".

CHAPTER III

* First published in F. van Anrooij et al. (eds), Between people and statistics; Essays on modern Indonesian history presented to P. Creutzberg, pp. 33-47. The Hague, 1975.
1. Picis from Old-Javanese Pisis. Caixa (cash) is a Portuguese term. In this article preference is given to the Javanese word. See also Rouffaer and IJzerman 1929:216-38.
2. Meilink-Roelofsz 1962; Van Leur 1967; Blussé 1975; De Jongh and Van Naerssen 1977; Fruin-Mees 1920.
3. "The port of trade is Polanyi's name for a settlement which acts as a control point in trade between two cultures with differently patterned economic institutions - typically, between a market and a non-market economy, or rather between a non-market society and professional traders, who may belong to the market pattern even if the society from which they come, as a whole, does not." (Humphreys 1969:191.) See also Polanyi, Arensberg and Pearson 1957 and Polanyi 1963.
4. The best contemporary description has been given by John Saris (Purchas 1903 III:506): "Observations of Saris on the Eastern trade".
5. Bakker 1936:3: "Voor het geld-karakter is deze munt hier niet duurzaam genoeg [...]".
6. Rouffaer and IJzerman 1929:20 mention a crop of 25,000 bags. Saris (c.1610) speaks of 32,000 bags of pepper (Purchas 1903 III:506).
7. Plakaatboek II:377: "met de luyden niet en con teregt komen". This plakaat is an order to start the manufacture again.
8. VOC 3127, f.1034 verso.
9. Personal communication from Peter Carey, Trinity College, Oxford. See also Appendix IV, "Comparative values of paper and metal currency circulating in Java in 1811", in Carey 1980:199.

CHAPTER IV

* First published under the same title in Itinerario 9-2(1985):3-41. [Special issue "All of one Company; Essays on VOC history presented to Prof.dr. M.A.P. Meilink-Roelofsz".]
1. Coppel 1983; Salmon 1981; Suryadinata 1972 and Wang Gungwu 1981.
2. Notarial document in the Daniel Hudde collection dated March 19, 1635. Arsip Nasional, Jakarta. This explanation seems more plausible than the rather fanciful one offered by Schlegel 1899:529.
3. Fines were paid by those gamblers who were caught trying to evade the regulations: 12 rials for losers and winners involved, one third of the stake money devolved to the tax farm lessees (Coen III:654; Plakaatboek I:78, 29-10-1620). According to the local Gazetteer of Amoy gambling was the pursuit of sailors who had been corrupted by contacts with foreigners overseas (HMC 1980 V:653).
4. Res GG and C 21-3-1622 in Hoetink 1923:17 and sentence of the Council of Aldermen, 4-3-1622 in De Haan 1935 II:J 5.
5. Resolutions of Raad van Defensie, 13-10-1622 and 8-11-1622 in Coen IV:97 and 100.
6. For a description of this pomp-and-circumstance affair see Daghregister 1624:1-2.
7. Since May 1623 the Chinese had contributed 60,700 guilders (Opkomst V:91).
8. Letters of 5-11-1624 (Hoetink 1923:5) and 3-3-1625 (VOC 1085).
9. VOC 1101, 27-1-1630; 1101, 2-4-1630; 1101, 7-5-1630; 1101, 23-5-1630.
10. Resolution Governor and Council of Taiwan, 15-10-1630, VOC 1102.
11. VOC 1102, letters by Governor Putmans of 22-2-1631, f.446-55 and 10-10-1631 f.464-85. Putmans adds: "If we may believe the Chinese, Jan Con is a man whom we can trust, but, alas!, we cannot and dare not do so" (VOC 1102, f.485).
12. Concerning his departure: VOC 1102, letter of Governor Putmans, 20-2-

1631; about his arrival: Coolhaas 1947:72.
13 See letter of Governor-General Specx to Governor Putmans, 31-7-1631, VOC 1103, f.493.
14 For the problematical relations with Cheng Chih-lung see Blussé 1981.
15 See for instance the contract for the digging of a canal along the southern city wall, dated 28-5-1630 (Hoetink 1917:362).
16 There was corruption at the building-sites, for example, Chily Gonthing tried to bribe the Company surveyor of the public works, Jan Roelofsz. van Deutecom. See Res GG and C 20-6-1633, VOC 112, f.605.
17 "We the Chinese citizens of Batavia have gladly and with good reason presented, in perpetual memory of our gratitude, this small gift to the excellent hero Jacob Specx, General of the East Indies, our venerable patron, November 25, 1632, Batavia." A silver copy of this medal has been preserved in Teylers Museum, Haarlem. A short accompanying motto in Chinese characters has been unrecognizably distorted by the Dutch mintmaster (Brandes 1901:248).
18 Res GG and C 17-7-1634 and 29-8-1634, VOC 112, f.760, 781. "Caymans [!] devour the poultry, ducks, young geese and other cattle of the citizens."
19 This canal was to measure 48 feet wide and 9 feet deep. VOC 119, f.313. See the accompanying map.
20 Bencon intended to return home, but actually settled down in Taiwan and eventually returned to Batavia in 1639, where he died on April 8, 1644. See Hoetink 1917 and 1923.
21 "De suikerindustrie op Java onder het bestuur van de VOC", in Van den Berg 1904:311. For Jan Con's complaints about theft, see Res GG and C 27-7-1639, VOC 662.
22 See letter of GG Van Diemen to the Governor of Formosa, 19-5-1638 (Hoetink 1917:396).
23 Res GG and C 5-9-1639. In his capacity of Director-General, Philips Lucasz. was responsible for inviting tenders for the execution of the public works.
24 Request in Res GG and C 27-7-1639, VOC 662.
25 On the western gate of the citadel the coat of arms of Batavia was fixed in 1652. The sword piercing through a laurel was in later years seen as an omen of the Chinese massacre in 1740 (Hsü 1953:30).
26 Concerning the administration of justice to the Chinese of Batavia see Vermeulen 1956.

CHAPTER V
* First published under the same title in Journal of Southeast Asian Studies 12(1981):159-78.
1 De Roo de la Faille 1924; Iwao 1975; Nakamura 1969; Vermeulen 1956:2-12.
2 For a succinct analysis of the text, see Boin 1984.
3 See for instance Wittram 1954 and Ligers 1946.
4 "Andere consideratiën" in Coen I:641. The Spanish dependence on the Chinese was admitted by Governor-General Tavora who wrote in a letter to king Philip IV that "the country cannot get along without the infidel Sangleys [Chinese], for they are the ones who bring us food from China" (Blair and Robertson 1903-09 XXIII:108).
5 To express their gratitude, the Chinese gave the Governor-General a present (Daghregister 1648:149). In 1657 the poll tax was again increased (Daghregister 1656-57:344).
6 P. van Hoorn, "Praeparatoire consideratien", in Opkomst VI:130; De Haan 1910 I:67, 95.
7 Letter from manuscript Isaac de Saint-Martin, KITLV collection, Leiden, no. H 6.
8 Crawfurd 1820 II:427-30; Van Hoëvell 1840:447-557; Raffles 1817 II:210-4; Barrow 1806:219-22; Vermeulen 1938; Hoetink 1918; Opkomst IX:xlvii-lxxvi; De Haan 1935 I:381-2.

Notes

9 Since this essay was published in 1981, the adherents of the "Dutch conspiracy" theory, have found an enthusiastic spokesman for their cause in A.R.T. Kemasang, who has over the past years published several articles on the subject, and intends to write a book about it (Kemasang 1985). For reasons unknown to me he has steadfastly ignored my viewpoint.
10 For the sugar cultivation, see Opkomst VIII:cxxix, 157; Van den Berg 1904:305-49.
11 Joan Everhard van der Schuur en Rogier Thomas van Heyningen, "De toestand der Bataviase suykermolens [...] en de gedane klachten over enige knevelarijen in de leverantie der suyker" with appendix and register, 18-12-1728 (VOC 2119, f.5932-6009).
12 "Berigt van Directeur-Generaal Douglas", letter of 24-12-1710 (VOC 1782, f.1152-7).
13 "Droom", in Verzameling van verscheide echte stukken 1742.
14 ARA, eerste afdeling, Aanwinsten 1895, LXX-2:5.

CHAPTER VI

1 A quantitative analysis of the data in the ARA concerning shipping movements, and the import and export of commodities will by published by J. Oosterhoff, A.C.J. Vermeulen and the present writer in the Intercontinenta series of the Centre for the History of European Expansion, Leiden University. The documentary materials on imported and exported commodities of the junk trade give a partial portrayal of the trade. They concern the goods sold to, or purchased from the VOC, and consequently should be studied in correllation with the transactions of the VOC in Canton.
2 The yachts were only used on the Batavia-Macao link. Three examples of junks owned by "Javanese" Chinese taken at random from the Resolutions of GG and C: Tan Tjinko, lieutenant of the Chinese of Semarang, asked permission to build a junk measuring 80 by 25 foot with "a Dutch rudder" (Res GG and C 1-7-1774, VOC 804). Tan Wanseng asked to be exempted from paying the tolls for his new junk Toa-son-i (Res GG and C 26-5-1758, VOC 788). Lieutenant Kouw Hong-liang asked to be allowed a larger crew than usual on account of the size and the heavyness of his junk built of teak in Eastern Java, which could carry a freight of 12,000 piculs or 720 tons (Res GG and C 27-6-1769, VOC 709, f.731).
3 The "Shun-feng Hsiang-sung" (Fair winds for escort) has been dated as of about 1430 (Needham 1971 IV-3:581). The "Chih-nan Cheng-fa" (General compass-bearing sailing directions) appeared according to its modern editor in the final years of the K'ang-hsi period (c. 1720). This rutter also contains a description of the route the junks followed between Batavia and Nagasaki. The two rutters have been re-edited together under the title "Liang Chung Hai-tao Chen-ching" (Two rutters) (Hsiang 1961).
4 A rare documentary example of a Dutch citizen hiring houses to Chinese nachodas is Isaacq Jansz's "memorieboekje" of 1709 in ARA, eerste afdeling, Schepenbank VOC 11999 D, "Varia uit het archief der Bataviase schepenbank".
5 Concerning the early porcelain trade, see the survey drawn up by T. Volker from the "Daghregisters" (Volker 1954). An interesting glimpse into the holds of a Chinese junk carrying porcelain in the 1640s, has been provided by Michael Hatcher who discovered a shipwreck near the Strait of Singapore in 1984. The 23,000 odd pieces were auctioned at Christie's Amsterdam in the same year (Jörg 1984).
6 1639 - 9102 piculs (GM II:9); 1640 - 6000 piculs (GM II:105); 1641 - 170 last (about 340 tons) (GM II:149); 1642 - 500 last (about 1000 tons) (GM II:181).
7 These three embassies have been described by contemporaries in two beautifully illustrated volumes (Nieuhoff 1665 and Dapper 1670).
8 See De Hullu 1917:102, who quotes from a letter dated 5-9-1730 in which several Chinese in Canton are mentioned who had resided and traded for

many years in Batavia, and as a result had acquired command of Dutch.
9   On an average the total shipload of tea brought in by 14 junks was enough to fully load one VOC tea ship (De Hullu 1917:42-4). For a comparison of the costprice in Canton and Batavia see Glamann 1958:218.
10 Res GG and C 2-3-1717, VOC 1876, f.2454-5: thee Songlo (green tea) 40 rixdollars per picul; thee Bing (emperor's tea) 60 rixdollars per picul; thee Boey (black Bohea tea) 80 rixdollars per picul.
11 Edict of 3 November, 1728 (CCT:459). In an earlier edict (March 7, 1717), every sailor had been allotted 2 sheng of rice (à 31.6 cubic inches) a day (CCT:457).
12 See CWT:7465-6 and Hoetink 1917:372.
13 VOC 2216, f.6610-4, 18-3-1733; the interest rate of 40% is also cited by Crawfurd (1830 III:179), who speaks of profits amounting to several hundred percent. This is confirmed by the Amoy Gazetteer (HMC V:644).
14 See for instance the lists of tea prices of 13-3-1737 on which the names of the nachodas as well as of the owners of the lots shipped on the vessel are mentioned (VOC 2366, f.3054). Also in the porcelain trade the Chinese officers played an important role.
15 Ni Hoekong, for instance, was banished to the island of Ambon (Hoetink 1918:501).
16 On May 11, 1792, an edict was issued which once again permitted the transport of tea on board of Company ships (Plakaatboek XI:427).
17 This was the outcome of a protracted legal battle waged by a Dutch merchant, Jan Oldenzeel, against nachoda Ong Koquan. The lawsuit was lost by Oldenzeel, and the High Government wrote a letter to Canton informing the Chinese shipowners in that city of the new procedure (VOC 788, Res GG and C 26-5-1758 and 11-4-1758).
18 Makassar constitutes a fine example of these changing policies. Navigation to this port was closed on 25-11-1746 (Plakaatboek V:426), opened on 14-3-1752 (Plakaatboek VI:688), closed on 24-12-1762 (Plakaatboek VIII:29), and opened once again on 21-7-1768 (Plakaatboek VIII:519).
19 For this extraordinary case, "dit criante geval", see VOC 798, Res GG and C 27-5-1768, 14-6-1768, 17-5-1768. VOC 799; Res GG and C 13-1-1769, 10-3-1769, 8-6-1769, 20-6-1769, 27-6-1769. The ship was finally given up on 23-3-1770 (VOC 800, Res GG and C 23-3-1770).
20 Realia II:81, 9-4-1778; in the "Plakaatboek" two instances are mentioned, respectively in 1754 and 1756, in which pepper was sold at a reduced price to the junk traders from Ningpo and the country traders from Manila "whose navigation is of much importance to Batavia" (Plakaatboek VI:665 and VII:190).
21 Chinese skippers exported, for instance, tahi minyak (!) (squeezed kacang cakes) in order to spend their remaining capital (Plakaatboek XI:145-6, 2-6-1789).

CHAPTER VII
*   First published under the same title in Itinerario 7-1(1983):57-85.
1   "Vertoogh van de staet der Vereenichde Nederlanden in de quartieren van Oost-Indiën" (24-11-1623) in Coen IV:594; see also for his earlier plans for instance Coen VI:199.
2   In a letter dated February 3, 1626, Governor-General Pieter de Carpentier, who replaced Coen during his absence between 1623-1627, reported the progress of the school as follows: "Boys and girls are separated and well-lodged, under the guardianship of teachers and a governor, and under the supervision of masters and mistresses, they are educated in good manners according to the school ordinances. Apart from the children of the local citizenry, 60 boys and 49 girls (of the Dutch as well as several Indian nations) are educated (VOC 1086, f.29v). For more details on the school, see Taylor 1984:24-6.
3   Boxhorn 1654:81. On the infertility of European women see also Josaphat

Geerdings, "Cort discours over de populatie van Indien opgedragen aan de Heeren Meesters bij Josaphat Geerdings", VOC 1110, f.503-8 and De Jonge 1858:136.
4 The Sara Specx case is particularly well-documented. The most incisive remarks about this drama are without doubt those by Gerretson 1944:52-96.
5 "Indian" in this context of course meant Asian. Letter of 2-9-1634, VOC 316, f.46.
6 Letter of 31-8-1643 in KITLV collection, H 54, Leiden.
7 For a short history of the Portuguese church see De Haan 1898.
8 See Plakaatboek I:82, 99-101; Opkomst IV:241-2.
9 A native of Papangan in the Philippines.
10 Resolution of Governor-General and Council 7-10-1639, VOC 662. Catrina must have been a charming woman in many respects. In the Acta it is mentioned on 20-10-1625 that Van Diemen and Specx conversed with her too frequently (Bouwstoffen I:224).
11 Resolution Heeren XVII 15-1-1654, VOC 149; Bouwstoffen I:53.

CHAPTER VIII
1 Manuscript collection, Maritiem Museum Prins Hendrik (MMPH), Rotterdam, dossier D. van Lennep, letter dated January 1802.
2 De Haan has written the standard work on ancien régime Batavia: "Oud Batavia"; Taylor 1983.
3 Pictures of all these objects can be found in Yamaguchi 1978.
4 In 1961 this painting was purchased by the Rijksmuseum from the Amsterdam antique dealer, Nico Israël. It had belonged to the well-known Russian collectioner, Paul Delaroff, who sold it at a Paris auction in 1914.
5 For Formosa see, for instance, the studies by Ginsel (1931) and Campbell (1903). Contemporaries saw ziekentroosters in a different light. Witness Nicolaus de Graaff, who described them as the private traders and smugglers par excellence, because they were absolved from the oath that they would not infringe the strict prohibition of the Company concerning private trade (De Graaff 1930:28). In light of these facts, Coeman may have used his occupation as a perfect alibi to engage in artistic pursuits (De Loos-Haaxman 1937).
6 This information is derived from the Van Delden Collection, eerste afdeling, ARA; a very rich source of information on Company servants for the 1602-1660 period.
7 The biographical data on Van Nijenroode have been drawn mainly from Terpstra (1938), Groeneveldt (1898) and Wijnaendts van Resandt (1944).
8 The best historical description of the Dutch-Japanese relations in this period has been made by Justus Schouten (Blussé 1985).
9 Letter by Pieter Nuyts to Philips Lucassen at Batavia dated 30-9-1632, VOC 1110, f.473.
10 "Memorie van donatie die d'E. van Nijenroode saliger aen sijn kinderen als andere heeft gelegateerd, 23-9-1632", VOC 1124, f.89 and VOC 1110, f.398.
11 "Inventaris van de goederen van Cornelis van Nijenroode", VOC 1110, f.386-91.
12 "Testament van Cornelis van Neyenroode opgetekend door J. Schouten, 13 Febr. 1633", VOC 1124, f.87 and VOC 1110, f.399-400. One tael is equal to 45 or 57 stuiver; one stuiver is equal to 8 duiten or 5 cents.
13 15-8-1633, GM I:373. It is not altogether clear whether the total sum of his income was also included in this seizure. The Dutch text reads: "Ende also van Nijenroode met het vergaeren van soo considerable middelen notoirlijck heeft gepecheert tegen de teneur van den algemeijnen artijckelbrief, soo sijn alle sijn naergelaten middelen bij den advocaet fiscael van de Raet van Justitie betrocken, ende verclaert verbeurt ende geconfisqueert".
14 "Instructie voor den E. Nicolaes Couckebacker", 31-5-1633, in Bataviaas Briefboek, VOC 856, f.226 as well as Hirado Diaries I:330.
15 This becomes clear from the testament of Joan de Harde and Cornelia Cou-

ckebacker in which mention is made of juffrouw Schemon van Maccauw, her half-sister (Arsip Nasional, Jakarta, Notarial Archives Huysman). "Juffrouw Schemon" most likely is the Suzanna who was married to the Captain of the Japanese in Batavia, Nicolaes alias Schemon (see De Haan 1910 I:197).

16 Letter of N. Couckebacker to GG Brouwer dated 20-10-1633 in ARA, Aanwinsten 1886, 225, f.7.
17 Letter of N. Couckebacker to GG Van Diemen dated 20-11-1633 in ARA, Aanwinsten 1886, 225, unfoliated.
18 The decree for the banishment was promulgated on May 9, 1639 (Verseput 1954:xxxiv). The mothers of Cornelia and Hester were exempted from banishment because they had married Japanese men in the meantime. See also for the description of the arrival of the refugees in Batavia GM II:97-8, 8-1-1640.
19 According to G.F. Meylan cited in Hesselink 1984:73.
20 Resolution GG and C 23-8-1625, VOC 1085. The instruction for the Orphanage can be found in Plakaatboek I:173-87. The weeskamer was established on 1-10-1624.
21 Iwao 1978:149 and ARA, eerste afdeling, collection Van Delden: Pieter Cnoll. See note 6.
22 See De Haan 1910 I:216-7. According to Iwao 1978:143, one of the godmothers, Maria Verburgh, was the Japanese daughter of Pieter van Santen, but this is highly unlikely. See Wijnaendts van Resandt 1944:130.
23 Gingan, gingham, cotton stuff of the Coromandel coast. Chintz also, a printed or spotted cotton cloth. One Kin or catty weighs about 0.6 kilogramme. "Testament tusschen de heer Pieter Cnoll van Delft, eerste oppercoopman dezes casteels ende d'eerbare juffrouw Cornelia van Nieuwenroode geboortigh van Firando in Japan, echteman en vrouw" (Arsip Nasional, Notarial Archives Huysman, 15-2-1672, f.22). I would like to thank Prof. Iwao for lending me his copy of the testament.
24 The Hamada Sukeeimon mentioned in the letter was a Christian Japanese from Nagasaki, living in Batavia. In Dutch sources he is known as Jan. Yoshitsugi Kuzaeimon was his wife's younger brother (Iwao 1978:151).
25 Kana writing includes Hiragana and Katakana. They are alphabetical systems developed during the Heian period. Katakana was used by Buddhist priests in reading their scriptures. Hiragana was used by women.
26 Palcalle and Salempoory cotton are both a kind of chintz, according to Iwao, extremely highly valued items in Japan at the time (Iwao 1978:154). Batik is printed cloth from Java. One tan is a roll of cloth of about twelve yards.
27 Dai-feitor literally opperkoopman, a conjunction of the Japanese word Dai = large and feitor, the Portuguese word for factor or merchant.
28 The representative and spokesman of the Japanese burghers of Batavia.
29 For the instructions of the super-merchants see Plakaatboek II:80-5, 214-7, 380, 398; 9-4-1644, 11-2-1656, 25-11-1664 and 22-9-1665.
30 See Daghregister 1666:80, June 4. An overview of Pieter Cnoll's career can be found in the alphabetical Personalia index to the Resolutions of Governor-General and Council (VOC 828).
31 This particular decision played a major role in later developments. As long as no neat inventories existed or could be shown, distrust could be easily raised among parties involved. Due to the absence of the inventory it cannot be established how wealthy Cnoll actually was. Judging from the figures that we shall encounter in this narrative, the estimate of a contemporary who thought Pieter Cnoll good for 2 million guilders, "20 Tonnen Goldes" seems a bit above the mark (Meister 1692:293).
32 She could remain legal guardian only until she remarried. Thereupon the guardianship would pass to her husband or a specially appointed guardian. See De Groot 1926 I:16.
33 This is how we know that Hester had a son called Joan from her second marriage with Abelis Bentingh.
34 Res GG and C 20-2-1672 (VOC 687, f.5 and 101). For a very detailed

genealogical study of the Nobel family, see the study by Van Schouwenburg (1986).
35 Neither in Kumar 1976 nor in Klooster 1984, is any effort made to lift the veil that hangs over his early career. The contemporary evidence presented by Georg Meister would seem the most reliable as a source. He explains Surapati's decision to run away as follows: "While Surapati had ultimately been promoted to the rank of parasol bearer by the father he was soon pressed by the son [Cornelis, after his father's death] into all kinds of services [that were below his status]". Moreover, the son was only a burgher; no wonder the slave chose to flee, Georg Meister adds. He concludes "although, according to custom and the 'Bataviasche Statuten', super-merchant Cnoll left his slaves and the other movables to his son, he would have been wiser to manumit Surapati on account of his faithful service, as is often done by the well-to-do upon their death" (Meister 1692: 293). As bearer of his master's insignia - the payong or parasol was only permitted to those of the rank of super-merchant and above - only Surapati would have been allowed to carry his master's banner.
36 These data have been obtained from the "Genealogical notes on related families" in the Van Boetzelaer family archives, kept at provincial archives of Utrecht (RU), no.6. Johan Bitter, born on September 20, 1638, was the son of Arnold Bitter and his second wife, Aaltje Scholten of Arnhem. Bartha Eygels was the daughter of Arnold's sister, Warburg (?), who was married to a Strassburg wine seller, Anthony Eygels. Johan and Bartha married on August 1, 1660.
37 The "Album Promotorum" mentions this occasion on February 16, 1662; "Johannes Bitter Arenaco-Gelrus, post habitam publicam disputationem in conclavi promotus, promotore d. Arnoldo Schonaeo" (O.S. Schutte 1980:23).
38 "Barta born on Wednesday afternoon four o'clock at Harderwijk July 10, 1661. Eva born on February 21, 1663 at Amsterdam, died one year later. Arnolt born on Sunday evening half past nine, September 21, 1664 at Amsterdam. Aletta I died in her first weeks. Aletta II born on Saturday morning five o'clock July 21, 1668 at Amsterdam. Eva I died in her first weeks. Eva II born on Tuesday morning, six o'clock December 30, 1670. Johanna died after a few months. Johanna II born in 1673, died three years old" [in Batavia or on board the ship Ceylon]. Quotation from: "Aantekeningen over de geboorte van de kinderen van Joan Bitter en Barta Eygels" RU, Van Boetzelaer Archief, no.482 and "Genealogische aantekeningen van verwante families", no.6. I would like to thank K.L. van Schouwenburg for pointing out the existence of these sources, in addition to those mentioned in M.P.H. Roessingh's formidable "Sources" (Roessingh 1982).
39 See note 2 and Lubberhuizen-van Gelder 1945:98.
40 HR 783:85. As such, a representative example of the means by which the Dutch burghers at the time invested money: housing or bottomry.
41 Inscrutable indeed, the ways of the Lord must have been to the lawyer! In clerical punishment procedures it was not the individual rights which were primordial but the well-being of the Community which had to be protected against Ira Dei. The defendant was not allowed to be accompanied by a defender. He was not shown the evidence nor was he informed of the names of his accusators. One had to accept the total Church Council as the juridical court, even in case of a personal conflict with a parson (Van Deursen 1980 IV:50).
42 In his interesting article on Andreas Cleyer, De Haan touches upon Speelman's speculative transactions (1903:442) and concludes: "the shrewd politician, the valiant, determined admiral and general, was also a thorough cheat, who could even debase himself to the meanest kind of usury while dealing with the natives" (1903:448).
43 Hochepied had to do so for "no director is allowed to correspond directly or indirectly for himself or anyone else, with any servant of the Company in the East Indies" (Stapel 1927-43 III:383).

44 Pieter van Dam has devoted one chapter to the strictly forbidden private trade of Company servants. Concerning the trading in diamonds he asserts that the directorate had not followed the same line of policy over the years (Stapel 1927-43 III:384).
45 Here the 1683 edition, published by Johannes Steucker, has been used.
46 The article on the prohibition of private trade is referred to in the artikelbrief, to which every Company servant, with the exception of the clerics, had to swear on oath.
47 Dirk Tulp (1624-1682), the father of the famous doctor Nicolaes Tulp; Louis Trip (1605-1684), burgomaster of Amsterdam in 1674, 1677 and 1679, merchant and gunfounder. His daughter was married to Valckenier's son, Wouter.
48 On the procedure of the administration of justice at the lawcourt of Holland in the 17th century, see Ketelaar 1971.
49 Here we recognize the letter by Over't Water who had described Bitter as a diligent person, the letter by the Governor-General addressed to the Church Council, and the papers collected at that institution prior to Bitter's departure.
50 Van Alphen 1683 II:325. The member referred to is probably Cornelis Speelman, who had mediated in the earlier settlement.
51 Pieter van Dam occupied the position of Advocate, "managing director", to the Company during the years 1652-1706. He compiled for the Heren XVII the "Beschrijvinge", a description of the activities and policies of the VOC, which was kept secret from all outsiders. The manuscript was published in 7 volumes by F.W. Stapel and C.W.Th. van Boetzelaer between 1927-1947. Coolhaas considers it an excellent work (1980:27).
52 Van Alphen 1683 II:318. The text mistakenly says March 24.
53 Of the 25,000 rixdollars, she received 14,901 and 7/8 rixdollars back, consisting of 12,000 rixdollars deposited at the Company's treasury, the sale of a house (2,600 rixdollars) and the sale of some slaves (301 and 7/8 rixdollars). On March 13th, 1680, two freeburghers, Mattheus van Lugtenburg and Jacob Does served a subpoena on Cornelia van Nijenroode on account of debts made by her husband. She was sentenced to pay them respectively 7,330 and 4636.5 rixdollars (HR 783:71).
54 By coincidence the Civiele Rolle of 1681-2 has been preserved at the Hague. The above discussion as well as the contents of Bitter's letter can be found in extenso in VOC 9236, 6-11-1681, f.151.
55 I should like to thank F.S. Gaastra for informing me on this issue from his forthcoming thesis.
56 As a matter of fact, De Graaff throughout his book deems any superior to whom he harbours no particular grudge "wise and modest".
57 The "geweldiger" who arrested and guarded with his eight kaffers (blacks from Angola or Mozambique) the suspects on the orders of his direct superior the advocaat-fiscaal, the public prosecutor. See La Bree 1951:31-2, 53.
58 Of the 42 articles of her contra interrogatorium only 11 were answered, the remaining 31 articles were deemed impertinent and irrelevant and therefore were removed. Cornelia's lawyer was condemned to pay one hundred rixdollars to the poor relief (HR 783:82).
59 The eldest two children are mentioned by De Haan (1910 I:198). For Jacobus Wijbrant, see note 77.
60 On December 11, 1685 Bitter had remitted 8,500 rixdollars to Floris Ouwelsz. Prins and Johannes Stolp in the North Holland town of De Rijp; 3,500 rixdollars to Catharina de Swart (widow of Cornelis de Jager) and Paulus van Durven (a lawyer of Delft); 765 rixdollars to Lambert Lambertsz. of Amsterdam (HR 783:74). None of these people appear to have had any close relationship with Bitter. It is not unlikely that the transfers were merely meant to divert the attention. When hard pressed by the interrogators Bitter asserted that he had kept promissory notes of the same

people in Batavia (HR 783:79).
61 De Bevere here refers to a decision of the Batavian Court under the date September 10, 1678, that I have not been able to find in the evidence available.
62 For a closer look at Speelman's estate which amounted to 400,000 guilders, see VOC 1431, f.736-51. The large amount of outstanding loans to the Batavian Chinese confirms the picture I have given in the earlier chapters of the Chinese who worked with money that the Dutch put out to them at high interest rates.
63 "Goed en gaaf van hout, wel ende na behoren gesloten ende verbonden zonder eenigh het minste manquement" (VOC 702, unfoliated).
64 Respectively by the resolutions of 18 November, 28 November, and 2 December 1687 (VOC 702).
65 See Resolutions Governor-General and Council December 5, 1687 (VOC 702).
66 Johann Wilhelm Vogel and Georg Meister travelled on board Waalstroom. Vogel gives a very vivid description of the departure of the ship, which on account of the large amount of pets and livestock for the kitchen, rather resembled Noah's ark. One of the entertainments for the crew during the long, dull voyage was to secretly feed burning pieces of coal to Bitter's cassowary, which ate everything in its vicinity (Vogel 1704:498, 523). Cassowaries indeed were great gluttons. Christoph Schweitzer narrates that one of the cassowaries which freely roamed within the walls of Batavia castle, ate all the bullets of the watch, only to reproduce them one day later, to the great relief of some soldiers who had been accused of thieving (Schweitzer 1931:29).
67 RU, Archives Dutch Reformed Church, Wijk bij Duurstede, no. 176, "Rekeningen van de administrerend kerkvoogd, 1702-1715".
68 RU, Archives Dutch Reformed Church, Wijk bij Duurstede, no. 176: "Rekeningen van de administrerend kerkvoogd, 1702-1715".
69 See RU, Staten van Utrecht, no. 364-217. Cortenraede provides a delightful anecdote about 63 year-old Johan Bitter and his 24 year-old fellow council member, Vosch, who disagreed on the planting of trees. Bitter: "Young lad, you do not understand me". Vosch: "Sir, so often I have heard this word jonge man used in such a patronizing way. I also know from hearing in Spain young horses are valued higher than old donkeys." Bitter: "Are you calling me an old donkey?" Vosch: "No". Bitter: "Do you compare an old man with a donkey?" Vosch: "That is how the proverb runs". Whereupon Bitter grabbed for his cane and would have attacked his colleague but for the intervention of the bystanders (Cortenraede 1983:54-5).
70 For the marriage settlement of January 14, 1704, see RU, Notarial Archives Van Sandick (Wijk bij Duurstede), Wij 008 a 009. Hendrick very reluctantly served as a burgomaster, witness his attempts to back out of his obligations. When he was called upon, he preferred to go carpentering in his garden. Finally he could only be installed on the magistrate's cushion by force. The VOC may be grateful that this lazy man did not carry out his ambitions to travel to the East as a "Councillor of the Indies". See: RU, Van Boetzelaer Archives, no. 475, "Verklaring voor het gerecht van Amersfoort afgelegd door de huishoudster van Hendrick Both, waarin zij getuigt van diens onwil om burgemeester te worden, 1703".
71 For the marriage settlement see RU, Van Boetzelaer Archives no. 484, "Acte huwelijkse voorwaarden Albert Jan van Lidth de Jeude en Aletta Bitter, 1707".
72 According to GM VI:262, Arnolt joined the Council of Justice in Batavia in the autumn of 1703 upon his arrival. In 1705 he was transferred as second-in-command and administrator to Malabar (GM VI:372, 475). In the Missive of November 25, 1708, he is reported to have been promoted to the post of advocaat-fiscaal. He returned home as the vice-admiral of the autumn fleet of 1715 (GM VII:166).
73 See for instance RU, Notarial Archives Van Sandick, Wij 008 a 004, 1697:

	Bitter received 1,200 guilders + 4% interest from Batavia; Wij 008 a 009, 1704: Bitter received 4,992 guilders from Batavia; Wij 008 a ·010, 1707: Bitter received 300 guilders in money bills from Batavia as well as 2,570 guilders in salary earned by Arnolt Bitter.
74	RU, Notarial Archives Nicolaes Keppel, Wij 007 a 001: July 30, 1698. As has been shown in the previous note he used these powers to cash his son's income.
75	Municipal Archives Amsterdam (GA) Weeskamer, "Register der voogdijen beginnende 21-10-1687 en eyndigende 9-8-1707", no. 5073-518; GA Weeskamer, "Inbreng register", vol. 38, f.31. The inventory of the Cnoll estate was executed by Notary Jacobus van Uylenbroeck on 12-4-1690. Unfortunately the notarial papers of 1690-1692 have been lost. According to the GM V:431, the Reverend Perreira transmitted to Hillegonda Dubbeldecop another 8,500 rixdollars belonging to her late husband in the spring of 1691.
76	RU, Wij 008 a 002, Notaris Van Sandick, 1694.
77	See GA, Notarial Archives Daniël Moors 247-6318, 1693-1719, f.829, Last will of Jonker Jacobus Wijbrant Cnoll, executed on August 23, 1702. Other beneficiaries of this estate were his nephew and godchild (2,000 rixdollars) and the two sisters Anna and Petronella Lossers (20,000 guilders). The place of decease, Vianen, gives rise to some wonder. This little town was a refuge for criminals and debtors. J.W. Cnoll's death was not communicated to the Orphan Board until March 31, 1706 (GA "Inbreng register", vol. 38, f.31).

LITERATURE

Alphen, Willem van
1683 Papegay ofte formulier-boek van allerhande requesten, mandamenten, conclusien, als anders, in de dagelijcksche practijcke dienende voor de respective Hoven van Justitie in Hollandt. 's Graven-hage. 2 Vols.
Apeldoorn, L.J. van
1925 Geschiedenis van het Nederlands huwelijksrecht voor de invoering van de Fransche wetgeving. Amsterdam.
Asser, C.
1957 Handleiding tot de beoefening van het Nederlands burgerlijk recht. Zwolle.
Audemard, L.
1957-71 Les jonques chinoises. Rotterdam. 10 Vols.
Bakker, P.
1936 Eenige beschouwingen over het geldverkeer in de inheemsche samenleving van Nederlandsch-Indië. Groningen/Batavia.
Barraclough, G.
1955 History in a changing world. Oxford.
Barrow, J.T.
1804 A voyage to Cochinchina in the years 1792 and 1793. London.
Basset, D.K.
1971 British trade and policy in Indonesia and Malaysia in the late eighteenth century. Hull.
Batavia
1782-83 Batavia, de hoofdstad van Neerlands O. Indien, in derzelver gelegenheid, opkomst, voortreffelijke gebouwen, Hooge en laage Regeering, geschiedenissen, kerkzaaken, koophandel, zeden, luchtsgesteldheid, ziekten, dieren en gewassen, beschreven. Amsterdam/Harlingen. 4 Vols.
Bataviasche Statuten
1862 "De oude Bataviasche Statuten", BKI 10:393-518.
Berg, N.P. van den
1904 Uit de dagen der Compagnie; Geschiedkundige schetsen. Haarlem.
Bierens de Haan, A.C.F. and L.L.
1918 Memorie boek van pakhuismeesteren van de thee te Amsterdam 1818-1918 en de Nederlandsche theehandel in de loop der tijden. Amsterdam.
Blair, Emma H. and James A. Robertson (eds)
1903-09 The Philippine islands, 1493-1898. Cleveland. 55 Vols.
Blakeney, W.
1902 On the coasts of Cathay and Cipango forty years ago. London.
Blécourt, A.S. de and H.F.W.D. Fischer
1967 Kort begrip van het oud-vaderlandsch burgerlijk recht. 's-Gravenhage.
Bloys van Treslong Prins, P.C.
1934-39 Genealogische en heraldische gedenkwaardigheden betreffende Europeanen op Java. Batavia. 4 Vols.

Blussé, Leonard
1975 "Western impact on Chinese communities in Western Java at the beginning of the 17th century", Nampo Bunka 2:26-57.
1979 "Impo, Chinese merchant in Pattani", in: Proceedings of the seventh IAHA conference, pp. 290-309. Bangkok.
1981 "The VOC as sorcerer's apprentice: Stereotypes and social engineering on the China coast", in: W.L. Idema (ed.), Leyden studies in Sinology, pp. 87-105. Leiden.
1985 "Justus Schouten en de Japanse gijzeling", in: Nederlandse Historische Bronnen, vol. 5, pp. 69-109. 's-Gravenhage.
Blussé, J.L., M.E. van Opstall and Ts'ao Yung-ho (eds)
1986 De Dagregisters van het kasteel Zeelandia, Taiwan 1629-1641. 's-Gravenhage.
Boetzelaer van Asperen en Dubbeldam, C.W.Th. baron van
1947 De Protestantsche kerk in Nederlandsch-Indië; Haar ontwikkeling van 1620-1939. 's-Gravenhage.
Bogaert, A.
1711 Historische reizen door d'oostersche deelen van Asia. Amsterdam.
Boin, Michèle
1984 The Khai-pa lèk-tai sú-kì; Chronicle of the Chinese community of Batavia, 17-18th centuries. [Unpublished paper 29th EACS Conference, Tübingen.]
Bonfield, Lloyd
1983 Marriage settlements 1601-1740. Cambridge.
Bontekoe, Willem Ysbrantsz.
1952 G.J. Hoogewerff (ed.), Journalen van de gedenkwaardige reysen van Willem Ysbrantsz. Bontekoe, 1618-1625. 's-Gravenhage. [Linschotenvereniging 54.]
Boxer, C.R.
1963 Race relations in the Portuguese colonial empire, 1415-1825. Oxford.
1975 Mary and misogyny, Women in Iberian expansion overseas 1415-1815; Some facts, fancies and personalities. London.
Boxhorn, M.Z.
1654 Commentariolus de statu confoederatarum provinciarum Belgiae. Hagae Comitis.
Brandes, J.
1901 "Een plattegrond van Batavia van 1632", TBG 63:248-74.
Braudel, Fernand
1979 Civilisation matérielle, économie et capitalisme, XVe-XVIIIe siècle. Paris. 3 Vols.
Bree, J. la
1951 De rechterlijke organisatie en rechtsbedeling te Batavia in de 17e eeuw. Rotterdam.
Breuning, H.A.
1981 Het voormalige Batavia; Een Hollandse stedestichting in de tropen anno 1619. Utrecht. [First edition 1954.]
Brunschwig, H.
1978 "French expansion and local reaction in black Africa in the time of imperialism (1880-1940)", in: H.L. Wesseling (ed.), Expansion and reaction, pp. 116-40. Leiden.
Bruijn, J.R.
1976 "De personeelsbehoefte van de VOC overzee en aan boord, bezien in Aziatisch en Nederlands perspectief", Bijdragen en Mededelingen betreffende de Geschiedenis der Nederlanden 91:218-48.
Bruijn, J.R., F.S. Gaastra and I. Schöffer (eds)
1979 Dutch-Asiatic shipping in the 17th and 18th centuries. The Hague. 2 Vols.

Literature

Burg, P. van der
1677   Curieuse beschrijving van de gelegentheid, zeden, godsdienst en ommegang, van verscheyden Oost-Indische gewesten en machtige landschappen. Rotterdam.

Campbell, W.
1903   Formosa under the Dutch. London.

Carey, P.B.R.
1980   The archive of Yogyakarta. Vol. 1, Documents relating to politics and internal court affairs. Oxford.

Castles, Lance
1967   "The ethnic profile of Batavia", Indonesia 9:153-204.

Chan Cheung
1967   "The smuggling trade between China and Southeast Asia during the Ming dynasty", in: F.S. Drake (ed.), Historical, archeological and linguistic studies on Southern China and Southeast Asia, pp. 223-7. Hongkong.

Chang Hsieh 張燮
1981   Tung-Hsi-Yang K'ao 東西洋考 [A study of the eastern and western oceans]. Peking. [First published in 1618.]

Chastelein, Cornelis
1855   "Invallende gedagten ende aanmerkingen", TBG 3:63-104.
1876   "Batavia, in het begin der achttiende eeuw", Tijdschrift voor Nederlandsch-Indië, New series 5:177-93.

Chaudhuri, K.N.
1978   The trading world of Asia and the English East India Company 1660-1760. Cambridge.

Chaunu, Pierre
1960   Le Philippines et le Pacifique des Ibériques. Paris. 2 Vols.

Chijs, J.A. van der (ed.)
1869   Catalogus der numismatische afdeling van het Museum van het Bataviasche Genootschap van Kunsten en Wetenschappen. Batavia.
1882-86   Realia; Register op de generale resolutiën van het Kasteel Batavia, 1632-1805. Leiden. 3 Vols.
1885-1900   Nederlandsch-Indisch Plakaatboek, 1602-1811. Batavia/'s Hage. 17 Vols.
1887-1931   (et al (eds)) Dagh-Register gehouden int Casteel Batavia vant passerende daer ter plaetse als over geheel Nederlandts-India 1624-1682, 's Gravenhage/Batavia. 31 Vols.

Chinese jonk Keying
1848   "De Chinese jonk Keying", Tijdschrift toegewijd aan het Zeewezen, second series 8:48-50.

Ch'ing-ch'ao Wen-hsien T'ung-k'ao
1936   Ch'ing-ch'ao Wen-hsien T'ung-k'ao 清朝文獻通考 [Ch'ing encyclopedia of historical records]. Shanghai. 2 Vols. [Reprint.]

Ch'ing Shih-lu
1959   Ch'ing Shih-lu Ching-chi Tzu-liao Chi-yao 清實錄經濟資料紀要 [A compendium of economic materials in the veritable records of the Ch'ing dynasty]. Peking.

Chou K'ai (ed.) 周凱
1961   Hsia-men Chih 厦門志 [Gazetteer of Amoy]. Taipei. 5 Vols. [Originally published in 1832.]

Ch'üan Han-sheng 全漢昇
1972   Chung-kuo Ching-chi-shih Lun-ts'ung 中國經濟史論叢 [A collection of essays on Chinese economic history]. Hongkong.

Colenbrander, H.T.
1925   Koloniale geschiedenis. 's-Gravenhage. 3 Vols.

Colenbrander, H.T. and W.Ph. Coolhaas (eds)
1919-53   Jan Pieterszoon Coen; Bescheiden omtrent zijn bedrijf in Indië. 's-Gravenhage. 7 Vols.

Commelin, Isaac
1646   Begin ende voortgang van de Vereenighde Nederlandtsche Geoctroyeerde Oost-Indische Compagnie. Amsterdam. 2 Vols.
Comte, L. le
1697   Memoirs and observations made in a late journey through the empire of China, and published in several letters. London.
Coolhaas, W.Ph.
1947   "Een Indisch verslag uit 1631, van de hand van Antonio van Diemen", Bijdragen en Mededelingen van het Historisch Genootschap 65:1-237.
1958   "Zijn de Gouverneurs-Generaal Van Imhoff en Mossel juist beoordeeld", BKI 114:29-54.
1960-85   (ed.) Generale Missiven van Gouverneurs-Generaal en Raden aan Heren XVII der Vereenigde Oostindische Compagnie. 's-Gravenhage. 8 Vols.
1980   A critical survey of studies on Dutch colonial history. The Hague. [First edition 1960.]
Coppel, C.A.
1983   Indonesian Chinese in crisis. Kuala Lumpur.
Cortenraede, Leon
1983   De Wijkse regenten: van timmerman tot rentenier; Een prosopografisch onderzoek naar de regenten van Wijk bij Duurstede in het tweede stadhouderloze tijdperk. Utrecht. [M.A. thesis Utrecht University.]
Crawfurd, J.
1820   History of the Indian archipelago [...]. London. 3 Vols.
1830   Journal of an embassy from the Governor-General of India to the courts of Siam and Cochin China [...]. London. 2 Vols.
Crow, Carl
1939   Four hundred million customers. Leipzig.
Cushman, Jennifer
1975   Fields from the sea: Chinese junk trade with Siam during the late eighteenth and early nineteenth century. [Ph.D. thesis Cornell University, Ithaca, N.Y.]
1978   Duke Ch'ing-fu deliberates: a mid-eighteenth century reassessment of Sino-Nanyang commercial relations. Canberra. [Papers on Far Eastern History 17.]
1981   "Siamese state trade and the Chinese go-between, 1767-1855", Journal of Southeast Asian Studies 12:46-61.
Dalton, George
1965   "Primitive money", American Anthropologist 67:44-65.
Dapper, O.
1670   Gedenkwaerdig bedrijf der Nederlantsche Oost-Indische Maatschappije, op de kuste en in het keizerrijk van Taising of Sina [...]. Amsterdam.
Davis, J.Fr.
1836   The Chinese: a general description of the empire of China and its inhabitants. London. 2 Vols.
Deursen, A.Th. van
1979-80   Het kopergeld van de Gouden Eeuw. Assen. 4 Vols.
Deventer, M.L. van
1886-87   Geschiedenis der Nederlanders op Java. Haarlem. 2 Vols.
Diaries
1974-85   Diaries kept by the heads of the Dutch factory in Japan 1633-1640. Tokyo. 5 Vols.
Enklaar, I.H.
1947   De scheiding der sacramenten op het zendingsveld. Amsterdam.
Feuerwerker, Albert
1968   History in Communist China. Cambridge, Mass.
Finley, M.I.
1977   "The ancient city: from Fustel de Coulanges to Max Weber and beyond", Comparative Studies in Society and History 19:305-27.

1985 The ancient economy. London. [First edition 1973.]
Fockema Andreae, S.J.
1953 "Staats- en rechtsleven onder de Republiek", in: J.A. van Houtte and J.F. Niemeyer (eds), Algemene geschiedenis der Nederlanden, Vol. 6, pp. 61-88. Utrecht/Antwerpen.
1969 De Nederlandse staat onder de Republiek. Amsterdam.
Fortune, R.
1853 The tea districts of China and India. London. 2 Vols.
Frazer, Antonia
1984 The weaker vessel; Woman's lot in seventeenth century England. London.
Fruin-Mees, W.
1919-20 Geschiedenis van Java. Weltevreden. 2 Vols.
Fu I-Ling 傅衣凌
1956 Ming-Ch'ing shih-tai shang-jen chi shang-ye tzu-pen 明清時代商人及商業資本 [Merchants and trade capital of the Ming and Ching dynasties]. Peking.
Fu Lo-shu
1966 A documentary chronicle of Sino-Western relations. Tucson.
Furber, Holden
1976 Rival empires of trade in the Orient 1600-1800. Minnesota.
Furnivall, J.S.
1939 Netherlands India; A study of plural economy. Cambridge.
Gaastra, F.S.
1982 De geschiedenis van de VOC. Bussum.
Gerretson, C.
1944 Coens eerherstel. Amsterdam.
Ginsel, W.A.
1931 De gereformeerde kerk op Formosa of de lotgevallen eener handelskerk onder de Oost-Indische Compagnie, 1627-1662. Leiden.
Glamann, K.
1958 Dutch-Asiatic trade, 1620-1740. Copenhagen/The Hague.
Godée Molsbergen, E.C.
1932-36 Tijdens de O.-I. Compagnie. Amsterdam/Bandoeng. 2 Vols.
Gorkom, W.J. van
1913 "Ongezond Batavia, vroeger en nu", Geneeskundig Tijdschrift voor Nederlandsch-Indië 53:177-227.
Graaff, N. de
1930 J.C.M. Warnsinck (ed.), Reisen van Nicolaus de Graaff gedaan naar alle gewesten des werelds, beginnende 1639 tot 1687 incluis. 's-Gravenhage. [Linschoten-vereniging 33.]
Groeneveldt, W.P.
1898 De Nederlanders in China. 's-Gravenhage.
Groot, Hugo de
1926 Inleidinge tot de Hollandsche rechtsgeleerdheid. Leiden. 2 Vols. [First edition 1631.]
Gützlaff, K.
1840 Journal of three voyages along the coast of China in 1831, 1832 and 1833. London.
Haafner, C.M. (ed.)
1820 Lotgevallen en vroegere zeereizen van Jacob Haafner [...]. Amsterdam.
Haan, F. de
1898 De Portugese buitenkerk. Batavia.
1903 "Uit oude notaris papieren II, Andreas Cleyer", TBG 66:422-52.
1910-12 Priangan; De Preanger-Regentschappen onder het Nederlandsch bestuur tot 1811. Batavia. 4 Vols.
1917 "De laatste der Mardijkers", BKI 73:219-54.

1935   Oud Batavia. Bandoeng. 2 Vols. [First edition 1922.]
Heeres, J.E
1912   "De 'Consideratiën' van Van Imhoff", BKI 66:441-621.
Hesse, Elias
1931   S.P. l'Honoré Naber (ed.), Gold-Bergwerke in Sumatra 1680-1683. Haag. [Reisebeschreibungen von deutschen Beambten und Kriegsleuten im Dienst der Niederländischen West- und Ost-Indischen Kompagnien 1602-1797, vol. 10.] [First edition 1690.]
Hesselink, R.H.
1984   Twee spiegels op Cambang. Utrecht.
Hoetink, B.
1917   "So Bing Kong; Het eerste hoofd der Chinezen te Batavia", BKI 73:344-415.
1918a   "De weduwe van kapitein Siqua", Chung Hwa Hui Tsa Chih 2-1:16-25.
1918b   "Ni Hoekong, kapitein der Chinezen te Batavia in 1740", BKI 74:447-518.
1922   "Chineesche officieren te Batavia onder de Compagnie", BKI 78:1-136.
1923   "So Bing Kong; Het eerste hoofd der Chinezen te Batavia; Eene nalezing", BKI 79:1-44.
Hoëvell, W.R. van
1840   "Batavia in 1740", Tijdschrift voor Neêrland's Indië 3:447-557.
1860   Uit het Indische leven. Zaltbommel.
Hogendorp, Dirk van
1799   Berigt van den tegenwoordigen toestand der Bataafsche bezittingen in Oost-Indiën en den handel op dezelve. Delft.
Hogendorp, C.S.W. van
1833   Beschouwing der Nederlandsche bezittingen in Oost-Indië. Amsterdam.
Hooyman, J.
1779   "Verhandeling over den tegenwoordigen staat des landbouws in de Ommelanden van Batavia", VBG 1:173-262.
Hsiang Ta (ed.) 向達
1961   Liang-chung Hai-tao Chen-ching 兩種海道針經 [Two Rutters]. Peking.
Hsieh Chao-che 謝肇淛
1972   Wu Tsa Tsu 五雜俎 [Five various components]. Tokyo. [Original edition published around 1600.]
Hsü Yün-chiao (ed.) 許雲樵
1953   "Kai-pa Li-tai Shih-chi" 開吧歷代史記 [A chronicle of Batavia], Nan Yang Hsüeh Pao 9-1:1-64.
Huet, P.D.
1718   Mémoires sur le commerce des Hollandois. Amsterdam.
Hullu, J. de
1917   "Over den Chinaschen handel der Oost-Indische Compagnie in de eerste dertig jaar van de 18e eeuw", BKI 73:32-154.
1923   "De instelling van de Commissie voor den handel der Oost-Indische Compagnie op China in 1756", BKI 79:523-45.
Humphreys, S.C.
1969   "History, economics and anthropology: the work of Karl Polanyi", History and Theory 8:165-212.
Huysers, A.
1789   "Het leeven van Reynier de Klerk", in: Beknopte beschrijving der Oostindische etablissementen verzeld van eenige bijlagen [...]. Utrecht.
Iwao Seiichi 岩生成一
1970   "Japanese emigrants in Batavia during the 17th century", Acta Asiatica 18:1-25.

1975	"Jakaruta no Hsin-chien yang-chi-yüan Li-fu-hu-chüan-chin-hsing-shih no hi" ジャカルタの新建養濟院列福戶捐金姓氏の碑 [On the inscription of the Yang-chi-yüan in Jakarta], Nampo Bunka 2:13-25.
1978	"Kapitan no musume Cornelia no shogai" 甲必丹の娘コルネリヤの生涯 [The life of the captain's daughter Cornelia], in: Rekishi to jinbutsu [History and people], pp. 142-55. Tokyo.

Johnson, Marion
1970 "The Cowrie currencies of West Africa", Journal of African History 2: 17-49, 331-53.

Jonge, J.K.J. de
1858 "Geschiedkundig onderzoek omtrent de vroeger genomen proeven van volksplanting in de Nederlandsche Oost-Indische bezittingen", in: Verslag aan den koning uitgebragt door de Staats-commissie [...] betreffende Europesche kolonisatie in Nederlandsch-Indië. 's Gravenhage.
1862-1909 (et al. (eds)) De opkomst van het Nederlandsch gezag in Oost-Indië; Verzameling van onuitgegeven stukken uit het Oud-Koloniaal Archief. 's-Gravenhage. 13 Vols.

Jongh, R.C. de and F.H. van Naerssen
1977 The economic and administrative history of early Indonesia. Leiden.

Jörg, C.J.A.
1982 Porcelain and the Dutch China trade. The Hague.
1984 De Hatcher schenking; Chinees exportporselein uit een wrak in de Zuidchinese zee. Groningen.

Kan, J. van
1943 "Het rechtsmiddel der revisie voor den Raad van Justitie des kasteels Batavia", BKI 102:1-40.

Kat Angelino, P. de
1921 "De Kèpèng op Bali", Koloniale Studiën 5:67-83.

Kemasang, A.R.T.
1985 "How Dutch colonialism foreclosed a domestic bourgeoisie in Java: The 1740 Chinese massacres reappraised", Review 9-1:57-80.

Ketelaar, F.C.J.
1971 "De procesgang bij het Hof van Holland, Zeeland en West-Friesland", in: Verslag en Bijdragen van de Rijks Archiefschool, 1969-1970, pp. 33-63. Utrecht.

Keuchenius, W.M.
1875 "Beschrijving der Bataviasche jurisdictie en onderzoek naar de oorzaken der meerdere ongezondheid van Batavia en deszelfs rhee", TBG 22:390-531.

Keuning, J. (ed.)
1938-51 De tweede schipvaart der Nederlanders naar Oost-Indië onder Jacob Cornelisz. van Neck en Wijbrant Warwijck. 's-Gravenhage. 6 Vols. [Linschoten-vereniging 42.]

Klooster, H.A.J.
1984 "Abdoel Moeis' roman over Surapati", Jambatan 3-1:3-15.

Kolff, D.H.A.
1984 "La nation chrétienne à Surate au début du XVIIe siècle", in: R. Goutalier (ed.), La femme dans les sociétés coloniales, pp. 7-16. Aix-en-Provence.

Kroeskamp, H.
1953 "De Chinezen te Batavia (± 1700) als exempel voor de Christenen van West-Europa", Indonesië 3:346-71.

Kumar, Ann
1976 Surapati, man and legend: A study of three babad traditions. Leiden.

Lannoy, Ph. de and H. Vanderlinden
1907 Histoire de l'expansion coloniale des peuples européens; Portugal et Espagne. Bruxelles.

Leguat, François
1708 Voyages et avantures de François Leguat et de ses compagnons en deux isles desertes des Indes Orientales [...]. Londres/Amsterdam.
Lekkerkerker, C.
1918 "De Baliërs van Batavia", Indische Gids 40:409-31.
Leonard, Jane Kate
1984 Wei yüan and China's rediscovery of the maritime world. Cambridge, Mass.
Lequin, F.
1982 Het personeel van de Verenigde Oost-Indische Compagnie in Azië in de achttiende eeuw, meer in het bijzonder in de vestiging Bengalen. Leiden. 2 Vols.
Leupe, P.A.
1878 "Rapport over een onderzoek naar den toestand der Bataviasche Groote Rivier na de aardbeving van den 5en Januari 1699", BKI 26:494-506.
Leur, J.C. van
1967 Indonesian trade and society. The Hague.
Ligers, Z.
1946 L'historie des villes de Lettonie et d'Estonie. Paris.
Linschoten, J.H. van
1910 H. Kern (ed.), Itinerario; Voyage ofte schipvaert van Jan Huygen van Linschoten naar Oost ofte Portugaels Indien 1579-1592. 's-Gravenhage. 2 Vols. [Linschoten-vereniging 2.]
Loos-Haaxman, J. de
1937 "Jacob Coeman, ziekentrooster en schilder", TBG 77:590-601.
1968 Verlaat rapport Indië; Drie eeuwen westerse schilders, tekenaars, grafici, zilversmeden en kunstnijveren in Nederlands-Indië. 's-Gravenhage.
Lubberhuizen-van Gelder, A.M.
1945 "Hendrik Veeckens, een ambtenaar van den ouden stempel", Cultureel Indië 7:89-106.
Mac Leod, N.
1927 De Oost-Indische Compagnie als zeemogendheid in Azië. Rijswijk. 2 Vols.
Madrolle, C.
1901 Les premiers voyages francais à la Chine; La Compagnie de Chine (1698-1719). Paris.
Mastenbroek, W.E. van
1934 De historische ontwikkeling van de staatsrechtelijke indeeling der bevolking van Nederlandsch-Indië. Wageningen.
Maunier, René
1932 Sociologie coloniale; Introduction à l'étude du contact des races. Paris.
Medhurst, W.H.
1840 "Chronologische geschiedenis van Batavia", Tijdschrift voor Neêrland's Indië 3-2:1-145.
Mees, W.C.
1952 Maria Quevellerius, huisvrouw van Jan van Riebeeck, en haar omgeving. Assen.
Meilink-Roelofsz, M.A.P.
1962 Asian trade and European influence in the Indonesian archipelago between 1500 and about 1630. 's-Gravenhage.
Meister, Georg
1692 Der Orientalisch-Indianische Kunst- und Lust-gärtner [...]. Dresden.
Mill, John Stuart
1981 The subjection of women. Cambridge, Mass.
Millies, H.C.
1871 Recherches sur les monnaies des indigènes de l'Archipel indien et de la Péninsule malaie. La Haye.

Mills, J.V.G. (ed.)
1970		Ma Huan, Ying-yai Sheng-lan; Overall survey of the ocean's shores, 1433. Cambridge.
Mollema, J.C.
1935		De eerste schipvaart der Hollanders naar Oost-Indië 1595-1597. 's-Gravenhage.
Montanus, A.
1669		Gedenkwaerdige gesantschappen der Oost-Indische Maatschappij [...] aan de Kaisaren van Japan. Amsterdam.
Mooij, J.
1923		Geschiedenis der Protestantsche Kerk in Nederlandsch-Indië; I. 1602-1636. Weltevreden.
1927-31	(ed.) Bouwstoffen voor de geschiedenis der Protestantsche Kerken in Nederlandsch-Indië. Weltevreden. 3 Vols.
Muijzenberg, O.D. van den
1965		De "Plural Society": Een onderzoek naar gebruik en bruikbaarheid als sociologisch begrip. Amsterdam.
Murakami Naojiro 村上直次郎
1917		Boekishi-jo no Hirado 貿易史上の平戸 [Hirado in trade history]. Tokyo.
Nakamura Takashi 中村孝志
1969		"Batavia kakyo no chozei ukeoi seido ni tsuite" バタヴィア華僑の徴税請負制度について [Concerning the tax farm system in Batavia], Toyoshi Kenkyu 28-1:52-79.
Needham, Joseph
1954-71	Science and civilisation in China. Cambridge. 4 Vols.
Nieuhoff, J.
1665		Het gezandtschap der Neêrlandtsche Oost-Indische Compagnie, aan den grooten Tartarischen Cham, den tegenwoordigen Keizer van China [...]. Amsterdam.
Nieuwenhuys, Rob
1984		"Heimwee naar het archief: over dr. F. de Haan (1863-1938), in: F. de Haan, Uit de nadagen der 'Loffelijke Compagnie', pp. 7-16. Amsterdam.
Ng Chin-keong
1983		Trade and society, the Amoy network on the China coast, 1683-1735. Singapore.
Oba Osamu 大庭脩
1972		"Hirado Matsuura Shiryo hakubutsukan-zo 'Tosen no zu' ni tsuite" 平戸松浦史料博物館蔵唐船の図について [On the scroll of China ships in the possession of the Matsuura Museum], Bulletin of the Institute of Oriental and Occidental Studies, Kansai University 5:13-49.
Ong Tae-hae
1849		The Chinaman abroad. Shanghai.
Oost-Indisch-praetjen
1663		Oost-Indisch-praetjen voorgevallen in Batavia, tusschen vier Nederlanders. Amsterdam.
Owen, R. and B. Sutcliffe
1972		Studies in the theory of imperialism. London.
Parry, J.H.
1963		The age of reconnaissance. London.
P'eng Hsin-wei 彭信威
1958		Chung-kuo Huo-pi Shih 中國貨幣史 [A history of Chinese currency]. Shanghai.
Polanyi, Karl
1963		"Ports of trade in early societies", The Journal of Economic History 23-1:30-45.
Polanyi, Karl, C.M. Arensberg and H.W. Pearson
1957		Trade and market in the early empires. Glencoe, Ill.

Purchas, Samuel
1903-05   Hakluytus Posthumus or Purchas his pilgrimes containing a history of the world in sea voyages and lande travells by Englishmen and others. Glasgow. 20 Vols.
Purcell, Victor
1951   The Chinese in Southeast Asia. London.
Quiason, Serafin D.
1966   "The sampan trade, 1570-1770", in: Alfonso Felix (ed.), The Chinese in the Philippines, pp. 160-74. Manila.
Raffles, T.S.
1817   The history of Java. London. 2 Vols.
Reed, R.
1967   "The colonial origins of Manila and Batavia: desultory notes on nascent metropolitan primacy and urban systems in Southeast Asia", Asian Studies 5:543-62.
Robinson, Joan
1970   Freedom and necessity; An introduction to the study of society. London.
Robinson, R.
1972   "Non-European foundations of European imperialism: sketch for a theory of collaboration", in: R. Owen and B. Sutcliffe (eds), Studies in the theory of imperialism, pp. 117-42. London.
Roessingh, Marius P.H.
1982   Sources of the history of Asia and Oceania in the Netherlands; Part I: Sources up to 1796. München.
Rogers, Woodes
1712   A cruising voyage around the world. London.
Roo de la Faille, P. de
1924   "De Chineesche Raad te Batavia en het door dit college beheerde fonds", BKI 80:302-24.
Roorda, D.J.
1978   Partij en factie. Groningen.
1983   "Het onderzoek naar het stedelijk patriciaat in Nederland", in: W.W. Mijnhardt (ed.), Kantelend geschiedbeeld, pp. 118-42. Utrecht.
Rouffaer, G.P. and J.W. IJzerman (eds)
1915,   De eerste schipvaart der Nederlanders naar Oost-Indië onder Cornelis
1925,   de Houtman 1595-1597. 's-Gravenhage. 3 Vols. [Linschoten-vereniging
1929   7, 25, 33.]
Salmon, Cl.
1972   "Un Chinois à Java (1729-1736)", Bulletin de l'Ecole Française d'Extrême-Orient 59:279-318.
1981   Literature in Malay by the Chinese of Indonesia: a provisional annotated bibliography. Paris.
Salmon, Cl. and D. Lombard
1977   Les Chinois de Jakarta; Temples et vie collective. Paris.
Sato Dokusho 佐藤獨嘯
1910   "Jagatara-bun no shin hakken" ジャカタラ文の新発見 [A new discovery of Jakarta-material], Rekishi Chiri 16:75-81, 164-75, 472-85.
Schlegel, Gustave
1899   "Bookreview of W.P. Groeneveldt's De Nederlanders in China", T'oung pao 8:518-31.
Schouwenburg, K.L. van
1986   "'Over de Nobels'; Genealogie en geschiedenis", De Nederlandsche Leeuw 103:3-71.
Schurz, W.L.
1939   The Manila galleon. New York.
Schutte, G.J.
1974   De Nederlandse patriotten en de koloniën. Groningen.

Schutte, O.
1980   Het Album Promotorum van de Academie te Harderwijk. Arnhem.
Schwarz, Georg Bernhardt
1751   Reise in Ost-Indien. Heilbronn.
Schweitzer, G.
1931   S.P. l'Honoré Naber (ed.), Reise nach Java und Ceylon 1675-1682. Haag. [Reisebeschreibungen von deutschen Beamten und Kriegsleuten im Dienst der Niederländischen West- und Ost-Indischen Kompagnien 1602-1797, vol. 11.]
Semmelink, J.
1885   Geschiedenis der cholera in Oost-Indië voor 1817. Utrecht.
Sjoberg, Gideon
1960   The pre-industrial city: past and present. Glencoe.
Sombart, Werner
1916   Der moderne Kapitalismus. Leipzig. 2 Vols.
Souza, G.B.
1981   Portuguese trade and society in China and the South China Sea, 1630-1754. Cambridge. [Ph.D. thesis.]
Stapel, F.W.
1927-47 (ed.), Pieter van Dam; Beschrijvinge van de Oostindische Compagnie. 's-Gravenhage. 7 Vols.
1936   "Cornelis Janszoon Speelman", BKI 94:1-222.
Stavorinus, J.S.
1798   Voyages to the East Indies. London. 3 Vols.
Steur, J.J.
1984   Herstel of ondergang; De voorstellen tot redres van de V.O.C. 1740-1795. Utrecht.
Suryadinata, Leo
1972   Prominent Indonesian Chinese in the twentieth century; A preliminary survey. Athens, Ohio.
Tavernier, J.B.
1682   De zes reizen van de heer J. Bapt. Tavernier [...]. Amsterdam. 2 Vols.
Taylor, Jean Gelman
1983   The social world of Batavia; European and Eurasian in Dutch Asia. Madison, Wis.
Telkamp, Gerard J.
1978   Urban history and European expansion. Leiden.
Terpstra, H.
1938   De factorij der Oostindische Compagnie te Patani. 's-Gravenhage.
Tien Ju-kang 田 汝康
1956   "Shih-ch'i shih-chi chih shih-chiu shih-chi chung-yeh Chung-kuo fan-ch'uan tsai tung-nan Ya-chou hang-yün ho shang-yeh shang te ti-wei" 十七世纪至十九世纪中葉中國帆船在東南亞洲航運和商業上的地位 [The place of Chinese sailing ships in shipping and trade of Southeast Asia from the 17th to the mid-19th centuries], Li-shih Yen-chiu 8:1-21.
1957   "Tsai lun shih-ch'i shih-chi chih shih-chiu shih-chi chung-yeh Chung-kuo fan-ch'uan-yeh te fa-chan" 再論十七世纪至十九世纪中葉中國帆船業的發展 [Another study of the development of the Chinese junk trade between the 17th and 19th centuries], Li-shih Yen-chiu 12:1-12.
1982   Causes of the decline in China's overseas trade between the fifteenth and eighteenth centuries. Canberra. [Papers on Far Eastern History 25.]
1985   The Chinese junk trade: merchants, entrepreneurs, and coolies, 1600-1850. [Unpublished paper, International Historical Congress, Stuttgart.]

Valentijn, F.
1724-26　Oud en nieuw Oost-Indiën [...]. Dordrecht/Amsterdam. 6 Vols.
Vermeulen, J.Th.
1938　De Chineezen te Batavia en de troebelen van 1740. Leiden.
1956　"Some remarks on the administration of justice", Nan Yang Hsüeh Pao 12-2:4-12.
Verseput, J. (ed.)
1954　De reis van Mathijs Hendriksz. Quast en Abel Jansz. Tasman ter ontdekking van de Goud- en Zilvereilanden (1639). 's-Gravenhage. [Linschoten-vereniging 56.]
Verzameling van verscheide echte stukken
1742　Verzameling van verscheide echte stukken van Batavia herwaarts gezonden. Dordrecht.
Vienne, M.-S. de
1979　Les Chinois dans l'archipel insulindien au XVIIe siècle. [Thesis University of Paris.]
Viraphol, Sarasin
1977　Tribute and profit: Sino-Siamese trade 1652-1853. Cambridge, Mass. [Ph.D. thesis.]
Vogel, Johann Wilhelm
1704　Zehen-Jährige Ost-Indianische Reise-Beschreibung [...]. Altenburg.
Volker, T.
1954　Porcelain and the Dutch East India Company as recorded in the Dagh-registers of Batavia castle, those of Hirado and Deshima and other contemporary papers 1602-1682. Leiden.
Wall, V.I. van de
1923　Vrouwen uit de Compagnie's tijd. Weltevreden.
1943　Oude Hollandsche buitenplaatsen van Batavia. Deventer.
Wang Gungwu
1981　Community and nation; Essays on Southeast Asia and the Chinese. Kuala Lumpur.
Wang Hsi-ch'i (ed.) 王錫祺
1877　Hsiao-fang-hu Chai Yü-ti Ts'ung-ch'ao 小方壺齋輿地叢鈔 [Collected texts on geography from the Hsiao-fang-hu Studio]. Shanghai. 3 Vols.
Wesseling, H.L.
1978　Expansion and reaction. Leiden
Weitzel, A.W.P.
1860　Batavia in 1858; Of schetsen en beelden uit de hoofdstad van Neêrlandsch Indië. Gorinchem.
Wills, John E.
1984　Embassies and illusions; Dutch and Portuguese envoys to K'ang-hsi, 1666-1687. Cambridge, Mass.
Winius, George Davison
1985　The black legend of Portuguese India; Diogo do Couto, his contemporaries and the "Soldado Prático". New Delhi.
Wittram, R.
1954　Baltische Geschichte. München.
Wijnaendts van Resandt, W.
1944　De gezaghebbers der Oost-Indische Compagnie op hare buitencomptoiren in Azië. Amsterdam.
Yamaguchi Yasuo 山口康夫
1978　Hirado-to no rekishi 平戸島の歴史 [A history of Hirado island]. Hirado.
Yamawaki Teijiro
1976　"The great trading merchants; Cocksinja and his son", Acta Asiatica 30:106-16.

Yokoi Tokifuyu 横井時冬
1927   Nihon Kogyo-shi 日本工業史 [History of Japanese industry].
        Tokyo.

INDEX OF PERSONAL NAMES

Aarden, Maurits van 94
Agung of Mataram, Sultan 23
Alberts, Martje 168
Albuquerque, Alphonso de 159
Almeida, Dom Francisco de 159
Alphen, Willem van 213, 216-8
Alting, Willem Arnold 143, 149-50, 260 n.10
Amangkurat II 248
Anda, Simon de 103
Antwerpen, Adriaan van 230
Aria Rana di Manggala 45
Aristotle 17
Audemard, L. 107-8

Backer, Cornelis 212
Bakker, P. 42-3
Barrow, John 106, 108
Bartholomeus, Grietgen 166-7
Batavia, Natalia van 170
Baukes, Nicolaas 211, 219, 245
Becom, Adriaen van 211, 244-5
Bencon (Su Ming-kang) 46, 51, 53-5, 60, 63-4, 69, 81, 84, 262 n.20
Bengalen, Monica van 170
Benting, Abelis 187, 266 n.33
Berg, N.P. van den 25
Bergsma, J. 29
Bevere, Gerard de 237-8, 243-4, 258
Bingam 80
Bitter, Aletta 253, 255, 267 n.38
Bitter, Arnolt 253, 255-6, 267 n.38, 269 n.73, 270 n.73
Bitter, Bartha 230, 253, 255-6, 267 n.38
Bitter, Eva 253, 255-6, 267 n.38
Bitter, Johan 178, 196-9, 201-3, 205-35, 237-51, 253-6, 258-9, 267 n.36, 268 n.49, n.60, 269 n.66, n.69
Blakeney, William 113
Blieck, Jan 223-4
Blom, Dirk 214
Blom, Wijbrand 135-7
Bloys van Treslong Prins, P.C. 7

Boetzelaer van Asperen en Dubbeldam, C.W.Th. baron van 11
Bogaert, Andries 188, 214
Boin, Michèle 96
Bolk, Daniël van der 244, 246
Bollemeijer, Albertine 9
Bonfield, L. 258
Bontekoe, Willem IJsbrandtz. 181
Bort, Balthazar 179, 214, 231-2
Both, Hendrick 255-6, 269 n.70
Both, Pieter 80, 158
Boxer, C.R. 159, 173, 199
Braam, J.P. van 150
Braam Houckgeest, A.E. van 107
Braudel, Fernand 33
Bree, J. la 197
Brelius, Theophylus 209
Breuning, H.A. 7
Broecke, Femmetje ten 188
Bronckhorst, Vincent 250
Brouwer, Hendrick 46, 61, 74, 81, 115, 162, 184, 189
Brunschwig, Henri 73
Brunswick, Duke of 188
Bruijn, J.R. 30

Camphuys, Joannes 87, 236-7, 239, 246, 259
Camps, Leonard 184
Cansius, Hendrick 174
Caron, François 188
Carpentier, Pieter de 50, 57-8, 63, 115, 264 n.1
Casembroot, Catrina 166-7
Casembroot, Nicolaes 166
Chastelein, Cornelis 24, 26-7, 88
Chang Hsieh 104
Charles, Catalina 168
Chaudhuri, K.N. 128
Chaunu, Pierre 103
Ch'en Hung-mou 134
Ch'en I-lao 134
Cheng (family) 117, 119-20
Cheng Ch'eng-kung (Coxinga) 85, 117, 119
Cheng Chih-lung 59-60
Cheng Ho 99

Index of Personal Names

Chien-lung 138
Chili Gonting 60
Ch'ing Fu, Duke 138-9
Ch'üan Han-sheng 104
Chijs, J.A. van der 48
Cleyer, Andries (Andreas) 232, 267 n.42
Cnoll, Anna 187, 240, 256
Cnoll, Catharina 179, 187
Cnoll, Cornelia see Cornelia van Nijenroode
Cnoll, Cornelis 187-8, 195, 205, 224, 233, 240-4, 247-8, 255-6
Cnoll, Elisabeth Catharina 187-8
Cnoll estate 243, 270 n.75
Cnoll family 179, 188, 192, 197, 233
Cnoll, Hester 179, 187-8
Cnoll, Jacobus Wijbrant 240, 256, 270 n.77
Cnoll, Martha 187-8
Cnoll, Pieter 179, 187-91, 193-6, 211, 234-5, 240, 266 n.31, 267 n.35
Cnoll, Pieter Jr. 187, 240
Coeman, Jacob Jansz. 179, 181, 189, 265 n.5
Coen, Jan Pietersz. 21, 24, 41-2, 45, 51-2, 54-5, 60, 73, 78-81, 105, 107, 158-61, 166, 169, 172, 181, 197, 264 n.1
Coenja, Lucia de 166-7
Coenja, Anthonijder 166
Coetenburgh, Adriaen 219
Comte, L. le 111
Con, Jan 8, 46-7, 49-60, 63-5, 67-72, 80, 261 n.11
Cook, James 29
Coppel, Charles 49
Correia, Germano da Silva 159
Cortenraede, Leon 253-4, 269 n.69
Couckebacker, Nicolaes 184-5, 188
Couper, Jacob 233, 248
Couperus, A. 15, 19
Couperus, P.T. 153
Couto, Diogo do 159
Coxinga see Cheng Ch'eng-kung
Cramers, Andries 166-7
Crawfurd, John 106, 109, 175
Crow, Carl 71
Cuneus, Joan 24
Cushman, Jennifer 101-3, 110, 138-9

Daendels, Herman Willem 16, 34
Dalton, George 35
Dam, Jacob van 209
Dam, Pieter van 10-1, 209, 212, 220, 228, 267 n.44, 268 n.51

Demmer, Gerard 24
Deursen, A.Th. van 257
Diemen, Antonio van 24-5, 47-8, 50, 63-4, 67, 69, 70-2, 162, 189, 265 n.10
Disponteyn, Davidt 202
Does, Jacob 206, 212, 214-5, 246-8, 268 n.53
Douglas, Abraham 93
Dubbeldekop, Hillegonda 240, 256, 270 n.75
Durven, Diederik 28, 89, 93

Es, Van 239, 242-3

Febvre, Lucien 9
Fockema Andreae, S.J. 257
Frazer, Antonia 173, 187
Frisius, mrs. Andries 188
Fu I-ling 99
Furber, Holden 3, 7, 147, 173-4
Furnivall, J.S. 5

Gaastra, F.S. 227
Gade, Frans 235
Glamann, Kristof 91, 130-1
Godric (of Finchal) 72
Goens, Rijckloff van 211-2
Goes, Martin van der 219
Graaff, Nicolaus de 172, 174-5, 229-30, 265 n.5
Gützlaff, Karl 106, 111

Haan, Frederik de 6-7, 9-11, 20, 51, 58, 63, 89-90, 168, 173, 211, 267 n.42
Haji of Riau, Raja 150
Hamada Sukeeimon 190-1, 266 n.24
Hamengku Buwono IV 48
Hammion 36-7
Handa Goeimon 190-1
Hartsinck, Hester 188, 202
Hay, Jan 212
Henderson, Alexander 256
Hermite, Jacques l' 21
Hertoge, M. de 219
Hesse, Elias 10
Heurnius, Justus 74
Heijningen, Rogier Thomas van 93
Hinlopen, Aletta 232
Hochepied, Isaacq 212, 267 n.43
Hoetink, B. 50-1, 75, 89, 94
Hoëvell, W.R. van 89, 94
Hogendorp, C.S.W. van 16
Hogendorp, Dirk van 33
Holte, Zegher ten 219
Hoorn, Joan van 88
Hoorn, Pieter van 24, 85
Hooyman, J. 91

Hope, Thomas 250
Houtappel, Hendrick 198
Houtman, Cornelis de 36
Hsieh Chao-chih 108
Hullu, J. de 130
Hurdt, Anthoni 224, 237-8
Huysers, Ary 95
Huysman, Anthony 193-4

Imhoff, Gustaaf Willem van 29, 31, 94, 141-2, 147
Intche Mouda 55
Iwao Seiichi 50, 177-8, 185, 187, 191

Jacobs, Leendert 167
Jan 205
Jan Con see Con, Jan
Jansz, Elsgen 167
Johnson, Marion 35
Jonge, J.K.J. de 31, 89, 91
Judith 207

Kainosho Kizaemon 190
Kan, J. van 197, 228-9, 259
K'ang-hsi, Emperor 119, 133-5, 263 n.3
Kao Ch'i-cho 133
Kao-tsung, Emperor 106
Kat Angelino, P. de 43
Keppel, Nicolaes 255
Ketting, Pieter 224
Keuchenius, W.M. 16
Keijsers 208-9
Kipling, Rudyard 15, 34
Kolff, D.H.A. 175
Kouw Hong-liang 148

Lackmoy 57
Leendersz., Andries 255
Leenderts, Aernout 167
Leguat, François 75
Lennep, David van 172, 175, 198
Leonard, Jane Kate 121
Lequin, F. 7
Leur, J.C. van 103
Li Ching-fang 139
Lim Khee-qua 125
Lim Lacco 55-6, 60, 63-5
Lin Heng-t'ai 96
Linschoten, Jan Huygen van 36
Lodewijcksz., Willem 42, 44
Lombard, D. 73
Loos-Haaxman, J. de 179
Lucasz., Philips 67, 69-71, 262 n.23
Luchtenburgh, Mattheus 215, 268 n.53
Lucretia 238

Lijn, Cornelis van der 26, 75, 83, 85, 117

Maetsuijcker, Johan 117, 192, 208-10, 214, 228
Manuel 168
Maria 168
Mastenbroek, W.E. 5
Matelieff, Cornelis 158
Matsu 111
Matsuura, family 108, 176-7
Maunier, René 169
Meilink-Roelofsz, M.A.P. 43
Meister, Georg 269 n.66
Ment, Eva 161
Mesquita, Maria 168
Michault, Frederik 243
Minne, Mr. and Mrs. 168
Modave, Duke of 33
Montesquieu, Ch.L. de 258
Mooy, J. 168
Moquette, J.P. 37
Mossel, Jacob 27, 31, 33, 147
Munter, Eghbert 212
Murakami Buzaemon(donne) 190-2
Muijzenberg, O.D. van den 6

Nakamura, T. 82
Neck, Jacob van 42
Nederburgh, S.C. 33, 150, 154
Ng Chin-keong 102-3, 119, 134
Ni Hoe-kong (Hoekong) 87, 89, 94, 137, 264 n.15
Nobel, Constantijn 193-5, 230, 253, 255
Nuyts, Pieter 182
Nijenroode, Cornelia van 3, 13, 172, 177-9, 182-5, 187-90, 192-4, 199, 201-3, 205-8, 210-2, 214-8, 220-6, 228, 230-2, 234-44, 247-8, 250-1, 254-6, 258-9, 268 no.53, n.58
Nijenroode, Cornelis van 177, 181-4, 189, 203
Nijenroode, Hester van 182-5, 187-8, 190-1, 203

Oba Osamu 108
Oentoeng see Surapati
Oeij Hingko 143
Ong Tai-hai 108, 112, 151
Ongtiko 110
Oosterhoff, J. 9, 263 n.1
Outgers, Christoffel van 24
Outhoorn, Willem van 123-4, 126-7, 136, 211, 223, 237, 239, 244-5
Overstraten, Petrus Gerardus van 34
Over't Water, Jacob 207-8, 268 n.49

Index of Personal Names

Palliacatte, Ursula van 170
Paravicini, J.A. 27
Parry, J.H. 3
Passigan, Alexander van 248
Pauw, Pieter 193
Payart see Thijssen Payart
Pays, Cornelius 205
Pirenne, Henri 72, 77
Pit, Marten 245
Pittavin, Abraham 85
Plutarch 11
Poelenburg, V. 220
Polanyi, Karl 38, 261 n.3
Putmans, Hans 59-60

Que Koenqua 125
Quiason, Serafin D. 102

Raffles, Thomas Stamford 16, 27, 89, 102
Ranst, Constantijn 198, 202, 237
Reed, R. 78
Reyersen, Cornelis 55-6, 181
Rhijne, Willem ten 244, 246
Riebeeck, Abraham van 93
Riemsdijk, Jeremias van 148-9
Robinson, Ronald 73
Rogers, Woodes 75, 129
Roman, Johan 169
Roorda, D.J. 254, 257
Roosenboom, George 225, 250-1
Roy, Nicolaes de 2201

Salmon, Claudine 49, 75, 77
Santen, Pieter van 184
Saris, John 40, 42, 105
Sastroamidjojo, Ali 97, 99
Sato Dokusho 190
Schaep, Dirck 198
Schagen, Nicolaas 245-6, 254
Schellebeecq, Christiaan van 256
Schlegel, G. 37
Scholten, Jan 166
Schouwenburg, K.L. van 255
Schrieck, Joan van 194
Schurz, William Lytle 103
Schuur, Joan Everhard van der 93
Schwarz, Georg Bernhardt 95
Scot, Edmund 41, 43
Shih Lang 121
Silva, Annika da 167
Silva, Paula da (alias Brouwa) 167
Siqua 87
Smith, Adam 4
Soecko 54
Solemne, Sarah de 188
Sombart, Werner 20
Sonck, Martinus 56, 181
Specx, Jacques 60-1, 161-2, 182, 262 n.17, 265 n.10
Speelman, Cornelis 174, 202, 211-2, 223, 231-2, 237, 240, 245, 267 n.42, 269 n.62
Spillebout, Maria 194
St. Martin, Isaac de 85, 88
Staets, Isaacq 213
Stapel, F.W. 10
Stavorinus, John Splinter 29, 108
Stepel, Johan 219
Sterrevelt, Adriaen van 225-6, 248-50
Stertemius, Joannes 168
Strantwyck, Gijsbrecht David 220-1
Su Ming-kang see Bencon
Succadana, Anna van 168
Sukeeimon see Hamada Sukeeimon
Sultan 23, 34, 38, 48, 73
Surapati 195, 267 n.35
Surishia 177, 182-3, 190
Suryadinata, Leo 49
Swaardecroon, Hendrick 93
Swoll, Christoffel van 93, 131

Tavernier, Jean-Baptiste 17, 175
Taylor, Jean Gelman 7, 10-1, 173
Tayouan, Paulinha van 170
Teggouw 57
Thrale, Mrs. 187
Thijssen Payart, Jan 117
Tien Ju-kang 97, 99-102, 106, 141, 151, 154
Tokeshio 182-3
Tresoir, Michael 187
Trip, Louis 216, 227, 268 n.47
Ts'ai Hsin 138, 154
Ts'e Leng 139
Tulp, Dirk 212, 216, 268 n.47

Usselinx, Willem 158
Uylenbroeck, Abraham van 256
Uylenbroeck, Jacobus van 256

Valckenier, Adriaan 138
Valckenier, Gilles 196-8, 202, 214, 216, 226, 268 n.47
Valdero 168
Valentijn, François 15, 25, 131, 154, 160, 211, 222, 232
Verbeek 203
Verburg, Nicolaes 117
Vermeulen, A.C.J. 9
Vermeulen, J.Th. 75, 89, 94, 263 n.1
Versluys, L. 220-1, 224
Verstegen, Willem 179
Vienne, Marie-Sybille de 8, 75, 120

Vinck, Cornelis 225-6
Viraphol, Sarasin 101-3
Vogel, Johann Wilhelm 269 n.66
Vosch, Balthazar Anthoni 269 n.69
Vrieslandt, Gerrit 195
Vuijrborn 207

Wall, V.I. van de 7, 173, 178
Wang Chih-i 151
Wang Gungwu 49
Wang P'i-lieh 134
Wangsan 107

Wei Yüan 121
Weitzel, A.W.P. 15
Westpalm, Michiel 137
Wicquevoort, Pieter 212, 214
Wills, John E. 120
Wit, Frederik de 58-9
Wonderaer, Petronella 223, 232
Wijnaendts van Resandt, W.Z. 173-4
Wijtens, P. 224

Zas, Theodorus 207-10, 223, 232
Zeeman, Gualtherus 214, 246

INDEX OF GEOGRAPHICAL NAMES

Aceh (Achin)   126, 128, 147, 150
Africa(n)   35-6, 45, 73-4, 99, 110, 161, 198
Ambon(ese)   5, 19, 23, 26, 148, 158, 165, 170, 179, 264 n.15
America(n)   102-3, 147, 199
Amoy   6, 9, 56, 59, 97, 100, 102-6, 108-9, 112-3, 117, 119-22, 125, 130-1, 133-4, 138, 142-3, 145-51, 153, 261 n.3
Amsterdam   15, 24-5, 117, 132-3, 140, 158, 162, 179, 196, 212-3, 216, 220, 229, 251, 255, 257, 268 n.47; see also Chamber of Amsterdam
Ancol (Antjol)   24, 128, 189
Anhai   59
Anké (Ankee)   24, 128
Annam(ese)   37
Antjol   see Ancol
Archipelago (Indonesian)   3, 8, 19-20, 30, 36-7, 47-8, 51, 55, 73, 78, 80, 83-4, 95, 99-100, 102-5, 120, 128, 141, 147-50, 153-4, 157, 159-60, 163, 165, 170, 181
Arnhem   196, 253
Asia(n)   3-4, 6, 9-11, 17, 24, 26-7, 30-1, 35, 42, 73-4, 78-9, 81, 91, 93, 97, 99, 105, 127-8, 130, 154, 156-8, 160, 162-3, 165-6, 172-3, 181
Austria(n)   132-3
Ayutthya   181

Bali(nese)   5, 18-9, 23-4, 26, 43, 48, 81-2, 84, 89, 165
Baltic   77-8
Banda(nese)   67, 148, 165, 168, 170
Banjar(masin)   129, 148
Banka   113, 148
Banten(ese)   3, 8, 21, 23-4, 36, 38-40, 42-8, 52-5, 57, 60, 64, 73, 80, 83-5, 90, 104-5, 114, 121, 128-9, 188, 248
Batavia(n)   1-13, 15-21, 23-31, 33-4, 44, 46-55, 57-61, 63-5, 67-8, 70-5, 77-81, 83-5, 87, 89-91, 93-7, 102-5, 107-8, 110-7, 119-42, 145-51, 153-63, 165-6, 168-75, 177-9, 181-5, 187, 190-1, 195-9, 202, 205-6, 210, 212, 214-30, 235, 238-9, 242, 246, 248, 253-5, 257-260 n.10, n.12, n.14, 262 n.17, n.20, n.25, 263 n.2, n.3, n.8, 264 n.9, n.20, 266 n.24, n.28, 269 n.62, n.73; seel also Oud Batavia
Batavia Castle (Casteel Batavia)   3, 8, 15, 21, 23, 34, 60, 63-4, 69, 74, 78-9, 82, 89, 93, 114, 135, 141, 165, 169, 174, 179, 188-9, 193, 195, 197-8, 223, 226-7, 269 n.66; see also Castle
Bengal(i)   19, 91, 123, 128
Bima   116
Bombay   33
Borneo   44, 46, 54, 106, 129, 147-8, 190
British   33, 147, 150, 153; see also English
Brunei   106
Bugis(nese)   19, 94, 150
Burma   23

Cairo Genizah   153
Calcutta   30, 33, 147
Cambodia   106
Canton(ese)   6, 37, 51, 70, 96-7, 100-1, 113, 119-20, 122, 129-33, 135-8, 140, 142, 146-8, 153, 263 n.1, n.8, 264 n.9, n.17
Cape Town   198, 246, 248
Casteel Batavia   see Batavia Castle
Celebes   44, 148
Ceram   248
Ceribon   see Cirebon
Ceylon(ese)   19, 94, 128, 165
Champa   106
Chan-Pi-Lo-shan (Pulau Cham)   113
Chang-chou   115
Chekiang   106, 119, 122, 132-3
Chenhai   97
Chi-chou   113
Chi-lung   125
Chin-chiang   117
China   9, 36-8, 42-5, 49, 51, 55, 57-

60, 68-70, 75, 80, 83, 87-9, 91, 96-7, 99-106, 110-1, 113, 115-7, 119-125, 127-30, 132-7, 139-41, 146-51, 153-4, 179, 181, 192, 262 n.4
China Sea see South China Sea
Chinese 1-6, 8-10, 13, 18-20, 24, 26, 36-40, 42-7, 49-54, 56-61, 63, 65, 67-75, 77-85, 87-91, 93-7, 99-111, 113-7, 119-20, 123-40, 142-3, 145-51, 153-4, 159, 161, 163, 165, 168, 175, 182, 190, 192-3, 202-3, 261 n.11, 262 n.17, n.25, n.4, n.5, 263 n.2, n.4, n.8, 264 n.14, n.17, n.21, 269 n.62; see also Overseas Chinese
Chiu-kang 113; see also Palembang
Ch'üan-chou region 36
Ciliwong 17, 23, 27, 60
Cirebon (Ceribon) 28, 46-8, 260 n.10
Cochin 132
Coromandel 165, 172, 188, 266 n.23

Danish 77, 130
Delft 179, 181, 184
Demak 38
Denmark 115
Depok 88
Deshima 166, 174, 176, 185, 190, 192
Duizend Eilanden (Pulau Seribu, Thousand Isles) 67, 91
Dutch 1-11, 16-7, 20-1, 23-6, 29, 31, 34, 36, 39, 42-3, 45-7, 49-53, 55-61, 63, 65, 68, 70, 73-5, 78-85, 87-8, 90, 94-6, 100, 103-9, 113, 115-7, 119-21, 125-32, 135-6, 138-41, 147-51, 153-4, 156-62, 165-74, 176-9, 181-2, 184-5, 188-90, 192, 194, 196, 199, 201, 203, 216, 228, 246, 249, 253, 259, 262 n.9, n.17, n.1, 265 n.13, 266 n.24, 267 n.40, 269 n.62
Dutch Republic 9, 21, 24, 31, 48, 50, 158, 163, 165, 169, 228, 244

East, the 158, 165, 172-4, 198, 213, 229; see also Orient
East Indies 37, 128, 158, 163, 216-7, 228, 262 n.17, 267 n.43
Edo 184
Egmond aan Zee 229
England 47, 173, 187, 198, 258
English(men) 21, 34, 39-41, 45, 47-8, 64, 75, 103-6, 109, 113, 115, 130, 132, 147, 150, 153, 185, 187, 189, 196, 198; see also British

Europe 29, 31, 34-5, 72, 95, 124, 128, 130-1, 135, 172, 201, 227
European(s) 2, 4, 8, 10, 15, 24, 26-7, 30, 35-6, 43, 73-4, 78-9, 91, 94, 99-102, 105, 108-9, 120, 123-5, 127-32, 135, 137, 140, 156, 173, 248

Far East 133, 217
Firando see Hirado
Formosa 58, 85, 125, 179, 181-2, 188
Fu-chou (Foochow) 100, 119, 121, 125
Fukien(ese) 37-8, 45, 52, 55-6, 58-60, 99, 102, 104-6, 109-10, 115, 117, 119, 122, 128, 130-5, 138-9, 147, 151, 153

Gelderland 64, 249-50
Goa 6, 36, 116, 159

Hague, The 7, 103, 188, 218-21, 225, 246, 249, 251
Hai-ch'eng 59, 104
Hainan(ese) 106, 113
Hirado 108, 176-8, 181-2, 184-5, 188, 190, 193
Holland (Low Countries, Netherlands) 3, 9, 15-6, 20, 25, 36, 42, 50, 64, 80, 83, 96, 119, 123-4, 132-3, 135, 137, 140-1, 154, 158, 160, 162-3, 172-3, 176, 178, 183-4, 188, 199, 201, 205-6, 212-6, 219-20, 223-9, 235, 239, 241, 243-5, 248-50, 253, 255-6, 258-9
Hsi Yang (western ocean) 104
Hsia-kang 104; see also Banten
Hsin-chou (Qui Nhon) 113
Hsin-ning 38
Hué 113

Iberian 73, 157
India(n, ns) 4, 31, 54, 81, 103, 105, 128-9, 135, 156, 158-60, 162, 165, 167, 172, 192, 196, 199, 228-9, 242-3
Indian Ocean 104-5, 123, 128, 135, 157
Indies 5, 25-6, 33, 80, 135-7, 154, 160-1, 168-9, 174, 179, 181, 184, 188, 193, 195-8, 207, 210-1, 213-4, 219-20, 226-9, 231-2, 235-7, 241-3, 245, 250, 255-6, 258, 269 n.70
Indonesia(n) 8, 11, 23, 42, 47-8, 51, 73, 77-8, 94, 97, 99-100, 102, 105, 142, 147, 157, 163, 165, 182, 242

Index of Geographical Names

Jakarta 3, 7, 21, 23, 36, 45, 52, 73, 77, 80, 104-5, 156
Jakatra 18, 24, 189
Jambi 43, 46-7, 105, 116
Japan(ese) 5, 79, 83, 104, 106, 117, 119, 121, 132, 142, 157, 159, 161, 166, 174, 176-8, 181-2, 184-5, 187-93, 232, 266 n.24, n.26, n.27, n.28
Japara 46-7, 116
Java(nese) 1, 4, 8, 16, 19, 23, 26-8, 33-6, 38-9, 41-2, 44, 46-8, 57, 64, 73, 77-8, 80, 83-5, 88-91, 97, 104-5, 109-10, 115, 121, 134, 137, 139, 143, 148-9, 151, 154, 195, 248, 263 n.2, 266 n.26
Johore 117, 126, 128, 149

Kedah 147
Kiangsu 132-3
Krawang 84-5
Kuala Selangor 147
Kun Lun (Pulau Condor) 113
Kwakiutl Indians 35
Kwangsi 138
Kwangtung 38, 106, 119, 122, 134, 138-9
Kyushu 176

Leiden 188, 194, 244
Li Mountains 106
Ligor 117
Ling-shan (Cape Varella) 113
Lisbon 159
London 109
Low Countries see Holland
Luzon 104, 132

Macao 116, 119-20, 123, 132, 159, 263 n.2
Macassar see Makassar
Madeira 27
Madras 33, 147
Madura 34, 48
Makassar(ese) (Macassar) 19, 47, 84, 108, 116, 148, 264 n.18
Malabar 19, 93, 165, 172, 269 n.72
Malacca see Malaka
Malaka (Malacca) 19, 75, 80, 117, 128, 132, 148-50, 159, 165
Malaka, strait of 105, 113
Malay(s) 19, 104, 148-9, 165, 170, 211, 244
Maldive islands 128
Manchu(s) 117, 119, 121, 127
Mangga Dua 84
Manila 78-9, 96, 102-4, 107, 132-4, 159, 264 n.20
Mardijker(s) 18, 67, 163, 165-6, 168-70
Maronde 128
Martapura 47
Mataram 23, 25, 42, 83-5
Matsuura 108, 176-7
Meester Cornelis 24
Mexico 78
Middelburg 196-7
Middle Kingdom (China) 124, 165
Moluccas(ans) 104-5, 158, 165, 169, 244
Mongol 99
Mookervaart 27-8
Moor(ish, s) 84, 242

Nagasaki 75, 119, 166, 190-1, 259, 263 n.3
Nagasaki Bay 176, 185
Nanking 100
Nanyang 60, 99-100, 102, 106-7, 121, 133-4, 139, 151, 154
Netherlands, the see Holland
New York 109
Nieuwe Poort 202
Ningpo (Ning-po) 97, 100, 125, 142-3, 146, 148, 264 n.20
Noordwijk 15

Ommelanden 8, 16-8, 20-1, 23-8, 64, 84-5, 88-91, 93-4, 96, 121, 126, 131, 136, 189, 195
Onrust Island 174
Oosthoek 48
Orient 30, 36, 158-9, 172, 175, 181, 227
Ostend 132
Overseas Chinese 49-50, 55, 99, 120, 134-5, 139; see also Chinese

Palembang 46-8, 113, 116, 148
Pasisir 114
Patani (Pattani) 116-7, 181
Pearl River 113, 119, 129-30
Pekalongan 75
Peking 107, 119, 122, 133
Penang 150
Persia 91, 93
Pescadores 55-6, 181
Philippines 58, 99-100, 102, 265 n.9
Portsmouth 198
Portugal, Portuguese 1, 24, 36, 105, 116, 119, 123, 126, 132-3, 156, 158-63, 165, 170, 172-3, 185, 187-8, 192, 195, 199, 239, 266 n.27
Priangan 6
Pulicat 165

Qui Nhon 113

Quinam   184

Riau (archipelago)   147, 150
Riga   77
Rijswijk   15, 24
Ryukyu Islands   104

Salak volcano   16-7, 27
Sangora   117, 181
Semarang   38, 48, 114, 260 n.14
Shanghai   100
Siam(ese)   23, 47, 100-2, 106, 111, 117, 181
Singapore   102, 153, 263 n.5
Solent   198
Solo   34
Solor   58
South America(n)   35, 104, 158
South China Sea   6, 102, 105, 109, 135, 147, 153, 157
Southeast Asia(n)   3, 5-6, 10, 12, 38, 49-50, 59, 70, 74, 78, 85, 97, 99, 104, 110, 113, 115-7, 120, 128, 133-4, 139-40, 147-9, 153, 177
Southern Ocean   60, 99, 131, 139; see also Nanyang
Spanish (Spaniards)   57, 79, 100, 102-4, 159, 192, 199, 262 n.4
St. Helena   109
Sukadana   148
Sulawesi   19
Sulu Islands   104
Sumatra   19, 38, 42, 44, 46, 48, 54, 113, 148
Sumenep   48
Sunda, strait of   38, 80, 105
Sunda Kalapa   36, 38, 104-5
Surabaya   34, 48
Surakarta   248
Surat   214

Swatow   6

Taiwan(ese)   55-60, 69, 116-7, 119, 121, 262 n.20
Tallinn   77
Tanah Abang   94
Tangerang   24, 189
Tangerang river   27, 128
Tanjongpura   24
Tartar(s, y)   88, 127, 132
Ternate   148, 246
Texel   198, 248
Thousand Islands   see Duizend Eilanden
Timor(ese)   19, 58, 116
Tioman Island   113
Tonkin (China)   132, 188
Tung-an   147
Tung Yang (eastern ocean)   104
Tijgergracht   15, 189, 224, 233-4

Ujung Pandang   8
United Provinces   160; see also Dutch Republic
Utrecht   253, 255

Vietnam(ese)   37, 100, 106, 113

Wai-Lo-shan (Pulau Canton)   113
Weltevreden   15-6, 29, 34, 155
West Indies   27, 91, 158
Westerkwartieren   123
Whampoa   130
Wu-hsü Island   112
Wu I Mountains   131

Yemen   157
Yung-chun   115

Zeeland   196, 218
Zeelandia Castle   59, 116-7, 119

SUBJECT INDEX

ARA see Algemeen Rijksarchief
acculturation 156, 163, 168
Acta (of the Church Council) 2, 11, 156, 168-70, 178, 207, 265 n.10
administration 1-2, 4-6, 8-10, 16-7, 38, 52, 54, 58, 65, 67-71, 77, 79, 88, 91, 95-7, 102, 104, 115, 121-2, 124, 127-8, 139, 158, 161-3, 165-6, 170, 185, 193, 197, 202, 207, 217, 228-9, 232, 234, 241, 243-5, 247, 250-1, 257-8
administrator 109, 201
admiral 55, 99, 121, 150, 158, 181, 230, 248, 267 n.42
adultery 54, 167-8
advocaat 212, 255, 268 n.51
agriculture (al, alists) 20, 26, 39, 74, 84-5, 95, 121, 127, 145
alderman 198, 212; see also Bench of Aldermen
Algemeen Rijksarchief (ARA) 3, 9, 246, 263 n.1
ambassador(s) 55-7, 101, 107, 188
ammunition 46, 94
ancien régime 1, 9-10, 12-3, 31, 156, 172, 256
armistice 23, 54, 64
army 94, 119, 195, 240
arrest(s) 220-1, 224, 226, 242, 246, 250-1; see also mandate of arrest
Arsip National 3, 77
assimilation 163, 165
attorney(s) 198, 220, 223, 250

bail 249, 251
bailiff 88, 207, 218, 220, 224
bakufu 192
bamboo(s) 108, 131
ban 117, 121-2, 127, 132, 150, 223; see also maritime prohibition
bankrupt(cy) 93, 96, 138, 153
baptism(s) 170, 173, 177, 187-8, 240
barbarian(s) 55, 96, 135, 139
barracks 169, 240
barrister(s) 178, 197, 219, 243, 245

"Bataviasche statuten" 25, 71, 162, 185, 228, 267 n.35
batik 191, 266 n.26
Bench of Aldermen 3, 5, 26, 87, 166-7, 197, 202, 224, 241-2, 254, 258; see also alderman
Bench of Magistrates 81, 88; see also magistrate
"Beschrijvinge" 220, 228, 232, 268 n.51
betel nuts 10, 156
bill(s) of exchange 212, 226, 235
biography(ical) 11, 52, 71-2, 179, 257
bird's nests 54, 116
blockade 45, 53, 57
boedelmeesters 70, 82, 87; see also curators
bookkeeping 104-5, 158, 179, 193, 211
bribe(s) 89, 91, 95
brigands 64, 121
broker(s) 49, 52, 60, 77, 83, 87, 140, 175
burgher(s) 5, 10, 20, 24-5, 29, 31, 61, 65, 67, 70, 95, 126, 161-3, 171, 189-90, 257-8, 266 n.28, 267 n.35, n.40
burgomaster 196, 254-5, 268 n.47

caixa(s) (caxas) 36-7, 41-2
camphor 54, 190
canal(s) 15-6, 23, 27-8, 34, 52, 58, 60-1, 63, 67-8, 80, 189, 260 n.9, 262 n.19
cannon(s) 94, 106, 229
capitation tax see head tax
Captain 51, 53-4, 65, 75, 81-2, 84, 87-91, 93-6, 104, 109-11, 114, 125, 127, 137, 143, 145, 148, 188; see also chief
cargo(es) 97, 103, 105, 109-11, 116, 120, 122, 125, 132, 142-3, 146, 150-1
carriage(s) 189, 222
Casa de Misericordia 159, 162
cash crops 26, 99, 104, 154
cashier(s) 174, 179, 211, 226
cassowary 248, 269 n.66

Castellenije 249, 251
castle 45, 77-80, 82, 176, 253; see also Batavia Castle
catty(ies) 48, 106, 266 n.23
caxas see caixa
census 9-10, 18
Ceylon (ship) 198
Chamber (of Amsterdam) 135, 196-7, 212, 214, 216, 226, 248
Chia-ch'ing period 153
chief(s) 4, 24-5, 79, 81, 96, 104, 108, 174, 195; see also Captain
chief-merchant(s) 10, 179, 184, 189; see also head-merchant; opperkoopman
ch'ien 36-7
"Chih-nan Cheng-fu" 112, 263 n.3
China Town 73, 79
Chinese massacre 20, 26, 31, 73-5, 89, 96-7, 138, 262 n.25
Ch'ing dynasty 100-1, 117, 119-21
"Ch'ing-ch'ao Wen-hsien T'ung-k'ao" 134, 139
christian(s) 103, 162-3, 165-6, 168-70, 192, 215, 217-8, 223, 231-2, 251, 266 n.24
chronicle(r, s) 75, 89, 178
Ch'u-hai 107, 109-10
Church 11, 23, 159, 162-3, 165-71, 173-4, 187-9, 205, 211, 224, 232, 238, 241, 244, 253, 258; see also Reformed Church
Church Council 2, 11, 156, 163, 167-9, 171, 178, 205-11, 215, 217, 219, 223-4, 231, 235, 238, 267 n.41, 268 n.49
citizen(s, ry) 79-81, 91, 97, 107, 115, 124, 159, 162, 165, 181, 263 n.4
citizen soldiery 25, 165; see also soldier
city 18, 20, 51, 78-80, 89-91, 94, 96
City Council (vroedschap) 24, 31, 159, 254-5
city wall(s) 65, 67-9, 71, 77, 79-80, 84, 89, 189
clan(s) 114, 117
clergyman (men) 165, 167, 170, 179, 207-8
cleric(s, al) 11, 74, 158, 163, 173, 258, 268 n.46
clerks 110, 165
cloth 105, 116, 125, 192, 212, 266 n.23
cloves 105, 110, 116, 124-6, 135, 140
coconut 53, 168
coffee 20, 26, 43
coin(s) 2, 8, 36-9, 42-6, 48, 63-4, 116, 135, 138, 151

collaboration 73-4, 87, 96, 103
colonial(ists) 3, 8, 10, 13, 18, 50-2, 70, 73-4, 77-9, 99-100, 102-3, 124, 131, 155, 161, 165-6, 170, 179, 187, 197, 238, 253
colonization 80, 157-60, 162-3, 172
colonize(rs) 73, 78, 156, 158, 161
colony(ies) 21, 24-5, 81, 85, 94-5, 105, 127, 140, 148, 157-9, 162-3, 168, 228
commander 58-9, 181
commissary(ies) 88-9, 193
commission(ers) 93, 220, 250-1
Commissioner-General 33, 150, 154
committee 140, 208, 223
communion see Holy Communion
Company (Dutch East India Company, East India Company, Verenigde Oost-Indische Compagnie) 3-6, 8, 10, 16, 18, 20-1, 24-6, 30-1, 33-4, 46, 48, 50-1, 54-5, 58-60, 64-5, 67-8, 71-5, 77, 79-85, 87, 89-91, 93-5, 103, 105, 115-7, 119-21, 123-7, 129, 132, 135-7, 140-2, 148-50, 154-5, 158-63, 165-6, 170-1, 173-5, 179, 181, 184-5, 189, 192, 195-9, 206, 211-2, 214, 220, 226-8, 234-6, 241, 243-4, 250-1, 258, 264 n.16, 265 n.5, 268 n.51, n.53
Company official(s) 16, 20-1, 24-5, 65, 80, 87, 120
Company personnel 30, 157, 198
Company servants 1, 10, 23, 29-30, 33, 67, 69, 74, 81, 83, 87, 94, 124-5, 128, 161-3, 165, 173-5, 181, 184-5, 197, 199, 208, 210, 215, 228, 259, 267 n.43, n.44, 268 n.46
concubinage 159, 161, 166, 169-70, 173
concubine(s) 163, 177, 182
confiscate 146, 184, 187
consultation 219-20
consumers' market 51, 71; see also market
contract(ors) 49, 60, 65, 68-9, 80, 201-2, 245
coolies 26-7, 48, 52-5, 58, 94, 97, 114, 122
copper 31, 36-8, 43-4, 46, 48, 142
corruption 89, 91, 95-6, 159
corvée 24, 28
cotton 191-2, 266 n.23, n.26
Council 17, 56, 65, 68, 71, 77, 82, 87-9, 93, 127, 133, 135, 141-2, 146, 148, 159, 161, 163, 166, 184-5, 197-8, 206-11, 215, 219, 223, 227-32, 235-46, 259; see also Church Council, City Council
Council of the Indies 25-6, 135-6, 154,

Subject Index 295

193, 195, 197, 207, 211, 214, 235-7, 241-3, 245
Council of Justice 3, 196, 198, 202, 207, 210, 214, 227-9, 254, 269 n.72
councillor(s) 94, 135-6, 205, 211, 238, 244, 246
councillor of the Indies 179, 188, 211, 232, 258, 269 n.70
councillor of justice 198-9, 238, 243, 245, 259
counsellor(s) 39, 57, 188
counterfeit 37-8
country houses 7, 85
country traders 147, 150, 264 n.20
court 89, 94, 99, 107, 134, 138-9, 151, 188, 197, 207, 213-21, 224-7, 235, 237, 239-40, 243, 245-6, 248-9, 251
Court of Holland 3, 205, 216, 219-20, 225-7; see also High Court, Provincial Court
Court of Justice 175, 178, 184, 197, 201, 205-9, 211, 213-4, 217-20, 223, 226-8, 234-40, 242, 244-6, 258
cowrie(s) 35, 44-5
craftsmen 52, 57
credit 39, 43-4, 51, 67, 69-71, 93
curators 50, 69-70, 243-4; see also boedelmeesters
currency 42, 45-6, 63
customs 114, 122, 125, 127, 134, 142-3, 145

Daghregisters 8-9, 47, 75, 120
dai-feitor 191, 266 n.27
deacons 167, 223
decree 201, 242
deity(ies) 110-1
desa(s) 28, 88-9
diamond(s) 31, 54, 181, 183, 206, 212-6, 222, 226-7, 267 n.44
Director-General 67, 69-71, 88, 93-4, 137, 193, 211-2, 223, 231, 237-8
directorate 17, 25, 31, 129, 158, 227, 267 n.44
directors 9, 20, 42, 64, 117, 121, 124, 130, 136, 154, 158, 162, 194, 196, 198, 206, 212-4, 216, 226, 228-9, 258
disease(s) 8, 16, 33, 173, 182-3
divorce 206-7, 213-5, 240
dollars 109, 194, 201, 250; see also rixdollars
domestic(s) 19, 205-6, 217
dues 115, 134
duiten 46, 48
Dutch East India Company (Company, East India Company, Verenigde Oost-Indische Compagnie) 1, 9, 15, 17,
21, 36, 46, 50, 106, 114, 128, 130, 133, 156-7, 178, 212, 226
Dutch Reformed Church see Reformed Church
duty(ies) 104, 114-5, 122, 130, 136, 141-2, 153

East India Company (Company, Dutch East India Company, Verenigde Oost-Indische Compagnie) 11, 73, 95, 129, 147, 158, 172, 174, 195-6, 213, 216-7, 220, 225-6, 229
East Indiaman 99, 198, 206, 229
ecology 7, 15, 17, 21, 26-8
edict(s) 25, 125, 132, 141, 145, 192, 221, 264 n.16
Eenhoorn (ship) 248
elder(s) 87, 167, 207, 209, 231
elephant (tusks) 115-6, 150
élite 1, 8, 10, 20, 73-4, 87, 127, 154, 174-5, 189, 192, 198-9, 246, 257
embezzle(ment) 212-3, 242
emigrant(s) 109-10, 135, 158
emigrate(ion) 94, 134, 147, 160
Emperor of China 37, 55, 88, 99, 119, 131-6, 138-9
empire 129, 132, 138, 150, 192
emporium 19-20, 48, 150
ensign 80, 188, 194
entrepot 147, 150, 153-5
Essex (ship) 132
estate(s) 7, 50, 69-70, 88, 184, 193-4, 232, 241, 243-5, 256, 258, 269 n.62, 270 n.75, n.77
Europa (ship) 206, 212, 216
exactions 123, 129
exemption 81, 84
expansion (European) 3, 9, 13, 99
expedition(s) 135, 179, 181, 195

factor(y, ies) 116, 149, 161, 174, 177, 181-2, 185, 214; see also trade factory
farmer(s) 3, 26, 52, 115, 126, 133, 138, 159
fish(ing) 20, 38, 52, 63, 74, 106, 149, 176, 199, 229
fleet(s) 23, 95, 99-100, 103, 147, 159, 181, 198, 215, 223, 230, 239, 246, 248
fortress(es) 55-6, 79, 157, 181
fraud(s) 50, 69
freeburgher(s) 1, 10, 20, 24, 79-83, 85, 119-20, 158, 162, 174, 195, 197, 235, 240, 268 n.53

Galjas (ship) 185
gambling 53-4, 68, 82, 125, 261 n.3

gardening 23-4, 26, 52, 84, 145, 150
garrison 23, 34, 77, 82, 117, 159-60, 165
Gazetteer(s) 102, 105-6, 153, 261 n.3
Generale Missive(n) 9, 50, 61, 67, 123, 126, 132, 184, 239; see also missive
Gentlemen XVII (Heeren XVII) 9, 20-1, 24-6, 41, 46, 48, 50, 70, 80-1, 89, 91, 105, 115, 117, 119-20, 124, 126-8, 130, 132-3, 135-7, 140, 153-5, 158, 160-2, 172, 184, 189, 196-7, 213-6, 226-9, 231, 258-9, 268 n.51
gold 57, 142, 148, 151, 250
gongs 58, 111
Goudestein (ship) 174, 246, 248
Governor(s) 19, 55, 58-60, 103, 117, 133-4, 138, 151, 188, 190-1, 264 n.1
Governor of Fukien 55, 133-4, 151
Governor of Malacca 19, 117
Governor of Taiwan 58, 60, 117
Governor(s)-General 9, 16-7, 21, 24-9, 31, 33-4, 46-7, 50, 54-60, 63-5, 68-71, 74-5, 80-1, 83, 85, 87-9, 93, 115, 117, 123-7, 131, 133, 135, 138-9, 141-3, 146-50, 154, 158, 161-3, 172, 174, 182, 184-5, 189, 192, 195, 197, 206-11, 214-5, 219, 227-32, 235-46, 255, 259, 260 n.10, 262 n.4, n.5, 264 n.1, 268 n.49
gracht 15, 63, 189, 224, 233-4
guardian(s, ship) 194, 201, 243-4, 250-1, 255-6, 264 n.1
guilder(s) 36, 120, 126, 130, 133, 136, 176, 179, 183, 185, 195, 198-9, 214, 253-4, 256, 266 n.31, 269 n.62, n.73, 270 n.73
guilds 75, 107; see also Yang-hang

Hakka 147
handicraft 20, 74, 99
harbour (payments) 115-6, 125, 136
harbourmaster 67, 114, 145
head-merchant 179, 181, 190, 193; see also chief-merchant; opperkoopman
head tax(es) (capitation tax) 10, 58, 114, 125-7
heathen(s) 163, 168-9
Heeren (Heren) XVII see Gentlemen XVII
Heusden (ship) 182-3
High Court (of Holland) 3, 250-1; see also Court of Holland, Provincial Court
High Government (of Batavia) (Hoge Regering) 3-4, 9, 26, 54, 56, 60, 63-5, 67, 69-70, 72, 119, 124, 127, 130, 132-5, 137, 140-1, 143, 145-50, 154-5, 219, 236, 260 n.14, 264 n.17

Ho-ho-ch'eng Yang-hang 153
Hoge Regering see High Government
Holy Communion 167, 169-71, 178, 205, 209, 223-4, 231-2
Honsei temple 177
horticulture(alists) 74, 165
hospital(s) 29-30, 70, 75, 79, 83, 87
"Hsia-men Chih" 9, 105, 153
Hsien-ping period 37
hua-chiao 49-50, 52

immigrants 82, 85, 87, 91, 102, 105, 115, 131, 145, 187
immigration 3, 80, 85, 90-1, 95, 97, 127-8, 141, 145
imperial 73, 99, 102, 121, 132, 138
imperial court 104, 119, 132, 138-9, 154
imperial government 26, 100-1, 117, 119
import(s) 122, 142, 145, 153, 192-3, 263 n.1
Indischman 10, 244
inheritance(s) 82, 87, 179, 184, 194, 202, 245, 248, 256, 258
interpreter(s) 59, 104
irrigation 16-7, 27
Islam(ic) 52, 168

Jan Compagnie 1, 177
Jesuit(s) 159, 169
judge 215, 225, 236-7, 241, 243, 258
junk(s) 10, 39, 41-4, 46, 52, 57-9, 63, 68, 75, 80, 83, 87, 91, 97, 99-103, 105-11, 113-7, 119-43, 145-51, 153-5, 263 n.2, n.3, n.5, 264 n.9, n.20
jurisdiction 228, 249
justice 167, 228, 257; see also Council of Justice; Court of Justice

"Kai-pa Li-tai Shih-chi" 68, 75, 96
kampong(s) 24, 26, 77, 84, 89
Keicho period 192
kèpèng 43, 48
keris 54, 182
Keying (ship) 109
king(s) 36-7, 75, 96, 101, 104, 158
kingdom 124, 165, 195
kinship 75, 102, 163
koopvrouw 201-2
kraton 21, 54-5

labour(ers) 28, 52, 60, 83, 85, 90-1, 94, 110, 121, 127, 165
Land van Schouwen (ship) 214
landowner(ship) 20, 24, 26
's Lands Welvaren (ship) 246

Landsarchief 3, 6, 185
Law Court 89, 213-4, 220, 235
lawsuit(s) 166, 209, 224, 255, 264 n.17
lawyer 196, 198-9, 205, 208, 215, 231, 234, 248, 255, 257
lead(en) 2, 8, 35-9, 43-8, 63-4, 126, 136
legislation 3-4
letter (carriers) 83, 111, 146
licence(s) 104, 114, 148
lieutenant(s) 81, 87, 90-1, 93, 125, 127, 134, 148, 187-8, 263 n.2
lime 61, 63, 67, 69
lineage(s) 102, 117
lumberjacks 53, 67

magic 167, 242
magistrate(s) 79, 81, 199; see also Bench of Magistrates
mandarin(s) 51, 59, 65, 110
mandate of arrest 216-9, 225, 248; see also arrest
manumission 195, 207, 215, 267 n.35
marauder 53, 85, 88
marital affairs 188, 193
maritime prohibition(s) 26, 38, 99, 131-4, 136, 138, 176-7; see also ban; prohibitions
market 4, 8, 19, 21, 23-4, 26-7, 36, 38-40, 42-6, 48, 51, 55, 58, 63-4, 71, 74, 77-8, 82, 84, 91, 96, 100, 102-5, 115, 120, 123-5, 128, 130, 132-3, 135-6, 140-1, 143, 147, 150-1, 154, 159, 253, 261 n.3; see also consumers' market; staple market
marriage(s) 159, 161, 166-70, 172-4, 176-8, 185, 187, 194, 199, 201-3, 217, 227, 240, 250-1, 254-5, 257-8; see also marry
marriage settlement(s) 207, 215, 217-9
marry 162-3, 166-7, 169, 171, 173, 175, 199, 201, 251; see also marriage
massacre see Chinese Massacre
merchant(s) 4, 10, 31, 36, 40, 44-5, 47, 50-1, 55, 58-9, 64, 68, 70-2, 74, 87, 96-7, 99-101, 103-10, 114, 120, 122, 128-36, 139-40, 142, 145-6, 148-9, 151, 153, 157, 159, 161, 163, 166, 173, 176, 179, 181-2, 184, 189-90, 192, 212, 264 n.17, 266 n.27, 267 n.35, 268 n.47
mestizo(s) 1-2, 5, 8, 26, 84, 163, 165, 170, 172-3
middlemen 49, 53, 71, 87, 100, 125, 150

migrant(s) 81, 161
migration 15-6
military 34, 59, 77, 81, 159, 163, 165, 171
militia 58, 188, 195
Ming dynasty 38, 85, 99, 104, 117, 119, 121, 127, 133
mission(ary) 11, 106, 156
missive 221, 224; see also Generale Missive
money 35, 38-9, 42-8, 50-3, 55, 58, 67-8, 81, 85, 93, 125, 132, 139, 141, 146, 150-1, 155, 168, 174, 184, 192, 201, 203, 206, 211-5, 217, 226, 234-5, 241, 243, 245, 251, 255-6, 267 n.40, 269 n.62, n.73
money lenders 70, 83, 126, 162, 175
monopoly(ies) 31, 33, 39, 45, 47, 63, 74, 77, 83, 97, 101, 103, 105, 115, 117, 119-20, 128, 132-3, 136, 147, 155, 157-9, 163, 192
monsoon(s) 27, 38, 56, 59, 64-5, 109, 111, 114-5, 133, 145, 222
mortality 17, 27-31, 260 n.12
mortgage 201, 203
murder 88, 95, 139, 167
Muslim(s) 38, 169

nachoda(s) 10, 57-8, 63, 87, 91, 109, 114-7, 123, 125, 127-8, 131-2, 143, 145-6, 149-50, 263 n.4, 264 n.14, n.17; see also skipper
Nieuw Hoorn (ship) 160
notarial archives 3, 77, 185, 253, 256
notary 198, 202, 208-9, 212, 224, 234, 239, 242-3, 255-6
numismatic(al) 36-7
nutmeg 105, 116, 140

opium 31, 99
opperkoopman 191, 193, 195, 266 n.27; see also chief-merchant; head-merchant; merchant
orang baru 114, 127, 146, 215, 244
ordinance(s) 25-6, 97, 143, 194, 264 n.1; see also plakaat
orphan(age) 5, 79-80, 82-3, 87, 159-62, 185
Orphan Board (Weeskamer) 3, 162, 185, 187, 194, 241, 256, 270 n.77
"Oud Batavia" 6-7, 9, 51, 90, 156
outlaws 91, 93, 132
Ouwerkerk (ship) 108
Overgekomen brieven en papieren 9, 123, 145

pagoda(s) 110, 177

pangeran 21, 23, 38, 42, 45, 52, 54-5, 57, 73, 80, 105
"Papegay" 213, 216, 219, 224
parson(s) 207, 219, 267 n.41
pasar 39, 44, 46, 63
passage 145, 198, 241, 246, 248, 256
passenger(s) 91, 97, 109-11, 115, 124, 127-8, 131, 136, 143, 145-7, 150, 160, 198
patrol(s) 148, 153
payong 195, 267 n.35
peace (treaty) 24, 57, 85, 90, 115, 188
peku 40, 42
pepper 26, 31, 36, 38-41, 44-6, 53, 55, 59, 104-5, 110, 115-6, 124-6, 130, 135-7, 140, 147-9, 264 n.20
pepper cultivation 38-9, 44
perioeci 78, 159
physician 172, 174
picis 8, 19, 35-48, 63
picul(s) 46-7, 59, 64, 109-10, 125, 134, 137, 141, 148-9, 263 n.2
pilot(age) 109-10
piracy 104, 106, 132, 151
pirate(s) 59-60, 104, 113, 133, 153, 176
plakaat 26, 127, 131, 141, 145; see also ordinance
Plakaatboek(en) 2, 9, 75, 145, 153, 193, 213
plantation(s) 52, 64, 68, 85, 90-1, 94, 126, 137
planter(s) 43-4
plunder(ing) 55, 94-5
plural society 5-6
pogroms 78, 95-6
poison(ing) 166-7, 169
Polder Board 3, 26, 240
poll tax(es) 80-1, 83-4, 87, 89-91, 262 n.5; see also tax
poor relief 65, 127
porcelain 43, 104-5, 115, 124-6, 128, 135, 137, 143, 149, 153, 192, 256, 263 n.5, 264 n.14
port 78, 80, 142
porters 48, 150
pothia 90-1
potions 166-7
Potlatch 35
prahu 67, 126
priest(s) 110, 242
prince(ly, s) 34, 52, 77, 87, 260 n.10
private trade 20, 31, 33, 59, 87, 104, 119-20, 126, 137, 141, 158, 174, 184, 191, 201, 211, 213-4, 226, 258, 265 n.5, 267 n.44, 268 n.46

privileges 159, 241
prohibition(s) 133-4, 138-9, 151, 154, 173, 192, 214; see also ban; maritime prohibition
Provincial Court (of Holland) 216, 218, 248-50; see also Court of Holland, High Court
proxy 221, 255
public prosecutor 214, 246

rampart(s) 64, 68-9
real(s) 36, 41-3, 46-8, 54, 80, 226; see also rial
"Realia" 2, 75, 213
reconciliation 238, 243
redemption (fees) 142-3, 149
Reformed Church 156, 162-3, 165-7, 169, 185, 188, 253; see also Church
regent(s) 39, 190, 192, 253, 255
regulation(s) 17, 163, 184
religion 156, 162-3, 165, 167, 170, 192
rent(s) 20, 93
Resolutieboek 67, 212
resolution(s) 131, 141, 146, 148, 166, 185, 207, 209, 215, 227, 239, 246, 263 n.2
revenue(s) 114, 116, 151
reverend 74, 168, 205, 207-9, 223, 232, 238, 270 n.75
revision 227-9, 231, 242-3, 245, 249
revolt 84, 94, 119
rial(s) 46, 50, 55, 58-60, 63-5, 67-71, 83, 99, 104, 109, 116, 131, 151, 168, 189; see also real
rice 23-4, 26, 34, 57-8, 95, 104, 106, 110-1, 132-4, 143, 264 n.11
Ridderschap (ship) 229-30
river(s) 23, 27-8, 60, 104, 113, 119, 128-30, 253
rixdollars 43, 110, 114, 124-5, 127-8, 131, 133, 136-7, 141, 143, 145, 148-50, 194, 199, 201-3, 206-7, 211-2, 214-5, 220, 226, 231-2, 234-6, 240-1, 246-8, 250-1, 254-6, 268 n.53, n.58, n.60, 270 n.75; see also dollars

sacraments 169-70
sailor(s) 30, 36, 44, 55, 74, 80, 95, 97, 99, 106, 108-11, 114, 125, 127, 129, 131, 134, 139, 141-2, 145, 150, 158, 160, 166, 181, 198, 212, 234, 246, 261 n.3, 264 n.11
salina(s) 64, 68
salt 63-4, 69
sampan(s) 102, 111
sandbank 16, 27
sanitary(tion) 17, 29, 82

sappanwood 136-7, 140
school 160-1, 179, 264 n.1
secretary(iat, ies) 69, 81, 114, 169, 188, 206-8, 213, 224, 232
sentence 229, 243-4; see also verdict
separation (from bed and board) 217, 222, 231, 237, 244, 250, 258
sequestration 244, 246
settler(s) 3, 81, 97, 105, 157, 159, 161
shahbandar 36, 38-9, 48
sheriff 5, 88-91, 93, 95, 229, 234
shipowner(ing, s) 105-7, 127, 132, 134, 145
shipping 97, 102-3, 105, 114, 122, 128, 130-2, 137-9, 141-2, 147, 149-50, 153-4, 165, 181
shipping lists 9, 123
shipping routes 147-8, 151
shogun(al, ate) 176, 182, 187-8
"Shun-feng Hsiang-sung" 112, 263 n.3
silk(s) 56, 99, 104-5, 115, 124-6, 137, 147, 149, 151, 153, 191-2
silver 8, 35, 39, 42-6, 99, 104, 116, 130, 133, 135, 138, 147, 151, 182-3, 199, 250, 262 n.17
Sion (ship) 246
skipper(s) 67, 87, 91, 110, 125, 130-1, 137, 143, 181, 192, 203, 264 n.21; see also nachoda
slave(s) 5, 10, 19-20, 24, 26, 29, 31, 40, 52, 65, 81, 83-4, 88-9, 127, 132, 156, 159-60, 165-6, 168-70, 172-3, 179, 189, 195, 199, 205, 207, 215, 217, 236, 238-9, 241, 246, 250-1, 267 n.35, 268 n.53
slavery 25, 55, 166, 170
smuggling 31, 38, 110, 119, 135, 142, 148, 212-6, 222, 227, 265 n.5
Sofi dynasty 91
soldier(s) 30, 34, 65, 67, 80, 94, 99, 158-60, 165, 167, 169, 195, 197-8, 238, 269 n.66
spelter 124, 126, 137
spice(s) 26, 31, 105, 116, 129, 159
spinsters 158, 161, 255
staple market 73, 102, 104-5, 150, 159
States-General 24-5, 48, 83, 220, 228
stepfather 241-2
stepson 241-2, 247
stuiver(s) 46, 48, 63, 194, 199, 250
sugar 20, 24-5, 27, 44, 64, 69, 85, 90-1, 93, 95-6, 104, 115, 149
sugar cultivation 17, 24, 26-7, 63-4, 85, 90, 121, 136

sugar mills 23, 27, 64, 90-1, 93-4, 121, 126, 145
sugar plantation(s) 52, 64, 68, 85, 91, 94, 137
Sung dynasty 37, 99
Susuhunan 34, 248

tael(s) 106, 138-9, 153, 182-5
tariff(s) 101, 142
tax(es) 10, 20, 33, 53-4, 58, 68, 70, 74, 77, 81-3, 87, 93, 114, 116, 125-6, 133, 136-7, 139, 142-3, 145, 149-50, 165, 182, 184, 227; see also capitation tax; head tax; poll tax
tax farm(er, ing, s) 8, 10, 52, 54-5, 68, 72, 75, 82, 87, 101, 125-6, 136, 142, 261 n.3
tea 99, 124-6, 128, 130-2, 135-7, 141-2, 147-50, 153, 264 n.9, n.14, n.16
teak 54, 106
temple(s) 75, 110-1, 177
tenants 20, 24
tenders 69, 262 n.23
testament 183, 185, 193, 232
testimony(ies) 208, 234, 241-3
textiles 31, 104, 115, 124, 150, 179
timber 23, 27, 34, 53, 106, 108, 149
tin 110, 116, 135, 136-7, 148-9
Toa-son-i (ship) 263 n.2
tobacco 125-6
toll(s) 47, 79, 81-2, 123, 137, 141, 143, 149-50, 165, 182, 263 n.2
tonnage 103, 123, 147
towkay 49, 51-2, 54, 58, 60, 64, 67-9
town hall 80, 205, 214, 253
Townsend (ship) 132
trade(rs) 3-4, 6, 9, 19, 25, 31, 35-6, 38-9, 41-3, 45-6, 48-9, 52-3, 57-60, 63, 71-5, 77-8, 80-1, 83-5, 87, 91, 93, 95-7, 99-105, 107-9, 114-7, 119-24, 126-43, 145, 147-51, 153-5, 157-63, 165, 168, 174-5, 181-2, 184, 191, 216, 227, 261 n.3, 263 n.1, 264 n.14, n.20
trade factory(ies) 18, 21, 58, 105, 148, 157, 176, 181; see also factory
trading company(ies) 99, 130, 154, 161
treasury 139, 179, 181, 212, 234, 241, 244, 250-1, 268 n.53
trial 228, 246
tribute (payments) 73, 79, 99, 101-2
trustees 26, 82, 244-5
"Tung-hsi-yang K'ao" 38, 104, 111-2

umbrellas 104, 114-5
University (of Harderwijk) 196
urban 1, 5, 173
usury(ers) 84, 89

VOC see Verenigde Oost-Indische Compagnie
vagrants 131, 138
verdict 209, 211, 214-5, 231, 241-2, 245, 251
Verenigde Oost-Indische Compagnie (VOC) (Company, Dutch East India Company) 1-9, 13, 17-20, 24-6, 30-1, 33-4, 36, 44-8, 50-3, 56, 59, 63, 70-1, 97, 103, 105-6, 109-10, 115-7, 119, 121, 123-4, 127-33, 135-7, 141, 145, 147-51, 153-4, 156-8, 161, 163, 165-6, 172, 174-7, 179, 181-2, 184, 187-8, 192, 197, 216, 263 n.1, 264 n.9, 268 n.51
viceroys 31, 37, 119, 139, 159
village 15, 26, 38
vroedschap see City Council

Waalstroom (ship) 246, 248, 253, 269 n.66

Wan-li period 37
wangkang(s) 67, 97, 128
war 46, 55, 73, 84-5, 94, 106, 117, 147, 150, 173, 185
ward(s) 9-10, 87
wardmasters (wijkmeesters) 10, 87, 127
warehouse(s) 15, 23, 45-6, 71, 74, 80, 93, 114, 154
wayang 82, 113
Weeskamer see Orphan Board
weighing house 125-6, 143
widow(s, er) 166, 168, 172, 174-6, 179, 191, 198-9, 203, 217, 255
Wilgenburg (ship) 24
witch(craft) 166, 242
wontai 36-7
wijkmeesters see wardmasters

Yang-hang 107, 134, 146, 149, 153; see also guilds
Yüan dynasty 99
Yung-cheng period 133-5

Zallant (ship) 246
ziekentrooster(s) 179, 265 n.5

SOURCES OF THE ILLUSTRATIONS

J.T. Barrow, A voyage to Cochinchina in the years 1792 and 1793. London, 1804, p.177.   32
Leonard Blussé and Jaap de Moor, Nederlanders overzee. Franeker, 1983, p.229.   13
J. Brandes, "Een plattegrond van Batavia van 1632", TBG 63(1901), p.248.   61
H.A. Breuning, Het voormalige Batavia; Een Hollandse stedestichting in de tropen anno 1619. Utrecht, 1981, pp.35, 53.   28, 66
I. Commelin, Begin ende voortgang van de Vereenighde Nederlandtsche Geoctroyeerde Oost-Indische Compagnie. Amsterdam, 1646, Vol.I, p.76.   40
J. Crawfurd, History of the Indian archipelago [...]. London, 1820, Vol.III, p.140.   152
Ivon A. Donelly, Chinese junks; A book of drawings in black and white. Shanghai, 1920, p.22.   129
J. Haafner, Reize in eenen palanquin; of lotgevallen en merkwaardige aanteekeningen op eene reize langs de kusten Orixa en Choromandel. Amsterdam, 1808, Vol.II, p.393.   157
Hsü Pau-kwang, Chung-shan Chuan-hsin Lu. 中山傳信錄 n.p. [c.1718].   122
J. de Marre, Batavia, begrepen in zes boeken. Amsterdam, 1740, title page.   14
A.J. van der Meulen, Platen-atlas voor de vaderlandsche geschiedenis. Groningen, 1911, p.98.   247
A. Montanus, Gedenkwaerdige gesantschappen der Oost-Indische Maatschappij [...] aan de Kaisaren van Japan. Amsterdam, 1669, p.28.   183
J. Nieuhoff, Het gezandtschap der Neêrlandtsche Oost-Indische Compagnie, aan den grooten Tartarischen Cham, den tegenwoordigen Keizer van China [...]. Amsterdam, 1665, pp.128, 138.   90, 41
J. Nieuhoff, Zee en lant-reize, door verscheide gewesten van Oostindien [...]. Amsterdam, 1682, pp.196, 197, 199, 200, 204, 205, 216.   22, 230, 233, 222, 82, 186, 164
G. van Rijn, Nederlandse historieprenten (1550-1900); Platenatlas. Amsterdam, 1910, pp.49, 54, 54, 55, 115.   21, 221, 225, 249, 56
Marwyn S. Samuels, Contest for the South China Sea. New York/London, 1982, p.39.   112 (adapted map from Wei Yüan, Hai-kuo T'u-chih 海國圖志
W. Schouten, Oost-Indische voyagie [...]. Amsterdam, 1676, Vol.I, p.23.   113
W. van Toorn, Wijk bij Duurstede; Stad aan het water. Nieuw Vennep, n.d., p.19.   254
F. Valentijn, Oud en nieuw Oost-Indiën [...]. Dordrecht/Amsterdam, 1724-26, Vol.IV-1, pp.235, 253.   204, 76

ARA. The Hague: map collection no.1244   86
Atlas van Stolk, Rotterdam: contemporary print depicting the fighting in the Ommelanden and Batavia   92; late 18th century water colour by an anonymous artist   144
Christie's Amsterdam: Nanking treasure collection (1986)   140

Koninklijk Instituut voor de Tropen, Amsterdam: Andries Beeckman, Gezicht op Batavia, early 17th century   62
Matsuura collection, Hirado: "Tosen no zu"   107
Pau collection, Amsterdam   118, 177, 178
Rijksmuseum, Amsterdam   180
Rijksprentenkabinet, Rijksmuseum Amsterdam: drawings by anonymous 17th century artist (Cornelis de Bruyn?)   53, 76, 200, 240
Stichting Cultuurgeschiedenis van de Nederlanders Overzee, Rijksmuseum Amsterdam   171